The LORD foils the plans of the nations;
he thwarts the purposes of the peoples.
But the plans of the LORD stand firm forever,
the purposes of his heart through all generations.

PSALM 33:10-11

THIS
REBELLIOUS
HOUSE

American History & the Truth of Christianity

STEVEN J. KEILLOR

InterVarsity Press
Downers Grove, Illinois

InterVarsity Press® is the book-publishing division of InterVarsity Christian Fellowship®, a student movement active on campus at hundreds of universities, colleges and schools of nursing in the United States of America, and a member movement of the International Fellowship of Evangelical Students. For information about local and regional activities, write Public Relations Dept., InterVarsity Christian Fellowship, 6400 Schroeder Rd., P.O. Box 7895, Madison, WI 53707-7895.

Cover illustration: Snark/Art Resource, NY

ISBN 0-8308-1877-4

Printed in the United States of America

Library of Congress Cataloging-in-Publication Data

Keillor, Steven J. (Steven James)
    This rebellious house: American history and the truth of
Christianity/ by Steven J. Keillor.
        p.   cm.
    Includes bibliographical references.
    ISBN 0-8308-1877-4 (pbk.: alk. paper)
    1. United States—History—Religious aspects—Christianity.
I. Title.
E179.K25   1996
973—DC20   96-21546
                                                                              CIP
                                                                              AC

21 20 19 18 17 16 15 14 13 12 11 10 9 8 7 6 5 4 3 2 1

13 12 11 10 09 08 07 06 05 04 03 02 01 00 99 98 97 96

For Aldridge and Eleanor Johnson,
and in memory of their son Philip Johnson

93441

Acknowledgments

I am greatly indebted to several people who helped me in one way or another to write this book. Bob Clark, Pastor Kevin Carr and Dr. Daniel Johnson read the manuscript and offered helpful suggestions, as did J. Philip Keillor. Dr. Aldridge and Eleanor Johnson of Isanti, Minnesota, provided most of the funding that enabled me to do the research and writing. I am deeply grateful for their support, and this book is dedicated to them. My wife Margaret did not rebel at the fanciful notion that her absent-minded husband could recall enough U.S. history to reinterpret. My thanks to her and to Jeremy, William and Amanda for tolerating a husband and father who was preoccupied with the mystery of American history when they had more pressing concerns. Thanks also to David and Wendy Nelson, to Pastor Dave Tyree and Dr. Howard Lindskoog, and to my editor, Rodney Clapp, to James W. Sire, and to the staff at InterVarsity Press. They may not recognize the views here advanced, but I am grateful to my professors at the University of Minnesota for my graduate education in history—especially to John R. Howe Jr. and George D. Green. Raising and educating a historian is like growing walnut trees—it takes time before there is any harvest. My parents, John and Grace Keillor, have shown patience, and I thank them.

Preface

This book's novel perspective and approach may deserve—some would say, demand—an explanation; and I will give one, but it will be brief. The interpretations of American history found in the following chapters must be judged on their own merits or demerits. I cannot, by some philosophical or theological argument, prove them to be worthy of consideration, nor can they be proved false and ruled out of bounds by some opposite a priori argument. They will have to be judged mainly by whether they satisfactorily explain the American past and present.

In this Christian reinterpretation, I have simply tried to stand on basic evangelical, Christian assumptions and the best contemporary historical scholarship in order to see what American history would look like from that vantage point. I make no claim that this is the only possible Christian interpretation of the American past, nor that it is based on some special revelation given to me. It rests on religious views that are common among American evangelicals: scriptural inerrancy; a trinitarian belief in Father, Holy Spirit and Jesus Christ the Son of God, who died for our sins, was raised and will return bodily and visibly; a premillennial view of his return, absent any doctrinaire stand on prophecy.

What would American history look like if we stood on these beliefs, got down off less essential or incorrect ones and used the best available research and writing on the subject? That is the question this book seeks to answer.

But why do we need to ask that question? It seems to me a matter of great urgency that we do so. In the college classroom of the 1990s, professors and students assume that current historical scholarship on U.S. history disproves the exclusive truth claims of Christianity. Evangelical faith is assumed to be a provincial, local viewpoint—dominant in some regions and in certain eras of U.S. history and thus worthy of study—but not a universal, divine revelation and probably fated to wither away as a cosmopolitan, global outlook becomes everywhere dominant. Instead of attacking the seven supposed proofs of God's existence, professors are now more likely to point to American history—to white American males' behavior toward everyone else—as proof that what these males believed cannot be true for anyone else.

None of these assumptions is correct. The white males were often rebelling against Christianity, not advancing it, and it's not a local belief system but a rival cosmopolitanism at war with a secular one. Christianity has long ceased to be a Eurocentric faith. This book looks at U.S. history from the perspective of, say, a Chinese believer, in order to avoid the ethnocentrism and nationalism for too long associated with evangelical views of American history. Its purpose is not to secularize or to be "politically correct." Quite the opposite!

A more consistently Christian view allows us to state more emphatically that the claim "Jesus Christ is Lord" is not a private value but a public fact. Several authors have noted evangelicals' retreat from the public world of "facts" to a private world of "values." I first encountered that idea in Lesslie Newbigin's *Foolishness to the Greeks.* History is a good academic discipline in which to reverse that retreat: history describes public facts, the Christian faith is a historical one, and the doctrine of the Lord's return makes claims about the public world and its future. That is why this book is not so much a Christian view of U.S. history—a historical story we evangelicals can tell ourselves to prop up our faith—as it is a *truer* view of U.S. history, one that uses revisionist scholarship but offers a metanarrative that is truer to the facts than are revisionists' metanarratives. I do not accept the postmodern critique of metanarratives and "truer" views, so I offer this one without apology.

That current scholarship—revisionist, multicultural, feminist, neo-Marxist, whatever—has itself uncovered truer facts and interpretations, but its metanarrative directly or implicitly seeks (yet fails) to disprove the exclusive truth claims of Christianity. In these chapters I occasionally point out these scholars' unwarranted conclusions. Some go beyond their evidence, but most do excellent work that disproves only an ethnocentric, nationalistic view of U.S. history, not a Christian one, properly understood. So I have relied heavily on their work and am grateful for it. Of course these authors would not necessarily approve and should not be held responsible for my use of them. I have cited their books and articles with the understanding that they support my factual and general historical points, but of course they are not cited as support for the specifically Christian interpretations I draw from those points. I remain responsible for all points made, whether Christian or secular.

If I have failed to cite work, especially interpretive work, done by evangelical historians, it is because this book's apologetic purpose is best accomplished by using secular historians' work. And it is best done by taking a Christian view of all of American history rather than focusing on the history of evangelicalism in America or of particular denominations. Chapter four, especially, departs from the popular evangelical view that the United States was founded as a Christian nation. I do not belabor the point. I simply try to show that we make a stronger public claim that "Jesus Christ is Lord" if we acknowledge that many of the Founders did not believe that he was.

The title *This Rebellious House* is taken from Ezekiel 2 and 3, where Yahweh repeatedly calls the nation of Israel a "rebellious house." The specific phrase "this rebellious house" is used in Ezekiel 24:3. By using it I do not at all intend to suggest that the United States is somehow Israel's successor as God's chosen people. Nor do I suggest that Americans have rebelled against God in some manner peculiar to themselves. The rebellion that is the major theme of this book is the same rebellion against God commonly displayed by all humans. More specifically, Americans of European descent share in the general Western rebellion against the Christianity that Western civilization claims to defend and promote. Yahweh's words to Ezekiel could be applied to most any nation, certainly to most any European nation and its colonial offspring, including the United States: "A rebellious nation . . . has rebelled against me; they and their fathers have been in revolt against me to this very day" (Ezekiel 2:3).

There have been redemptive moments as well as rebellious ones in American history, as in all national histories. This book examines some of them. Yet the Lord's success in foiling his enemies' plans and making his own plans stand firm does not at all depend on having the redemptive moments outnumber or outweigh the rebellious ones. Human rebellion is a much stronger causative engine driving American history than is human repentance. God can use human rebellion to accomplish "the purposes of his heart," so revisionists' emphasis on the negative aspects of U.S. history does not at all negate the truth of

Christianity—it tends to confirm it.

The study of history is inevitably caught up in larger debates. Anti-Christian spokespersons use a revisionist view of American history as an argument, a secular "apologetic," against Christianity every day. Christians have little choice but to engage in this debate and to use history in the process.

That does not mean that I have rummaged through current historical writing to grab whatever fits Christian apologetic—and then discarded the rest. One of the sad features of our current cultural debates is that we pick out the weakest arguments of our opponents and then focus exclusively on those. We are like snipers who shoot when the enemy takes one or two steps into the open. I have tried to take secular, revisionist, feminist or neo-Marxist historians at their strongest points. I have tried not to be taken captive by any particular political or ideological viewpoint. The reader must judge the degree to which I have succeeded. Other Christian interpretations of the same evidence are possible.

The book comes in four parts. The first three chapters look at America under European colonial rule. The next three examine an American republic of rebellious male individualism. Chapters seven to nine deal with social, economic and international developments largely outside the control of the republic's government. The last three chapters are chronological in order and describe how U.S. society adjusted to "realism," then rebelled against it and, in the process, splintered into the fragmented consumer society of the 1990s. The book closes with an argument that the Lord's return is essential to a Christian interpretation of U.S. history—and that it is certain.

As a historian, I realize that in today's fragmented consumer society, books are like wall plaques—only longer. They are marketable goods, sold in a market niche, to a select audience that is warmed or inspired or reassured by their words. Yet, as I tell my American history classes, the workings of history cannot be ended, like some mistaken marketing idea, by consumers' dislike for the results. Like the Energizer bunny, history just keeps going with its causes and effects, despite consumer disinterest. The Lord of history keeps working too, to foil plans and to thwart purposes and, we should add in this consumer age, to ignore purchases: "The plans of the LORD stand firm forever, the purposes of his heart through all generations" (Psalm 33:11).

1

1492
The Seven
Deadly Sins Tumble
out of Europe

AT DAWN ON FRIDAY, OCTOBER 12, 1492, Christopher Columbus landed at an island that the indigenous Taino called Guanahani. With the captains of the *Niña* and *Pinta,* he "went ashore in the armed launch," displayed King Ferdinand and Queen Isabella's flags, with the cross prominent, and took "possession of the said island for the king and for the queen his lords."

Some Taino witnessed this ceremony, but they likely saw no reason why this stranger should take possession. Nor did they understand his actions in the next weeks: planting crosses as symbols of conquest, naming places and natural features, eyeing the Taino as potential slaves, looking for gold and reconnoitering for good sites for forts.[1]

The Revisionists' Critique of Columbus, Europe and Christianity
During the recent quincentennial, Columbus's acts, though understood, have been condemned. In *The Conquest of Paradise* Kirkpatrick Sale ridiculed him as a bumbling navigator, a deceptive captain, an incompetent gold-obsessed

explorer who misidentified flora and fauna, "a man rather lost in a world that he cannot come to know."[2] Everything about his "discovery" is controversial. How can we say that Europeans "discovered" a land which was quite familiar to its inhabitants? How can we call it a "New" World when its civilizations were quite old or its peoples "Indians" when they lived far from India? How can we celebrate what resulted in the deaths of millions of "Indians"? How can we call Columbus a hero?

This controversy dismays many Americans, who view it as an unwelcome manifestation of "political correctness" spoiling the old-fashioned American history they fondly remember from their school days.[3] Yet these are legitimate questions. By trying to answer them apart from politicizing polemics, we Americans can learn much about ourselves and our past.

On some points we can agree. Others can be left to specialists to debate. We need not cross swords over the term *discovery*. Let's think of it as a first encounter between peoples or, as Mexican historian Silvio Zavala argues, "a multiplicity of encounters between peoples and cultures." If *encounter* sounds too peaceful, think of it as a head-on collision. We need not argue over calling this a "New" World. It was merely a different one, quite unlike Europe and Asia. (For convenience, we will consider Africa's contribution in the next chapter.) We need not fight over guessing the Americas' pre-1492 population, a task likened to "extract[ing] Sun-Beams out of Cucumbers."[4] That is not vital for our broad-brush discussion.

We must, however, attend seriously to arguments that the Americas' indigenous cultures were somehow superior to European culture in ways that discredit the exclusive truth claims of Christianity. The Columbian encounter is said to have proven that all cultures and religions are equally valid—with European Christianity perhaps least valid in light of 1990s concerns about the environment, the status of women, human equality, peace and social justice.

Many scholars and popularizers make this argument. From an environmentalist's perspective, Sale criticizes "the Hebraic Yahweh" for "using [nature's] elements to wreak vengeance on His flock" and for remaining aloof from nature. He perceives a "long history of Christian antagonism to nature." Calling Christianity "the core of European thought and culture," David E. Stannard considers this "theocratic culture" to have been "obsessed with things sensual and sexual" and committed to holy war. He holds Christianity responsible for "the horrors that were inflicted by Europeans and white Americans on the Indians of the Americas." Their violent path was "paved in the earliest days of Christendom."[5]

Writers of college textbooks are more circumspect. In *The American People* historian Gary Nash argues that Europeans, who "came bearing the crosses of their religion, were a volatile and dangerous people." He links their crosses to their volatility: "European settlers . . . saw a holy necessity to convert—or destroy—these [Indians who were] enemies of their God." Indigenous societies were environmentally sensitive, communal, egalitarian, committed to "the sharing of power between male and female" and "less structured in their religious views." All the contrasts work to Europeans' disadvantage, but Christianity is not identified as the main disadvantaging factor. James Kirby Martin, in *America and Its People,* praises "group-oriented" natives and faults Europeans for "cultural superiority," but he does not attribute these to the absence and presence of Christianity in the two groups.[6]

In the classroom, professors can make explicit what is only implicit in the texts—and many undoubtedly do. The Columbian encounter becomes their object lesson in cultural relativism to start the year's work in American history. Here is the creation myth of American cultural relativism: the foolish Europeans who thought theirs were the only crops, animals and gods discover a completely new set, as valid and useful as theirs—even more so. Yet looking at the evidence we find that, far from being a proof text for cultural relativism, the Columbian encounter powerfully argues for the exclusive truth claims of Christianity. But we cannot see that without looking at the evidence. The historian "proves" an argument by crafting a credible explanation of past events, not by crafting a syllogism or conducting an experiment or solving an equation.

The first step is to take the anti-Christian revisionist argument *at its strongest point,* not its weakest. Sale and Stannard do romanticize indigenous peoples: Stannard, for example, devotes only two paragraphs to Aztec human sacrifice. Historian William Cronon notes that Sale's "Indians are so perfectly in tune with nature, such paragons of ecological wisdom, that they glide right out of history and back into noble savagery."[7] Yet, like snipers, critics often take aim when the revisionist steps out a little too far. Sniping (that is, answering only the weaknesses in opponents' arguments) is too much a part of our current cultural debates. Confronting opponents' *strengths* will prove more helpful.

Let us confront the fact that polytheistic, animal- and star-worshiping indigenous peoples *were* generally less violent, more generous, more egalitarian, less aggressive and more in tune with nature than Christian Europeans. Then we will gain new insights into European society on the eve of colonization.

Then we will see—as we go along—that this paradox confirms rather than disproves God's revelation in Christ and in Scripture.

Critics of Christianity, such as Sale, Stannard and Martin, err in equating European culture and the Christian faith. From their secular perspective, they see the Hebrews constructing creation myths about their tribal god Yahweh and Christianity as a cultural artifact formed by Europeans. Nothing could be further from the truth. The Old (or Hebrew) Testament is one long *argument* between Yahweh and his often-rebellious people. European history also reveals an *argument* between the triune God and rebellious Europeans. They desired the benefits of the faith they professed but avoided the rigorous demands accompanying the knowledge of God. When Columbus brought European history to the Western Hemisphere, he brought this argument with him. That accounts for much of the resulting conquest, slavery, war, exploitation and misery. Yet tragedies caused by rebellion against Christianity and its God cannot logically be blamed on that faith or that God.

Before examining Europe and the Columbian encounter, we must backpedal and look at the pre-Columbian world of the Americas. Can we summarize the diverse characteristics of its many indigenous peoples and cultures?

Human-Centered Belief Systems Versus God-Centered Christianity

There is much truth in the romanticizers' portrayal, despite differences from place to place and changes over time. Pre-Columbian societies were not homogeneous or static. Rich fishing societies along the Pacific coast of Canada, communal agricultural Pueblo villages on the upper Rio Grande, migratory buffalo-hunting Plains tribes, settled Mississippi Valley corn-growers, small scattered groups of hunters and gatherers north of the St. Lawrence, urbanized Aztec imperialists—these varied greatly one from the other. Also, one group might at times change the other. Some time before A.D. 1000, Mayan-speaking traders spread a Caddo cult to the Mississippian culture in the lower river valley and altered that culture's religious system.[8]

Indigenous cultures did, however, share certain characteristics. Each used religion to locate "human life at the center of reality," with everything else "bounded and controllable by reference to that center." Each used a creation myth and anthropocentric gods to integrate a culture. The Pueblo conceived of the female god Iatiku as a helper who gave humans corn and assistance but made few demands on them. The Huron created two anthropocentric deities— Aataentsic, the mother of humanity, and Iouskeha, people's helper. Many *oki,* or "guardian spirits," assisted humans as well. In Incan and Aztec societies, human-created gods were more demanding. The Aztec god Huitzilopochtli demanded sacrificial victims. Therefore the Aztecs continually warred to secure captives for their sacrificial rites. Incan mythology also strongly drove the Incas to militaristic expansion. They believed that their rulers were immortal gods. When one died, his mummy was worshiped: he kept his palace, his possessions and his servants. Deprived of these, his "successor" had to conquer new territories to acquire palace, property and servants.[9] Past human life became a "center of reality" as deceased kings kept on ruling.

These indigenous belief systems were constructed by humans to achieve human goals. In the case of the Incans, the goal was royal immortality. In Huron culture, commoners achieved their desires once a year in a dream-fulfillment festival called Ononharoia. More communal, the Pueblos sought the group's long-term good. Since humans had designed the belief system to meet human needs, rebellion was folly. It did occur, but rarely. Religion integrated indigenous societies and regulated every facet of daily life. It was "the one great force in behavior,"[10] and it was all-pervasive. Many Native American peoples lived in a spirit-filled world in which trees, animals and landscapes had spiritual personalities. That encouraged proper care for the environment.

Note the contrast between these belief systems and Christianity, which is God's revelation to humanity, not a human construct. (Again, we cannot prove that here; we can only see if it helps us explain events.) By contrasting them, we are not denigrating indigenous cultures or saying that they were somehow less "advanced" than European ones. Many were complex, with sophisticated states conducting diplomacy and ruling vast areas and with complex economies and beautiful arts and crafts. Nor was Christianity a European invention that reflects credit on Europe. It was not invented by humans, nor was it primarily designed to meet human needs. Humanity is not its "center of reality." Because it is not anthropocentric, rebellion against its God is the normal human response to being replaced as the "center of reality." Already, in the Hebrew Testament, Yahweh announced that rebellion was his people's characteristic response:

I reared children and brought them up, but they
    have rebelled against me.
The ox knows his master,
    the donkey his owner's manger,
but Israel does not know,
    my people do not understand.

Even when they claimed they were not rebelling, he knew they were:
> These people come near to me with their mouth
>> and honor me with their lips,
>> but their hearts are far from me.
> Their worship of me
>> is made up only of rules taught by men.[11]

Running through Old and New Testaments is the stark reality that human rebellion produces a split between those who falsely claim to be his people and those who truly are his people. The latter characteristically obey him, but sometimes they rebel too.

That is not the case with human-centered belief systems. It makes no sense to speak of Hurons rebelling against Iouskeha, the helper of humans, or of false, professing Aztecs versus true Aztecs or of Pueblo who did not believe in Pueblo religion. The Pueblo did not think in terms of outward behavior versus inner attitudes. Religion *was* outward behavior. What were indigenous religions if not "rules taught by men"? What else was there?

Europeans, by contrast, were inextricably enmeshed in all these dichotomies, dilemmas and rebellions. Rather than being pious followers, God's dutiful schoolchildren living to teach others of him, they were often in active rebellion against the God they professed to obey. Their religion was not an integrated, harmonious human-centered belief system but a traveling argument between their God and them. Contrasting Aztec and Spanish religions, Tzvetan Todorov captures this truth: "The Spaniards' God is an auxiliary rather than a Lord, a being to be used rather than enjoyed." These conquerors' self-proclaimed goal was to advance their religion, but actually they used religion to conquer—"ends and means have changed places."[12]

Europe Rebelling Against Christianity
Revisionists' unfavorable picture of fifteenth-century Europe is largely correct. Sale sees it as "uniquely a culture in flux." It was "far less stable and conservative in its religious customs or political systems than those ancient, encrusted regimes of long-sanctioned rule and unquestioned authority" in Mesoamerica. To Stannard, Spain appears "a land of violence, squalor, treachery, and intolerance . . . no different from the rest of Europe."[13] That is an exaggeration, but, compared to indigenous societies, Europe *was* unstable and dynamic to the point of being destructive, aggressive, unbalanced and contentious. Its religion did not integrate fully its economy,

politics and society as did Native American religions. That is the key.

But we must not oversimplify. Western Europe was a large area with many competing states, language groups, cities and classes—all of which made for dynamism and discord. It had two conflicting cultural roots—Greco-Roman and Judeo-Christian—which caused a "flexibility of mind" but also instability.[14] Before Christianity, Greek and Roman cultures were dynamic and imperialistic. When Renaissance Italians used classical Greek and Roman heritage to authenticate their rebellion against medieval Christianity, their dynamism stemmed from both their rebellion and their classical models. Europe's flux had many causes, but rebellion against religion was crucial in preventing full cultural integration. To be sure, a common Christianity caused cultural similarities throughout Europe and between the linked realms of church, economy and state. But rebellion against the Christian God caused similarities to fall short of integration. Parts did not function smoothly as a whole.

We must not fault Europeans too strongly. Christianity was not designed to accomplish a human purpose such as integrating a culture, a polity or an economy. Implicit in the Scriptures were the right of private property (theft is condemned) and the God-ordained right of rulers to rule (submission to governments is commanded). Within a society permeated by total obedience to God, those two ideas would be controlled by a more powerful one—the knowledge of God. In a society rebelling against God, they could not be. Avarice and ambition ran rampant. Medieval Europeans attempted to integrate their society around a popular lay religiosity and a bureaucratic church, but they failed to restrain individual self-seeking. Their religious-political-economic mix satisfied many people's interests, but it did not make for a harmonious, integrated society.

Lack of full integration meant that few European institutions really worked to accomplish their supposed goal. Instead, they used proclaimed goals to achieve aggrandizement, personal wealth and power as ends in themselves: to reiterate, "ends and means changed places." We can see this if we examine in more detail European churches, governments and economies. The purpose is not to preach at the past or urge the deceased to repent but to understand Europe's impact on the New World and on history. If rebellion is a driving force in history that helps to produce capitalism, democracy, imperialism and other driving forces, then we must understand it.

The role of religion. Instead of seeking the salvation of souls and the worship of God as ends, the fifteenth-century Catholic Church often used people's hunger for salvation and for God for its own profit. Pope Leo X sold two thousand church offices yearly for five hundred thousand ducats. With the annual income from their purchased offices, officials hired deputies at much lower salaries to do the spiritual tasks and pocketed the difference. One cleric often held many offices. Already archbishop of Magdeburg, Albert of Branden-burg desired another archbishopric (he had to support several mistresses), for which he owed Leo X about thirty-one thousand ducats. To raise the money, he sent the notorious Johann Tetzel to sell indulgences with the jingle

As soon as the gold in the basin rings,

Right then the soul to heaven springs.

In saints' relics, the church had another consumer good to sell.[15]

The laypeople—the consumers—supported this system. Church profiteers were partly responding to laypeople, who created a human-centered religion for their solace. Historian Euan Cameron notes, "Most lay people were less worried about saving their souls, than about everyday security." Thus "they used an arsenal of supernatural charms" to solve "the immediate pressing concerns of human survival." Like indigenous peoples, they used material objects, festivals, images and paraphernalia to manipulate the supernatural world. "Firebrands from St. John's day bonfires were regarded as talismans, as were eggs laid on Good Friday." Popular religion stressed externals, not attitudes or understanding: "All the most popular activities of late medieval religion were based on *doing* something . . . on experiencing an event more than on learning or understanding a message." This lay religion corrupted the church and prevented true reform. The wealthy poured money on the reformed relig-ious orders—hoping to buy the benefits of their greater holiness but corrupting them in the process.[16] Mutually reinforcing were people's eagerness to buy and the church's eagerness to sell. The result was what two Dutch historians "kindly disposed to Catholic Christianity" describe as "a religious consciousness that can hardly be called Christian."[17]

Pope and church sought political power as well. The pope ruled the Papal States in central Italy. To obtain funds to finance construction in Rome and the States, Pope Sixtus IV in 1476 ruled that purchased indulgences could reduce a soul's time in purgatory. Upon seeing Pope Julius II in 1506 triumphantly parading through Bologna with his army, Erasmus reputedly asked, "Whose successor is this Julius, Julius Caesar or Jesus Christ?" Popes intervened in European politics. "The bequests of the devout, largely in the interests of their departed souls," made the church the largest landowner. Popes used "spiritual sanctions" to give their Papal States a monopoly on the sale of alum in Catholic Christendom.[18] Spiritual powers became means to political ends.

In the first week or two of an American history course, these familiar examples are used to explain Martin Luther and the Reformation. Yet, as Cameron notes, they don't come close to explaining the Reformation. Europeans did not complain about this popular, human-centered religion "adapted to the needs, concerns, and tastes . . . of the people who created it." They grumbled about the church's appetite for funds and the clergy's privileges, not about shrines, rites, pilgrimages, saints, relics, indulgences and festivals.[19]

True, this human-created distortion of Christianity did not integrate society fully or control the powerful drives of political ambition and economic avarice. Yet the ambitious and the avaricious hardly complained. As we shall see, the Reformation resulted from *God's* complaints about medieval religion, not *Europeans'* grumblings about it. Medieval distortions did not pit some Europeans (clergy) against others (the devout laypeople), but almost all of them against a God who condemned human pride, ambition, lust and greed. Almost all conspired in a conquest of a Christianity whose original, pacific, self-denying, all-embracing character was as unfamiliar to them as any New World island. The church's spiritual functions and people's spiritual needs became mines to be worked for individual profit like the Potosi silver mines of Peru.

The role of government. Because religion did not integrate European society, government did not perform functions which religion assigned it. Government's purpose was to maintain order and to dispense justice (Romans 13:1-7). If Christianity had integrated European society, as Pueblo religion did its society, then European Christian rulers would have maintained order and provided justice out of a motivation to serve their God. But most rulers needed other motives.

After the collapse of the Roman and Carolingian Empires, local governmental powers were parceled out to the leaders of roving military bands in exchange for their allegiance to the king. To motivate these lords to govern and to help them feed and clothe their private armies, the king gave them extensive lands ("fiefs") to farm and serfs to work them. This meant "the passing of public power into private hands" for private economic gain. These lords dispensed private justice in their own courts. Their knights swore allegiance to them, not because they were just or the knights were Christian but because they offered protection, booty and small fiefs. At first the church criticized this "disintegration of the Christian empire." Soon, however, church officials saw that they could profit from it by becoming lords, estate owners and dispensers of private justice. Thus they legitimized it with "the usual Christian façade."[20]

This feudalism did not serve monarchs' long-term interests. Kings sought to regain functions they had farmed out. If Christianity had integrated European society, then the church's impressive coronation ceremony, its anointing of a new king, would have won lords' loyalty to the Lord's anointed. But the rulers' authority to grant lands won their fealty instead. Recognizing a new king safeguarded their land titles. Self-interest spoke louder than the church.

As kings expanded their powers and created nation-states, they used economic motives to bind their subjects to their cause. England's King Edward III secured military services by promising a share in the spoils or new government posts in conquered territories. "The soldiers in Edward III's armies were men on the make and military considerations seldom clouded their selfish intentions." His "war with rich France" was "more popular than war with poor Scotland." Edward showed his men how a government post could be milked for money: when he returned to England from France in 1340, he lodged accusations of misconduct against his subordinates "partly in order to levy large fines from them." Justice was prostituted for mercenary profit.[21]

Taxes were a king's main source of revenue. Scripture authorized them: "This is also why you pay taxes, for the authorities are God's servants, who give their full time to governing" (Romans 13:6). Tax revenues paid them for their work of governing. When they collected taxes, though, they were not to collect more than was due (Luke 3:12-13). French taxation glaringly revealed how little these principles were respected. The French king authorized taxes (*aide, taille, gabelle* and so on) but farmed out tax collection to private "tax-farmers." They purchased the rights to collect taxes in a given region for a sum much less than the anticipated revenue, then pocketed the difference. By the eighteenth century, they squeezed as much from peasants as possible with little regard for legal rates. The public power of taxation was sold into private hands for private profit.[22]

Viewed in terms of European history, unrestrained self-interest seems unremarkable. However, Europeans stood poised to break out of parochial European history into new worlds where self-interest *was* restrained. In the Incan empire, "state-administered labor taxation was governed by ancient Andean principles of reciprocity." Taxpayers paid in labor, but while working they had to be fed and entertained. That limited the ruler's ability to increase taxation: the more labor, the more food and entertainment.[23] When transported to this world of reciprocity, where there was no countervailing power, Europeans' unrestrained self-interest would prove immensely destructive and dynamic.

The role of merchants. In exploiting their functions for profit, rulers and church officials were ably assisted by merchant bankers. When Archbishop Albert sent Tetzel to sell indulgences, the Augsburg merchant bankers (the House of Fugger) sent along an accountant. They had loaned Albert money for the down payment on his second archbishopric and were to be repaid from Tetzel's sales receipts. Despite the church's rules against interest-bearing loans, the Medici of Florence earned interest from the pope's alum monopoly and sales of offices.

Merchant bankers profited from loans to rulers who outspent their revenues. In the Italian city-states, government debt "held promises of returns" for lenders. Servicing debt was more lucrative than collecting taxes, so public "finances were in a disastrous state." Merchant bankers took 40-60 percent of city-state revenues as interest payments. The resulting hyperinflation and doubtful coinage drove Italians to deposit money in banks, thus giving bankers more capital to loan out at interest.[24]

Easy profits from lending to church and government pulled the economy from its proper functions. In Florence, "the net loss to productive investment" from financing the public debt "was enormous." In Christian terms, investment, production, employment and trade should enable people to acquire necessities at reasonable prices. Naturally, people who invest, produce, hire and trade expect to earn a profit, but profit should not be exorbitant or so high as regards luxury goods that production of necessities is neglected. Production of necessities for everyone in society is crucial. Tax-farmers, papal bankers and indulgence sales accountants did not produce anything. The larger merchants mostly dealt in luxury goods or in money as a commodity. That was where large profits lay. The European capitalist, says historian Fernand Braudel, "did not commit himself wholeheartedly to production" but eyed the main chance and the easy profit. He "only took an interest in production when necessity or trading profits made it advisable."[25]

Millions of European peasants lived close to starvation, while merchants, princes and clerics exploited political and spiritual institutions for private profit. Self-interest was the great integrating motive. Important consequences resulted from organizing society around self-interest rather than religious, communal or reciprocal principles. When Europeans left Europe, those consequences became clear. Countervailing self-interests restrained each other in Europe, but, since indigenous peoples lacked that power, European self-interest ran riot in the conquered world.

The role of the Renaissance. Europeans lacked an ideology justifying self-interest. In Renaissance Italy, elites and intellectuals used the Greco-Roman heritage to free themselves from a medieval Christian worldview and to integrate their society. In the Italian city-states, lack of cultural integration was especially marked. Rather than one set of rules, there were separate sets for separate "games" of politics, trade, church and art. Capitalists, politicians and thinkers such as Machiavelli developed rationales that justified existing rules.

The Dane Johannes Sløk argues, "The Renaissance meant that humanity seized power in a radical liberation from all traditions and authority." Acquiring power and accumulating capital became justifiable ends, unlimited ends. There was no limit to the power and capital that could be accumulated. By accumulating, elite individuals and families differentiated themselves from society and its interests. Individualism justified accumulation. Limitlessness created uncertainty (especially for those subject to elites), which encouraged dynamic innovation. Individualistic, innovative, respecting no limits, humans were in control.[26]

Renaissance Europeans did not invent rebellion against God. They only tried to justify and regularize it, then build a society around it. They groped for ideas to explain and justify rebellion and for human-centered ideologies to integrate their culture.[27]

The European Conquest of Another World: The Columbian Encounter
Starting in 1492, many of these limitless, innovative, individualistic self-seekers were tumbled out of Europe and set loose on generous, communal, stable and nonaggressive societies. They were tumbled out of their homelands to reveal what was really in their hearts. The sight was not a pretty one.

They had enormous military advantages: cannon, firearms, the horse, the caravel, armor, navigational instruments. In their aggressive, innovative, monotheistic *mentalité,* they had an added advantage. The Spanish "wore their religion like a sword . . . against all who were not, or who did not rapidly become, Christians." (In many ways they were not Christians themselves, but the conquistadors were not much given to introspection.) The effects were catastrophic. The Aztec population had declined 95 percent seventy-five years after the conquest, and that percentage was typical of other societies! By far the largest losses were to European diseases, for indigenous peoples lacked immunity to them. The Pilgrims' friend Squanto was the last survivor of his Patuxet tribe, once numbering two thousand, which was devastated by disease.[28]

We have to be clear in how we describe this catastrophe. As historian James Axtell cogently argues, it was not genocide: the spread of disease, the main killer, was unintentional. No European state tried to destroy Indians as a race. If for no other reason, profit-seeking Europeans found Indians valuable as workers and trading partners. To describe these Europeans as genocidal is to demonize them, to exaggerate their racist violence, to make them safely unlike our modern selves so that we need not confront the darkness in our own souls. Their violence was not a uniquely European problem, for the Iroquois tried to destroy the Huron in 1649.[29]

That is not to downplay the conquest's horrible reality. On Columbus's second voyage, after he fell sick his Spanish forces lost all self-control: they "went wild, stealing, killing, raping, and torturing natives, trying to force them to divulge the whereabouts of the imagined treasure-houses of gold." Recovered, Columbus systematized the terror by ordering that the hands be cut off any adult Indian who did not bring the Spanish a set quantity of gold. Supposedly in the Aztec capital on a peaceful mission, Cortés's conquistadors suddenly began to massacre Aztecs. Throughout their famous campaign, they killed, destroyed, raped and terrorized with attack dogs, which ate slain Aztecs. Elizabethan English explorers "wished to emulate the conquistadors, by subduing native cities and kingdoms." They used their military superiority to kidnap, steal, rape and murder.[30] It was as if the seven deadly sins had escaped Europe, taken to horseback and galloped across the Americas.

With his superior weapons, every European adventurer could now hope to acquire the wealth, booty, women and lordship previously available only to the European elite. He was freed from restraints imposed by king, church or public opinion, now thousands of miles removed. He could "profit beyond the reach of the king." Europe had few constraints on self-interest, but the Englishman or Spaniard away from home was freed even from these.[31]

More than military weakness hindered indigenous peoples in resisting this assault. Their human-centered, traditional, naturalistic, polytheistic, generous worldview weakened them. In 1614-1618, Indians who first encountered English ships off the New England coast took them to be floating islands complete with trees (masts), thunder and lightning (cannon). Others took the English for *manitous,* spirit beings, who had to be placated. A century earlier, the Aztecs briefly had "the paralyzing belief that the Spaniards [were] gods." They saw the Spaniards' ability to write and to decipher written messages as godlike.

Cortés took advantage of the Aztecs' polytheistic uncertainty as to whether the Spaniards' horses were gods or animals. He secretly buried dead horses at night to encourage a belief that horses were immortal. An English captain magnetized his sword "to cause [the Indians] to imagine some great power in us . . . and for that to love and feare us." Indians felt a paralyzing awe of European objects. They lacked a strengthening belief that their deity was above such material objects.[32]

Europeans' belief in one invisible God gave them a temporary advantage. They could never mistakenly venerate objects or take indigenous peoples for gods. They did not fear and obey this invisible God, but they used the doctrine of his invisible nature to free themselves from a limiting veneration of visible objects. They were limited by reverence for neither God nor objects.

Veneration of objects also weakened the natives when Europeans used consumer goods to win their friendship and secure their dependence. Quick to learn the relative worth of goods, they as quickly became dependent on European consumer goods. For them, objects had communal and religious, as well as individual, meanings. Europeans normally did not use objects in self-abnegating worship of God; they used them for self-exalting pleasure. In the process, Europeans created goods that were more appealing and accessible to Indians than their abstract religious ideas. For example, a mirror powerfully appealed to human vanity. Young warriors wore small mirrors around their wrists or on their shoulders and constantly altered their face-paint, hair, necklaces and so on in a "preoccupation with personal fashion."[33]

Traditionalism and communalism left them ill-prepared to deal with Europeans' limitless, individualistic innovation. Aztec culture was very ordered, past-oriented and communal: "The individual's future is ruled by the collective past." Believing that history repeats itself in cycles, they consulted the past to determine how to respond to the Spanish, for surely this had happened before.

Improvising was difficult for them. Cortés improvised brilliantly, inventing conquest's goals and means as he went along. Nominally obedient to Christendom's evangelizing mission, he claimed to have come "to extol and preach faith in Christ." To that motive he added "honor and profit," which he admitted was an innovation, for these "seldom fit in the same bag." He threw them all together: "Let us go forth, serving God, honoring our nation, giving growth to our king, and let us become rich ourselves; for the Mexican enterprise is for all these purposes."

Means became ends, and ends means, as Cortés's conquistadors used religion "to give themselves courage" for the dangerous, self-seeking conquest.[34]

Communicating the truth of one invisible God proved much harder than selling mirrors. Commerce and conquest were usually higher priorities than conversion. Yahweh seemed a very abstract idea to people used to gods in nature, and he did not appeal to their human vanity. In 1605, the English briefly left one Owen Griffin among the Abenaki. The Abenaki laughed at this "Igrismannak" when he denied worshiping moon, sun or stars—though he lifted his hands toward heaven. Indigenous peoples could not easily comprehend the concept of sin either, since their morality derived from human social needs, not from divine command.[35]

Missionary work was frustrating for the Spanish, French and English. Spanish efforts were greatly hindered by the legacy of their forcible expulsion of Muslims from the Iberian peninsula and their forced conversion of Jews there. That left a "confusion between conquest and Christianization." Conversion was involuntary. Before proceeding, a Spanish conqueror had to read to natives the infamous *Requerimiento*. It grandly announced Christianity's and the pope's worldwide supremacy and Pope Alexander VI's grant of most of the Americas to Spain. They had to obey the Catholic Church and the Spanish king. If they refused, the document threatened them with war, slavery, loss of property and imminent destruction. As Bartolomé de Las Casas, an early Spanish missionary and defender of the Indians, wrote, this made "mockery of truth and justice and [was] a great insult to our Christian faith and the piety and charity of Jesus Christ." It was more like Simon Peter cutting off the ear of the high priest's servant. Thus Spanish Franciscans burned Pueblo religious materials, whipped nonbelieving Pueblos and required daily attendance at Mass for baptized Pueblos. Not surprisingly, the Pueblo externally acquiesced to Christianity while maintaining the old religion within their small groups.[36]

The French were more understanding of indigenous cultures and more cynical about papal decrees. Hearing of Pope Alexander VI's decree, King Francis I of France exclaimed, "I would be pleased to see the clause in Adam's testament that excludes me from a share in the globe." French missions were led by the Jesuits, who adapted Christianity to appeal to receptive elements in each indigenous culture. They achieved great success with the Huron, for example, but their pragmatic approach led to many Huron converting for pragmatic reasons: to keep family ties with prior converts, to obey dreams about being baptized or to obtain preferential treatment from French traders.[37] The Huron were shrewd too.

Puritan missions produced fewer converts in New England. Products of the Protestant Reformation, Puritans concentrated too obsessively on their argument with Catholicism to be very missions-minded. They were reverse images of the Jesuits—intolerant of everything in indigenous culture lest it recontaminate their own Christianity. They focused on their own survival. Despite their demand that converts make a total cultural change, they convinced a surprising number of Massachusets and Wampanoags to break with their past and become "praying Indians."[38]

New World Mirror and Old World Bible

Their behavior while conquering the Americas ought to have convinced Europeans that *they* needed to be converted to Christianity. Instead, what caught their attention after 1492 were surprising aspects of indigenous cultures. Some European writers now saw their culture as deficient in light of indigenous cultures. Rather than seeing Europeans' rebellion against God as the cause, these writers blamed European ideas about property and the state.

In *New Worlds for Old,* William Brandon portrays "attitude toward property" as "the greatest dividing difference" between European and indigenous societies. Europeans were quick to notice it. In the Americas there was no "mine and thine." A stay-at-home compiler, Peter Martyr, summarized explorers' accounts in 1504 (here translated in Tudor English). Land was held communally, "in open gardens, not intrenched with dykes, dyvyded with hedges, or defended with waules. They deal trewely one with another, without lawes, without bookes, and without Judges." Europeans' stress on "mine and thine," Brandon argues, created a stratified society of haves and have-nots, and a powerful state was needed to protect property rights. By contrast, many indigenous societies stressed group ownership of land and generosity with food and goods. This produced an egalitarian "masterlessness" by comparison. Europeans thought the natives amazingly free.[39]

The root problem was Europeans' lack of obedience to the God who instituted property rights and government, not those institutions themselves. In a state of rebellion that rendered their religion unable to integrate their society, Europeans made property and power ends in themselves. European writers did not focus on the root problem but on its surface manifestations. Without realizing the revolutionary implications of their argument, they favorably contrasted indigenous propertylessness and "masterlessness" with European avarice, tyranny and bondage. They used the myth of human goodness in a New World state of nature to liberate themselves from the Christian belief in innate human depravity.

In reality, there were inequality and some private property and some rulers in the Americas.[40] European thinkers such as Jean-Jacques Rousseau and Michel de Montaigne ignored that fact and used indigenous societies as models whose libertarian nature Europeans might copy. Here were human-centered societies they could imitate in order to create a more human-centered Europe free of the old medieval argument between God and man. The New World mirror showed them their defects in light of their relationships to each other, not in light of their relationship to God.

So the Columbian encounter did not change their minds about their argument with God or even show them they were arguing with him. It did not cause the Protestant Reformation, for initially seafaring and settling had secularizing effects. Also, as Cameron argues, lay dissatisfaction with some church abuses did not logically lead to the Reformation. The laypeople were generally satisfied with "the predictable cycle of sin and forgiveness, the breathtaking shrines and sparkling festivals, the sensuous, tangible piety" they had created.[41] The Reformation was not anthropocentric but theocentric. It used the mirror of Scripture, not of exploration or experience.

Martin Luther's emphasis on justification by faith alone powerfully undercut human means to salvation: indulgences, good deeds, masses and prayers for the dead. Thus it undercut the mining of the church's spiritual functions. It powerfully restored God's preeminent role in human salvation:

> The saving of fallen souls was *not* a process of little lapses and little rituals to correct those lapses. Rather, it was a question of real sin, of a massive, all-corrupting inability to do right, which only God, by utterly gratuitous, self-sacrificing mercy, first covered with his grace, and then gradually . . . replaced with his own goodness in the Christian, in a process completed only in death.[42]

Reformers told Europeans that God was "a being infinitely vaster and more mysterious than the God of current anthropomorphism."[43] They powerfully restated God's side in his argument with Europeans.

Instead of reintegrating Europe, this restatement further divided it into bitter factions. Far from motivating exploration and colonization, the Protestant Reformation delayed them in countries such as England, where people were preoccupied for generations with religious strife. Later, the Reformation supplied a religious motive for emigration, but that was not its immediate effect.

The engine driving European overseas expansion was not religious zeal but capitalism, so we must examine the roots of European capitalism to understand expansion. Those roots are intertwined with the fact that, given Europeans' rebellion against God, the Christian religion did not fully integrate European societies.

We must recognize the paradox that the Reformation tended to strengthen, not weaken, the capitalist spirit unshackled in Renaissance Italy. First, it further destroyed any ability the Catholic Church and Catholic monarchs had to restrain merchants' behavior by secular or religious authority. Second, by reconnecting some Europeans to the transcendent God, the Reformation created the ascetic, intensely striving, calculating, saving Calvinist, whom Max Weber and others have seen as *the* personality type in capitalism's origins and growth. Protestants dignified all labor—not just the priest's or monk's labor—as service to God, to be done diligently and well, thus "producing a zeal for work unlike anything the world had yet seen." Calvinists seemed like Italian merchants—motives varied, but, as Stephen Innes notes, outwardly "the diligent saint (working for God's glory only) was indistinguishable from the diligent worldling (working for himself or herself only)."[44]

Innes describes Puritan Massachusetts Bay, but his words apply to all of Calvinist Europe: "The settlers' providentialism—the belief that they were participating in the working out of God's purposes—made all labor and enterprise 'godly business,' to be pursued aggressively and judged by the most exacting of standards." This Protestant providentialism was outwardly similar to yet inwardly opposite from Renaissance individualism: it stressed individuals (their consciences, not their desires); it was innovative; it was limitless in a way (God asked *total* obedience, but to well-marked rules); it did not condemn the accumulation of capital (the Bible had little to say on wealth creation but much on its distribution). Thus in economics two opposite movements worked to the same end.[45]

European Capitalism: Amoral, Abstracting, Accumulating, Limitless

Following Braudel, we can define *capitalism* as the "realm of investment and of a high rate of capital formation," where multiplying capital is the all-consuming goal, private property rights are assumed and markets and prices govern economic actions. Here, *capital* means either fixed assets used in production or circulating assets such as raw materials, unfinished goods and, most of all, money.[46] Accumulating capital was the goal which integrated European society. That was not predetermined or inevitable; it was the result of people's choices—

though once made they could not easily be unmade by later generations.

This drive to increase capital took off in the towns, especially Italian city-states and Dutch and German cities. Towns had more freedom for innovation apart from princely control, for Italian and German cities often ruled themselves. The country's fertile land could increase capital only very slowly. Harvest came once or twice a year, and the capitalist who wanted a quicker turnover of his investment could not speed it up. It was hard to increase the amount of tillable land, and demand for foodstuffs was limited too. Governments tended to control the price, lest food riots break out.[47] Farming was not abstract or limitless.

The drive to increase capital found release in the long-distance trade of luxury goods, not in the trade of necessities such as foodstuffs, which could not be transported far. Luxury goods made by city craftsmen and traded by city merchants were in great demand, and governments did not normally regulate their price. Their production was not limited by the seasons. They were less perishable and could be traded over long distances. Capitalists were less interested in producing them than they were "in distribution, marketing—the sector in which real profits were made."[48]

By stressing profit, not production, by trading luxury goods, not necessities, and by setting the highest prices, capitalists circumvented God's purposes for the economy and trade. The prophet Amos warned Israel of God's anger against unjust profiteering:

Hear this, you who trample the needy
    and do away with the poor of the land, saying,
"When will the New Moon be over
    that we may sell grain,
and the Sabbath be ended
    that we may market wheat?"—
skimping the measure,
    boosting the price
    and cheating with dishonest scales,
buying the poor with silver
    and the needy for a pair of sandals,
    selling even the sweepings with the wheat.[49]

Avaricious capitalism was not the result of private property but of a rebellious priority on accumulating property above worshiping God or supplying one's neighbor with necessities. Merchants did not corrupt European society with capitalism. They used capitalism to integrate a society which could not be integrated fully through politics or religion. They were the priests of the self-interested religion of ambition and avarice. Generalists who used the easily translated language of money, they effortlessly crossed political and religious boundaries to finance and coordinate the vices that existed: simony, sale of indulgences, tax-farming, wartime raids and ransoms, rulers' prodigal spending.

Bills of exchange show how merchant bankers integrated European society and flaunted their superiority over the church and their immunity from its rules. A bill of exchange was a merchant banker's promise to pay a certain amount "after a stipulated period in another place with a different currency." A merchant in Florence might write up a bill promising to pay three hundred Venetian ducats in six months in Venice. The merchant banker then sold the bill for money in one currency (ducats), and it was redeemed later in another currency (florins). The currency exchange rate between ducats and florins was set such that the banker made a profit (really, interest) on the exchange *and* a profit by investing the purchaser's money for the stipulated period. This increased capital and avoided the church's ban on usury (earning interest).[50]

The Medici, the pope's bankers, used bills of exchange in conducting his business, thus using church funds to evade the church's ban.[51] Though perhaps unreasonable, this ban and merchants' evasion symbolized the church's failed attempt to control economic life and to integrate European society. Yet the bill of exchange showed the merchants' successful attempt to integrate business dealings in distant places—Florence and Venice, for example.

As Braudel points out, "The bill of exchange, . . . the key weapon in the armoury of merchant capitalism in the West, was still . . . circulating almost exclusively within the bounds of Christendom." That similarity in creed and church created a minimal level of trust needed to accept bills from distant places.[52] Yet widespread similarity was not full integration. The bill might earn interest or buy slaves, and both were practices condemned by the church.

Bills of exchange, exchange fairs, stock exchanges, joint stock companies and other devices abstracted the merchant from the particularities of locality, product, people, nation, religion or language. Such financial devices flowed across these barriers. The merchant was distanced from the morality or immorality of any particular transaction. He profited from distant investments without feeling responsible if his agent was "buying the poor with silver and the needy for a pair of sandals." He had learned the wisdom "of never allowing oneself to be deterred in the pursuit of profit by moral, religious or sentimental considerations." He rejected "traditional values," which held that long-distance trade "served no legitimate social purpose" and threatened "the salvation of the soul." The abstract, generalized nature of his business allowed him to engage in many forms of trade. He did not have to know the details of any one craft, only the prices. Thus he could integrate European trade across craft and industry lines as well.[53]

These devices were developed in Italian city-states mainly engaged in Mediterranean trade with Egypt and the Levant. The long-distance luxury trade in Asian spices, medicinal plants, jewels, ivory, dyes and herbs was the most profitable. It drove the growth of city-state capitalism. Slaves were also traded. Columbus's home city, Genoa, dominated the long-distance slave trade. Its merchants bought slaves in the Balkan Black Sea ports and sold them in Egypt or in Genoa.

Italian and Moslem domination of long-distance Mediterranean trade drove Portugal and Spain to seek other trade routes. In 1492, Columbus was seeking a shortcut to the Orient to horn in on the spice trade. The Spanish brought to the Americas these capitalist devices. The resulting plantations were conquest institutionalized. Braudel calls them "capitalist creations *par excellence:* money, credit, trade, and exchange tied them to the east side of the Atlantic." They were "remote controlled" from Europe by means of capitalism's abstract devices with few misgivings about their harsh exploitation of human life.[54]

This amoral capitalism resulted from the failure of religion or the state to integrate and control European society. That is clear when we consider the example of China, which did not develop capitalism despite its advanced market economy. Using Confucian culture, the Chinese state integrated and controlled Chinese society. According to Braudel, it did not allow merchants to nourish great ambitions: "The state uncompromisingly controlled everything and expressed unmistakable hostility to any individual making himself 'abnormally' rich." It controlled the economy in a nearly Christian manner: guarding against famine, controlling markets and opposing "excessive wealth." Only the state, not the individual, could accumulate capital.[55]

Theoretically, Christian doctrine encouraged similar moral control of Europe's economy. As pious individuals exercised self-control, renounced greed and considered their neighbor when buying or selling, the economy would come under control. However, Christianity was not heeded in Europe as Confucianism was in China. Moreover, Confucianism was "a state ideology as well as a personal ethic." It explicitly justified and upheld the social order.[56] By contrast, Christianity was a personal ethic strangely unconcerned with exactly what government or economy its followers lived under. Its "kingdom of God" was not a blueprint for a specific nation or empire, and its God-centeredness provoked rebellion among its own adherents. Absorbed in their pursuit of riches and power, Christendom's pope, church officials and rulers did not use Christian doctrines to integrate European society.[57]

Integrated mainly by capitalist devices and common self-seeking, this European society was almost destructively dynamic, innovative, aggressive and expansionist. Describing it at a later stage, historian Theodore Von Laue calls it "a singularly prolific cultural hothouse in which all human accomplishments were advanced at a forced clip." Even by 1500, it was a hothouse in the making.[58]

The European Conquest of the New World: Synopsis

Freed by monotheism from a paralyzing worship of objects, Europeans rebelliously argued with that one God in ways that added to their destructive dynamism. Divinely revealed, Christianity denied innate human goodness, diagnosed humanity as sinful and rebellious and exalted a God whom humans could not manipulate. Its once-for-all text, Scripture, stood as a barrier to any attempts to alter it for human purposes. Even its Reformation exacerbated the dynamism: Calvinist saints' seeing eternal consequences in daily deeds were nearly as intense and dynamic as rebellious merchants. The Reformation also showed that any religious monopoly would face competition. Bishops and rulers could not make Christianity as secure a support for their status quo as Confucianism was for Manchu and mandarins. It provoked Europeans to rebellion or to holy zeal, so it could not integrate European society.

Try though they might, using New World "noble savages" as examples, they could not return to pre-Christian "innocence." They could not invent a human-centered creation myth and religion which everyone would accept and use to achieve integration. They could not manipulate Christianity indefinitely, and they could not escape it. They would have to hurtle into the future "at a forced clip" with a society and culture that was not integrated or controlled. As Sale notes, Europe's "increasingly vigorous capitalist system" was "more materialist, for sure, than any other economy, more expansionist, more volatile and energetic . . . and almost everywhere without the kinds of moral inhibitions found in the world's other high cultures."[59]

It was apocalyptic in its destructive dynamism, a proof of history's linear character, a guarantee that one day history would come to an end. It was impossible to project this "cultural hothouse" advancing at "a forced clip" and avoiding some kind of catastrophe indefinitely. Even sixteenth-century Europeans, who had hardly seen the start of new accomplishments, understood that "the almost miraculous sequence of events which led to the discovery, conquest and conversion of the New World" tended "to reinforce the linear and progressive" view of history.[60]

A student of biblical prophecy, Columbus believed that by reaching new lands he was hastening the end of the world. The prophet Isaiah and Jesus the Messiah had stated that the end could not come until the gospel had been preached to all nations. Pauline Watts notes that "Columbus's apocalyptic vision of the world and of the special role that he was destined to play in the unfolding of events that would presage the end of time was a major stimulus for his voyages."[61] Without justifying his actions, or those of other explorers and conquerors, we can say that Columbus was correct here. By starting the process whereby this dynamic European culture became globally dominant, Columbus made global history an irretrievably linear history.

His advancing of God's purpose in history was somewhat inadvertent, however, for he thought God's purpose was inextricably linked to his and to Spain's. It was not, for they were engaged in an argument with him. He used them to accomplish his purposes anyway but did not excuse their actions. Columbus's view of biblical prophecy does not justify his actions toward the Taino, but neither do his actions make biblical prophecies erroneous. One can have a right idea and still do wrong. One can have truth and still rebel against it. Europeans were doing just that. God's ends did not justify their means, even if they had been pursuing his ends, which they were not.

So, paradoxically, both Columbus and the revisionist writers who condemn him are correct. His voyages advanced God's long-range goals and yet were profoundly ungodly. That is so because of a deeper paradox: the Christianity carried by Europeans to the New World was divinely revealed truth, yet those who carried it were in serious rebellion against it. As divine revelation, it provoked human rebellion. Exploration brought rebellion to a world that had not known rebellion as destructively dynamic as was Europe's.

2

Africa Comes
to the Americas,
Christ Comes to
the Slaves

NEW WORLD SLAVERY WAS EURO-
pean conquest institutionalized and perpetuated, with one addition: Africans
were imported to serve as the permanently conquered. Forcibly transporting an
estimated 11.5 million Africans to the Americas and Atlantic islands between
1451 and 1870, Europeans brought a third people, race and culture into the
momentous Columbian encounter.[1] Here we have a positive story—Africa's
contribution to America's mix of peoples and cultures; but we also have a
human tragedy—the inhuman means used to bring Africa to America and keep
it there. We necessarily start with tragedy, with capitalism, the slave trade and
plantation slavery—the motives, means and ends which brought it here.

As the conquest is cited to criticize Christianity, so some historians blame
slavery partly on Christianity. Gary B. Nash calls it the religion of the "master
class"—implying that Christianity is linked to mastering slaves. Howard Zinn
claims that masters used "the lulling effects of religion" to secure obedience.
Many writers note that, in Europe, Christians were forbidden to enslave other
Christians, but in the Americas Africans who converted were not thereby freed.

Yet Europeans continued to rationalize slavery as a means to convert them.[2]

Plantation Slavery a Product of Capitalism, Not Christianity

The acts of Europeans who argued against their God cannot be blamed on Christianity, its Scriptures or its God. It did not *advocate* slavery. It commanded believers to work with their own hands and to serve others. An obedient Christian was stripped of the motives for acquiring slaves. In one of his lists of "the ungodly" the apostle Paul included "slave traders." In his list of ungodly Babylon's merchandise, John included the "bodies and souls of men."[3] Jesus Christ was executed, as were Roman slaves, by flogging and crucifixion. How could honestly following him lead to slaveholding?

Jesus was crucified toward the end of the first of "three explosive surges of imperial expansion" which enslaved "captives on a scale unmatched in human history": the Roman conquests that created the Roman Empire, the Arabian conquests of 630-730 and the Spanish-Portuguese conquests of 1450-1550. Roman slavery was different from New World plantation slavery, though sometimes as cruel. It was not based on race, and Romans did not make it into a vast business. They sometimes gave trusted slaves important administrative or educational roles.[4]

Critics correctly note that the New Testament did not explicitly condemn Roman slavery; indeed, Paul commanded slaves to obey their masters. We can quickly see why that was so. First-century Christians were a small, persecuted minority sometimes tossed to the Coliseum's lions or lit up as human torches in Rome. The apostles did not waste quills or parchment writing to their scared flock about ideas to reform Roman society. No matter how noble the ideas or well-intentioned the believers, they could never carry them out. That applied to the economy as well: the New Testament hardly addresses the issue of capital accumulation, for the early believers were poor peasants and fishermen.[5] That does not excuse later Christians who achieved majority status and prosperity from a duty to abide by the antislavery implications of the gospel.

In a deeper sense, the biblical revelation of God acting in Jesus Christ does not contain a divine blueprint for an integrated, idyllic society and economy. The kingdom has come "now" in the person of the King, but its full realization is "not yet." As Richard John Neuhaus notes, the New Testament's "view of riches . . . is not so much ethical as eschatological and theocentric." These are the last times; an idyllic society is "not yet" possible until the King returns.

Meanwhile, the divine plan is to bring humans, one by one, to salvation and "the knowledge of the glory of God in the face of Christ"—*not* to bring human society to utopian equilibrium *short* of the hoped-for goal of everyone knowing God. Slavery was a symptom of the human rejection of God. Once the runaway slave Onesimus and his master Philemon had, one-by-one, come to salvation, Paul urged Philemon to treat him leniently, perhaps to free him.[6]

Since we are primarily examining U.S. history, where the overwhelming majority of slaveholders were Protestants, I will focus on the relationship between Protestantism and slavery. We will find it a complex relationship. Portraying it as mutual hostility or acceptance is simplistic.

Historian David Brion Davis reminds us that slavery was linked to the human desire for progress (not to any divine desire): "Plantation slavery . . . was a creation of the most progressive peoples and forces in Europe." In ancient Greece and Rome, slavery freed the master class from manual labor to concentrate on politics and culture. In Renaissance Europe, merchants integrated slavery into their limitless, amoral, individualistic, innovative capitalism. Genoa engaged in the prohibited trade in Christian slaves—even selling them to Muslims in Egypt—as "part of a general defiance of traditional restraints and limits that made Genoa a crucible of economic and maritime innovation."[7] Europe innovated its way out of the fourteenth-century economic doldrums into the capitalistic expansion of the late fifteenth and sixteenth centuries, and slavery helped greatly. It was one of the engines driving European expansion and prosperity. We need not determine here whether it was the main engine.[8] We are asking whose servant slavery was—Christianity's or capitalism's? We are not asking how important its services were to the latter; few would claim that they were insignificant.

The Causes of Plantation Slavery

Why did European merchants and colonizers get involved in slavery in the Americas? Merchants sought immediate high profits through trading, not lower, slower returns from long-term investments in production. Colonizers sought to bring European emigrants, not Africans, to their newly found lands. Why, therefore, did they end up doing what they first did not intend to do?

In the New World, Spanish and Portuguese explorers and captains were often frustrated to find "no preexisting trading networks" to plug into. Indigenous traders did not stand on the shore offering to trade gold or silver or much of anything the Iberians wanted. They would have to steal, mine, grow or make it themselves. Natural resources were abundant—arable land, minerals, forests—but who would do the manual labor? European explorers, merchants and adventurers did not intend to do it, and their diseases decimated the Native Americans, who were unwilling to be slaves anyway. They also could not convince enough lower-class Europeans to migrate and to labor. Historian Barbara Solow summarizes their dilemma: "Voluntary labor was slow to immigrate; capital was hard to attract or generate; promising export crops were slow to emerge; and when they did, free labor was reluctant to grow them."[9]

The French, Dutch, English and others faced the same dilemma. Desperate, the English sought a Northwest Passage in order to leave this tradeless area and reach the lucrative Asian trade. They also preyed on Spanish ships returning to Spain with Peruvian silver.[10] Both had diminishing returns: the first never succeeded and the second led to war with Spain. Two continents blocked the way to Asia, and their inhabitants would not trade or make the goods Europeans wanted. Merchants had to solve the problem of production first.

To explain why they turned to slave labor to solve it, some historians advocate the "free land" hypothesis. Land was "free" (cheap and abundant) in the Americas. (Of course, it already belonged to indigenous peoples, but Europeans generally ignored that fact.) A merchant or other European could acquire huge landholdings. Yet labor was scarce, so he found it hard to exploit the land or its natural resources. Free (nonslave) laborers demanded high wages, then quit to start their own farms on "vacant" lands once they had saved enough to pay start-up costs. That further reduced the labor supply, and the only solution for the large landowner was "unfree" labor—unpaid and immobile.[11]

This hypothesis is disputed, but both its supporters and critics miss the importance of *religious* motives. "Free" land and scarce labor are problems only to the capitalist investor seeking maximum profits through production of a staple crop for export. Supporter Solow criticizes the dispersal of free labor: "The immigrants will just replicate their family-sized farms across the vast landscape." To religiously motivated colonists seeking to worship God, there's nothing wrong with that. It's only undesirable to the merchant-capitalist.

Two critics complain that the "free land" hypothesis cannot explain "why slavery was central to the economies" of the southern colonies and "only peripheral in New England, the Middle Colonies, and the southern backcountry."[12] That's easy to explain. Enough religiously motivated Protestants migrated to the Americas that the Dissenting colonies' labor force was adequate to meet their goal of replicating religious communities across the landscapes of New England and the Middle Colonies. (The southern backcountry is a more complex case.) The cohesive nature of religious communities limited population dispersal. No scarcity of labor meant little need for slave labor.

When done earnestly by enough people, serving and worshiping God have great social and economic effects. In the Northern colonies they largely solved the "free land" problem and made slave labor unnecessary. Historians do not give Puritans and other Dissenters credit for how their religious motives solved or forestalled problems. Solow admits, "The success of the Massachusetts Bay Colony rested on the strength of its noneconomic motives," but she does not specify religious ones. Seeming reluctant to credit Christianity, one textbook author attributes the northern colonies' relative lack of slave labor to "colder climates" that kept settlers from growing "labor-intensive crops." Quite the contrary, Massachusetts' Puritans could have grown tobacco, but they chose not to rely on this cash crop. David Hackett Fischer claims that high African death rates in cold New England "partly" kept slavery limited there. Yet West Indies sugar planters hardly let high African death rates *there* stop their slave owning.[13] No, the desire to serve and to worship caused Dissenters to come, to plunk themselves down in a strange place, to work with their own hands and to stay together, not wander off to seek profits.

There were exceptions. Religious motives did not preclude economic motives. Puritans and Quakers sought profits, and some dispersed to the high seas to find them. Both participated in the slave trade, and some African slaves were imported into New England and the Middle Colonies.[14] Protestantism did not forbid slavery and seventeenth-century Dissenters did not abstain from it altogether. The picture was more complicated. Dissenters had a strong motive for emigration, compact settlement and creation of a semisubsistence, small-farm economy, which tended to keep slavery "peripheral." Later, they produced a strong antislavery movement.

By looking at the Puritan nobles' colony at Providence Island in the Caribbean, historian Karen Ordahl Kupperman tries to demonstrate that Puritans had economic, individualist motives too, that Massachusetts Bay succeeded because it allowed these motives, making it little different from Virginia and Maryland. Yet Providence colony differed from Massachusetts Bay in ways that make her argument unconvincing: leadership by "grandees" with nationalistic as well as religious motives, and a firm control over Providence that discouraged settlers' initiatives and kept them tenants.[15]

Profit Motives Create the Slave Trade

We see the importance of religious motives or the lack thereof when we look at colonial Georgia. Founded in the early 1730s next to settled South Carolina, it was started by idealistic trustees for noble motives: to provide useful goods for the English market, farms for debtors and petty criminals and a military buffer for South Carolina from Spanish attacks. It would be an egalitarian society without extremes of wealth or poverty. Here the "free land" hypothesis would be defeated by limiting landholdings, delaying population dispersal and banning slavery. (Of course, the trustees were unaware of the "free land" hypothesis.) Like Chinese mandarins, the trustees tried to control profit seeking and wealth accumulation and avoid the moral and social costs of unrestrained avarice.[16]

The problem was that many Georgia colonists did not share the trustees' ideals. In neighboring South Carolina, they had a visible example of the wealth which landowning slaveholders could accumulate. "South Carolina exhibited all that the Georgia trustees wished to avoid, but its example and propinquity proved too powerful." Georgians began a twenty-year battle of pamphlets, petitions and pressure to convince the trustees to reverse their mandarinlike measures. Interestingly, the trustees' main supporters were the Salzburgers, German Dissenters who came for religious motives. The others were profit seekers who saw slavery as the answer to Georgia's economic stagnation. The trustees gave in, and slavery became legal by 1751.[17] Idealism worked only if it was shared by settlers. Only a strong Christian faith caused settlers to practice the virtue of working their own land with their own hands.

One of Georgia's proslavery pamphleteers argued that slavery was an economic necessity: "It is clear as light itself, that negroes are as essentially necessary to the cultivation of Georgia, as axes, hoes or any other utensil of agricultures." Like an economic historian, he calculated the "comparative profitability of black and white labor." He concluded that "a Man at the end of 8 years, who plants with white men is £715.9[shillings].9 [pence] worse [off], than he would be were he to use Negroes." Like many economic historians, he assumed profit motives as a given and ignored social and moral costs in this tidy, narrow accounting. Plantation slavery was a calculated choice, but a profit-motivated mentality came before the calculation.[18]

We must avoid economic, environmental or geographical determinism. "Free" land, scarce labor, warm climates or staple crops did not produce New World slavery. Europeans did. In the Canary Islands, Barbados and Virginia, they pursued their idea of progress: capital accumulation and investment at high rates of return with little manual labor on their part. In the Canaries, Spanish "conquerors needed quick profits to pay for their expeditions, mainly financed on credit," so they sold Canarians as slaves and used slaves to tend sugar plantations. On Barbados, profit-seeking Englishmen tried one staple crop after another before mastering sugar-cane production. Not warm climate but materialism was the "historical force" at work there. After much bungling and high mortality, English gentlemen's disdain for work and regard for profit triumphed in Virginia. Tobacco tended by indentured servants became the staple crop by the 1620s. But large-scale slavery did not begin for another fifty years.[19] The motive of profiting greatly from others' labor came long before slavery.

Profit seekers are notoriously impatient. Ironically, notes historian Philip Curtin, European landowners in the New World could have solved the labor shortage by waiting for disease immunity to build and the native-born population to reproduce. Given migrant slaves' high mortality rates, that waiting would not have slowed the solution much. "A plantation society willing to accept this slow natural increase could have avoided the slave trade, with its high mortality for all concerned." But merchants and investors were not willing to wait or to postpone production. Part of capitalism's limitlessness was its urge to transcend the slow limits of time, of seasons, of human growth spans. So merchants turned to the slave trade.[20]

The demand for bound individuals to labor on plantations increased enormously,[21] so Europeans looked to Africa for slave labor. Why didn't they enslave other Europeans? Their use of Africans was not predetermined. Enslaving criminals or prisoners of war might have been more cost-effective.

Here again, Christianity limited Europeans' ability to act from profit motives only. It produced similarity, not integration, in Europe. Other Europeans were similar enough to be ineligible for enslavement. They were "insiders" belonging to the same society. The greater universality of Christianity produced a wider circle of inclusion than did localized tribal religions in Africa. There, members of other tribes were often defined as "outsiders" eligible for slavery. Yet Western Europeans had a very human-centered view of Christianity. They equated it with culture, inherited status, race and ethnicity more than with conversion to a faith in Jesus Christ. So they refused to free African slaves who converted. Paradoxically, the more Europeans were unable "to think in terms of slavery for other Europeans, the more" they were "likely to contemplate coerced labor for non-Europeans." Drawing the circle of insiders left Africans outside.[22]

Here we come to the second story: Africa's contribution to the peopling of America. The overwhelming majority of Africans transported to the Americas as slaves came from West Africa, so we must briefly examine that area's history, culture, religion and economy.

West African History

West Africans shared some characteristics with Native Americans. They belonged to many tribes and nations, so it is hard to generalize about them. They too "seem to have shared a special reverence for the natural world and a belief that spirit power inhabits it." For many of them, "rocks, trees, and rivers held power and could be the abode of gods" or "spirit forces." They too created human-centered religions to integrate their societies. Like the Aztecs, their religions stressed a cyclical view of history: innovation was abhorred; the individual sought to recreate the past in the present; "through rite and ritual the African strove for the goal of repeating the mythical past." In large kingdoms such as Ghana and Kanem, as in the Incan empire, the king was a religious figure integrating present with past, and people with "spirit forces." In Ghana, as Muslims disapprovingly noted, the king was "exalted and worshipped instead of God. . . .They believe that it is the kings who bring life and death, sickness and health."[23] Living in integrated cultures, West Africans also lacked Europeans' destructively dynamic argument with their God.

Unlike Native Americans, West Africans lived close to an aggressive, monotheistic, proselytizing people—the Muslims, who had a more advanced civilization than Europe's during the Middle Ages. The Sahara Desert separated black West Africa from Muslim North Africa, but this sea of sand was narrower and more easily traversed than the Atlantic. Traders' caravans brought West Africa into the Muslim trading network and stimulated manufacturing, trade, learning and political ambitions throughout the region. Some West African societies had achieved much even before the Muslim trade encouraged greater achievements. By the eleventh century A.D., West African societies were more advanced than most in the Americas and some in Europe. In the north-south trade, Muslim traders exchanged horses, weapons, salt and general merchandise for West African gold, kola nuts, ivory and slaves.[24]

This trade encouraged mining and manufacturing throughout West Africa. It encouraged kings to expand their domains in order to control the trade and the goods needed for it. Trade primarily benefited the ruling classes, who used it to obtain horses and weapons to increase their military power. In Ghana, for example, the trade in gold was "virtually a state monopoly." As in China, state control greatly limited the chance that merchant capitalism would develop. Individuals had less incentive to pursue new trading opportunities, since rulers would seize a great part of the profits. However, this insured that West African societies maintained unity and resisted the individualistic temptations of limitless trade.

The "free" land hypothesis was true of West Africa, which was "chronically underpopulated; land had little value without people to work it." The need for exports, labor scarcity and abundant land led to the use of slave labor. Yet rulers' control and seizure of profits limited economic motives and prevented wholesale conversion to slave labor. West African slavery was more humane than New World plantation slavery. It was not based on race. Slaves often married and joined their adopted tribe. Some were given administrative positions. They were not "articles of commerce" but "means by which" rulers created "larger and more effective units of population . . . than resulted from kinship ties." Yet they were still slaves.[25]

The Atlantic Slave Trade as a Capital-Accumulating Business

European merchants did not initiate, but rather exploited, an existing slave trade and made it incomparably worse. West African kings could regulate the African end of the Atlantic slave trade, but they could never regulate plantation slavery across the Atlantic. There, European capitalism created enormous demand for slave labor, purchased some 11.5 million Africans, transported them thousands of miles and used them in a new type of slavery—racial, hereditary, degrading, permanent, commercialized. Plantation slavery was "capitalism away from home."[26] Europeans were distanced from its destructive consequences. For three centuries they exerted little pressure to humanize the New World slave plantations.

The slave trade was a business in which Europeans often used the new methods developed by Italian merchants. England's Royal African Company (RAC) was a joint stock company capitalized at £100,000 and dominated by London merchants. King Charles II gave it a trading monopoly and governmental powers to make war and dispense justice along the African coast. But it lacked military supremacy there, so it bribed West African kings to renew its privileges. Sometimes it only transported slaves and did not assume "ownership" of them. The abstracting devices of capitalism allowed London merchants to form syndicates, which contracted with the RAC "to buy slaves at a fixed price and sell them in the West Indies." Merchants took most of the risks but did not have to dirty their hands with the disreputable details of slave trading, which were "laundered" through the abstracting devices of syndicates and contracts. The West Indian planter then paid the syndicate with a bill of exchange drawn on his London agent.[27]

These devices helped slave traders finance voyages and manage, subdivide or contract out the substantial risks: high mortality rates, insurrections, pirates, price changes and normal sailing hazards. Marine insurance was costly, but it helped to spread the risks. The business could never have been conducted on such a large scale over such great distances without stock companies, syndicates, bills of exchange and insurance. Profits averaged only about 8-10 percent.[28]

The slave trade loomed so large to the merchant and his nation because it stimulated European production of exports to Africa, forced the Americas to produce goods to pay for slaves and allowed them to pay for imports from Europe. It set up a complicated, mutually reinforcing network of trading partners. The key was the African slave, whom the merchant saw as a "commodity" which could be traded for profit but which could also produce other commodities.[29] Within capitalism's narrow accounting, the African's suffering, the family's loss and the disruptions of slavery in Africa and the Americas did not show up on the profit and loss statement. They were "externalized" and borne by others, not the merchant.

In 1745, the slave trade's importance was described by an RAC member with the wonderful name of Malachy Postlethwayt. In *The African Trade* he argued that Britain's naval power and maritime prosperity rested on it because Britain's colonies depended on it. "Are we not indebted to that valuable People, the Africans, for our Sugars, Tobaccoes, Rice, Rum and all other Plantation Produce?" Britain imported these from her colonies and exported manufactured goods to Africa to trade for slaves. "The Negro-Trade . . . may be justly esteemed an inexhaustible Fund of Wealth and Naval Power" and is "the mainspring of the machine which sets every wheel in motion."[30]

It set wheels in motion in West Africa, where it was "the business of kings, rich men, and prime merchants" seeking wealth and power. Slaves were exchanged for European goods: cloth, guns, knives, metals, tobacco, alcohol and gold. Using European firearms, "upstart potentates" organized new kingdoms or city-states to control and profit from the slave trade. Some kingdoms collapsed when the disruptive trade increased too rapidly. In some, an "anarchic free for all" erupted over the trade in slaves, worth far more than before. African rulers controlled European traders, who had to pay head-taxes, fees, commissions, rents, entertainment expenses and bribes to the rulers and to African brokers, slave-caravan leaders, "porters, guards, water carriers, criers, and so forth." Many Africans prospered from it, but Europeans who sold both slaves and the sugar and tobacco they produced earned more.[31] West Africa had traded for centuries, but a high demand for its slaves magnified trading's importance and disrupted its traditional integration of politics, religion and trade.

Plantation Slavery Distorts Family, Church and Government

Both the cause and result of the slave trade, New World plantation slavery set wheels in motion in the Americas too. Here it did not disrupt traditional integration; European conquest had accomplished that. It attempted a new integration of New World societies around the all-important master-slave relationship. Family, church and government all orbited around this relationship with harmful effects for all three.

As we have seen, the English who settled at Jamestown in the early seventeenth century disdained work as beneath a gentleman's dignity. In proportion to its population, Virginia had six times the number of gentlemen England had. The Virginia Company had some noble motives: to give farms to the farmless and employment to the unemployed. Unlike Puritans' religious motives, though, the Company's motives were not shared by its settlers and did not limit their economic motives. When Virginians discovered tobacco in the early 1620s, Company idealism was swamped. High tobacco prices set off a boom-town atmosphere, complete with "floating taverns" in the James River, frenzied buying and selling of indentured servants, neglect of gardens and crops and sudden fortunes. The governing Company was cheated by its own Virginia officials, who sold Company servants for their own profit.[32]

Government was more bent to plantation owners' purposes in Barbados, the home of and model for many South Carolina settlers. King Charles I had granted the island to the Earl of Carlisle as a virtual fief. The Earl could "make laws, select clergymen, erect courts, appoint judges, enforce obedience by corporal punishment or sentence of death." He ran the island for his personal economic benefit, to maximize his rents from planters. Very early, however, his government lost control of the planters, who had their own economic interests to pursue: first tobacco, then sugar. Masters abused their slaves with no intervention from the government. Private persons had public powers of judge, jury and executioner on the plantation.[33]

In what historian Gary Puckrein calls the "frenzied, bonanza climate" of a sugar-cane boom, neither family, church, government nor economy fulfilled their divinely ordained functions. The economy provided neither food nor work for the lower classes. Food prices soared as land was planted in sugar cane. Slavery meant that the poor could not find employment, for slaves were cheaper than hired hands. If they worked the land as tenants, skyrocketing land values evicted them and doomed the landless man's hope of getting into sugar production. Slavery, high mortality rates and a high ratio of males to females hampered family life among blacks. The last two distorted the whites' family life too.

Anglicanism was bent by the planters for their purposes. "Playing on African religious beliefs, planters made Christianity appear to be a secret society that endowed all its adherents with great knowledge and privileges." Like West African kings arranging to be fed secretly to inspire awe, planters told slaves to leave the room when prayers were said to make them believe that Christianity was sorcery and the planters sorcerers who should not be opposed. Planters fought attempts to evangelize their slaves. To them, religion was a convenient device "to distinguish superior from inferior persons." All this was turning true Christianity upside down.

A similar distortion occurred in Virginia and South Carolina once slave plantations became the norm. Through each Anglican church's governing board or vestry, wealthy planters denied clergymen economic security and controlled their religious functions. When it came to evangelizing slaves, the master's priorities were clear: "The economic profitability of his slaves, not their Christianization, held top priority for the colonial planter." He worried that baptized slaves could claim their freedom, that religious instruction was too time-consuming, that conversion would change his relationship to his slaves and make them harder to control. It is not true, as historian Jon Butler claims, that evangelical Christianity established and supported slavery in the South. Christian doctrine challenged slaveholders to change the system but did not remove their right to refuse. Where doctrine and economics conflicted, the planter insisted that the church back down. One minister said it all in his sermon title: "Trade preferr'd before Religion and Christ made to give place to Mammon."[34]

So Anglican ministers backed down. Colonial legislatures passed laws declaring that baptism did not bring freedom. Bowing to planters' priorities,

Anglican ministers justified evangelization on the grounds that the gospel would make better slaves. The resulting efforts were human-centered "churchianity"—painfully intellectual, creedal, dry, condescending and tedious. One Anglican minister described his Sunday sessions with slaves: "We begin and end our particular assembly with the Collect *Prevent us O Lord* etc. I teach them the Creed, the Lord's Prayer, and the Commandments." Where Christianity was tied to planters' interests, many slaves refused to convert.[35]

Because they assume that people designed Christianity to meet human needs, many historians presume that masters were unaffected by their choice of trade over Christ. But that was not the case. Christianity is a living, dynamic faith in a living, personal God. Masters who chose trade over him could not have the same relationship with him as those who chose him over trade. Christianity was not a faith where the "master class" called the shots no matter what power it had over the vestry. With another meaning in mind, a nineteenth-century writer said it best: "Christianity and slavery cannot live together; but churchianity and slavery are twins."[36] When Anglican ministers had to offer slaves a "churchianity" tailored to slaveholders' interests, the masters ended up with "churchianity" too.

In Virginia the Anglican Church was established, but Christianity was very weak. Many parishes lacked ministers. Only about 40 percent of white families attended church in the early eighteenth century. Communion was given only four times a year. In 1724, only 25 percent of those in attendance took Communion. Sunday church was a social event, whose proud ostentation and conviviality undercut the Christian message. "Gentlemen arrived late and made a grand entrance just as the service began and left in a body after all others had departed." They flaunted their power. Before church began, reported one local tutor, they mingled, "giving and receiving letters of business, reading Advertisements, consulting about the price of tobacco" and discussing horses. Church was a quick reading of prayers and a twenty-minute sermon. Afterward they spent nearly an hour "strolling around the Church among the crowd," giving and receiving social invitations. Judging by the sheer number of words, Christianity was severely limited, profit-seeking unlimited. The planter was not humbled for even a few short minutes on Sunday, but exalted himself. No wonder one "young Gent" in South Carolina said "that he is resolved never to come to the Holy Table while slaves are Rec[eive]d there."[37]

This proud racial prejudice had been present since the English first stepped ashore, though one historian claims they did not have "a racial ideology" then.[38]

Racial prejudice they had, and, when the profit motive led them to use slave labor, it was African labor they purchased. Slavery, in turn, strengthened racial prejudice. It placed blacks in inferior, menial roles at which they had no real motivation to excel. Whites concluded that they were naturally lazy. Whites' implicitly violent role as masters earned them the hatred of some African-Americans. That hatred and the fear of slave revolt increased whites' prejudice against them. Racial prejudice served as a convenient reason to keep them enslaved—and that use strengthened prejudice. It was a never-ending cycle.

The First Great Awakening Challenges Plantation Slavery

In the late 1730s and early 1740s, some African-Americans and some whites tried to break that cycle. Spearheaded by the Anglican revivalist George Whitefield, a great continental revival, the (First) Great Awakening, swept the Thirteen Colonies. It was totally unlike the previous highly intellectual, institutional efforts at religious instruction. Those were ineffectual human efforts; this was Spirit-powered and strikingly effectual. One powerful sign that God's Spirit was at work was the revival's impact among African-Americans. Their response to the revival helped shape it.

Preaching in the South, Whitefield was touched by slaves' acceptance of his message: "God will highly favour them to wipe off their reproach and shew that He is no respecter of persons." Whitefield insisted on meeting with slaves and made a special appeal to them at the end of his sermons. Other white preachers were also moved by blacks' response. Later, one Methodist preacher reported, "the number of blacks that attend the preaching affects me much."[39] African-Americans were actors in the revival even before some began preaching and exhorting. Revivals are spread by avowals and stopped by refusals. Black slaves helped spread this one. The sight of illiterate African-American slaves converting, exhorting, preaching and worshiping with whites was a major wonder of the revival, encouraging supporters and enraging detractors.

Revival did not end racial prejudice, but it brought whites and blacks together in ways that undermined prejudice. "The tendency of evangelical religion to level the souls of all men before God" was shown in preachers' powerful emotional appeals to all. African-Americans responded to those appeals more than to intellectual catechizing. Once converted, they came into churches, into "religious reciprocity" with whites. All born-again believers were equal in Virginia's early Baptist churches. Here, God could partially redeem the evils of slavery. Here, slaves could complain about masters' brutality. Here, sexually immoral masters and those who sold slave husbands away from their wives could be disciplined (if they were church members). One brutal master was disciplined, repented and became a teaching elder in a largely black congregation! Virginia Baptists took a stand against slavery.[40]

What caused slaves to accept their masters' faith? Some historians claim that it was the preachers' egalitarianism. The evidence suggests the reverse: slaves' response prodded preachers to include slaves as equals in audiences and congregations. Some claim that slaves identified with the Israelites and their exodus out of Egyptian slavery. Yet that was not the preachers' message: Whitefield's hellfire-and-brimstone sermons hardly stressed equality (in a positive sense), Egypt or emancipation from slavery. Some see parallels between conversion experiences and traditional African "spirit travels." Yet hell, Scripture, conversion and preaching were concepts foreign to West African religions.[41] With African-American personalities, with a different style of worship, with different tastes in music, slaves accepted this theology. They left the meetings as converted African-Americans, not new-baked Europeans. (The theology was not European either.) The white preachers' message did not automatically fit their personalities, their style, their tastes.

Orlando Patterson convincingly argues, "Jesus and his crucifixion dominate the theology of the slaves and not, as recent scholars have claimed, the Israelites and Exodus story." That theology was very similar to whites' theology. It began with God's anger at all races' sinfulness. It called the individual to accept Christ as the Substitute who bore God's punishment for sin. It brought converts into a close relationship to Jesus Christ. Slaves may have identified more with the Jesus who died a Roman slave's death. "In the figure of Jesus Christ, they found someone who had suffered as they suffered, someone who understood, someone who offered them rest from their suffering."[42]

Here we must note modern, secular historians' failure to make any sense of slaves' sufferings. A Christianity of the cross proclaims that innocent suffering can be redeeming and ennobling in ways that neither degrade the sufferer nor excuse the perpetrator. Writing to encourage persecuted believers, Peter presents several ways in which "even if you should suffer for what is right, you are blessed." Without this view, historians have debated several interpretations of African-American slaves: Sambos whom suffering has stripped of the capacity to resist, constant rebels for whom shirking work was rebellion or proud people proving their manhood by running away or revolting. Some historians seem to wish for a bloody slave uprising to prove African-Americans' manhood and will to resist. Some analyze slavery in economic terms and leave suffering off the final profit-and-loss statement.[43]

Here is an inability to make sense out of suffering. Of course, even from the Christian view that suffering can achieve some redemptive goal, we cannot say in individual cases exactly what goal might be achieved. Nor can we say that in every case it achieved anything. Nor can we deny that there may have been better ways to achieve those goals. But we know that for those who love him God can turn suffering to some redemptive use without excusing the perpetrator or turning the sufferer into a degraded personality. We can reject the common view that only by resisting or revolting can a slave retain his or her personality and self-respect. The suffering slave had a greater model than Nat Turner and a higher destiny than to be another Denmark Vesey. Christ, the suffering Servant of Isaiah, was the model; the destiny was to be Christlike. By following "the figure of Jesus Christ . . . who had suffered as they suffered," the slave could become like the King of kings. That's the hope Christianity offered to individual slaves.

We must not be simplistic and see plantation slavery as some course in discipleship, whose pain and degradation were all worthwhile because of the end result. Nor does the end result somehow excuse slaveholding. But this view denies that slaves lost their personhood or dignity if they did not revolt or resist. In a Christian view, Pontius Pilate and his Roman soldiers were not the final victors, nor were African-American slaves final losers. African-American history cannot be understood without understanding that suffering need not be dehumanizing but can be redemptive and ennobling.

Although we cannot say with certainty what African-American slaves' identification with Christ in his crucifixion meant for individuals, we can know what it meant for the church. It partly fulfilled Jesus' saying "But I, when I am lifted up from the earth, will draw all men to myself." Whites and African-Americans meeting in Baptist churches fulfilled Paul's pronouncement: "There is neither . . . slave nor free . . . for you are all one in Christ Jesus." The centrality of the cross in slaves' theology and interracial Baptist churches lets us apply Paul's words concerning Jews and Gentiles to masters and slaves:

> For [Christ] himself is our peace, who has made the two one and has destroyed the barrier, the dividing wall of hostility. . . . His purpose was to create in himself one new man out of the two, thus making peace, and in this one body to reconcile both of them to God through the cross, by which he put to death their hostility.[44]

Reconciliation was a powerful vindication of Christianity. Did African-Americans and whites accept the revivalists' message in order to achieve racial reconciliation? No, that was a consequence of the message, not the message itself. Far from being human-centered or attractive, it was a humbling, fearful message of judgment and the need for repentance. Only through the humbling did the racial healing come.[45]

Rejection of Revival but the Start of an Antislavery Movement

Most Southern slaveholders rejected the message. They refused to humble themselves. Since revivals are spread by avowals and stopped by refusals, this revival, with its antislavery instincts and its racial reconciliation, was stopped in the South by the gentry. Men accustomed to marching up the church aisle in a proud body did not come humbly one by one. By the late eighteenth century, they had turned increasingly violent in their opposition to antislavery talk from Baptists and Methodists. Mob threats, beatings and tongue-lashings met antislavery preachers, so by the 1790s Baptists and Methodists had backed away from antislavery.[46]

The South's chance to choose racial reconciliation and to allow revival to work a gradual emancipation was largely gone, but we must not be deterministic about this. One historian argues, "The egalitarian trend in evangelicalism which" produced antislavery acts by some white evangelicals "foundered on the intransigency of that institution [slavery] in the South." But *people's* intransigence, not an *institution's,* stopped reconciliation through revival. True, plantation slavery was deeply entrenched in Virginia and South Carolina, and it would have been hard to dislodge it. Pursuing profit singlemindedly had consequences hard to undo. It created a plantation society dependent on a staple crop and deeply in debt to London merchants. White Virginians were caught in a "tobacco mentality" in which "the quality of a man's tobacco often served as the measure of the man."[47] But the fact that some converted whites emancipated their slaves shows that it was not impossible for white Southerners to renounce slavery.

Once rejected, this chance would not come again. During the revolutionary struggle with Britain, planters embraced republicanism, which gave them a rationale for their pride and their slaveholding. As Edmund Morgan has shown, republicanism and slavery were closely linked and mutually reinforcing. Paradoxically, revolutionary republicanism highlighted the contradiction between white Americans' liberties and African-Americans' slavery, but it greatly reduced the chance for slaveholders to repent over slavery. It gave them an ideology that justified slavery, which they had lacked before. It gave them a doctrine of rights. By giving them an independent nation, it created an internal, sectional politics which hardened their hearts against any talk of emancipation and made slavery a sectional-political, not religious, issue.

Of course, slavery also existed in the Northern colonies, though not plantation slavery. Here, whites purchased slaves to work in urban workshops and to be domestic servants. Nowhere were blacks more than 20 percent of the population. Only in a few areas of "large-scale agriculture" such as Rhode Island's "Narragansett region" were blacks heavily involved in agriculture. In Pennsylvania, slavery was most prevalent in Philadelphia, though some rural entrepreneurs such as millers, tavernkeepers and tanners used slaves once their "labor needs were beyond the capacity of family members."[48] Family labor was the first resource, and slave labor was used only when more help was needed. In the South, however, slave labor was fundamental, not supplemental, and the white family might not labor at all.

In the North, Christian antislavery activists made a promising start. Quaker opposition to slavery predated the Great Awakening. As early as the 1690s, some Quakers spoke out against fellow Quakers who imported slaves into Pennsylvania. Products of the Reformation, the Quakers stressed nonviolence and the virtues of the simple life. Both beliefs led some Quakers to antislavery, for the slave trade involved violence, and plantation slavery was built on the trade in luxury goods such as sugar and tobacco. In 1754, the Philadelphia Yearly Meeting issued a Christian attack on slavery: "To live in Ease and Plenty by the Toil of those whom Violence and Cruelty have put in our power, is neither consistent with Christianity, nor common Justice. . . . Where Slave keeping prevails, pure Religion and Sobriety decline." The Yearly Meeting sent a committee to warn Quakers against slaveholding. In 1761, the Pennsylvania Assembly enacted a £10 tax on slave imports. Consequently the number of slaves in Pennsylvania began an accelerating decline. Some Quakers freed their slaves, and many stopped importing slaves.[49]

Still, outside Pennsylvania and western New Jersey, antislavery work did not make much progress before the Revolution. Paradoxically, the same republicanism that hardened Southern masters against antislavery softened Northerners and led to the creation of many antislavery societies. (We will examine republicanism in a later chapter.)

African-American Culture and Contributions to American Life

In Africa's arrival to the New World, we have both a human tragedy, which the antislavery movement tried to stop, and a positive contribution, especially to life in what is now the United States. African-Americans constructed their own culture, which enriched American society, although slaves in the North were less able to build their own culture. Northern masters had far fewer slaves, so African-Americans had more daily contact with whites and less with each other. In the South, slaves on smaller plantations adapted to white ways faster than those on larger plantations, where African Americans in the slaves' quarters had greater autonomy. Everywhere, they contributed to colonial society. In South Carolina, they may have taught whites how to grow rice, unknown to the English but familiar in parts of West Africa. In Virginia, they persisted in African agricultural methods and induced white overseers to use them. They brought home-building patterns, which likely became models for constructing the smaller log homes in Virginia.[50] They made their greatest contribution to American churches with their spirituals, their preaching and worship styles and their strong faith amid suffering. They contributed even though they were mostly deprived of normal human control over government, economy and family life.

It was in their own churches, "quarters" and families that African-Americans could best develop their own culture. Here, textbook writers overemphasize the African contribution and underestimate Christianity's role in African-American culture. In *Nation of Nations,* Christine Heyrman argues that they "began to build stable families and communities only late in the eighteenth century," but she does not note that this was *after* the revivals, which were a contributing factor. She incorrectly asserts, "Christianity won few converts among eighteenth-century slaves. . . . Most blacks preferred traditional African religions." She does not give black Christianity and black preachers credit for strengthening the family or for discouraging the violence of slave revolts. In *The American People,* Gary Nash argues that "black Christianity . . . blended African religious practices with the religion of the master class." He emphasizes West Africans' traditional kinship ties as strengthening the African-American family, but he ignores Christianity's stress on the family, monogamy and parenting.[51]

It is hard to believe that the strong Christian emphasis on the family did not impact the African-American family, even if slavery threatened marriages' permanency. When we consider the fear and guilt that often preceded conversions during revivals, we can hardly believe that those so stricken by God's

Word consciously carried former African religious beliefs forward into their new life. They repented with African-American personalities—not white ones—but they did repent.

Some textbook writers subtly use plantation slavery to criticize the traditional family. They link slaveholding to *one form* of patriarchalism: a master thought of his slaves as part of his "family," with himself as the head. They then portray colonial families as patriarchal without pointing out the vast difference between the two senses in which the word is used.[52] They load the word *patriarch* with the negative connotations of a slave plantation, then carry it to the nuclear family and dump the negatives there. The slave-owning patriarch ruled his extended "family" in cruel and often immoral ways, very unlike the colonial father's behavior toward wife and children. Any comparison of the latter to slaves is greatly exaggerated. That is only one area where historians use the presence of slavery in a professedly Christian society to discredit Christianity.

Plantation Slavery in the Americas: Synopsis

As we have seen, professing Christians were often arguing against their God, and slavery was capitalism's servant, not Christianity's. True Christians with religious motives for settlement were often able to avoid slaveholding. They were willing to work their own land with their own hands. Christian revivals such as the Great Awakening showed a strong antislavery impulse and some racial reconciliation. Christian groups such as the Quakers led a Northern antislavery movement. Through an emphasis on the cross of Christ, many African-American slaves strongly identified with the Christian faith. The importance of the black church and minister in African-American life can hardly be overemphasized. It is not true that Christianity was the religion of the "master class." Many masters did not practice it, whereas many slaves embraced it.

3

Born from Above
Puritans,
Conversions,
the Great Awakening

G ENERALLY SPEAKING, HISTORIANS
and social critics have pilloried few Americans of the past as much as they have
the Puritans. Placed in the stocks and scourged, Puritans have had many
execution sermons preached over them before being led to the gallows and the
graveyard of historical failures. Oddly, their New England is condemned as a
failed experiment, yet its role in American history is exaggerated. Perhaps a
condemned man is a more compelling figure than an innocent Quaker or
Pilgrim, so different than the Puritan. Perhaps the Puritans spoke, wrote and
read so much that historians stress this articulate minority because they left
more evidence behind. Perhaps proving Puritan New England a failure is
considered a way to prove America a failure.

No myth is so oft repeated and so ill-founded as the myth that the Puritans'
"City upon a Hill" forms the basis of the American experiment. Generalist
historians, social critics and popularizers are more guilty of these sins of
exaggeration and distortion than those historians who specialize in the history
of New England and of Puritanism.

Many writers of college textbooks in American history are especially guilty.

Their Puritans are often depicted as zealots fired with a utopian religious mission to save Europe and bring in the millennium by growing oats, children and churches in the rocky soil of Framingham and Dedham, thus "planting the seeds of a belief in America's special mission in the world." Some devote twice as many pages to Puritan New England as they do to New York, New Jersey and Pennsylvania combined. The portrait is strikingly negative:

> a determined band of zealots . . . [with] the aggressive, martial spirit of a crusade; a people charged with messianic zeal . . . [and a] need for moral surveillance, or "holy watching" . . . [with] an ideology of control; proud and driving, and as demanding of themselves as they were of the world about them. They sought power . . . and they sought it untiringly, intolerantly, and successfully.[1]

Here they are portrayed in terms normally used by liberal media to describe the Religious Right of the 1990s. Supposedly, their religious zeal stemmed from their fear of social and economic change in England. Having "cringed at the crumbling of traditional restraints" on individualism there, they set sail "to banish diversity on a [new] continent." Here, they spied on and coerced their neighbors, persecuted heretics, repressed women who dared rise above a "subordinate position," ravaged Indian tribes, preached a dour doctrine of predestination and hanged suspected witches. Two texts have special sections on Puritans' alleged obsession with death. Their successes—stable families and communities, literacy, education, rapid population growth—are not attributed to their religious faith. Neither is their success in largely abstaining from the use of slave labor. Apparently, faith persecutes, but does not prosper, a people.[2]

It would take us some time to get through this list of myths, omissions, exaggerations and misinterpretations. Puritans are pictured as proud, self-righteous zealots, especially when facing heretics. Yet John Winthrop briefly questioned his own faith when he saw that Anne Hutchinson and her followers "were able to testify to a livelier experience of Christ than he was able to do at the time." Few textbooks portray Cotton Mather as he "threw himself on the floor and 'humbled and loathed' himself before God, for 'former Iniquities, and . . . present Infirmities.' "[3] Few point to John Eliot or David Brainerd's self-sacrificial work among the Indians or to New England's greater success at getting along with Indians compared to Virginia's failure.

The Myth of Puritan Exceptionalism: The "City upon a Hill"
The basic myth is that Puritans came to America on a messianic mission to save

the world. That myth arises from the most misused quote in American history, John Winthrop's "City upon a Hill." Here is the quote from his sermon "A Model of Christian Charity," delivered on board the *Arbella* in 1630:

We must Consider that we shall be as a City upon a Hill, the eyes of all people are upon us; so that if we shall deal falsely with our God in this work we have undertaken and so cause him to withdraw his present help from us, we shall be made a story and a by-word through the world.

Not a utopian call to redeem the world by New England's example, the phrase "a City upon a Hill" was "a rhetorical commonplace," a quote from Matthew 5:14 used by many Protestants. The context shows that Winthrop meant it in a *negative* sense, as a warning. Possible failure is in view here, not utopian success. True, Winthrop talks of success prior to this passage, but success as a model for "succeeding plantations" in America, not for all Europe or all humanity.[4]

The work of specialists in Puritan history is helpful in correcting such myths. Theodore Bozeman demolishes the notion that Puritans came believing that "God had assigned them a special task in his plan for the redemption of humankind"—"the building of a religious commonwealth" as an example to "decadent England." The real Puritans regarded that idea as presumptuous. They humbly saw themselves as "poor exiles of Christ" seeking refuge from persecution by Archbishop Laud and King Charles I. They came to New England to preserve their idea of pure first-century Christian worship and church order. This was no forward-looking experiment but an attempt to recover and preserve the ancient practices of the early church. It was not an attempt to hasten Christ's second coming and the millennial kingdom, for Puritans (before 1640) were deeply skeptical of millenarian enthusiasms.[5] There was no millennial experiment to fail at. They never sought utopia.

As "poor exiles of Christ" and the Reformation's children, Puritans resembled French Huguenots, Moravians, English Quakers, Pilgrims and various German sects who sought refuge in the New World. The main difference was the Puritans' success in achieving political, social and religious control over such a large region as New England. They could attempt on a regional level what others could try only on a local level.

Textbook authors exaggerate Puritan exceptionalism. But specialist Charles Hambrick-Stowe notes that "Puritanism was from the start a devotional movement," part of an "Augustinian tradition of personal experiential devotion" to Christ. Puritans used Catholic devotional books such as the *Imitation of Christ.*

As Calvinists, they shared Reformed theology with Dutch, Swiss, French and other Calvinists. They eagerly looked abroad for news, books and correspondents because they saw themselves as part of an international Protestant movement. "As a habit of mind, Puritanism required a special kind of cosmopolitanism transcending the intensely local and regional loyalties by which most Englishmen gained their identity."[6]

It was not a continual, morbid anxiety about one's salvation. Though beginning in anxiety ("conviction of sin"), it "was capable of producing experiences of great spiritual satisfaction." It did not begin in anxiety over social or economic change. Historian Stephen Foster observes, "Modern scholarship has a curious penchant for locating the motor force of Puritanism" in anxiety over change, "more or less equating 'Puritan' with 'stress,' 'transition,' or 'discontinuity.' " That assumes "that the function of religion is always anodynic or manipulative."[7]

Puritans were children of the Reformation, which was not an anodyne soothing the nervous but a powerful challenge to a lifelong pilgrimage toward the knowledge of God, a restatement of God's side in his argument with humans. Only divine grace producing human faith could work salvation in believers. Only the Scriptures and the Holy Spirit could guide them. The logic of Reformed theology did not stop change but intensified it by splitting society between converted and unconverted. When Puritans saw themselves as "besieged knots of the faithful in the wilderness of antichristian England," that was true to Scripture (for example, Philippians 2:15) and European experience, not paranoia. When Puritans stressed human depravity, attacked "innovations" such as saints and images and preached *sola Scriptura,* they repeated Reformation themes. They stressed holiness and zeal, but the knowledge of God had always demanded that of ancient Hebrew, first-century Christian and medieval saint alike.[8]

As we have seen, Reformed religion was no anodyne, no narcotic that soothed people and stabilized society. Saints proved as hardworking and innovative as city-state merchants, because they saw eternal consequences in daily work. Given the eschatological and apocalyptic nature of Christianity, which had no blueprint for an ideal human society short of the Lord's return, they could not have redesigned Western politics and economics along more stable lines if they had wanted to. Like all revolutions, theirs tended to demolish traditional constraints—even ones it intended to preserve. It also provoked more human rebellion against God. The Reformation accelerated the dynamism of Western civilization—and that was a problem for Puritans who sought to return to first-century Christian principles.

Primitivism: An Attempt to Return to the First-Century Church

Bozeman stresses this desire to return to the "primitive" first-century church as the defining quality of Puritanism. To him it was a thrust backward in time, an attempt "to live ancient lives." This is a valuable insight, which I shall make use of later. However, Bozeman's skepticism about divine revelation leads him to a subtle distortion of Puritanism.[9]

Fundamentally, it was a doctrinal, not chronological, thrust—a vertical reach up to the knowledge of God more than a horizontal reach back to first-century human practices. Bozeman seems to feel that a vertical reach is impossible, so he focuses on the horizontal one. True, God's revelation in Jesus Christ came in the first century and was proclaimed by first-century apostles. So the vertical reach toward the purest form of God's revelation would seem to be chronological, back to an earlier time. But first-century teachings were sought because of their divine source, not their antiquity. Puritans attacked human additions to them because people ought not to add to God's truth, not because sixteenth-century people ought not to add to first-century people's religiosity.

Puritans differed from most European Protestants in their longer struggle to restore first-century truth and practice. They were children of the more protracted English Reformation, which lasted from the 1530s until the late seventeenth century, when the doctrine and organization of the Church of England were finally decided. Henry VIII's Reformation only partially ended Catholic practices and beliefs. Puritans wanted to finish the job, to "purify" the Church of England from all Catholic practices that seemed unscriptural and to return fully to first-century practices.[10] Thus in some ways Puritanism is more a residue of English history than a shaper of American history. It looks back to Henry VIII and Thomas Cromwell more than forward to Calvin Coolidge and Ronald Reagan. Puritans aimed to finish a Reformation, not to start a utopia. In this sense Bozeman is right: Puritans looked backward, not forward.

Prolonged argument can distort a disputant's views: one tends to take a position contrary to one's opponent and to hold views more dogmatically. Lasting for 150 years, the English Reformation sharpened Puritanism to the point of dogmatism. Puritans engaged in sixteenth-century religious disputes long after other European Protestants had moved on to other issues. In church polity, church membership and worship, they carried Reformation principles further than some other Protestant groups. Reliance on the Bible as sole spiritual authority *(sola Scriptura)* was a Protestant principle, but Puritans went beyond that. They refused to use composed hymns. They would sing only the Psalms, though these contained only veiled references to Jesus Christ and no Pauline theology. They recognized that Christ's birth had advanced truth to "a higher plane," but they still regarded many Old Testament laws and rules as binding.[11] Having the English-language Bible was so precious a privilege, and the medieval additions to Scripture so distasteful an innovation, that they hesitated to allow the Lord himself to add the Gospels and Epistles so as to supplant the Old Testament law and prophets.

The Puritan Integration of Church and State

Reliance on prince or Parliament to make the Reformed church the nation's only church (state church) was another Protestant principle. Puritans were so long frustrated in their search for an English monarch who would purify the state church that they became even more zealous to fulfill this principle. Yet delay meant that they must struggle for decades as "besieged knots of the faithful," a sect of the most godly ones. As a result, they came to advocate two ideas in precarious, paradoxical combination: a state church of all the English people, yet a pure one led by the pious alone.[12]

After the anti-Puritan Stuarts came to the throne in 1603, they placed their hopes in Parliament. When King Charles I dissolved Parliament in March 1629, many Puritans decided that a purified state church could only be erected in the New World, far from Stuarts and archbishops. With the help of the Massachusetts Bay Charter granting them governing powers, they took their hopes to a new locale. They still felt that the state had to set up the church, but in the New World *they* would be the state, far from king and Parliament.[13]

Recalling medieval Europe's lack of integration, we can see that the Puritans who came to New England in the 1630s sought to create a society integrated by religion. That society could not be in rebellion against God, nor its churches filled with those who only professed, but did not possess, faith. They sought to have a purified church that controlled family, economy and government. Not a church hierarchy but church members who were truly converted would truly integrate this society.

The first generation came close to achieving this goal. Exile simplified their task. Emigrating exiles were a self-selected group; Winthrop and other leaders carefully screened the 1630 emigrants. No king or bishop threatened their program: to build pure churches of visible saints supported by taxes, ministering to and hopefully converting the entire society. Only church members could vote in the early years of the Massachusetts Bay colony. The congregation met for worship in the town's meetinghouse. At first it decided the town's affairs too. Only when it could no longer handle all town business was the separate, "secular" town meeting established. New Englanders did without some of the English church's governmental functions. They had no church courts, no clergy in the legislature, no clergy in public office. Yet they could do without these because church members controlled the government.[14] Actually this was a church-state.

In this church-state they could carry out their two main principles: adherence to the Bible and establishment of one purified church with a state monopoly in each local community. They used parts of the Mosaic law in their legal code. That might mean more severe penalties (for example, the death penalty for adultery) or less severe ones (for example, eliminating the death penalty for theft) than in England. When the Reverend John Eliot drew up a plan of government for the "praying towns" of converted Indians, he exactly copied Mosaic precedent and set up a ruler for each ten people, a ruler for each group of fifty and one for each group of one hundred. He even suggested that this literal Mosaic scheme would be used in the coming millennial kingdom![15] In New England nothing prevented the literal use of biblical precedents. Here was religious integration of society carried to an extreme, almost like the Aztec use of the past as a guide for present decision-making. Here was the backward-looking primitivism which Bozeman describes.

We see the two principles combined when we examine their belief that New England was also a New Israel. They applied to themselves the rules and warnings Old Testament prophets addressed to Israel: the special covenant relationship with Jehovah, the blessings of covenant obedience and the curses of disobedience, the interpretation of historical events as blessings or curses. Their success in settling and ruling a community of pious believers in a large territory encouraged—almost required—this identification with Israel. Nothing in Jesus' sermons to Jews oppressed by Rome or in Paul's letters to Christians persecuted by Rome gave precedents for governing a territory. So a people valuing biblical precedents turned to ancient Israel for guidance.[16]

For the first fifty years, they largely succeeded. Their communities were remarkably stable compared to other seventeenth-century Western societies. Common faith, close-knit communities, democratic government, relative prosperity—all bound them together. They emigrated in sufficient numbers to avoid, largely, the use of slave labor. Abundant, cheap land and the cattle-raising business led to some dispersal of population: ministers worried that "an insatiable desire after Land" led some "to live like Heathen, only that so they may have Elbow-room enough in the world."[17] Still, such "hivings-out" to new areas were within the Puritan orbit. Settlers formed new churches. The first generation were God-seekers or God-fearing enough not to challenge the believing majority.

Yet primitivism had its dangers. One problem in a church-state was the implicit need for the state to make and enforce laws against competing churches. No matter how visibly saintly its members were, the church looked un-Christian when it used the magistrate's sword to punish those who disagreed with it. Enforcement of the Congregationalist (Puritan) monopoly culminated in the deaths of four Quakers from 1659 to 1661. Now seen as part of a centuries-long struggle for freedom of worship, the executions were really part of a mid-seventeenth-century religious conflict. Not martyrs for religious freedom, the Quakers were prophets of Quakerism. "They interrupted court sessions and worship services to chastise the populace and, especially, its leaders." They used a "violent rhetorical style" of predicting "divine retribution for all who remained unswayed." Puritan authorities had deported them with a warning that their return to Massachusetts Bay would bring the death penalty. The martyrs used their Christian acceptance of death, contrasted with the Puritans' un-Christian taking of their lives, as an argument for Quakerism. Many Puritans reacted with "public dismay" to the executions, the last ones carried out for religious nonconformity. The Puritan laity could not tolerate *this* consequence of the church-state principle.[18]

Economic Exceptions to Puritans' Religious Integration

We must not exaggerate the Puritans' success. Especially in economics, they had no divine blueprint that could control the economic growth which their work ethic, demographic growth, wide distribution of property and social stability produced. Cotton Mather described Plymouth colony's decline: "Religion begot prosperity, and the daughter devoured the mother." That occurred sooner or later in all New England. Puritan colonies were not capitalist in spirit. Historian Stephen Innes argues, "The Puritan covenant provided an essential counterweight to capitalist development," limiting capitalism's acquisitiveness and limitlessness, but Puritans' "countervailing institutions" actually helped capitalism by controlling "its destructive capacities." Puritanism was the first of many anticapitalist American movements that ended up strengthening capitalism.[19]

Capitalism tends to be parasitic; it needs a society with ethical, political and social qualities, which it can't build (and often undermines). Puritanism strengthened it by building a growing, family-centered, well-ordered society ruled by laws and constitutions, not traditions, and peopled by hard-working, inner-directed folk who obeyed laws and honored contracts for conscience's sake, not from a fear of force. Such a society was headed for prosperity and progress, and that threatened a faith that valued primitivism and the past.[20]

Also, not all 1630s emigrants came for religious motives; economic motives were dominant in some areas. The coastal towns of Gloucester and Marblehead were settled by English and Welsh fishermen and carpenters eager for profit. Springfield was founded by one Puritan who sought to control the fur trade. All three were slow to found churches or to heed ministers, and townspeople were quick to engage in conflict.[21]

In Gloucester and Marblehead, the Congregational church helped to bring stability after several decades of turmoil. They did not cease being profit-seeking towns, but the church fostered a localistic concern to spread economic benefits among most town residents, to avoid court battles between residents and to stress "conservative and cautious" economic development. Capital accumulation occurred slowly, from one generation to the next. This family-centered prosperity rested on the social stability brought by Christian faith. This was prosperity but not the limitless, amoral capitalism of the Italian city-states. In Marblehead, one minister worked for economic development and local control of the local economy.[22]

The Rhode Island "City-State" Uncouples Church, State, Economy

Gloucester, Marblehead and Springfield were more contentious and individualistic than subsistence farming communities, but the real contrast is with Rhode Island (a contrast Innes never makes). Massachusetts "Puritans often used the term Rhode Islandism to describe acrimonious, divisive conduct."[23] If we are seeking the roots of modern America, we will find them in colonial Rhode Island more than in Puritan Massachusetts. Rhode Island's original defining quality was lack of religious unity, lack of an established church. No church integrated society, so like the Italian city-states, Rhode Island pointed forward to modernity.

Rhode Island too was settled by "poor exiles of Christ," but in this case it was unorthodox Puritans exiled from Massachusetts Bay: Roger Williams, Baptists, Quakers, Anne Hutchinson's and Samuel Gorton's followers. Williams, its founder, rejected Massachusetts's church-state with its belief in Old Testament precedents and its claim to be a new Israel. For him, "the coming of the Messiah and a new and spiritual dispensation had relegated" these Hebrew antecedents "to mere history without precedential force." The other exiles did not intend to make Williams a new Moses either. They only agreed with Williams's followers on a list of negatives: no state church, no limits on freedom of Protestant worship, no oaths, no infant baptisms and no traditional clergy.[24] By necessity, religious toleration reigned. No sect was strong enough to rule the others. Rhode Island had the dynamism of a Puritan work ethic without Puritan magistrates to curb greed and cheating.

It had no modern theory of pluralism or diversity to justify or manage its remarkably modern situation. The colony was held together by two fears: fear of falling under the control of Massachusetts's Quaker-persecuting Puritans and fear of losing land titles if the colony collapsed. Fear does not unite for long. Rhode Island was a forerunner of modern, liberal democracy with its negative idea of freedom—freedom *from* compulsion, not freedom *for* some goal. Rhode Islanders' freedom rested on their common refusal to accept anyone else's positive goal. No goals were binding, and they were free.

Chaos came from this negative freedom. Land hunger and land speculation brought land quarrels. The "doggedly individualistic and mutually distrustful" towns retained so much power that the colony government was often powerless to collect tax monies or pass needed laws. Access to the sea and good harbors encouraged commercialized agriculture. Raising livestock for export to Barbados started a rush to trade, seafaring and mercantile pursuits. But unlike Gloucester or Marblehead, Rhode Island lacked a strong established church to control merchants' profit-seeking. Merchants integrated society and government around Newport's commercial interests; the colony became virtually the city-state of Newport. Like the merchants of Genoa or Venice, they disregarded moral or legal restraints on trade. Smuggling, slave trading, piracy and privateering were important sources of profit.[25]

Rhode Island experienced a very modern uncoupling of government, church and economy. The church did not oversee the government, and congregation and town meeting were not linked as in Massachusetts. Thus "councilmen shed much of the patriarchal identity of Puritan selectmen and assumed an identity closer to that of modern administrators." Very modern-seeming apathy and individualism often led to refusals to serve as town officers or to pay town taxes. Government did not oversee the economy for the public good, as Massachusetts's magistrates did. Newport's merchants ran the government for *their* good. They passed laws to discourage outside merchants from trading there, to encourage the slave trade, to grant subsidies for producing exports and to print paper money to solve a currency shortage. Rural towns willingly allowed this economic use of their colony government in exchange for a forty-year "tax holiday." Printing paper money became government's chief source of revenue. Farmers paid no property taxes for years.[26]

With its royal charter giving it self-government and with imperial authorities in London giving it virtual independence, Rhode Island became a merchants' republic, a city-state using democratic self-government for its economic advancement. It acted in opportunistic ways, benefiting from others' work or misfortunes and externalizing its own costs by throwing them on to others. During King Philip's War, Rhode Islanders let other New Englanders do the fighting, while they reaped the rewards. Taking advantage of Massachusetts's currency shortage, they flooded that colony with unredeemable paper money. When the money lost value in Puritans' hands, Massachusetts paid a "tax" to Rhode Island, while the latter's farmers escaped taxation. In its slave trade, Rhode Island externalized the social costs of rum consumption and slavery: Africa and the West Indies bore the consequences. Its commerce thrived under the virtually cost-free protection of the Royal Navy, while its merchants cheated the imperial government out of tax revenue by smuggling whenever possible and profitable.[27] This was not a church-state but an amoral city-state.

Coupling Church and State Distorts Christian Faith

Rhode Island horrified Puritans, who called it "the paganizing and perishing plantations." Yet Baptists and Quakers thrived there with many other Protestant churches.[28] Church control of government and economy was perishing there but not necessarily individual souls. Puritans in Massachusetts Bay and Connecticut held on to their Reformed belief that one state church should morally mold government and economy. They succeeded for a time. Church members dominated their towns, and royal charters protected their right of self-government. But their success and their church-state thinking distorted their Christian practice in ways that undermined their continued control.

The church-state depended on church members being a majority (of voters, at least) in the colony. To become a church member one had to testify to a conversion experience. To recruit new church members and retain members' dominance of the two colonies, Puritan churches had to produce new conversions continually. The Bible defines conversion as being born again or, more specifically, being "born from above."[29] The Holy Spirit works to convert people "from above." The Puritan church-state system depended on a supernatural phenomenon which could not be faked or manufactured.

Youth was the expected time for conversion. New England's amazing population growth—caused by high birth rates and low infant mortality— produced a very young population. Sometime in the seventeenth century, the median age fell to sixteen—the age when the young were expected to start converting and joining the churches.[30] Since the church-state depended on many youths being "born from above," when fewer did, Puritan leaders were concerned.

Yet forming a church-state and defining it as a new Israel hampered the Spirit's work of converting the young. The Israel analogy led second- and third-generation preachers to exalt New England's Founders as spiritual heroes almost equal to first-century Christians. Ministers added a return to first-generation principles to the Reformed return to first-century ones. They made the Founders like Moses and Aaron, laying down timeless standards for later generations. Here was an unscriptural primitivism, a desire to live Founders' lives.

Following the Israel analogy, they interpreted disasters as judgments from God for the descendants' failure to meet the Founders' standards. The logic of covenantal history was that the covenant people were purest when the covenant was made but declined later and had to be renewed. Ministers used this logic to accuse the young of lacking the Founders' piety and thus endangering the colony: the weight of responsibility rested on the young. They must keep the covenant even if they had never converted or joined the church: "they were automatically part of its promises and conditions" anyway.[31]

The resulting legalism is seen in the Halfway Covenant and the covenant renewal ceremony. The official solution to the problem of fewer conversions, the Halfway Covenant allowed unconverted adult sons and daughters of church members to become "halfway" members by publicly owning the covenant. Then their children could be baptized and they would be subject to church discipline. By relaxing the rule of testifying to conversion, Puritans ensured that church members would still be a majority. Covenant renewal ceremonies renewed each church's covenant. Participants "acknowledged their guilt for the latest disasters . . . and then pledged a new beginning . . . a more systematic religious life and special attention to the children of the church." Their main advocate, Increase Mather, intended covenant renewal ceremonies as the main means to bring the people back to the Founders' church-state traditions.[32] The Reforming Synod of 1679, which recommended them, admitted their legalistic nature: "Some that are but Legalists and Hypocrites, yet solemn Covenants with God, have such an Awe upon Conscience, as to enforce them unto an outward Reformation, and that doth divert temporal Judgements."[33] Viewing setbacks as God's judgments against covenant breakers, ministers sought individuals' outward compliance to avoid these dire judgments.

That was bound to create confusion, for the Scriptures taught that outward compliance was not enough. Mixed messages were sent. Ministers told the young to keep this covenant with Jehovah *and* preached that Christian ancestry or good works would not save them.[34] They were inside the fold and must keep the covenant, yet they might be outside the fold and need to be converted. Were they inside or outside? Had they mainly sinned against God or against parents and ancestors?

To charge the young with lacking the Founders' piety was to place a human, generational guilt trip on them. The Halfway Covenant and covenant renewal ceremonies subtly shifted the emphasis from the God-centered "pietist saga of the soul" to a human-centered "public concern" for the New England Way. In jeremiads delivered at election days, fast days, executions and militia training days, the young were confronted with their ancestors' deeds as much as with God's demands. [35]

Here was an intellectual and spiritual cul-de-sac. The answer to every problem was to return to the Founders' ways. Yet no youth could be as holy as the Founders seemed in the ministers' idealized portrait of them. Guilt over falling short of the Founders or failing to keep the covenant did not necessarily bring the young to repentance and faith in Christ. So ministers "sharpened the goad of rebuke when conversions were not forthcoming," but this human-centered guilt did not produce divinely worked conversions.[36] Youth did not need to be born *from the past* but *from above*. They needed to be brought face to face with a holy God, not with the Founders.

Some conversions did occur after spectacular crises which seemed to confirm ministers' claims that God was angry with New England: King Philip's War, the revocation of the Bay charter, the Dominion of New England, a major earthquake in 1727.[37] Catastrophes could plausibly seem sent from above when ministers' warnings, without them, seemed mere human nagging, but they were too rare to be counted on to convert the young.

Uncoupling of Church and State at the Colony Level

Revocation of the charter in 1686 shattered Massachusetts Bay's self-rule and church-state system. Puritan saints' political control had been the main difference between them and other Dissenting Protestants. Now that control of the colony was taken away, they were no different from the others. They too were a besieged group subject to a government which might turn hostile. To use the Israel analogy, this was the Fall of Jerusalem, the Babylonian Exile, the loss of independence.[38] It should have ended the analogy, but it didn't.

The uncoupling of church and state initially had a salutary effect. Puritans braced themselves for persecution, wrote "survival manuals," returned to the semi-underground tactics of their ancestors in Stuart England and stressed private devotion, not public ceremony. Ministers preached conversion, not covenant. A revival occurred in 1690. But Puritans ultimately rejected the idea of being demoted to the same status as believers elsewhere. "The Puritan colonies had been established too long and with . . . too much success for their inhabitants to refer to themselves only in terms of the travails of the church militant everywhere."[39]

They would not accept deliverance from the church-state's distorting effects. Instead, churches "became a shadow government" during the hated Dominion period as people flocked to join these patriotic symbols of resistance to tyranny. Increase Mather hastened to London to save the Old Charter, then secured a new one which restored the right to a representative assembly but mandated religious toleration and removed the provision limiting the vote to church members.[40]

The last two provisions effectively killed the church-state, though ministers and their allies tried to keep it alive at the local level. At the colony level, church, state and society were now separated. In election day sermons, "orators could speak of government in . . . secular terms because they had separated 'government' from its earlier theocratic identification with 'society.' " They "could describe it as a neutral referee or secular creation" and leave to the churches alone the responsibility to see that New England society remained religious. They had traveled part way toward Rhode Islandism. This uncoupling helped ministers deemphasize matters of governance, both civil and congregational, and reemphasize piety and morality.[41] They yet clung to the Founders' mission. Though it would have to be pursued without government's coercive arm, that only redoubled their efforts to preach sermons harking back to the Founders.

The cul-de-sac remained. The only way forward was the way back to the Founders. Yet the system had been weakened by the turmoil of the 1680s. Stirrings of youthful rebellion against it began to be heard, first from the mildly liberal Brattle Street group in 1699. With Puritan "intellectual energy and imaginative life" so "locked up in pursuit of a handful of time-honored themes, one of the few ways out was to find some wider concerns . . . that would show up the dominant obsessions as parochial or obsolete." Calling Increase Mather "the Reverend Scribbler," Brattle Street men adopted "the axiom that the prevailing dialogue was not worth talking about."[42]

Uncoupling Town, Family and Church: Stoddard's Solution

There was another way out, and it was first explored by the Reverend Solomon Stoddard of Northampton, Massachusetts, in the late seventeenth century. "Stoddard had no patience at all with reverence for tradition, and he didn't scruple to accuse the filiopietistic Mathers of leading New England churches into an abyss of spiritually arid formalism."[43] He tried to sidestep traditional, church-state formalism at the local level. Here, the integration of church, government and society meant a close link between church, town and family. That link still prevailed, and it distorted Christian faith and practice. That is clearly seen in the bitter disputes over where and when to build new meeting-houses and how to assign pews within them.

The town meeting and even the colony legislature became involved in these disputes. After 1700, Congregational churches moved away from using benches, on which people seated themselves in no special order, to building boxes or pews which were sold to individual families to help defray the costs of a new meetinghouse. Pews closest to the pulpit were more prestigious and commanded a higher price. They advertised a family's higher social status. The church or town meeting appointed a committee to assign pews according to a family's wealth: "worldly achievement was more laudable than experience as a humble Christian." Increasingly wealth alone brought a prominent pew, not public service, age or other factors. Often, "pews thus acquired became permanent family property."[44]

Puritanism's (and Christianity's) high priority on family life, when combined with the natural drive to accumulate wealth, had produced a hybrid family-centered capitalism. Seeking profit was deemed more acceptable if motivated by the desire to enrich one's family and heirs. Just as Puritans' religion became "tribal" and stressed converting their children, not Indians or strangers, so their capitalism became familial. In some towns, political offices belonged to a few families, who also dominated the major church offices. More and more, "family was a determinant of wealth and occupation" and status in the church. The family pew or box was the outward sign of that—"an affirmation of family and a public parade of economic rank." In it, family members sat facing each other—some with their backs to the pulpit.[45] Their status ratified in church, they need not listen to the gospel.

The Reverend Solomon Stoddard fought familial elitism. He greatly loosened the requirements for church membership and admittance to Communion. *He* decided who met them, not the congregation or a committee. Now membership and admittance conferred no social status. No pews came to Northampton while he was there. Families could not use the church to advertise their success. Stoddard vigorously preached the gospel to all alike. "There was no public designation of 'sainthood' to shelter the hypocrite," but every heart was "unprotected against the thunder of the Gospel." A powerful preacher, he "pressed his hearers for an immediate personal commitment." Consequently five local revivals resulted over a forty-year period.[46] The Holy Spirit was free to work where he pleased, regardless of family or social status, and many were born from above.

The (First) Great Awakening

Stoddard's solution was a local one. It was left to his more famous grandson Jonathan Edwards to develop a preaching style which would help trigger regional revival. Edwards went beyond Stoddard's steps to address the broader formalism, legalism, human-focused guilt and stereotyped conversion narratives that trapped many New Englanders in a cul-de-sac.

Jonathan Edwards helps trigger the (First) Great Awakening. He began poorly by exhorting the young, especially, to greater human effort on the hard pilgrimage toward salvation. That was a century-old Puritan theme that did produce an "increased religiosity" among some young people. But the 1734-1735 Northampton revival was sparked by a very different message, a series of sermons on "Justification by Faith Alone." In them, Edwards dropped his earlier call for human striving. With "luminous logic," he powerfully argued that God alone could save, for "the evil and demerit of sin is infinitely great." Human striving could not even help prepare the soul for sin's removal. Only "the soul's active uniting with Christ" would suffice, and that was not a human work.[47]

This message cut through all talk of covenant duties before conversion. It cut through human-centered guilt over failing one's ancestors and parents. In Edwards's new sermons, the sinner was starkly alone with God. By cutting out all distracting references to Old Testament characters or Puritan Founders, Edwards set the sinner before the judgment seat alone, not surrounded by a distracting crowd, and the sinner often repented. By late December 1734, Edwards reported, "the Spirit of God began extraordinarily to set in, and wonderfully to work amongst us" so that "a great and earnest concern about the great things of religion and the eternal world became universal in all parts of the town, and among persons of all degrees and ages." Family status, ancestors, parents, covenants—all were forgotten as people of all classes saw "their utter helplessness, & Insufficiency for themselves, & their Exceeding wickedness & Guiltiness in the sight of God . . . & they seem to be brought to a Lively sense of the Excellency of Jesus Christ & his sufficiency & willingness to save sinners."[48] The way out of religiosity's dead-end was to fly to Christ.

That is how we can best understand Edwards's famous, oft-anthologized sermon *Sinners in the Hands of an Angry God* (1741). It is less Edwards "preaching unmitigated terror" than it is Edwards powerfully restating the truth that his hearers' eternal destiny rested with God alone: "However you may have reformed your life in many things . . . and may keep up a form of religion in your families and closets, and in the House of God, it is nothing but his mere pleasure that keeps you from being this moment swallowed up in everlasting destruction."[49] It is not the swallowing up but "his mere pleasure" that is the major emphasis here.

Of course, human insufficiency and divine sufficiency had been preached innumerable times from Puritan pulpits. Yet the conflicting message of covenant duties, ancestral purity, use of "means" to grace and pride in the New England Way came from the same pulpits. The combination had been confusing. Edwards's preaching clarified by concentrating on conversion, not covenant. In addition, people are easily bored by oft-repeated themes. Edwards and other revival preachers used novelty to deliver an ancient message more effectively.

George Whitefield and the international, cosmopolitan Awakening. A different revival hit Northampton in October 1740. It was sparked by the preaching of the Grand Itinerant, George Whitefield, not Edwards. It was not local but was part of a continental, even transatlantic, revival often called the Great Awakening. Traveling preachers, or itinerants, were one novelty that aided this revival. "Preachers who were strangers were far more effective in arousing the congregation's emotions . . . than were the local pastors"; itineracy undercut the inhibiting effect which local social status had on religion. The "itinerant's unfamiliarity with his audience"—their status or their lack thereof—"and his lack of personal connection to local authority figures" enabled him to lay all hearts bare before God. Outdoor preaching, outside the social hierarchy of family pews in the meetinghouse, undercut social status too. When Whitefield and other itinerants criticized unconverted ministers, that undercut the clergy's presumed superiority to the layperson. If the minister had to answer to God, then all people must, regardless of social standing. If the religious specialist was not exempt, how could the magistrate, the lawyer or the wealthy farmer be exempt?[50]

Also novel to New England ears was the itinerants' preaching style. Whitefield and others spoke extemporaneously, without notes. The preacher's heart and mind touched the listener's mind and heart right at the moment of speaking. Audiences did not respond as readily to three-day-old thoughts, written essays read out loud, as they did to immediate thoughts.[51]

These novelties delivered many New Englanders from the cul-de-sac of venerating the Founders. The Great Awakening was a new work of God, not a return to the pristine past. Here was a fresh stress on the birth from above. Here was more immediate, less status-linked, less tradition-bound preaching. Of course, the novelties were not totally new. Edwards's series on justification by faith recalled Luther's emphasis in the early sixteenth century. Conversion had always preoccupied Puritans. It was not an innovation but a basic part of Protestantism. The novelty was largely in means and tactics.

Itinerants and stark preaching were not American innovations either. In Scotland and Ireland, nearly a century earlier, many of the same novel means were used. The Six-Mile-Water Revival (1625-1633) in Ulster was triggered by the "powerful" preaching of James Glendinning, who "preached to them nothing but law, wrath, and the terrors of God for sin." Itinerants traveled around Scotland in the seventeenth century.[52]

Some historians have seen the Great Awakening as a great cause that must have had some great effect—perhaps the effect of forming democratic attitudes, which in turn caused the American Revolution. Yet it was an international phenomenon, not merely an American one. Whitefield also drew great crowds in the British Isles. The 1741-1742 Cambuslang revival in Scotland matched the intensity of any in America.[53]

A transatlantic event like this 1740s revival is unlikely to have had unique consequences in the colonies, which were so closely tied to Britain. Also, its consequences are so closely tied to local responses to it that generalizing beyond the local level is hazardous. Both avowals and refusals were shaped by local conditions. In Gloucester and Marblehead, avowing it had the "basically conservative" effect of strengthening local churches.[54] In the South, as we have seen, the gentry's proslavery feelings and the revival's antislavery impulse meant that avowing it tended to foster racial reconciliation whereas rejecting it strengthened slavery. Neither of those effects was as prevalent elsewhere.

In New England, the Great Awakening meant that Puritanism returned to the cosmopolitan outlook it had in 1620s England. But the new cosmopolitan Protestantism was an evangelicalism that focused on the need for emotional, immediate conversion ("birth from above"). Puritan New England lost the last marks of its church-state uniqueness. Church splits arising from the Awakening ended the dream of one established, purified church for the entire society. New Englanders who supported the Awakening (New Lights) joined an international network of revivalists and Pietists stressing immediate conversion.[55]

The Awakening's true importance lies in its effects on the international evangelical movement, not in its reputed effects on New England or Britain's Thirteen Colonies. It was a religious movement with primarily religious effects. There were some political and social effects, but they varied from region to region, from town to town. By reconnecting to international evangelicalism, New Lights came in closer contact with other Dissenting Protestants in the North. As supporters of revival, these New Lights joined in a common cause to fight opponents of revival, the Old Lights. As the Awakening's central personality, Whitefield united its supporters.

Imitating Whitefield, other itinerants, such as Gilbert Tennant of New Jersey, traveled throughout New England preaching the Word. Pamphlets, books and sermons passed freely from the Middle Colonies to New England, and vice versa. Thomas Prince's revival newspaper, *Christian History,* communicated revival news from one region to another.[56] There had always been means of communication, but now the common, embattled cause of the Awakening gave New Lights a pressing reason to communicate.

This "evangelical network" extended beyond Presbyterians and Congregationalists. In Pennsylvania, Whitefield drew followers from many groups:

"Quakers, Congregationalists, some German Lutherans and Pietists, some unchurched, and a plurality of Presbyterians." Pietism was a broad movement originating in seventeenth-century Germany. It stressed heartfelt, biblical, earnest Christianity as opposed to formalistic, intellectualized orthodoxy. It was very influential. In the colonies, "leadership among Lutherans was increasingly exercised by ministers and laymen of Pietist persuasion," such as Henry M. Muhlenberg. Pietist institutions in Germany sent many ministers to serve German Lutherans in the colonies. They supported the Awakening, as did some Dutch and German Reformed ministers, often Pietists also. Outside this Pietist-New Light network were the Moravians and Quakers, whose doctrines were regarded with suspicion. Yet some of them undoubtedly participated in the revival meetings.[57]

Revivals are stopped by refusals and lead to divisions. The Awakening's effects were primarily religious: growing unity among New Lights who stressed heartfelt, immediate conversions and growing opposition from their rationalist, increasingly unorthodox, foes. Revival provoked some refusals, and the refusers formed a faction opposed to revival. A "revivalistic Pietism" confronted "rationalistic liberalism."

Many Old Lights remained orthodox on Christ and the Scriptures. Yet by stressing emotion, human depravity and human inability to attain salvation by means of prolonged rational reflection on Scripture, New Lights provoked some of their foes to a passionate defense of human reason and capacity. These rationalists drifted toward a naturalistic, human-centered theology. Human happiness was the chief end; human reason was the chief means. People were "naturally disposed toward Religion," they thought, because it promoted their happiness. Taking ideas from the Enlightenment, they dropped supernatural, God-centered Protestantism after the Awakening strongly highlighted its emotional and supernatural elements.[58]

Evangelicals and rationalists eliminated inessential differences *within* their respective camps and stressed instead essential differences *between* their camps. The bewildering religious pluralism in the Thirteen Colonies organized itself increasingly around the underlying split between two camps.[59] This split contributed to a secularization of colonial politics and culture, especially in New England. Those seeking to unify and integrate their society could no longer use religion. Religious disputes now split their society. More secular, less divisive ideas, such as the idea of liberty, would have to replace religion as the glue that bonded society's diverse factions together.

The rationalist, liberal Boston minister Jonathan Mayhew abandoned Calvinist theology, then adroitly turned it into a political theory of liberty: "The true saints were those who vigilantly protected their liberties and promoted the general good of their society." Secularizing their faith into a love of freedom allowed him to praise seventeenth-century Puritans for executing King Charles I. He abandoned their theology and praised their politics to regain popular support and to unify a society fractured by the Awakening.[60]

All New England moved toward the pluralism, diversity and secularity of Rhode Island. So it now needed some secular ideology as a glue to hold together the various "games" of politics, social climbing, mercantile ambition and learning. As we will see in the next chapter, republicanism became that ideology. That was true in other colonies as well.

That was the paradox of the Great Awakening. A great revival did not cause greater religious control over American politics and culture but greater secularization of both. Revival caused disunity, which rendered churches less able to integrate and dominate society. Revival starkly showed Christianity to be God's revelation, always at odds with society and its human-centered culture. That caused human rebellion against revival. The rebels became one faction; the revival's supporters another. The human mind might abhor dissension, but God often uses it to shake up a society.

But that is a little too neat and simple, for there are often more than two factions. Christianity is a delicate balance between faith and works, head and heart, authority and equality, preparing law and saving grace. People tend to become unbalanced, and that produces a faith faction, an authority faction, an equality faction and so on. So some dissension arises when a faction, not God, wants to shake up a church.

Faced with the task of governing society, gentry leaders became disgusted at "such a Spirit of Dogmatism and Bigotry in Clergy and Laity," as John Adams called it. They turned to more secular concepts to integrate society so that they could govern it. In all thirteen colonies, "some form of rationalism—unitarian, deist, or otherwise—was often present in the religion of gentleman leaders by the late colonial years."[61]

The Great Awakening's primary influence on the American Revolution came through the secularizing of those who refused the revival. Sometimes the key clue in a mystery is what did not happen—the dog that did not bark. Here, the people who did not convert are the clues to what caused the Revolution more than those who did convert. The refusers increasingly turned to republicanism, partly out of disgust at religious dogmatism and emotionalism, partly out of dissatisfaction with religion's failure to integrate society, partly because fashionable European thinkers were turning to republicanism. Republicanism became the new transatlantic cosmopolitanism for those who refused the evangelical kind. It was a rational religion for the gentry. Though they initially saw it as compatible with their loyalty to England's king, republicanism gradually eroded that loyalty and led to the Revolution.[62]

Yet this secularizing move to republicanism among the gentry leaders hardly proves that the Awakening did not accomplish God's purpose. Just as the New Testament gives no handy guide to ruling a society, so it offers no proof that God always prefers that rulers be Christians.

The Colonial History of New England: Synopsis

Puritan rule in New England distorted Christian faith and practice. It led to a veneration of the Founders and to the dead-end of seeing a return to their principles as the solution to every problem. It encouraged ministers to berate the young for failing their parents and ancestors as much as for failing the Lord. At the local level, it brought human pride and status into the church to hinder the gospel. Neither human-oriented guilt nor human pride was conducive to conversion, to being born from above. The Great Awakening brought mass conversions, produced enough discord to upend this church-state system and united Christians across denominations in a cosmopolitan movement. As a religious movement, it had the intended religious effects.

4

Gentlemen Think
Up a Revolution,
a Republic
& a Constitution

THE TURN TAKEN BY NORTHERN AND
Southern gentlemen away from revivals toward secular ideas had immense
consequences for American history. Within a few decades, they or their sons
would declare independence from Great Britain, form a new nation and write
its constitution. (Mothers and daughters as yet had little role in politics.) It is
vital that we examine the ideas occupying their minds as they acted, especially
their ideas on politics and government.

The young republic's aggressive expansionism, its failure to end slavery
short of civil war and its bumptious trigger-happy male individualism are often
partly blamed on the Christian faith of many of its citizens. Yet these gentlemen's ideas came out of a rejection, not revival, of Christianity. So we will have
to look elsewhere for the cause of violent proslavery conquest.

The Influence of Colonial Gentry on American History

Two objections to stressing gentlemen's ideas need to be answered. First, why
stress gentlemen and not all Americans? We may define gentlemen as men of

high social status who lived off rents or interest income if possible and did not conduct a business or trade but devoted themselves to culture, reading, society and public affairs. Those were ideals. Not all gentlemen fulfilled all of them, and they were impossible ideals for most Americans. Second, why stress ideas and not factors such as population and economic growth, social changes or westward expansion?

The gentry's commanding role in hierarchical, familial society. It is hard for contemporary Americans to comprehend an eighteenth-century society very different from our own. Today, government is separate from family, church, corporation and voluntary association. Church is distinct from corporation, corporation from voluntary association and so on. State government is separate from federal, state courts from state legislatures. Professionalization and specialization separate different roles according to impersonal, formal, bureaucratic rules.

That was not true of eighteenth-century colonial society. "The household, the society, and the state—private and public spheres—scarcely seemed separable." The Awakening separated New Light churches from a status-obsessed society, but other parts of that society were still linked. A social hierarchy linked everyone and every part: superiors had paternal duties to inferiors, who owed them dependent allegiance. Christianity offered no comprehensive model for integrating society, so the family became the pervasive model. Superiors (gentlemen) acted like parents: authoritative yet generous, condescending, loving in a stern way. Inferiors (commoners) tried to be good children: obedient, reverent, loyal, uncomplaining.

People acted out these roles in the economy (one merchant granting credit to a lesser merchant), government (a governor distributing jobs to his favorites) and society (a planter entertaining his less-wealthy neighbors). These three spheres were not separated but linked. The same man (for example, John Hancock) was merchant, politician and host at the same time. In this "paternal and face-to-face" society, no one accused him of conflict of interest for acting in several spheres. Yet only gentlemen had the money and connections to do so many things at once, and by doing so they tied society together.[1]

There are problems with using family as the model in politics, business and society. It encouraged partiality rather than impartial equity, for parents are naturally partial to their children. When partiality becomes a norm in government, injustice results. Thus governors gave preferential treatment to their clients and supporters. Also, most children have living parents, but not all colonists had a gentleman-sponsor to get them into business, into college or into a government office. Without the proper connections life could seem unfair and all roads blocked. Connections were not only modeled after family ties, often they *were* family ties: an uncle getting his nephew started as a merchant, a cousin finding his relative a government post. Also, as a distorted imitation of parents' almost unlimited power over children, gentlemen's considerable power over clients, servants and slaves led to serious abuses.[2] God did not design the family to be a model for society, economy and government. Even at church, family pride could block the gospel, as in Northampton's family pews.

The colonial church sanctioned this hierarchical, familial order "by preaching from Romans 13 that all were 'subject unto the higher powers' " and by stressing personal duties over abstract, contractual ones. However, gentlemen's values were anything but Christian. They abhorred work, especially manual labor (despite 1 Thessalonians 4:11). Their status as gentlemen depended on their reputation, and that fostered an ambition for honor and fame (despite Philippians 2:3). In spite of Paul's advice that "godliness with contentment is great gain," gentlemen were defined by their conspicuous consumption of luxuries. They also regarded themselves as superior to others (despite 1 Peter 5:5-6).[3] These contradictions led many of them to resist the Awakening. Though often not Christians, these gentlemen dominated colonial politics, society and economy. No commoner could compete with them.

The commanding role of Enlightened ideas among colonial gentry. So we must stress the gentry, but why their ideas? Ideas do not always cause events, nor do people always act to carry out ideas. But people may use ideas to rationalize greed, lust, ambition or anger. We saw how economic factors, more than ideas, produced the slave trade and slavery. European conquest of the New World was not just an idea, a cartoonist's light bulb in the European brain. Greed and ambition lay behind it.

Yet political ideas are very important in understanding the one generation (approximately) that protested the Stamp Act (1765), declared independence (1776), won the American Revolution (1783) and wrote the Federal Constitution (1787). It was the most politically influential generation in our history. That generation lived in an age of deference, when commoners deferred to the gentry in political and social matters. Social and economic causes continued to operate, but, given this deference, they did not as directly shape politics and government as they do today. Commoners then did not expect government to guarantee peace and prosperity, nor did they expect to tell the gentry how government should be run. Thus, socioeconomic turmoil did not produce revolution or "cause" new ideas. Gentlemen were somewhat insulated from turmoil. Armchair thinkers did not change their minds because of overcrowded workers' housing or lack of bread in the markets.

Those gentlemen were literate, educated men with some leisure to read Greek, Roman, French and English authors and to correspond with their peers. They lived in an age of exciting new ideas, the Age of Enlightenment. In Europe and America, men saw a chance to break through the crust of tradition and to establish a new social order consistent with the most Enlightened ideas. Founders' ideas became future Americans' copybook maxims. The Revolutionary generation became Americans' first-century church, their political Golden Age, the model to copy. We must take their ideas seriously—and the fact that their ideas came out of a rejection of Christianity.[4]

That generation lived in a far-off, provincial corner of the Western world, then experiencing the Enlightenment, which historian Peter Gay has called "the rise of modern paganism." A nearly religious worldview, the Enlightenment was built on "two propositions: first, that the present age is more Enlightened than the past; and second, that we understand nature and man best through the use of our natural faculties," rather than through divine revelation.[5] In its desire to create an integrated society through human-centered reason, not revelation, the Enlightenment resembled the Renaissance.

Yet things had changed since the fifteenth century. In seeking to center reality on themselves, humans now had more exact scientific knowledge, especially Isaac Newton's discoveries of the machinelike, mathematical workings of the universe and John Locke's theories of human psychology. Reason explained more than it used to. There seemed less need for revelation. Trying to reduce the tension between the two, Christian apologists argued that God could only act in a reasonable way. They imagined an anthropomorphic deity limited by any skeptic's definition of reasonable behavior. That apologetic only advanced secularization. Discovering New World peoples thriving without monotheism liberated European thinkers from revelation. Didn't these "noble savages" without property or masters disprove the doctrine of original sin? The Columbian encounter led thinkers to construct a myth of human origins in a "state of nature," in original virtue, contrary to Genesis.[6]

They saw divine revelation as a barrier to human progress. Partly, they were reacting to religious wars of the seventeenth century and to the excesses of the Protestant Reformation and Catholic Counter-Reformation. Reformed churches proved no more able to integrate European society than had medieval churches—less so, for they multiplied Europe's divisions. Of course, the Scriptures had never declared such integration to be a divine goal. And the seventeenth-century wars were largely caused by the notion that there could be only one established church in each country, not by Christian doctrine per se. Enlightened thinkers were not willing to give Christianity the benefit of these subtle distinctions. Consequently, the Enlightenment was more anti-Christian than was the Renaissance.

Many of America's "Founding Fathers" were not Christians in any orthodox sense. Many did not believe that Jesus Christ was the Son of God, that he performed miracles, that his crucifixion paid the penalty for human sins or that he was resurrected. Although retaining a quasi-Calvinist realism about human nature, John Adams thought it an "awful blasphemy" to "believe that great principle which has produced this boundless Universe, Newton's Universe . . . came down to this little Ball, to be spit-upon by Jews." In Philadelphia, the center of the American Enlightenment, Benjamin Franklin and other thinkers had long abandoned their Calvinist upbringings for a moralizing Deism. In Virginia and South Carolina, Deism and skepticism were fashionable among the gentry. In the soft Southern evenings, slaveholding gentlemen or students at the College of William and Mary pulled from their bookshelves a volume by the English skeptic David Hume or the French skeptic Voltaire. Gentlemen such as George Washington and Thomas Jefferson were expected to serve on the Anglican vestry, but vestrymen were often not believers. After a minister "preached a sermon in [his] presence" criticizing his refusal to take Communion, Washington stopped attending church for a time.[7]

Some of the Revolutionary leaders, such as Benjamin Rush and John Witherspoon, were devout Christians. And none, except Thomas Paine and Ethan Allen, were publicly anti-Christian. They confined unorthodox thoughts to their diaries and to their letters to other gentlemen. They thought Christianity socially useful because it taught commoners virtue. Their unorthodoxy they derived largely from what historian Henry May calls the Moderate (mostly English) Enlightenment, not from cynical, amoral French skeptics whose views were "unacceptable to most Americans." American evangelicals were slow to detect this private Deism. When Franklin donated a library to Franklin, Massachusetts, its pastor "urged his congregation to emulate the great man's life, with no suggestion that their benefactor had any dubious religious views."[8]

American gentlemen and college students (the would-be gentlemen) sat and read in a remote corner of the Western world. Theirs was still a religious corner—partly due to the Awakening they rejected. They avoided Enlightened authors who were too openly anti-Christian or read these authors' tamer works of history, not philosophy. They had "a clear preference for what was Protestant, Whiggish, moral and moderate." When reading Greek and Latin classics, they chose moralistic, historical works and avoided whatever advocated pagan immorality. New World remoteness meant that American gentlemen were behind on their reading. They did not read the latest, most antireligious authors until long after those books had been discussed in Europe.[9] Even many gentlemen were slow to realize the strongly anti-Christian nature of Enlightened thought.

The Rise of Radical Whig Republicanism in America

That was especially true because, in political thought, they greatly preferred a few English writers from the "Radical Whig" camp. All Whigs had supported Parliament's rights against the Stuart kings' claims to divine right. By the early eighteenth century most Whigs believed that the Glorious Revolution of 1688 had established the proper balance between Parliament and king. However, drawing inspiration from the Roman Republic and England's brief Puritan Commonwealth, the Radical Whigs disagreed: the king's ministers used bribery, corruption and patronage to influence Parliament and thus undo the balance. If the people did not show eternal vigilance and protest corruption, this aggrandizing power would lead to tyranny and a loss of natural rights. They must insist on a return to the first principles of the English constitution. To resist corruption required "virtue" in the people and in their gentry leaders.[10]

Just as Puritans wanted to take church purification further than their fellow Protestants, so the Radical Whigs wanted to take political purification further than their fellow Whigs. Believers in republicanism along with other Whigs, they were more zealous to return to first principles.

Republicanism was the creed of the Enlightened religion. With it, Europeans hoped to integrate their society around a political philosophy that would end the undesirable aspects of revealed religion, tradition, hierarchy and merchant capitalism. It was "as radical for the eighteenth century as Marxism was to be for the nineteenth century."[11] An exact definition is difficult. Most European thinkers did not use it in its literal meaning—a government controlled by citizens not by a king. Rather, they used it to celebrate the citizen, his virtuous participation in public affairs, his willingness to sacrifice his private interests to the public good and his equal relationship with other citizens. The virtuous citizen was the model for social, economic and political relationships. The parent-child model was largely dropped.

Some thought that the citizen could function in a constitutional monarchy. Gentlemen had a place too. Not pursuing a trade or business, they were better able to place the public good above their private interests. Much Enlightened republicanism tended to be sunny, optimistic, even utopian. Radical Whig republicanism was more Calvinistic: pessimistic, independent, zealous, oppositional in its stance to the world. That's one reason Americans accepted it so readily.

Radical Whig writings became "immensely popular and influential" in America. John Trenchard and Thomas Gordon's *Independent Whig* journal, their *Cato's Letters,* Joseph Addison's play *Cato,* Robert Molesworth's *Account of Denmark,* the Puritan writer John Milton, the republican Algernon Sidney— all were on gentry bookshelves. Though Radical Whigs came out of a zealous, militant Protestant tradition, they could not go to the New Testament for political blueprints for society. It had none. So they turned to Roman writers who praised the Roman Republic and deplored the lack of virtue leading to its downfall: Sallust, Tacitus, Cicero, Plutarch.[12]

Radical Whigs were not in the Enlightened mainstream, but colonial gentlemen emphasized their works anyway during the period of protests against imperial policies (1765-1775). In English politics, Radical Whigs were outsiders, and so were the colonists—provincials "alienated from the official world of cosmopolitan London." Radical Whig republicanism flattered Americans: they had the most virtue, the least corruption, the greatest liberty, no nobility, less royal influence, a more egalitarian society of self-sufficient farmers. They were model republicans. Europeans now saw "noble citizens" in the New World more than "noble savages."[13] Unlike Christian conversion, conversion to Radical Whiggery was pleasant for American gentry: one found virtues in oneself and vices in others (the English).

Radical Whig ideology ingeniously appealed to both sides in the fight over revival. It was "political Protestantism": pessimistic about human nature, opposed to the present worldly elite, suspicious of centralized authority and strongly moralistic.[14] That appealed to Dissenters and to the Puritans' heirs. With this ideology, partly derived from their Dissenting ancestors, colonial evangelicals could be political and yet Calvinist too. Or so they thought. And the Enlightened gentlemen who had abandoned orthodoxy for Deism or "rational" Christianity could still *sound* Protestant when talking politics. They could talk the same political language as their orthodox neighbors. They could still persuade commoners and retain their leadership role. Though no longer religious Protestants, they were political Protestants. Radical Whiggery worked for revivalist and rationalist alike.

For both groups, Radical Whig republicanism with its Greco-Roman roots offered underlying parallels to Protestant Christianity. These reassured the orthodox that they had not strayed from the faith and the unorthodox that they had jettisoned only religious dogmas and were otherwise following tried and true paths. Normally, some anxiety accompanies departure from Christian belief. "Political Protestantism" enabled rationalists to reduce that anxiety.

What were the parallels? The republican stress on virtue (sometimes called "public" or political virtue) resembled Christians' stress on virtue (personal morality). Corruption had a similar double meaning. Republicans' belief that rulers always lusted after more power resembled Christians' belief in human depravity. Republicans' struggle between rulers seeking power and the ruled seeking liberty was a dualistic battle similar to the war between good and evil, God and Satan, the church and the world. Republicans' fear of spreading tyranny recalled Protestants' fear of spreading Popery. Both saw conspiracies and plots advancing the thing they feared. Both believed in returning to first principles: republicans to the constitution, Protestants to first-century principles. Republicans' veneration for classical antiquity recalled Puritans' veneration for Old Testament Israel. Rationalists could take comfort: here was no foolish novelty. Puritans' national covenant became republicans' national constitution.

Since many colonists were descended from Puritans or other Dissenters, Radical Whiggism appealed to them. Radical Whigs were the most zealous republicans, just as their ancestors, they thought, had been the most zealous Protestants.

Radical Whig ideas give some Americans a reason to revolt. This common political language joined evangelicals and rationalists who had been split over the Awakening; now they were united by concepts that each understood differently. Evangelical New Englanders stressed moral behavior when they used the word *virtue;* the Virginia gentry stressed economic independence and property ownership, not piety, as the basis for virtue.[15] Parallels with Christianity reassured the former that they had not left it; the same parallels reassured some of the latter that they had only left its dogmas, not its culture, its distinct personality traits. Here, you could kill two birds with one stone. One ideology had two effects in two different groups.

The timing of many Americans' union around Radical Whig ideas was crucial. This alliance of misunderstanding could not last forever, but it lasted long enough to enable Americans to fight a Revolution, form a republic and write a constitution. By the mid-1790s it was coming apart.

Radical Whig ideas gave colonists a way of interpreting the actions of the imperial authorities during the 1760s and early 1770s. Otherwise this series of imperial steps—Sugar Act, Stamp Act, Townshend Duties, Tea Act, Coercive Acts and Quebec Act—would have been nearly as incomprehensible as they are today to millions of schoolchildren who read, memorize and recite them each fall. Mostly tax measures, they broke with the past, when London's benign neglect had allowed the colonies virtual autonomy at times. This was taxation without representation. But these were taxes, after all, and when was there ever a popular tax? Englishmen paid stamp taxes and custom duties too. Colonial protest against these measures was inevitable, but revolution was not. Radical Whig ideas enabled many Americans to interpret the measures as part of a conspiracy by powerful London politicians to upset the English constitution and reduce the colonies to political slavery. That interpretation triggered the revolution.[16]

Not that colonial or gentry opinion was unanimous. Some colonists with Radical Whig books opposed Patriots' anti-British protests and desire for independence. Some colonists recoiled at the results of protest: mobs wrecking stamp tax collectors' homes; extralegal committees enforcing extralegal decrees; disobedience toward the true "governing authorities" (Romans 13:1); disloyalty toward a beloved king and constitution; threatened disruption of lucrative economic ties to Britain. If the "logic of rebellion" led to these conclusions, it seemed illogical to them. So they became Loyalists, or Tories. The Revolution became a civil war.[17]

And what of those Americans who lacked bookshelves? Revolutions need followers as well as leaders. Their support could not be won by quoting Tacitus or Addison. Workers and farmers followed Patriot gentlemen for a variety of reasons. The Scotch-Irish hated the English. Dissenters feared that the Church of England would send an Anglican bishop to the colonies. New Englanders saw revolution as following the New England Way of autonomy from corrupt England. Egalitarian, participatory republicanism attracted urban workers and artisans. Some groups were Patriots because their enemies were Loyalists, and vice versa. Minorities in a colony supported the Crown to retain royal protection against local Patriot authorities.[18]

Many evangelical ministers supported the Patriot cause. As cultured, literate leaders exempt (in theory) from manual work, ministers could be seen as gentlemen. They read books, and their ideas counted. Political Protestantism enabled them to speak realistically about politics, to escape the cul-de-sac of a narrow, literal application of the Israel analogy. They no longer had to be John Eliots recommending captains for tens, fifties and hundreds. Yet they could remain safely Protestant, it seemed.

However, they saw republicanism through a seventeenth-century lens. The tree of English republicanism had Puritan roots, but it was unlikely to grow evangelical leaves in the rationalist climate of the late eighteenth century. Ministers assumed that they could interpret republican virtue to mean Christian morality, that they could persuade American society to accept that view. But republican virtue was embedded in a worldview that was Greco-Roman, rationalist, egalitarian, antiauthoritarian and basically non-Christian. Integrating society around a political philosophy was certain to marginalize religious truth and make the minister the odd man out. Yet opposing the Patriot cause would have marginalized them too.

Once most of them decided to support the Patriot cause, their faith led them to attach a religious meaning to a political event. With their optimistic worldview centered on God's redemptive plan, they could not limit republicanism to the negative function of averting tyranny. They almost had to give it a positive function. So they revised their millennial views to give it a role in bringing the millennium.[19]

Similarly, Whiggish gentlemen were not content merely to avert a tyrannical plot, though they had no religious millennium in mind. They hoped that revolution would yield positive fruits. Many had "a fervent belief in America's potential for greatness." A continental nation would have themselves as its honored founders. Since gentlemen sought fame and honor, what could bring more of both than that goal? Britain's victory over France in 1763 destroyed one rival for the continental interior, and Virginians had responded by crossing the Appalachians into Kentucky. Some Patriots were land speculators who hoped to profit from westward expansion under an independent United States.[20] It was no coincidence that in his famous pamphlet *Common Sense* Thomas Paine referred to the struggle of "the Continent" against the king. Republicanism was an ideology with which to conquer a continent. The year 1763 eliminated the colonial gentry's rival; 1783 would eliminate their ruler.

After decades of economic, geographic and demographic growth, the Thirteen Colonies already had the capacity to conduct a war against Great Britain, though growth did not guarantee victory. They had the Radical Whig language of republicanism to hold together a diverse coalition. Paine's *Common Sense* was the culminating argument. Using biblical allusions, harking back to Pilgrims and Puritans and adding hard-headed Calvinist realism, Paine carefully moved Americans beyond fears of conspiracies to "the excitement of a moment when men have a chance to form their institutions anew."[21] With this argument and these resources, they took the daring step of separating from England in the summer of 1776.

The Declaration of Independence was much less politically Protestant than was *Common Sense*. It was an Enlightenment project, grounded in "familiar theories of natural rights, the social contract, and the right of revolution." It contained no biblical allusions. "The god who appears in the Declaration is the god of nature rather than the God of Christian scriptural revelation." It described him in the vague, impersonal terms of Enlightened Deism: "the Supreme Judge of the world," "nature's God" and "Divine Providence." In a leap of reason, it grounded American politics in certain "self-evident" axioms which rested on thin air, not on divine revelation. The axioms paralleled the scriptural assertion that humans were created in God's image, but they did not deign to rest upon that revelation. They rested on the Enlightenment's scientific, optimistic, rationalist worldview. Yet they were stated with such authority as Reason's *ex cathedra* pronouncements, then backed up with such a victory—the world's first modern, successful revolution—that they gained extraordinary power.[22]

Republicanism fails to integrate or unite American society. Now that Americans had spoken and written themselves into existence as an independent republic, they set about to provide themselves with all the furnishings of a republic—or, rather, a coalition of small republics. The several states wrote constitutions to establish a set of first principles (Connecticut and Rhode Island kept their colonial charters minus all references to royalty). Constitution-making was a joy few modern students of these documents can share. John Adams exclaimed, "How few of the human race have ever enjoyed an opportunity of making an election of government, more than of air, soil, or climate for themselves or their children!" To make this election, they invented the constitutional convention.[23] By sending delegates to the Continental Congress, they elected a continental government, though it was more like a voluntary association with few powers over members. Upon writing a constitution—the Articles of Confederation—they had set up shop as republicans.

Business went badly from the start. It took a divided Congress more than a year to approve the Articles for submission to the states. Disputes over national ownership of Western lands, representation in Congress and state contributions to the Confederation delayed ratification. States refused to pay their allocated contributions. Congress lacked taxing authority. Rhode Island (and other states) blocked attempts to give it some. It could only print paper money and issue notes to pay expenses. The paper money became a proverb: "not worth a Continental." The resulting "spiraling inflation" distorted the economy. When Congress could not afford to give them back pay, a Pennsylvania regiment "surrounded the State House in Philadelphia" and "poked their muskets through the windows at such celebrities as James Madison and Alexander Hamilton." The gentlemen beat an "undignified" retreat to Princeton.[24]

A drawn-out war against a numerically superior British army and navy was a tough time to set up shop as a republic. Victory did not improve matters. To take effect, the peace treaty was to be signed and returned to England by March 3, 1784. Despite urgent appeals, Congress could not obtain a quorum of state delegates to ratify it until January 14, 1784, too late to get it back to London by the deadline! Fortunately, Britannia waived the rules.[25]

Republicanism did not function much better at the state level. In their hatred of British royal governors, Patriots wrote into state constitutions weak governors and strong popularly elected legislatures.[26] By gentry standards, state legislatures began to show themselves lacking in virtue, especially in Rhode Island.

Even before independence, Rhode Island was wracked by the Ward-Hopkins factional fight. The Ward faction would seize power, lay heavier taxes on Hopkins's towns and lighter ones on its own, appoint pro-Ward judges and govern with total partiality. Hopkins' men and towns refused to pay taxes or accept verdicts. They hoped for a reversal at the next election. Both factions used bribery and fraud at the annual elections. Should the Hopkins faction win, they would reverse tax assessments and verdicts, and the outcast Ward group would ignore both in hopes of another reversal.[27] Public powers were prostituted to private gain and private advantage.

The Ward-Hopkins fight was only a prelude. Inflation, state war debts, British occupation and the wartime decline in trade severely hurt this mercantile state. A debtor party seized control of the state government after the war ended.

Instead of taxing citizens to pay off its war debt, the state printed paper money not backed by reserves of gold or silver. This worthless currency was used to settle both the state's and individuals' debts. By law, creditors had to accept it as payment for debts or face severe penalties. Gentlemen who lived by loaning money and receiving interest were horrified. A New York paper called it "The Quintessence of Villainy."[28]

If only "Rogue's Island" was guilty of such rogueries! But gentlemen saw them spreading to other states. In Connecticut, the "land of steady habits," farmers refused to sell needed foodstuffs to the Continental Army in hopes that the price would rise further. The state government encouraged Connecticut men to stay in the state militia rather than enlist in the Continental Army. Their seven-month enlistment period up, Connecticut men abruptly left the siege of Boston and endangered Washington's army. In Massachusetts, farmers angry at postwar taxes and likely foreclosures gathered in armed bands and temporarily stopped court proceedings. Shay's Rebellion alarmed gentlemen far from the Bay State, who exaggerated its dangers, as they had Rhode Island's villainy.[29]

That learned gentleman James Madison served in Virginia's state legislature from 1784 to 1787. There, he was annoyed at "the endless quibbles, chicaneries, perversions, vexations, and delays of lawyers and demi-lawyers" who all had "a particular interest to serve" apart from the public interest. Virginia had its own "debtor-relief legislation" aimed at British creditors, who were required to accept depreciated paper money as payment and were denied access to Virginia's courts to sue debtors. On average, Virginia debtors (many of them gentlemen) got by with paying only $1 for every $18 they owed![30] That was using the state to pursue private interest.

The Southern gentry's debts to British merchants were an exception. Most gentlemen were creditors, not debtors, in their monetary relations to other Americans. As creditors, they were alarmed at pro-debtor laws and at inflation caused by the depreciation of paper money. Living off fixed amounts of interest and rent, they were hurt by inflation more than were farmers and tradesmen who could raise prices.[31] Gentlemen such as Madison were pursuing their private interests when they attacked villainies such as paper money and debtor-relief laws.

Throughout the new United States, everyone seemed to be sacrificing the public good to private interest. States ignored the Confederation's good, localities the state's good and individuals the local, state and national good. Separating from "corrupt" England and adopting republicanism had not created virtue in Americans. Republicanism's results were far from virtuous.

Southern gentry miss their second chance at ending slavery. Southern gentlemen sacrificed the public good to their private interests by refusing to take decisive action against slavery. Most had rejected the Great Awakening with its tendency toward antislavery and spiritual equality of the races. More congenial to their taste was the Enlightenment, but its cultured talk of liberty and equality had antislavery implications too. They saw the contradiction between talking liberty and owning slaves, and they were now free of an English king whom Jefferson, in an early draft of the Declaration, blamed for the American slave trade. Now they could abolish both slave trade and slavery. They had the ideology (republicanism) and the freedom to do so. Economically, the time was right in Virginia and Maryland, where depleted soils and low tobacco prices cut into their profits and forced them to grow more grain and less tobacco. Grains required less labor, hence, fewer slaves. The monetary value of a young adult male slave was less than $300 in Virginia in 1795.[32] Emancipation became a less costly option.

Under pressure from antislavery activists inspired by republican ideals, Northern states enacted laws mandating gradual emancipation: Pennsylvania (1780), Rhode Island (1784), New York (1799). These laws were less idealistic than they appeared. Northern society had less of an economic stake in slavery than did the South. These laws were *post-nati* emancipation: blacks born after a given date were freed after they reached a given age. Northern slave owners evaded the emancipating intent by selling soon-to-be-freed slaves in the South before that age.[33] Still, such laws were gradually creating a slaveless North, in marked contrast to the South, and gave Southerners a model for emancipation.

Jefferson pushed *post-nati* gradual emancipation gently and privately in 1783 as part of a new state constitution for Virginia. He wrote an amendment calling "for the freedom of children born of slaves after the year 1800" and convinced someone else to propose it publicly. It failed.[34] His fellow Virginia Deist St. George Tucker more openly supported gradual emancipation. Yet the record of Southern Enlightened gentlemen was strong on private laments about the evils of slavery and weak on any public action.

The key explanation is that they had no concept of sin and no scriptural belief in humans' spiritual equality before the Creator God. They could not regard blacks as equal to themselves, could not equate slavery with sin and could not take an unequivocal stand against it. "It was that sense of the very reality of sin that is lacking in Jefferson's religion." He and other Enlightened gentlemen had a sunny optimism about human nature that could not explain the existence of evil, much less slavery.

Jefferson's realism was scientific, not Calvinist. Rather than accept it on faith that blacks were equal, he scientifically scrutinized them to see if they were equal to whites. Disadvantaged by life under slavery, blacks could never conclusively meet his empirical test, for "the Negro's 'fundamental equality'—and the white man's for that matter—could not be confirmed by the empirical criteria of the Enlightenment." The "irony" was that though "the Enlightenment proposed to deliver modern man from 'religious superstition' . . . those steeped in religious tradition were better prepared to" emancipate blacks than were the Enlightened.[35] Denying sin's reality and evil's power was poor preparation for acting virtuously.

The Crisis of Republicanism Leads to the Federal Constitution

Republicanism could not produce virtue elsewhere on other issues. It lacked sufficient force to convince people to sacrifice self-interest for the public good. It did not integrate American society. Given Americans' preference for weak governments, the state lacked the grandeur and importance needed to excite citizens' self-sacrificing loyalty except in wartime. Americans opposed the standing army, military display, pomp and ceremony that impressed European citizens. Their state governments were not impressive, and their national government was often ludicrous under its weak Articles.

Republicanism was a good solvent but a poor glue. It dissolved the old hierarchical, familial bonds of obedience and paternalism that held society together. It required parents and other authority figures to earn respect by their reasonableness and generosity, which few succeeded in doing. Its notion of (white male) citizens' equality "tore through American society and culture with awesome power," undermining gentlemen's authority and liberating commoners' self-interest. Its notion of equality condemned gentlemen's proud strutting and ended up sanctioning that in everyone else. Proudly equal voters tossed gentlemen and their disinterested virtue out of office and sanctioned the use of public office for everyone's private interests.[36] Failing to replace old hierarchical values with a new self-sacrificing virtue, it freed Americans to pursue their interests apart from values or virtue.

By the mid-1780s, many gentlemen felt that the new nation was in a "wilderness of anarchy and vice," a crisis caused by an "excess of democracy."

Henry Knox was livid: "The vile State governments are sources of pollution which will contaminate the American name for ages. . . . Smite them, in the name of God and the people."[37] The crisis was exaggerated, for compared to other revolutions America's was remarkably tame. From decades of virtual autonomy before 1763, Americans had learned self-government. Without privileged nobility, despotism, oppressive taxation or military repression, their old regime was too mild for its overthrow to be tumultuous. Evangelical Christianity formed a sort of ballast keeping the ship stable. Christian beliefs had limited hierarchical paternalism in the old regime (many evangelicals never accepted gentlemen's authority). They now limited the acceptance of—and the dissolving power of—new republican values such as equality.

An Enlightened gentry creates the Constitution. Nevertheless, alarmed gentlemen called the Constitutional Convention to remedy the Articles' defects. The ship of state was placed in dry dock for major repairs. The Enlightened craftsmen who met at Philadelphia beginning in May 1787 were eminently qualified for the task. Their resulting masterpiece of the Whig "science of politics" proved that.

But here we see a paradox. The first (and sometimes second) generation to reject orthodox Christianity often finds the act of rejection intellectually liberating. They are freed from adherence to unchangeable biblical truth, freed from the cul-de-sac of always returning to forefathers' maxims, freed to invent and improvise. They often prove geniuses at it. However, their descendants end up stuck with inventions that are hard to modify, forced to tend and oil the "machine that would go of itself" without the help of the Christian faith they had rejected. Their failure to pass on Christian faith becomes more important in the long run than the supposed success of their inventions. The Federal Constitution is an example of this phenomenon. It was a brilliant document which failed to achieve its authors' goals, but their descendants were stuck with it. It was quickly outdated but could not be redone.

It was a product of bookshelves. James Madison prepared for the Convention by reading some twenty books on "ancient and modern republics, ancient and modern confederacies." Others did their homework too. The Constitution and the *Federalist Papers* defending it were "perhaps the greatest monument of the Moderate Enlightenment." A "remarkably secular" Convention produced "a perfectly secular text," whose only reference to God came offhandedly at the end, in the date, September 17 "in the year of our Lord" 1787. Compared to state constitutions, it was irreligious: it was a product of the irreligious Enlightenment, and states would not entrust the topic of religion to the nation.[38] Not by coincidence, this secular text ended up perpetuating slavery in the South.

The Constitution creates a nation and perpetuates slavery. With its checks and balances, separation of powers, extended spheres and filtration of talent, this gentlemen's Rube Goldberg machine was relentlessly balanced, orderly and compromising. It was brilliantly designed to curb democratic excess and control popular vice. Its semiaristocratic Senate would contain only gentlemen who could negate the self-interested schemes of the more popular representatives in the House. Even the latter were more likely to be gentlemen than were state legislators. Given much more power than a state governor, the president was to be chosen by an electoral college of gentlemen. The Constitution elevated Senate, presidency, House and Supreme Court until each, as it were, had the status of a gentleman, with the proper sense of honor, ambition for fame and refusal to display any dependence on the others.[39]

Most notably in the *Federalist Papers,* it was brilliantly marketed to the public as compatible with Radical Whig republicanism. Federalists had a republican answer to every question put by its opponents, the Anti-Federalists. Had it shifted ultimate power (sovereignty) from the states to the federal government? No, the people delegated only parts of their sovereignty. Did it shift too much power from the ruled to the rulers? No, the people were the rulers *and* the ruled. Would it reduce the people's power? No, even senators and presidents were to be elected and the Constitution submitted to the people for approval.[40] Convinced by these arguments, all but two states had ratified it by the end of July 1788.

Thus the Convention solved the immediate problem of creating a strong national government. The Framers compromised the thorny, yet nonmoral, problem of the balance of power between large and small states. Yet, unexpectedly, the most divisive issue turned out to be the moral one of slavery. "Throughout the summer of 1787 slavery would emerge to complicate almost every debate." Delegates argued over the slave trade and over slaves' place in the population count, which would determine each state's representation in Congress. Gouverneur Morris of Pennsylvania warned that if a serious North-South division existed, "instead of attempting to blend incompatible things, let us at once take a friendly leave of each other." When "an import tax on slaves" was suggested, John Rutledge of South Carolina threatened Southern secession: the "true question is whether the South[ern] States shall or shall not be parties to the Union."[41]

In true moderately Enlightened fashion, they compromised this fundamental moral issue. Without much sense of slavery as sin, these gentlemen could cut a deal. Northern delegates' opposition to slavery was more "political and economic" than moral. New Englanders wanted a national government to regulate interstate and foreign commerce; Southerners were reluctant to give it that power lest it tax their exports (tobacco, rice, indigo and so on). The "dirty compromise" was that the "South Carolina delegation would support the commerce clause if New England would support protection for the slave trade and a prohibition on export taxes." This was not hard to accept: Yankee ships carried imported slaves and exported products. Yankees surrendered their antislavery arguments to their commercial concerns. Their ancestors' faith played no role in their choice. The Constitution counted slaves as three-fifths of a person, allowed the slave trade until 1808 and ordered Northern states to surrender fugitive slaves to their owners.[42]

Thus many parts of this Rube Goldberg machine were partially designed to protect slaveholders. "The three-fifths clause . . . electoral college . . . prohibition on export taxes . . . slave trade clause . . . domestic violence clause . . . limited nature of federal power and the cumbersome amendment process"—all protected slavery. American independence now protected slavery from English authorities. Radical Whigs' stress on rights, not responsibilities, gave the slaveholding gentry a rationale for their right to own slaves. When equality was for whites only, they could use the idea of equality to link white commoners to themselves. That protected them against any possible alliance of poor whites and blacks like the spiritual one begun by the revivals. "Racism became an essential, if unacknowledged, ingredient of the republican ideology that enabled Virginians to lead the nation."[43]

The Constitution was the capstone to political protection for slavery. It gave slaveholders constitutional rights. It channeled discussion of slavery away from practical morality toward abstract constitutional hair-splitting. It almost guaranteed that the issue could not be resolved peacefully.

The Constitution fails to perpetuate virtue or gentry rule. That was the irony. The document perpetuated slavery, which few meant it to preserve, and failed to perpetuate gentlemen's rule, which its framers meant it to preserve.

The gentry tried to use it to maintain their rule. When the new federal government organized itself in Philadelphia in the spring of 1789, the Federalists tried to clothe it with an awe-inspiring, loyalty-evoking grandeur. President Washington's trip from Mount Vernon to Philadelphia was a triumphal procession. His arrival set off a round of posturing. Condescending to entertain visitors at weekly "levees," the new president was annoyed when "people came, saluted him, and otherwise ignored him while freeloading on the refreshments he provided." When he went to the Senate to obtain its "advice and consent," passing carriages drowned out his statement. He "grew visibly irritated" when senators debated rather than consented. Posturing for posterity, debating senators "seemed scarcely able to speak without citing a dozen ancient authorities, so as to display their erudition." It was more like a debate "between Polonius and a Greek Chorus." They debated at length over what title to use when addressing the president.[44]

Within a few short years, this gentlemen's government and Constitution were hopelessly outdated. Powerful forces undercut commoners' deference to gentlemen. Equality (that great solvent), westward expansion, commercialized agriculture and increased manufacturing, a growing spirit of democracy, attacks on aristocratic pretensions—all meant that Federalists could not "prolong the traditional kind of elitist influence in politics." The very role of a gentleman came under attack as labor was now valued, not leisure.[45] By the early 1790s, rival gentlemen and their artisan followers in the Republican faction opposed Federalists' quasi-monarchical presidency and British-style financial program.

The republican gentry's rule was further weakened when republicanism took an extreme form in the French Revolution. Begun in 1789 and partly inspired by the American Revolution, it entered a more violent stage with the September Massacres of 1792, the execution of King Louis XVI in January 1793 and the Reign of Terror (1793-1795). Radical Jacobins proclaimed the "Republic of Virtue," declared Christianity to be contrary to the revolution, turned churches into "Temples of Reason" and replaced Catholic saints with "Revolutionary saints" such as Voltaire. The "new Revolutionary calendar began time itself with the first year of the Republic" rather than with the birth of Jesus Christ. To the radicals, Jean-Jacques Rousseau was "a new Christ, preaching a revolutionary redemption." Robespierre ordered a deistic "Festival of the Supreme Being," but it was human reason that was worshiped. Utopian hopes were expressed as the French called each other "citizen" and changed their dress.[46]

Three hundred years of pent-up hunger to erase Christianity, inequality and monarchy from Europe was suddenly released, and a flood of radical republicanism swept France and other European societies. Humans and human reason were finally to be placed at the center of reality.

Americans were polarized by this extreme version of the republicanism they had adopted. Many passionately supported their fellow republicans in France, even while the guillotines were busy. When Citizen Genêt, the French ambassador, arrived in Philadelphia in May 1793, pro-French demonstrations swept the capital: banquets, toasts, the Marseillaise, liberty caps, burning the English flag. At the College of William and Mary, some students called each other "citizen" and adopted the Revolutionary calendar. The cabinet split: Thomas Jefferson favored France; Alexander Hamilton favored England.[47]

The nation split also. Some Americans strongly opposed the French Republic, now that its anti-Christian colors were flying and it was at war with England. Evangelicals were slow to oppose the French Republic: the Jacobins were anti-Catholic, and republicanism had been linked to the Protestant cause since the seventeenth century. The past can blind one to present realities, and American evangelicals had been slow to perceive the anti-Christian nature of the Enlightenment. Avoiding extreme authors, praising moderate ones in a bid for respectability in an Enlightened age, they were caught by surprise when extreme French Deism and atheism hit the United States in the 1790s. Thomas Paine published *Age of Reason,* his attack on biblical Christianity, in 1794-1796. Many Republican leaders were Deists or skeptics: Philip Freneau, Joel Barlow, John Randolph, John Breckinridge, David Rittenhouse and Charles Wilson Peale. What seemed a sudden sprouting of skepticism alarmed some evangelical leaders, who struck back in the late 1790s.[48]

In a philosophical sense, the Constitution was outdated in ten years. Amidst a polemical war between evangelicals and Revolutionary Deists, the Moderate Enlightenment dissolved. Gone was the evangelical-rationalist alliance built on Radical Whiggery, on political Protestantism. The Founding Fathers had seized a narrow window of opportunity. Historian Henry May writes that it is "doubtful whether the Constitution could have been framed or adopted if the Convention had been held only a few years later."[49] The document soon became an outdated relic.

It also became a relic in a demographic and geographic sense. Generally, Federalist strength lay in Tidewater areas within fifty miles of the Atlantic; Anti-Federalists were stronger in regions farther inland.[50] Westward expansion carried Americans away from Tidewater Federalism into inland and trans-Appalachian areas that had fought the Constitution.

Political parties resulting from the 1790s strife were another reason it was outdated. The Founders had not designed it to accommodate political parties. When the House, Senate and presidency were controlled by the same party, partisan ties meant officeholders cooperated rather than checked each other as the Founders intended. When they were controlled by different parties, partisan wrangling aggravated the checks and balances. Electioneering Republicans recruited candidates from the artisan class. That interfered with the filtration of talent and threatened to end gentry rule.[51]

The Constitution was further outdated when Jefferson's Republicans won the 1800 presidential election. Applauding the move to democracy and popular politics, they quickly abandoned Federalists' monarchical style and governmental grandeur. Antigentry feelings came to dominate the Republicans (soon to be called Democrats). As Federalists faded, the Constitution's authors and other gentlemen were kicked out of office.

In a religious sense also, the Constitution was soon outdated. Evangelical leaders such as Timothy Dwight, president of Yale College, bitterly opposed the Deist Jefferson. His election helped to discredit their strongly biased Federalism and ill-informed conspiracy charges. "What an effort, my dear Sir, of bigotry in Politics & Religion have we gone through!" Jefferson wrote to the English Unitarian Dr. Joseph Priestley after his inauguration. "The barbarians really flattered themselves they should be able to bring back the times of Vandalism, when ignorance put everything into the hands of power & priestcraft." Yet Dwight, not Jefferson, was the victor. In a great irony, the longest sustained revival in American history erupted at Cane Ridge, Kentucky, five months after Jefferson was sworn in.[52]

The American Enlightenment began in opposition to the First Great Awakening and was ended by opposition from the Second. Not republican virtue but evangelical piety became the great glue holding American society together. All that was left of the American Enlightenment were a few copybook maxims of practical morality and common sense, a sort of *Reader's Digest* simplification of eighteenth-century Scottish philosophers.[53]

The Gentry-Led Creation of a New Nation: Synopsis

As democratic, religious, frontier America sailed past its outdated Constitution, many Founders felt disillusioned. Benjamin Rush tossed "all the notes and documents for his once-planned memoir of the Revolution into the fire." Washington lamented the rise of democracy. "John Adams spent much of his old age bewailing the results of the Revolution, including democracy, religious revivals, and Bible societies." Jefferson complained of a Richmond revival: "[The women] have their night meetings and praying parties, where, attended by their priests, and sometimes by a hen-pecked husband, they pour forth the effusions of their love to Jesus."[54]

The Framers' descendants felt the opposite. They came to venerate the Constitution as they grew less able to comprehend its Enlightened authors or its spirit. Misunderstanding both, they thought its failure was success. Disillusioned Founders seemed political prophets wisely legislating for all future generations. The glory and crown of America seemed to lie in Americans' political skills and in their ability to form republican governments. Both were greatly exaggerated. Abundant land, new immigrants, no nobility or established church, evangelical moral values—these caused the United States' prosperity and progress more than an outdated Constitution. They were gifts from the one whom the Deists called the Supreme Providence, who had his own purposes to fulfill. The Constitution was the work of their ancestors' hands, yet their descendants were tied to it. Its defects became their limitations. Americans would never summon the unity to write another.

5

Rebel,
Young Patriarch,
& Go West
with the Country

WESTWARD EXPANSION WAS ONE cause of the Constitution's rapid obsolescence. It moved Americans across the Appalachians and away from the Tidewater gentry who wrote the document. This westward expansion is also misrepresented in textbooks, often in a section called "Manifest Destiny," which describes post-1840 expansion west of the Mississippi River. One text alleges that Americans believed that "the country's superior institutions and culture gave" them "a God-given right, even an obligation, to spread their civilization across the entire continent." This "sense of uniqueness and mission" is seen as "a legacy of early Puritan utopianism" and "John Winthrop, who assured his fellow Puritans that God intended them to build a model 'city upon a hill' for the world to emulate." One historian blames Puritans' sexual repression and Indian hating instead.[1]

Thus westward expansion becomes a replay of the Columbian encounter, for textbooks portray greedy, violent, profit-taking Christians conquering peaceful Native Americans, hunting buffalo to near extinction, despoiling a fragile environment and shooting each other as they went. Texts imply or directly state that Christians' proselytizing zeal was a major cause of this disaster. So Puritan zeal helped drive the conquerors onward.

This is misleading or mistaken. By 1845, when John L. O'Sullivan coined the term "Manifest Destiny," westward expansion had almost run its transcontinental course. By 1849 the United States had acquired lands all the way to the Pacific. Why draw a line between settlements east and west of the Mississippi? The great river was a highway, not a barrier. The real barriers were the Appalachian and Rocky mountains; the first was crossed before 1776, and national glory did not motivate Americans to cross it. As we saw, Puritans did not come to Massachusetts Bay to set up a utopian "City upon a Hill." Most Americans did not move West for religious motives at all.[2]

They shared Columbus's excitement if not his motives. One pioneer praised "the pleasing and rapturous appearance of the plain of Kentucky," which was "a sight so delightful to our view and grateful to our feelings" that it "almost inclined us, in imitation of Columbus, in transport to kiss the soil of Kentucky, as he hailed and saluted the sand on his first setting his foot on the shores of America."[3] Rebellion against Christianity helped to tumble Americans out of the Tidewater, but it was different from that of 1492. This was patriarchal rebellion seeking family gain, not medieval rebellion seeking merchants' profit. It was agricultural more than mercantile, land-seeking more than profit-seeking, democratic not aristocratic.

Revisionist historian Francis Jennings calls this trans-Appalachian expansion "a landborne repetition of the seaborne colonizing of the seventeenth and eighteenth centuries," albeit "less controlled and more individualistic."[4] It was not. To seek minerals, trade and empire, merchants and monarchs had financed seaborne exploration and colonization. Insufficient European emigration, a lack of indigenous goods to trade and abundant, cheap land led them to introduce slave plantations to grow staple crops. Later, religious persecution and economic depression led to a great European emigration to Britain's colonies.

Trans-Appalachian expansion was very much the opposite. Religious toleration in the new United States meant that almost no one except Mormons went west for religious freedom. Masters hesitated to move valuable slaves to a lawless, unstable frontier. Merchants were not pioneers who traveled beyond markets: the Atlantic was their market highway, the Appalachians their barrier. Like Spanish and French kings, gentry leaders talked empire, but their government was less able than France's or Spain's to make one. It was largely their economy that made one.

Immigration, Tidewater plantations and British naval protection, however, made an American *economy* better able to support expansion than Quebec's, Mexico's or Louisiana's. The French in Quebec and Louisiana lacked the European immigrants needed to expand. Spain's major weakness was economic: "Spain simply could not deliver the goods, either to its own subjects or to Indians, and its North American holdings stagnated." Settlers and Indians looked to France, then to the United States, for goods that Spain could not deliver. Spanish growth north from Mexico was slow, government-controlled, lacking in incentives for the individual. By contrast, the United States was "not so much a democracy as a huge commercial company for the discovery, cultivation, and capitalization of its enormous territory." It was "primarily a commercial society . . . and only secondarily a nation."[5]

That analysis by a French political scientist appeared in 1891, long after the deed was done. The commercial company could capitalize on territory only after someone claimed and cultivated it. Neither activity offered much initial profit. We must return to the free land hypothesis to see why capitalism alone could not push American settlement across a continent. (The land was cheap, not free, and had been seized from Native Americans.) Cheap, abundant land meant that few migrants would consent to work for wages, for they could afford to start their own farms. "The immigrants [would] just replicate their family-sized farms across the vast landscape."[6] For a time they would be largely self-sufficient—poor customers for any merchants foolish enough to accompany them. With few markets, customers, workers, surplus crops or transportation arteries, few merchants moved west with them.

Historians have erred in describing merchants and markets as history's dynamos and self-sufficient pioneers and family-sized farms as history's dead weights. The latter powered amazing geographic and demographic growth from the 1770s to the 1840s. The U.S. birth rate in 1800 exceeded 50 births per 1,000 people; it "may have reached 65 in some areas of fresh settlement." By contrast, it was 15.4 per thousand in 1979. By 1800 more than 40 percent of Americans lived on lands that had been unsettled by whites in 1760.[7] Westward expansion occurred in a single lifetime. With astounding speed, Americans settled parts of the vast landscape from the Appalachians to the Pacific in seventy-some years (c. 1775-1849). Merchants capitalized on this growth, but they did not initiate it.

Patriarchal Rebellion Against Church-Centered Rural Life

John Mack Faragher's recent biography of Daniel Boone allows us to describe one major reason for westward expansion: patriarchal rebellion, as seen in that archetypal American pioneer Daniel Boone and his father, Squire Boone. (Another example is found in Alan Taylor's biography of William Cooper, archetypal frontier promoter, fellow rebel against Quaker faith and builder of his own patriarchal domain.)

Squire Boone emigrated to Quaker Pennsylvania in 1713 with his English Quaker siblings and parents. After the Quaker meeting gave him permission, he married a fellow Quaker of Welsh background, Sarah Morgan, in 1720. Sarah bore him eleven children, including Daniel in 1734. They moved farther west up the Schuylkill River, within sixty miles of Philadelphia but at that time on the frontier. It was a peaceful one, for Quakers had exemplary relations with the Indians. Here, Boone "clannishness" took geographical form: "Squire's farm was bounded on all but one side by the land of three brothers, and three others lived within a mile or two." But clan was constrained by church. The Quaker meeting supervised individuals and extended family.[8]

In the 1740s the meeting twice reprimanded Squire and Sarah for allowing a son and daughter to marry non-Quakers. The second time Squire argued back, "penned an angry letter to the meeting" and was expelled. Sarah "remained [a member] in good standing" and took the children to meeting, "but Squire Boone was finished with the Quakers." Three years later he left Pennsylvania for backcountry Virginia and North Carolina. Rebellion against religious authority and the lure of cheap land caused him to lead his married and unmarried children down the Allegheny Trail and Virginia Road. At very low prices, he bought 1,280 acres in western North Carolina and soon owned "several square miles of land." As the patriarch, he gave each maturing child enough farmland to get started. They re-created their Pennsylvania "landscape of kinship" in North Carolina. Here the Boone farms were also adjacent, though the farm sizes were much greater than in Pennsylvania.[9]

Daniel took rebellion against the religious communalism of a Quaker village meeting further than Squire had. After marrying Rebecca Bryan in 1756, he too became a patriarch—she bore him ten children—but he was an irresponsible one. Almost addicted to "long hunts" in the fall and winter, he spent months hunting and trapping while Rebecca cared for the children and the farm. He squandered money from fur and hide sales on one three-week frolic in Philadelphia, and later lost money gambling and cavorting in St. Augustine. Closer to home, he competed in shooting matches and other "rough male sports" at nearby Salisbury. His 1760-1762 "long hunt" separated him from his family for almost two years. When he returned, Rebecca had delivered a child who was certainly not his. After leaving Pennsylvania, "he remained unchurched until he died."[10]

Rebelling against the church did not end his patriarchal role of ruling his family and providing land for his grown children. To avoid debts, acquire cheap land for his children and move closer to his beloved hunting grounds, Boone led successive family migrations to the Upper Yadkin Valley (1766), to Kentucky (1773 and 1775) and to Missouri (1799).[11]

These patriarch-led migrations of extended families were the cutting edge of westward expansion. Neither religious nor profit motives caused them; rather, patriarchs needed to find cheap land for rapidly multiplying offspring. Historian Charles Sellers notes, "Cheap land . . . swelled patriarchal honor to heroic dimensions in rural America. The father's authority rested on his legal title to the family land." Only he could provide land the son or daughter needed for marriage and family formation. "Supreme on his domain, he was beyond interference by any earthly power," or so it seemed.[12]

The male drive to achieve a patriarchal role on extensive land and to rule an extended family made semisubsistence family farms dynamos, not dead weights, in early America. This drive was powered by a rebellion against churches and clergy who limited patriarchal power. (Many historians claim that the drive was to make money off commercial farming in the West, yet where profit came before religion, that too showed male rebellion. Thus this debate over the *form* that rebellion took need not concern us here.[13]) This male rebellion differed from medieval Europeans' rebellion against Christianity. It was democratic, egalitarian.

Many patriarchs felt that they were beyond interference from the heavenly Power, whose role seemed unchanged since Puritan days, when it was harnessed to a community's religious goals. Then, writes Sellers, "worship of an Absolute Patriarch stabilized this patriarchal society by restraining patriarchal abuse" as "congregations enforced communal horror at marital infidelity and punished male drunkenness and violence."[14]

But that overemphasizes God the Father as Patriarch. The New Testament emphasizes Jesus Christ as the Christian's Brother and the Father's obedient Servant. He is an example, not a martinet. The major passage on the Christian family (Ephesians 5:21—6:4) begins with a general command: "Submit to one another out of reverence for Christ." Commands to submit to husband and father are given in the context of obedience to Christ and his broader goals. The apostle

Paul orders husbands to love, feed and care for their wives "just as Christ does the church." Fathers are to rear children "in the training and instruction of the Lord." The male leads as a servant guiding other servants of Christ in a joint mission to follow him. Mission and Master are "restraining patriarchal abuse," and restraints were strong in Dissenting and Puritan villages.[15]

Restraints limited male independence. Many males rebelled against a Christianity that failed to place them at the center of reality, that paradoxically demanded that their leadership be servanthood. They rebelled against the Christ who endured the paradoxes of being a rejected Messiah, powerless King and humble Lord.

They rationalized their rebellion. The minister was the professional specialist in Christlikeness, they might argue. That standard was too high for laymen. Yet they chafed at the minister's resulting moral authority and rebelled against religious, communal values. Most did not move directly from religious communalism to rebellious individualism. The intermediate step was familism: family came first.[16] Yet the patriarch defined what the family's interests were, so this was male individualism thinly disguised. Patriarchal power meant having your cake and eating it too: your individualism *and* your family, your male autonomy *and* women and children's fealty to you. That seriously distorted the Christian concept of the Christlike male leader-servant.

Rebellion against restraints and standards could be partial or complete (or partly justified by local pastoral misconduct). The patriarch might be the village agnostic, Sunday-morning absentee or nominal churchgoer. He might allow his wife and children to attend church or he might not. One Southern patriarch tried to escape Methodist preachers:

> I quit Virginia to get out of the way of them, and went to a new settlement in Georgia, where I thought I should be quite beyond their reach, but they got my wife and daughter into the church. Then . . . I found a piece of good land, and was sure that I would have some peace of preachers; but here is one of them before my wagon is unloaded.[17]

Rebellion could be more subtle than that. The patriarch might help start a new church in the West, but his relationship to the church was subtly altered. In migrating, he had placed the family's interests in acquiring hundreds of acres of cheap land above the church's interest in not having the westward dispersal of population outrun its ability to plant new churches. Church was secondary, family primary. That was far different from Puritan fathers' risking their families' well-being to establish a pure church in the New World.

Household Economy and Society on the Patriarchal Frontier

The resulting economy and society rested on land ownership, not church membership. The Puritan congregation *was* the key to land ownership: Puritan towns distributed parcels of land to church members, but common, undivided land was used by all. By contrast, late-eighteenth-century patriarchs bought large (often 640-acre) parcels which they owned in "fee-simple"—without restrictions, except taxes, road work and militia duty. The Land Ordinance of 1785 called 640 acres a "township" (later "section"). Yet "government was not creating townships in any functional social or economic sense." It "was not in the business of community formation" but in "the business of peddling land." One patriarch might buy the whole township and be his own community.[18] Fee-simple land in abundance "sustained his honor and untrammeled will" and "extraordinary independence."[19] He did not allow the church to limit these.

True, land brought difficulties, whether it was prairie sod hard to plow or forest land hard to clear. Yet the semisubsistence farmer needed to clear and plow only a few acres. Pigs and cattle could forage in the woods. The corn-hog system of farming suited both pioneer semisubsistence agriculture and commercial agriculture. It took advantage of the greater productive efficiency of both corn and hogs to yield either an adequate subsistence or a marketable surplus—for relatively little labor. That was important in a land of labor shortage. One could move from subsistence to commercial farming with minimal and gradual increases in land, labor and capital.[20]

Why raise a large surplus when markets were so distant and transportation so primitive? In Sugar Creek, Illinois, in 1836, hauling corn fifteen miles to Springfield cost more than the sales proceeds! Freed from commercial agriculture's competitive demands (or engaged in a less demanding type of commercial farming), males spent their free time in hunting, fishing and "rough male sports." Since wage labor was scarce, children were the patriarch's labor force. Settlers on new lands produced children "about as fast as was naturally possible." "Fertility was enormously high as long as the young couple could form their own household on their own land."[21]

That imposed enormous childbearing and child-rearing burdens on women, who "paid a heavy price" to maintain males' independence. One Illinois immigrant noted that "a man can get corn and pork enough to last his family a fortnight for a single day's work, while a woman must keep scrubbing from morning till night" to complete her tasks. Gardening, cooking, canning, sewing, weaving, churning, caring for livestock, plus caring for children occupied her time. Distance isolated her and kept her from socializing with other women. Almost never did she share in the land ownership. Her income from butter and egg sales often went to buy necessities; her husband's grain sales proceeds went to buy farm machinery. "Men's product was for male use; women's product was for the family."[22]

Males dominated public life too. A "community" of patriarchal families was often a coincidence: the same site happened to advance each family's interests. Some families were linked by kinship. If there was a church, it had not created the community, nor did its interests come first. Nothing limited thinly disguised male individualism in these "ultra-virile" villages with Saturday drinking, fistfights, racing, bearbaiting and shooting contests. Indians called the whites' election day "the big drunk," for white males "went to town, voted, drank whiskey, smoked, swore, wrestled and fought, all for a little fun." Jacksonian democracy was for white males only. Universal white manhood suffrage was its creed. "The one public event that women claimed as their own was the religious meeting," but irreligious males came to camp meetings to mock the proceedings.[23]

This patriarchal economy's land hunger drove pioneers west. Hunting and trapping brought food and goods to sell but depleted the supply of fur-bearing animals and led hunters to look for new hunting grounds. Land was a commodity too. Speculators bought large tracts and upped prices. Pioneers balked at these prices. Moving west was the patriarch's answer to scarce animals and expensive land. He sold the farm and "used the proceeds to acquire a much larger tract of land farther west." Another westering motive was squatters' inability to purchase land they illegally farmed. They had to "squat" farther west. An observer reported that one Arkansas family in their shanty "appeared to have lived a roving rambling life ever since the battle of Bunker Hill when they fled to this wilderness."[24] The reduction of church influence over patriarchs meant the removal of one barrier to migration.

Native American Nations as Barriers to Westward Expansion
Though pioneers acted as if western lands were vacant, they were invariably occupied or claimed by Native Americans. The encounter between Euro-American settlers and indigenous nations was unlike the Columbian encounter. Europeans and Indians had changed greatly since Columbus. Indigenous peoples were no longer the powerless victims the Taino had been.

Native Americans in the interior of North America had adapted to Europeans' waterborne conquest and commerce. Europeans' success at oceanic trade and coastal settlement and their failure to settle the interior left Native Americans much economic and geographical "space." At the edges of the French, British and Spanish empires, according to Richard White, a "middle ground" developed where Indian and European met on more or less equal terms. These edges were "zones of interaction" primarily, a commercial exchange of goods. Both sides had "to behave themselves in ways expected of business associates." Playing off traders of different empires, nations such as the Cherokee and the Iroquois Confederacy gained some clout. Racial antagonisms existed, but they were restrained: trading was reciprocal; neither side had overwhelming power.[25]

Firearms and horses which Native Americans received in trade upset the balance of power between their nations and between genders within their societies. Guns and horses equipped them to fight whites on more equal terms and made the Indian interior as dynamic as whites' coastal settlements. Generally, the horse spread from the Spanish empire north and east to Indians living in the French and British empires; firearms spread west and south from the French and British empires to the Spanish. Eastern Indians who acquired firearms first gained an advantage over those farther west who lacked them. Coming from what is now Minnesota, the Dakota became armed nomads who conquered vast stretches of the Great Plains. In formerly egalitarian tribes a horse-owning hierarchy formed. Women lost power to men as "the benefits of the horse accrued disproportionately to men." Men's hunting duties were eased and their kill increased; women raised more corn to feed horses and worked harder "to treat and tan" more hides. "Europeans had unleashed forces they could not control."[26]

With their fleets confined to the oceans and their armies unused to highly mobile warfare, European powers could not conquer sharpshooting nomads on horseback. Indians could easily use guerrilla tactics against them. Governments did not want protracted wars in the interior against Native Americans. Besides, warfare interrupted profitable trade.

Racism has been exaggerated as a cause of Indian-white warfare. Traders harbored racial prejudices, but the profit motive overwhelmed other motives. Many took Indian wives. Farmers in the Thirteen Colonies had prejudices, but these produced racial segregation, not conflict. Farmers living near church-centered villages had little contact with Indians.

Faragher points to the paradox that "American conflict with the Indians came not because they were so alien to each other but precisely because they were so much alike." Or, rather, conflict came between Indians and those Euro-Americans most assimilated to Indian ways, not between those who found each other alien. Most assimilated were farmer-hunters who "interfere much more with the Indians than if they pursued agriculture alone," according to Indian agent Sir William Johnson. In hunting, whites adopted Indian ways, for they brought no European hunting tradition with them. In the forest they used a Euro-Indian "pidgin tongue," wore Indian breechcloth and leggings and went on "long hunts." Indians adopted the European long rifle and raised European livestock to supplement increasingly scarce game. Both groups hunted and trapped the same woods for the same purpose: to sell furs and hides to traders. Both made their women tend gardens and fields in their absence.[27]

Occupying the same woods and competing in the same fur market brought them into conflict more than did racism. A farmer in Connecticut might hate Native Americans but be so separated from them and so opposed to reckless westward expansion that he was no practical threat to them.[28]

Racial prejudice and conflicting notions of proper land use divided whites from Native Americans. Yet it was not inevitable that such differences would end in warfare. Indians had financial reasons to sell land if land sales were without fraud and did not endanger their survival. Enlightened gentry such as President Jefferson preferred a peaceful policy: negotiated treaties; slow, orderly settlement; continued residence of "civilized" Indians. Indian leaders such as Cornstalk of the Shawnee favored peace and negotiations. The Iroquois Confederacy opposed war. Quaker Pennsylvania was a precedent for peaceful relations. Religious and ethnic motives in the communal villages restrained dispersal of the white population until they were weakened by patriarchal rebellion.[29]

Much depended on the pace and type of settlement. Slow, orderly settlement following honest negotiations and land purchases, obeying distant governments' laws and leaving adequate land for Indian use—that need not have produced violence. But that was not the pattern typical of trans-Appalachian expansion. Kentucky is a good example of what did occur.

Rebelling Patriarchs Make Kentucky a Frontier Tragedy

Daniel Boone began by hunting there, for game was plentiful. He killed his first buffalo, shot hundreds of deer and bear and trapped "several hundred dollars' worth of beaver pelts." To the Shawnee hunters, "Americans like Boone were poachers." They trespassed, shot game in vast quantities and wasted the meat, for only skins were valuable in the market. Twice the Shawnee briefly captured

Boone and took his poached pelts and hides, but he ignored warnings to stay out of Kentucky. He brought his family across the Appalachians in 1773 in violation of Indian treaties and British Proclamation. Delaware, Shawnee and Cherokee warriors killed his oldest son James and others. The would-be settlers headed back home.[30]

They returned in 1775, sponsored by land speculator Richard Henderson, who had obtained dubious title to Kentucky lands from the Cherokee. The Shawnee denied that the Cherokee had any title to convey. With the colonies and Britain nearing war, colonial governments could not stop this fraudulent purchase and illegal emigration. Henderson offered land at the cheap rate of twenty shillings for a hundred acres, and each settler could buy up to five hundred acres. By April 1775, about eighty settlers were at Boonesborough to qualify for these generous terms.[31]

This makeshift town soon exhibited Jamestown's spirit, not Plymouth's. Land hunger and greed disrupted group discipline. Before the horses were unloaded, men hurried to locate the best land. Efforts to build a fort were abandoned despite the danger of Indian reprisals. An observer noted that Boonesborough "was all anarchy and confusion, [and] you could not discover what person commanded, for in fact no person did actually command anything." Men shot so many buffalo that game became scarce in the vicinity. "Disputes over land claims began immediately and threatened to escalate into violence." Settlers rebelled against Henderson's authority, which was in doubt once the Revolution began. "Many of the settlers had come west precisely to escape hierarchy and control, and in their radical notions of independent action they resembled no group more than the Indians."[32] The contrast to religiously motivated settlements in New England was marked. Patriarchal rebellion, greed and familism produced anarchy.

Another contrast was to the integrated, communal society of their foes, the Shawnee, who lived north of the Ohio River. Their capital, Shawneetown (Chillicothe), was more "civilized" than Boonesborough. It had "several hundred Shawnee homes," many of them log cabins set along streets laid out for protection against attack. Fifty miles north of Boonesborough stood the remains of Blue Licks, a mixed-tribe town once home to a thousand Indians. Kentucky was not a vacant wilderness—Native Americans used it. Boonesborough threatened their use; and they threatened the new town to stop the encroachment. Shawnee chiefs such as Cornstalk could not control this anger.[33]

Here we must pause to note that one result of westering patriarchs' rebellion against Christianity was their myopia regarding their sins. They did not see the wrongs they did to others but saw themselves as innocent victims when attacked.[34] The resulting warfare was brutal on both sides: Cornstalk was killed while on a peace mission; Indians and whites were tortured; bodies were mutilated; "Delaware Christian converts, two-thirds of them women and children," were murdered by whites. Males on both sides lived by a code of exaggerated honor and courage. "A man's expression of caution was likely to brand him a coward." Having rebelled against Christian restraints, frontiersmen became part Shawnee brave, part dueling Southerner. In August 1782, Boone guided a small army of Kentuckians pursuing an Indian force. Though he saw signs of an impending ambush, earlier his friend Hugh McGary had been accused of timidity for advising caution. Anxious to redeem himself, McGary now attacked Boone's cautionary warning of ambush as "cowardice." They yelled at each other. "McGary blew off like a keg of black powder." Shouting, "Them that ain't cowards follow me," he wildly charged into the ambush. They followed, and many were slaughtered, including Boone's second son, Israel. Daniel Boone escaped with other survivors, but the dead were left behind to be eaten by vultures. Male pride had a terrible price.[35]

Boone's quest for Kentucky land was a tragedy. Israel was shot before his eyes. When he visited James's grave site, he saw signs of wolves' digging. He dug up his son's and a companion's bodies, gazed on them and reburied them more securely. He "sat by the side of the graves in the rain and wept." By the mid-1790s he had lost all his Kentucky land.[36] Seeking land for his sons, the patriarch lost land and sons.

Rebelling patriarchs made Kentucky a frontier tragedy. They adopted the Indians' hunting-and-farming lifestyle without the conservation ethic. Each of them desired hundreds of acres of land. Without the religious motive for sticking together near the church-centered village, the government was unable to restrain them or to make them honor the terms of treaties with Indian nations. Indianlike whites battled whitelike Indians. Conflict increased race hatred, which bred more conflict.

Not all frontiers saw such bloodshed. Kentuckians raided into southern Ohio, but Ohio Company speculators preferred slow, steady settlement following negotiations. Small cleared tracts brought higher prices than large wild ones. Likewise, Connecticut speculators and settlers waited to survey and settle northern Ohio until the Treaty of Greenville (1795) had reduced the danger of Indian raids.

Pioneers from "the land of steady habits" did not see caution as cowardice. In an orderly way, they surveyed and allocated lands, established towns, churches and schools. Most of them did not move for religious reasons, and their commercial towns "did not quite add up to a replica of New England," but a bit of their ancestors' communal spirit lingered on and made them no replica of Kentucky either.

South of Kentucky and Tennessee, slaveholders had pecuniary reasons for caution: Indian warfare endangered their investments in slaves. Still, enough frontiersmen and cattle-raising farmers hungered after southwestern lands to spark white-Indian wars. Planters followed these pioneers.[37]

The often violent, aggressive hunter-farmers of backcountry Pennsylvania, Virginia and the Carolinas poured into Kentucky and Tennessee. They pushed ahead more rapidly than Yankees or cotton planters. By 1800 they had entered Missouri, southern Illinois and Indiana, when Yankees and cotton nabobs had hardly begun to settle their frontier regions. Backcountry pioneers led the way across the Mississippi and the Great Plains. Governments could not control them any more than the wind or the weather. Even with guns and horses, Indian warriors could not stop them. Their victories around the time of the War of 1812 "destroyed the last chance of effective Indian resistance."[38] By weight of numbers and sheer audacity, they swept west. Yet their rebellion against Christianity made their advance a tragedy, not a glorious epic.

Learning from Experience and the Land: "Going West" Changes

Once this westward advance became predictable, merchants and other capitalists could profit from what they could not have started. They recognized that the self-sufficient pioneer was only the first wave. Better customers were sure to follow. Entrepreneurs' services, in turn, greatly accelerated westward movement, which became specialized and commercialized, with better transportation and communication. Westering Americans learned from experience, and the profit motive spurred much of the learning. Huge profits awaited whomever could first anticipate the exact course of westward expansion.

Governments are often the slowest learners. The U.S. government was increasingly responsible for the first stage in expansion: Indian wars and Indian removal. From early settler-Indian conflicts, it deduced that Indians must be removed to lands west of the Mississippi. It assumed that east of the Mississippi it could not control settlers' "strong dislike to the Indians" and their land hunger. Rather than try to control them, it accepted defeat. Yet it assumed it could control them west of the great river, where "a permanent Indian country" could be denied to white settlement. That was not to be.[39] A democracy often assumes that citizens' lawless acts, if done in quantity, are an irresistible force. So it legalizes them. Democracy is worse than monarchy if democratic male individualism wins out over notions of public virtue and citizens' self-restraint.

What resulted was a great human tragedy. One-eighth of the Cherokees forced to move to Indian Territory along the "Trail of Tears" died from the trip. Removal occurred despite the fact that the Cherokees had largely adopted Euro-American ways: family farming, Christianity, republican government, a written alphabet. Conversion could not save them from whites seeking land rather than souls. Renouncing land, not sin, was the key to winning whites' (temporary) favor.

Soon settlers poured into the "permanent Indian country" beyond the Mississippi and Missouri rivers. Congress improvised an inconsistent policy of settling Indians on reservations. The Dakota and other nations, imperial powers who had conquered the Plains, refused to become colonial dependents. The resulting wars were as bloody as Kentucky's, but now the U.S. Cavalry, the military specialists, fought them more than did settlers.[40]

Specialization speeded westward expansion in other ways. Adventuresome males learned that the trans-Missouri West was too vast for jack-of-all-trades patriarchs such as Boone. No one person could hunt, trap, trade, explore, conquer and farm it. More individualistic than familial, men specialized in what interested them. The more diverse environments of the Great West also forced them to specialize, and the market encouraged them to. Using the natural resources specific to one's local environment was necessary to compete in the market. Self-sufficiency was less feasible west of the Missouri.

Thus mountain men such as Jedidiah Smith carried Boone's long-hunting, quasi-Indian lifestyle several steps further. They made no pretense of farming or familism. Some married Indian women, but they did not make family paramount. Many left American society for even longer periods or forever. Specialization in hunting and trapping encouraged a colorful individualism.

The 1849 California Gold Rush and other mineral finds turned thousands of single males into mining specialists. Once it was predictable, overland migration to California and Oregon encouraged entrepreneurs to specialize in outfitting, ferrying, supplying and guiding migrants. The opening of trade with New Mexico in 1821 led to the specialty of annual trading expeditions along the Santa Fe Trail. Potential profits were enormous. Specialization with its division of labor and efficiencies of skill speeded westward expansion: specialized explorers speeded trailblazing, and the guide and outfitter speeded overland travel.

Pioneer farmers became specialists: illegally squatting on government land, clearing it without intentions of staying, selling it to newcomers and moving on to the next frontier. In Iowa, some used democratic "claims associations" to intimidate newcomers into buying from them at inflated prices instead of from the government. They learned that the government had no real intention of enforcing its own land laws. Indeed, a job in the U.S. Land Office became a specialty, "a fief, a species of personal property that imparted to its holder a vested right" to personal profit. Land Office employees speeded the transfer of land into private hands as they defrauded the government.[41]

Land speculation was a specialty. Pioneering patriarchs avoided dependence on store-bought goods, but the market came to them in the form of land speculation. Land was a commodity too. Once westering became predictable, men tried to profit by anticipating it: buying land cheap and selling it dear. They gambled in a "futures market" in land. The pioneer farmer was part speculator: he expected to make more from land sales than from crop sales. The more predictable patriarchs' westward movement became, the more grandiose the speculative schemes. Huge sums could be earned by speculating in townsites. "Boomers" of paper metropolises filled the West with dreams. Creating real estate values where there had been none, they hastened development in most cases. Where speculators' high-priced land forced pioneers to seek cheaper land farther on, the leapfrogging accelerated the westward movement even more.[42]

Speculators and "boomers" sought improved transportation for their townsites: roads, canals and ultimately railroads. East Coast cities vied to be the eastern terminus of these arteries. New York's Erie Canal dramatically opened the trans-Appalachian West to market forces. Westering accelerated as investors leaped to conclude that railroads could be built ahead of settlement, which was sure to follow. Land values soared in areas that now had access to markets via rail lines. Manufactured goods flowed in; surplus crops flowed out.[43]

The "huge commercial company for the discovery, cultivation, and capitalization of its enormous territory" was in business now that a steady supply of Americans were freed from religious, communal restraints and were headed west in predictable numbers. Innovating and learning as it went, the company bounded across the continent with unprecedented speed. For his 1810-1811 long hunt, Daniel Boone, who had crossed the Appalachians in 1767-1768, "went high up the Missouri [River] trapping," perhaps as far as Montana. Back home, he met "John Jacob Astor's fur traders headed for the Columbia."[44] By the 1840s settlers were headed for the Columbia and California. The pace was breathtaking, but markets and merchants rapidly caught up with patriarchs fleeing west to escape them.

Individualism Fails to Free Males and Leads to Violence
The patriarch was now pressured by women and children wanting store goods, tempted by high wheat prices and shamed by neighbors' higher living standards. Rising land values increased his real estate taxes and decreased his children's chances of obtaining a farm. He had to adapt to commercial farming or head farther west.[45]

He sought independence from any earthly power, but his predictable, self-interested motives subjected him to the market's power. Merchants and markets thrived where self-interested acts became predictable. Where religious scruples or republican virtue led people to refuse to buy the most or the best for the least money—or made their purchasing unpredictable—merchants were hamstrung. But merchants had no need to worry, for the pioneering patriarch had rebelled against both Christianity's self-sacrifice for Christ's sake and republicanism's self-sacrifice for the common good. Markets easily captured him.

We must not suppose that male rebellion against Christianity occurred only among males going west. A parallel move toward male individualism occurred in a setting quite the opposite of the hunting-and-farming frontier. In large cities such as New York, young apprentices and journeymen, frustrated in their efforts to become masters, fashioned a similar male lifestyle. They largely skipped the intermediate stage of patriarchal familism and went straight to individualism.

Ideally, a boy learned the trade as an apprentice, a young man perfected his skills as a journeyman, and the mature man ran his own shop. Ideally, the common skills and interests of the trade united all three groups. In parades they marched together, a sign of the united "republic" of the trade.

The capitalist market destroyed ideals and unity. A few masters discovered the economies of scale and speed. They turned workshop into factory, divided skilled work into a sequence of less-skilled tasks and hired journeymen or apprentices at reduced wages to perform them. These employees had scant hope of ever becoming masters. This "bastardization of craft" sired figurative bastards, males lacking republican legitimacy because they had no hope of property ownership or the personal independence it conferred. They could not become true patriarchs. "The powerful assumption" was "that the honorable artisan expected to be the family breadwinner." Yet depressions and technological change often left him unemployed or compelled him to leave family to "tramp" from city to city in search of temporary work.[46]

Sometimes called Bowery Boys in New York, these artisans' male individualism often led them to drop patriarchal duties to women and children. Most "held to a profound and shameless indifference toward any kind of organized devotion." The centerpiece of their culture "was alcohol: at all times, in and out of the shops, New York's journeymen could be expected to drink." They formed gangs. Their fire companies frequently engaged in brawls and near riots.[47] Women and children suffered from Bowery Boys' brawls, alcoholism and tramping as they did from backwoodsmen's "big drunk" and "long hunt."

For economic relief, journeymen turned to unions. In politics they flocked to Andrew Jackson's Democrats or third parties such as the Workingman's Party. In backing Jackson they joined with westerners. Together, urban and frontier male individualists created the Age of the Common Man. "Universal [white] manhood suffrage" was its identifying slogan. To create a nation of equal, classless males, they fought the tradition of respect for gentry leaders. By moving west, pioneers distanced themselves from the gentry; by giving up hope of becoming masters, journeymen distanced themselves from masters' status as near gentry.

Rejecting gentry pretensions did not mean accepting minorities' aspirations. In practice, the idea of equality which "tore through American society and culture with awesome power" lowered the status of blacks, Catholic immigrants, Indians and women. Before, all had been subject to gentry leaders; now, white males' liberation from that only emphasized others' continued subjection.[48]

Male individualism, rebellion against Christianity and disrespect toward minorities lead to increased violence. The Age of Jackson and Common Men was one of America's most violent. Urban males' violence against blacks paralleled frontier males' violence against Indians. Mob violence was inherited from the Revolutionary era, when it was used by Patriots for political purposes. Jacksonian males used mob violence to uphold popular sovereignty, the idea that ultimate power remained in the people's hands. A mob was a majority acting "out of doors"—outside formal channels. In cities, it could bully "weak or unpopular minorities" or "punish them for their beliefs or their behavior" when the government failed to do so. On the frontier, vigilantes punished when government could not or would not.[49]

Frontier violence was more individualistic. True, groups attacked Indian and Loyalist minorities, but other racial and political minorities were well armed or less threatening. In California mining towns, "Chinese and Mexicans carried guns and knives, as did nearly everyone else . . . and were not averse to using them." That discouraged racist mobs. Crimes against women and crimes against property were also rare. The male code of honor caused most violence: "disputes over who was the better man, affronts to personal honor, careless insults, and challenges to pecking order in the saloon." Here was a society of young males who drank heavily, valued courage "above all else" and always carried a gun. They rejected a Christian code stressing piety, love and servant-hood and replaced it with a code stressing courage, honor and the need to avenge an insult. One person called them "Sons of Violence."[50]

Profanity was closely linked to male honor and violence. In frontier Kentucky, notes Christopher Waldrep, "Profanity was the emblem of manly self-assertion, of honor-as-language." Using God's name in vain showed frontier males' independence of the heavenly power. Swearing was used as a weapon against other males. Profane men "documented their mastery of other men by publicly cursing them." If they "dared not respond, it enhanced the swearer's reputation." If they did dare to respond, presumably that might lead to a duel. Here, too, anti-Christian rebellion led to violence-prone societies.[51]

The age's hero, Andrew Jackson, personified male honor, profanity, violence and individualism. Orphaned at fifteen, he became a wild young man, "the most roaring, rollicking, game-cocking, horse-racing, card-playing, mischievous fellow that ever lived in Salisbury," Boone's bachelor haunt in North Carolina. He used "curses and blood-chilling oaths" to intimidate others. At twenty-one he fought his first duel. As an Indian fighter, he was "bold, dashing, fearless, and *mad upon his enemies.*" He succeeded as frontier lawyer, speculator, politician and militia general, but he retained his sensitivity about his honor. Once an absurd misunderstanding over financial notes used as security for a horse-racing wager led to bitter exchanges of letters in local newspapers and a tragic duel. Though hit in the chest, the cool Jackson dispatched his opponent.

One encounter ended humorously. "Once, at a great outdoor banquet," he thought a friend was "under attack at the far end of the table." He "jumped on top of the table and strode toward his friend, wading through dishes and knocking food aside. 'I'm coming,' he shouted, 'I'm coming,' and his hand reached inside his coat." After the crowd urged him not to fire and he learned there was no need to, he stopped and revealed a tobacco box, not a gun, inside his coat pocket.[52]

Jackson was a slaveholding gentleman and land speculator, not the Common Man his followers imagined and his enemies feared. Much else in the Age of Jackson was illusion too. Westering patriarchs thought to escape gentry domination in a land and an age of equality. Yet they soon lost political control of Kentucky and Tennessee to speculating bankers and lawyers. The age of equality "experienced American history's sharpest rise" in inequality of wealth and consumption.[53] Some thought they would escape the market, yet it soon controlled their West. They thought a democracy of popular sovereignty and universal manhood suffrage insured victory over speculators, merchants and bankers. Yet capitalism seeped around all the barriers they erected against it. If the national government resisted, it used state and local governments. If legislatures hesitated, it used the courts, especially the Supreme Court. If popular movements rebelled against its markets, it co-opted them. Its markets, in turn, brought more inequality among supposedly equal males. Some patriarchs proved better farmers than others, and some prospered by specializing in storekeeping or a trade.[54]

The Church Pursues and Reforms Frontier Male Individualism

Many of the patriarchs thought they had escaped the church, its domineering clergy, its disciplining deacons, its moralistic sermons. Yet the Second Great Awakening brought church, clergy, deacons and sermons west.

Some historians link religion and expansion: "churches were a bulwark of support for the national imperial enterprise that brought Americans" across the continent; expansionism was "a legacy of early Puritan utopianism."[55] This is a misleading analysis which unites two different phenomena: the westward surge of settlers and churches' efforts to follow and minister to them. Heirs of the Puritans such as Timothy Dwight and Lyman Beecher did not lead the way west. They deplored the dispersal of people into areas lacking churches, schools, colleges and other Christian institutions. Bringing institutions west to the pioneers should not be confused with pioneering—nor initiators confused with reformers who trail behind.

Churches and ministers followed settlers into frontier regions such as Kentucky. Boonesborough's pioneers were hardly religious zealots like Boston's Puritans in 1630, and Boone's unchurched "spiritual condition was typical of many frontier Americans." Boone's brother-in-law noted, "Very few of the pioneers made any pretensions to religion." Many educated leaders of early Kentucky adopted the Deism then popular among the Virginia gentry. In 1800 "probably half of all Kentuckians [were] outside any organized congregations," and only about 10 percent were church members. Kentucky's great revival began in the late 1790s, more than twenty years after Boonesborough.[56]

When Christianity came to Kentucky, it brought ancient doctrines and century-old revival traditions. Later altered by frontier conditions, American preaching and worship did not begin that way. Early revivals were started by ministers such as James McGready, newly arrived from the East. He used the traditional, extended Scottish Communion service inherited from seventeenth-century Scotland and Northern Ireland. With its immense crowds, day-and-night outdoor preaching and strange physical "exercises," the famous Communion at Cane Ridge, Kentucky, was not a frontier innovation but a repeat of Ulster in 1624 and of Scotland in 1741-1742. Later, new leaders and settlers in new areas changed these services to create a camp meeting that met western needs and conditions.[57]

American history is occasionally the story of how God's Spirit acted in redemptive ways when people least deserved it. Using church, gospel, Scriptures and revival methods that were familiar to people, the Spirit acted autonomously. The Spirit's work was not shaped by the people's psychological state or by frontier conditions, nor did he sanctify the people's frontier lifestyle. He turned Kentucky upside down in the years 1797-1801.

Cane Ridge was the climax to six months of revival with a hundred thousand participants in central Kentucky. They did not come to be flattered but to be convicted by a gospel that challenged their lifestyle. At any one time ten thousand people listened to warnings of judgment and appeals for repentance from about twenty-five preachers. Moved by the Spirit, three hundred lay "exhorters" of both sexes and races, of all ages and classes, fervently urged the crowds to seek salvation. They sought it as frontier people, not as Philadelphia philosophers, and they suddenly did things such as exhorting that did not come naturally to them.

Revival turned Kentucky around; it did not confirm existing ways. One visitor found postrevival Kentucky "the most moral place I had ever been in." Swearing and quarreling had vanished; "a religious awe seemed to pervade the country." Temperance and antislavery ideas unpopular in prerevival Kentucky appeared. Evangelical preaching did not affirm but opposed westering patriarchs' lifestyle. "[James] McGready proved especially adept at felling adherents to the South's masculine code of behavior." Kentucky grand juries prosecuted profanity charges for fifty years after the revival.[58]

The new churches disciplined frontier males. Gilbert Dodds, Kentuckian and Presbyterian pastor, came to Sugar Creek in 1824 to start a church. He opposed frontier male culture, and his elders "hauled several affiliated men before the congregation and accused them of moral offenses": "Drunkenness and Frolicing" and "Dancing and Profane Cursing and Swearing." He pressured men to sign the temperance pledge, and he preached antislavery, unpopular in central Illinois.[59]

Frontier Male Individualism Alters American Religion

Over time, frontier conditions caused churches to modify their tactics. Methodists were particularly successful at adapting. They relied on young male circuit riders, often bachelors, who rode on extended "long hunts" after souls. "Thus the Methodists for example have a ministry admirably suited . . . to the new West—a kind of light artillery that God has organized to pursue and overtake the fugitives that flee into the wilderness from his presence." Uneducated and poor, the Methodist itinerants appealed to common men's antigentry feelings. They ridiculed the Calvinist clergy, and the patriarchs relished this criticism of the Eastern clergy whom they had sought to escape by moving west. Like frontier politicians, preachers such as Lorenzo Dow attacked pretentiousness, praised equality, exalted individual conscience and "championed popular sovereignty." They knew their audience.[60]

In adapting to that audience, American churches were changed. Positively, as Nathan Hatch points out, they learned to appeal to lower-class Americans and to avoid the middle-class ghetto of English churches.[61] They evangelized the successive Wests except the final Far West. They encouraged their members to cease the squatters' endless migration.

However, the people who adapted their faith to fit the frontier also moved it from its historic orthodox doctrines. The excitement of Cane Ridge and other revivals led one Presbyterian minister to join the Shakers and to accept Mother Ann Lee as prophet-messiah. Cane Ridge's local minister rejected the orthodox understanding of Christ's atoning death. Several critics of Calvinist clergy drifted into Universalism. Religious individualism found extreme expression in one Freewill Baptist leader who left that group: "I told them that I now stood alone, unconnected to or with any one."[62]

The heresy that most appealed to westering patriarchs was Mormonism. Its founder, Joseph Smith Jr., came from a poor, migratory Massachusetts clan. His grandfather led a "classic patriarchal migration to Vermont and then to" New York State. With an "ingrained aversion to evangelical religion," his father "led his growing family from tenant farm to tenant farm." They survived through "intense familism." Though mother Lucy was interested in the New York revivals, they rejected feuding denominations and got involved in treasure digging, divination and the occult. Young Joseph was angered when a local Methodist minister dismissed his 1820 vision. In 1823 he claimed that an angel (Moroni) had revealed to him the existence of gold plates containing a new divine revelation. In 1827 he claimed to have dug them up. He began to "translate" them, though he apparently allowed no eyewitnesses to see them. His *Book of Mormon* (1830) launched a new sect.[63]

Mormonism appealed to frontier patriarchs, especially poorer ones. America was not mentioned in the Judeo-Christian Scriptures; Smith put it at the center of his new reality, his "latter-day" revelation. The New Jerusalem would be "on the western Indian border," on the frontier. Echoing Puritan primitivism, he sold Mormonism as a return to pure first-century religious power, but with nineteenth-century males as its apostles. That appealed to young, propertyless males who sought empowerment.

His new faith was based on male equality, or equality of opportunity: "Men attained different degrees of godhood depending on how many descendants issued from their loins." Women owed any religious status to their husbands or male relatives. Even before Smith authorized polygamy, Mormonism was male heaven. Male individualism was sanctioned. Not only by familism, for males invented their own brand of religious communalism to sanction it. Having rebelled against Christianity's exclusion of them from the center of reality, they embraced a new faith that placed them there.[64]

Not surprisingly, males converted to Mormonism faster than did females. Not the gentry or the clergy or pietist females—*they* had authority to begin a new world. One male convert recalled that first year:

> I met the whole church of Christ in a little log house about 20 feet square . . . and we began to talk about the kingdom of God as if we had the world at our command. . . . We began to talk like men in authority and power—we looked upon men of the earth as grasshoppers. . . . We talked of such big things that men could not bear them.

Their neighbors could not bear them either. They were forced out: from western New York to Ohio to Missouri to Navoo, Illinois, where Joseph Smith was murdered by a mob in 1844.[65] They headed farther west, to the Great Basin, then part of Mexico. Persecution made Mormons the nineteenth-century equivalent of Puritans and Huguenots, moving in orderly, communal migrations to secure religious freedom. They were the exception to the nonreligious, noncommunal rule in westward expansion.

Religious motives and communal discipline enabled them largely to avoid conflict with Indians in Utah. They used patriarchal religious order to build an impressive empire there. They financed it by selling services to travelers on the Overland Trail. Yet they were no exception to the rule of patriarchal rebellion against Christianity. They kept males religious by creating a religion that was not Christianity.[66]

Rebellious Male Individualism: Synopsis

East of Utah, evangelicals Christianized frontier areas, but in the process their faith was bent to popular prejudices and habits. "The people insisted on a ministry linked directly to folk culture, separated neither by formal training nor professionalism."[67] It could often save the people from divine judgment but rarely from themselves. In the battle between Christianity and democratic, egalitarian, racially prejudiced, acquisitive, violent male individualism, a stalemate was reached. The adjectives were softened somewhat, yet males' drive to sanction their individualism through patriarchal familism, then through open individualism, was hardly slowed.

What was sanctioned for men would be for women too. Males would discover that a church that was denied the authority to restrain their individualism could not prevent female individualism either. And a church denied the authority to restrain Americans' westward move could not control their behavior within the nation's expanded borders or solve the problems created by expanded borders. But these discoveries would come only after westward expansion and violence-prone male individualism had helped spark a national tragedy.

6

The Great Duel
*North & South
Drop Debate &
Take Up Arms*

T HE SEDUCTIVE APPEAL OF NATION-
alism distorts Christian faith and separates believers by nation. If we Americans
are to resist this appeal, we must think realistically about our Civil War. Here
American nationalism wraps itself in its most appealing, sentimental, tragic yet
ennobling and politically idealistic robes. Recall Ken Burns's video series *The
Civil War* with its haunting violins, its brave privates recounting battles and its
adoring husband-soldiers writing love letters home to their wives. We Americans loved it. Yet romanticizing the Civil War makes the nation a substitute for
the church. Everything gets confused: the Union is viewed as suffering Lincoln's Bride.

The Civil War occurred on two levels: the Redeemer Lord answered slaves'
prayers for freedom, while Northerners and Southerners took political debates
from legislative chambers onto battlefields. We Americans combine the two
levels into one: a constitutional, democratic Union wins freedom for the slaves.
We know Northerners did not go to war to free slaves but to save the Union, so
we make principles the heroes: the Constitution and democracy end slavery and

save the Union. We find it hard to be realistic about Constitution, democracy or Civil War.

The mystic chords of romantic myth emanate from every battlefield, from every Union and Confederate grave, from thousands of Civil War books. They harmonize tragedy into ennobling, reconciling triumph. One textbook asserts that by 1865 "American democracy had proved itself." One claims, "Northerners and Southerners on the battlefields found each other to be not two alien peoples, but kindred peoples."[1] We nod in agreement. The Civil War becomes the nation's cross, a time of agony that freed slaves, reconciled North and South and gave the Union eternal life through soldiers' shed blood. Or Lincoln becomes the nation's Christ figure, a man of sorrows who bears a nation's grief, enters Richmond in triumph on Palm Sunday and dies a martyr's death on Good Friday.

Lincoln would reject our attempts to glorify him, to make political projects sacred, to confuse divine purposes with human plans. In his Second Inaugural he insisted, "The Almighty has His own purposes," different from Northern or Southern ones. Later he noted that his words were "not immediately popular": "Men are not flattered by being shown that there has been a difference of purpose between the Almighty and them." This humiliation, he wrote, "falls most directly on myself." He did not intend the war to do all that the Almighty did with it.[2]

Religionizing and romanticizing the Civil War ignores its harsh realities. "From the fearful day at Bull Run dates war," warned *Harper's Weekly,* "Not polite war, not incredulous war, but war that breaks hearts and blights homes." Nor was this suffering always ennobling. Like all wars, this one "corroded the discipline and order of society" and "corrupted morals." In the North, speculation, bounty-jumping and cheating on government contracts enriched a few. In army camps, alcohol, prostitution, gambling and swearing proved that sufferers weren't done with sin. Union soldiers didn't find Southerners a "kindred people." Their "letters home were a litany of complaint about" Southerners; they "found little to love in either" race and "felt they were risking their lives for undeserving blacks." The war freed slaves, but a resentful South did not accept their freedom or equality. A weary North abandoned them to segregation and sharecropping poverty.[3]

We are not flattered by comparing ours with other emancipations. "The world's most advanced republic could end slavery only by one of the bloodiest fratricides in human history." Less republican regimes in Latin America ended it peacefully. In 1833 imperial Britain ended it in the West Indies without bloodshed. Constitution, democracy and Union were largely responsible for failing to end it in the United States short of a war costing 620,000 lives. Why this failure when we have been admired for our political skill, our Constitution praised and our democracy copied? "The greatest puzzle in American history [is] exactly what caused the Civil War."[4]

The Duel and Gentlemanliness Versus the Cross and Godliness

We can start to solve the puzzle by recognizing the overall pattern: the Civil War resembles a great duel. Army officers introduced dueling during the Revolution. It lasted in the South after the North ended it.[5] Originally part of the gentry code of honor, it persisted as Common Men democratized it as a less formal, but still violent, frontier code of honor.

Historian Bertram Wyatt-Brown defines *honor* in terms quite different from Christian morality: "gentlemanliness; virtue . . . trustworthiness and honesty; entitlement; or class rank," or a reputation for these qualities. Honor wasn't internal, like conscience, but publicly claimed and bestowed, or denied. A gentleman insisted that others grant honor to his family, his town, his state and himself. Honor had racist overtones, for it was never given to blacks. Compared to them, all whites had some honor. A political idea, it gave the right to participate in politics, and such participation enhanced one's honor. It was a republican idea closely tied to "virtue," to the Founders' obsession with reputation. By 1850, Northerners' idea of honor diverged from Southerners' idea. In both regions, honor was democratized to include Common Men.[6]

The insult was the snake in honor's garden. It threatened honor as sin threatened godliness. It could be quite minor: a word such as *poltroon* or a rumor of dishonesty. Its appearance triggered a formal, inflexible chain of events, a "box" in which insulter and insulted were trapped. The insulted man demanded apology, clarification or satisfaction. Friends ("seconds") sought compromise. Failing in that, they prepared for the duel. For either side to back down then would be dishonorable. By facing each other, duelists confirmed their honor publicly. "Why should an exchange of shots wash away an insult?" Because, by "facing death, the duelist is reborn into the world" with his honor restored.

Each man honored the other by agreeing to duel, for only equals squared off. Duels were "a ritual of admission to a gentleman's club." You attained the social status of the man who shot at you. Duelists saved their correspondence and sometimes published it with an account of the duel. "Duelists needed to make their audience . . . aware of their honorable behavior in the encounter."[7]

Dueling was not Christian. Revealingly, "being closely associated with a religious group" was the one acceptable excuse for rejecting a challenge. Honor and duels were the opposites of Christian humility and peacekeeping.[8] The duel was a quasi-pagan ritual which offered a (potential) human sacrifice to cleanse both men of the stain of dishonor. It mimicked the cross: it "wash[ed] away an insult," gave duelists rebirth and born-again honor and transferred one duelist's status to the other (as Christ's righteousness is transferred to the believing sinner). Its dualisms of honor and dishonor mimicked "the dualisms of evangelical Protestant theology," yet its obsession with honor showed that gentlemen "loved praise from men more than praise from God."[9] They thus lost touch with the power of the cross to cleanse and reconcile without violent encounters.

The Civil War as analogous to a Great Duel can be traced in popular beliefs about it. First, Americans believe that both sides' courage and sacrifice brought them honor. Somehow 620,000 deaths wash away the dishonor of Southern slavery, Yankee self-righteousness, generals' bungling and politicians' short-sightedness. They give rebirth and cleansing to a Constitution and Union which helped cause the fratricide. They transfer Yankees' righteous, emancipating heroism to Rebels, who become heroes too. They turn political failure into success. There is another similarity, but it is factual. The lengthy disputes that led to the war also occurred within a formal, ritualized, inflexible system. Debating Northerners and Southerners were tightly restricted within a constitutional, republican system, a sort of "box."

Americans Boxed In by Constitutionalism and Republicanism

Chapter four discussed the construction of this "box." Any keys that might have peacefully ended slavery had been deliberately left out of it. Missing was any authority with the power to end slavery. Tidewater slaveholding gentlemen had rejected the antislavery impulses of the Great Awakening and the Enlightenment. That ensured that no appeal could be made outside the political system to religion or philosophy. The Awakening and the Revolution undermined the ability of external authorities to impose emancipation on the South. Throwing off Parliament's control meant throwing away chances of peaceful, Parliamentary emancipation like that in the West Indies.

The Constitution dispersed power between states and the national government and between three branches of government. A state could act against slavery, but only within its borders. The national government was too hedged in by states' rights and its powers too divided between its branches for it to act. Competition between branches, and between states and nation, made it unlikely that several authorities would cooperate to end slavery. The Constitution was a compromise that recognized the continued existence of slavery. The Founders' republicanism created a defiantly independent citizen suspicious of authority and protective of individual rights, including the right to hold slaves.

Denominationalism had similar effects in religion. After New Light—Old Light splits, Revolutionary disestablishment and the migration of thousands of sectarians, no one American church had the authority to stand against public opinion in a slave society. No denomination would ruin its chances in the religious competition by doing so. In the democratic Second Great Awakening, Americans denied a minister's right to decree doctrines that were so unpopular in local society. Southerners rejected the original antislavery impulses of the Second Awakening. Also, the Enlightenment reduced religion to a private value outside the public realm of facts such as slavery.[10] Finally, patriarchal rebellion against Christianity made it unlikely that slaveholders would submit to anti-slavery ministers.

Americans did not accept Christianity as authoritative in the public realm, but it was pervasive in the personal realm. Evangelicalism enjoyed unprecedented strength as a sort of glue holding a mobile, individualistic, antiauthoritarian society together.[11] Yet evangelical America had to express its political thoughts in the Enlightened, non-Christian language of the Constitution, adopted during piety's low point (1770s-1780s) but almost unalterable thereafter. By the 1830s, most Americans had rejected the Enlightenment except for a mild Scottish Common-Sense residue, but their political leaders still spoke the Constitution's Enlightened language.

Recent historians stress the masses, not the elites, and social and economic causes, not constitutional reasoning. Yet elites often framed the choices Common Men faced on election day. The Constitution framed the rules for candidates, parties and voters. Culturally and socially, the Constitution was as outdated by the 1830s as the knee-length breeches and powdered wigs worn in 1787. But it continued to shape politics, and the political leaders were those men most shaped by it.

Daniel Webster, John C. Calhoun and Henry Clay were the three great antebellum statesmen whom Merrill D. Peterson calls the triumvirate. Born during the Revolution, they represent a second generation trying to complete the Founders' work. Examining their careers allows us to identify Northern,

Southern and Compromise views of the "box." Like blind men describing the elephant, antebellum Americans developed very different estimates of the dimensions, color and texture of the political "box" into which they were jointly wedged.

The Northern perception of the "box." A descendant of Puritans, Webster was born in frontier New Hampshire to a family just moved out of their log cabin. His father was "a good Christian," a Congregational elder, a Bible reader. Young Daniel gravitated toward the Moderate Enlightenment while at Dartmouth College and later when studying law. He "spoke much of religion as necessary to the support of good government" but little of it as eternal truth.[12]

With his craggy black eyebrows and commanding presence, Webster was a superb orator who excelled at commemorative speeches. "Godlike Daniel" delivered the speech at Plymouth's 1820 celebration of the bicentennial of the Pilgrims' landing. Five years later he praised Revolutionary heroes at the fiftieth anniversary of Bunker Hill. After the seemingly providential deaths of John Adams and Thomas Jefferson on the same day (the fiftieth anniversary of the Declaration of Independence), he gave the eulogy at Boston's Faneuil Hall. Ancestor worship and civil religion were his themes in all three orations: New England's ancestors and the religion of republicanism.[13]

The second generation cheered when Webster placed the Founders (who were disillusioned with the Revolution's results) on a pedestal. More important than a landing, a battle or two coincidental deaths was the Union. Northerners now exalted the Union above its mundane origins in the bloody, divisive, almost accidental events of 1776-1783. In the 1820s many Americans still saw it "as a partnership, which might be dissolved when it became inconvenient." Webster's Second Reply to Hayne (1831) expressed Northerners' rejection of that view. With the words "'Liberty and Union, now and forever, one and inseparable,' " he "raised the idea of Union above contract and expediency and enshrined it" as an eternal reality. When Ralph Waldo Emerson noted that "the Union is part of the religion of this people," it was Northern worshipers he saw from his home in Concord.[14] Many Southerners had not bowed the knee to the Union.

Union worship did not produce character traits needed to preserve the Union: charity, mutual forbearance, patience. Yankees developed a proud, impatient honor that fit a modernizing, industrializing society outgrowing the rural, individual code of honor. They conferred honor on their governments and institutions, which repaid the compliment to individuals who obeyed the rules. The Union was the greatest institution. All lesser ones orbited around it and derived honor from their part in it. Especially honorable were the Union's principles: liberty and equality. The Union bestowed honor on all white males who showed ambition, self-control, industry, frugality and morality.[15] That a boy like Daniel from rural New Hampshire could be honored with high political office and gifts from the wealthy proved that character brought honor in Yankeedom.

The Southern perception of the "box." John C. Calhoun also came from a frontier—upcountry South Carolina—but he had other views on Union, Constitution and honor. Educated at Yale and at a Litchfield (Connecticut) law school, Calhoun believed in the Enlightenment too, but in its skeptical phase. In Litchfield's Congregational confines, he refused to attend church. He "was a sabbath breaker and probably a Jeffersonian infidel as well." A Man of Reason, he allegedly "could never write a love poem . . . because every line began with 'whereas.' " Clay described him as "haggard and intensely gazing, looking as if he were dissecting the last abstraction which sprung from metaphysician's brain." He was the Enlightenment's revenge on 1840s America: as others tried to maneuver within the constitutional box, Calhoun by deduction constricted its size and reduced their wiggle room.[16]

His religious views were not typical of upcountry South Carolina. After evangelical clergy abandoned their "avowed antislavery sentiments" to win a local hearing, evangelicalism glued together the upcountry's rough society.[17] Yet it did not fashion the South's idea of politics. Here, the religiously atypical Calhoun could be politically typical of Southerners.

He and they had a more accurate perception of the "box," for they guarded its blueprint from distorting changes. They knew that Constitution and Union were compromises on slavery. As one contracting party, they insisted that the original terms be fully observed. Southern political thinkers such as John Taylor of Caroline and John Randolph of Roanoke used key republican concepts, such as the return to first principles, to defend slavery. Return was needed, not to restore republican virtue, but to retain constitutional recognition of slavery. Checks and balances, the Senate's power, states' rights and limits on the president preserved slavery, not liberty or virtue. Union secured *sectional,* not individual, equality. It was temporary, and any of the contracting states could secede at will.[18]

The Founders built a box to ensure the domination of disinterested, virtuous gentlemen, but westward expansion and Jacksonian democracy displaced them. It now preserved the domination of slaveholders, a special class of gentlemen, not disinterested, not seeking the public good, but shielding slavery. Southerners preserved its dimensions and yet made its secondary purpose (maintaining slavery) into the primary one.

The Compromise perception of the "box." Henry Clay was positioned close to the center of this box. Westerner *and* Southerner, a cautiously antislavery slaveholder from the border state of Kentucky, he personified what historian Peter Knupfer calls the Compromise tradition of Constitutional Unionism. He personified the 1787 Compromise.[19]

Born in Virginia to a Baptist preacher who died when he was four, he studied law under George Wythe, Jefferson's teacher. In 1790s Richmond, "he embraced the city's ascendant Jeffersonian Republicanism as well as its moral and religious counterpart, deistic rationalism, so different from his father's faith." He acquired republican skills by joining a debating society, practicing oratory and reading law. Taking these to Kentucky, he prospered as a land-law and criminal trial lawyer. He adopted ideas of the radical and skeptical Enlightenments, influential among the Kentucky elite before Cane Ridge. He fought a duel, was elected to the legislature, to the House, then the Senate.[20]

A staunch defender of the Compromise of 1787, Clay best understood its weakness. "After 44 years of existence under the present Constitution what single principle is fixed?" he complained in 1833. "We are as much afloat at sea as the day when the Constitution went into operation." Slavery and other sectional issues created a periodic need for new compromises to preserve the Union. Yet new compromises were interpreted in different ways. North and South were too divided for any compromise to be unambiguous, comprehensive and final. A constitutional Union had been built on sand, with the plea that it was better than disunion. Each time the sand shifted, it had to be adjusted and the makeshift structure was again heralded as better than the alternative—disunion.[21]

The Union as courtroom, politics as perpetual trial. Webster, Clay and Calhoun were lawyers, though Calhoun disliked the law and left it. Lawyers were the clergymen of a constitutional republic, which showcased their talents and needed them. Supreme Court Justice Joseph Story noted, "The discussion of constitutional questions throws a lustre round the bar, and gives a dignity to its functions, which can rarely belong to the profession in any other country."[22] The Constitution's complexities—federalism, checks and balances, limited powers and judicial review—like Kentucky's notoriously confused land laws, created work for lawyers. The legality of citizens' deeds and governments' decisions was unclear. That required lawyers' arguments and courts' rulings. The number of litigants was expanded. Colonial politics had two main antagonists: colonial assemblies versus royal governors. The Constitution legalized many: states versus nation; president versus Congress; Supreme Court versus Congress and president; small states versus large ones; one section versus another.

Lawyers' adversarial, argumentative style was not too disruptive in courts trying crimes and lawsuits. Judge, jury and appellate court retained unquestioned authority here. In a political system that lacked one final authority, however, this style made compromise and conciliation difficult.

The Constitution gave the box dimensions much like a courtroom's, so we can modify the metaphor: the Union as courtroom, politics as perpetual trial. Here North, South and other litigants were represented by politicians who were the lawyers arguing the case. No one judge or jury heard them. Sitting on the room's four sides, four judges heard arguments and claimed authority: president, Congress, Supreme Court and state governments. Many juries listened. Northern politicians addressed a Northern jury, Southern politicians a Southern one, all politicians the local jury of their constituents. Out-of-court settlements and common-sense talk were not encouraged. Arguments were made in constitutional terms, even if these had little practical relevance. No final authority meant no final decision. When participants threatened to leave the courtroom, tentative settlements were cobbled together to keep the trial going. New issues perpetually undid done deals.

Slavery's revitalization and westward expansion created new issues. Compromising when tobacco and slave prices were low, the Founders assumed that slavery's days were numbered. But Eli Whitney's cotton gin and British textile mills' demand for cotton spread slavery to new southwestern lands and to a new cash crop.[23] The Founders did not foresee westward expansion taking the United States to the Pacific within sixty years after Washington's inauguration and creating continual competition between North and South, no longer fixed categories. Would new territories and states be Northern (free) or Southern (slave)?

The Founders had not planned for political parties, but these brought some coherence to a fragmented system. A Whig president cooperating with Whig senators, Whig governors and Whig judges could overcome the gridlock of the system. Parties needed issues to mobilize voters, and, since proslavery and antislavery were useful issues, they perpetuated the controversy.

Let's return to our metaphor. Consider our confusion when told that insiders knew that the trial was not really a debate of the issues but a competition between two social clubs (Whigs and Democrats) to see who was the best dressed and wittiest. No compromise could be final because it left one club behind and determined to prolong debate until it regained the lead. Later, we will see how this perpetual competition aggravated the debate over slavery and slavery's role in westward expansion.

Revivals Reintroduce Religious Ideas into a Political Debate

The Founders had not planned for revivals with "phenomenal increases in the number of Christian congregations," notably Methodist and Baptist ones that caught up with westering patriarchs. From 1780 to 1860, Methodist congregations grew from fifty to some twenty thousand; Baptists, from four hundred to more than twelve thousand. By 1855, 1.5 million Americans belonged to a Methodist church, 1.1 million to a Baptist one. Other denominations grew more slowly. Many nonmembers attended church. In the 1830s French observer Alexis de Tocqueville noted, "There is no country in the whole world in which the Christian religion retains a greater influence over the souls of men than in America."[24]

The Second Awakening differed from the First. Preachers still considered conversion a "birth from above," but they stressed the convert's personal choice and birth to personal holiness. They did not accept human imperfection but stressed immediacy in repentance, conversion and reform. Converts were to display Christian love in benevolent deeds as proof of conversion. The Second Awakening produced a "great profusion of voluntary societies" in which converts proved conversion: temperance, education, Sunday school, home missions, Sabbatarian, prison reform and antislavery societies. This Benevolent Empire was strongest in the North. Reform had antislavery overtones and was viewed with suspicion in the South.[25]

Unitarians and other liberals were strongly antislavery, but Northern evangelicals were crucial in mobilizing public support for the cause. They abhorred slavery's denial of slaves' free "moral responsibility for their own behavior." It corrupted masters with too much power: "Both master and slave were thus trapped in a relationship that inevitably led both down the path of sin and depravity." It began with man-stealing and continued with violence. One antislavery society called it "a sin—always, everywhere, and only a sin." Immediate abolition, not gradual emancipation, was needed.[26]

Abolition was hard for religious systems to accommodate. It threatened a revival-ending schism like the Old-New Light splits. Some Northern evangelicals disliked abolitionists: self-righteous, insubordinate, they ignored boundaries between church and state, tended to unorthodox views on Scripture, acted "beyond ordinary means of democratic control . . . and seemed impervious to, if not defiant of, the overwhelming public sentiment against them."[27]

A compromising political system could not abide these uncompromising seventeenth-century Puritans bursting into the nineteenth-century political courtroom. Recalling a visit to Virginia, Henry Adams described the effect on the New England mind:

> The boy [Henry] went back to Boston more political than ever, and his politics were no longer so modern as the eighteenth century, but took a strong tone of the seventeenth. Slavery drove the whole Puritan community back on its Puritanism. The boy thought as dogmatically as though he were one of his own ancestors. The Slave Power took the place of Stuart kings and Roman popes.[28]

A moderate, Enlightened, eighteenth-century Constitution could not abide seventeenth-century dogmatists, nor they it. Abolitionist William Lloyd Garrison called it "a covenant with death and an agreement with hell." Abolition "was at heart a theological conception" battling a very untheological Constitution.[29]

Trying to convince Americans that slavery was sin, abolitionists in 1835 mailed more than a million antislavery pamphlets, some to white Southerners. Claiming that these incited slave revolts, Southern postmasters refused to deliver them. A Charleston mob burned them. When abolitionists sent antislavery petitions to Congress, Southern congressmen insisted on a "gag rule" that kept Congress from considering them. Calhoun objected to the receipt of petitions that called Southerners sinners.[30] Like *poltroon, sinner* was seen as an insult to a Southern gentleman, not as a pastoral call to repentance. By his code, he need not seek satisfaction from abolitionists, whom he did not consider gentlemen, but he must demand an end to insulting petitions and pamphlets. So abolitionist appeals bounced off a Southern "Iron Curtain": no pamphlets, no petitions, no sermons, no repentance.

"The harvest is past, the summer has ended, and we are not saved."[31] By the 1840s, reformers and revivalists met other recalcitrant groups who refused to hear the message. From 1845 to 1854, 2.9 million immigrants entered the United States. That was 14.5 percent of the U.S. population in 1845, a percent-

age not equaled since. Native-born Americans did not know that this was to be a nation of immigrants, and many would not have been comfortable with the idea. The Catholic population increased tenfold from 1830 to 1860; many newcomers were Irish and German Catholics. That frustrated revival's purpose. As a preacher converted one man to Protestantism, two or three non-Protestants arrived from Europe. "Catholicism seemed hostile to everything" Americans valued, notes historian Tyler Anbinder. They "believed that the unlimited control which the Catholic hierarchy apparently exercised over its followers deprived Catholics of the independence necessary for participation in a republican government."[32] Culture and clerics helped Catholic immigrants resist the revival message.

They did more than reduce attendance at revival meetings. Catholic bishops opposed evangelicals' use of public schools to teach the King James Bible and Protestant values. They started parochial schools to shield Catholic children from such messages. For many Irish and Germans, alcohol was part of their culture. Temperance advocates ran into opposition from them and blamed them for the failure of voluntary prohibition. In New York City, the *New York Tribune* charged, "Ninety per cent of the rum-holes in some of the Wards are kept by foreigners." Some public drinking occurred on Sundays, so Sabbatarian reformers saw immigrant Catholics as unreachable opponents.[33]

In the late 1830s, frustrated reformers turned to the newly formed Whig party to seek reform through legislation. Whigs were friendly but reluctant to endorse their causes for fear of offending other voters. Reformers had to approach the Whigs, for Democrats openly courted immigrants, Catholics and drinkers and opposed their attempts to reform or coerce these groups. Some of them charged that priests insisted that Catholics vote Democratic and that almost all Irish and Germans did so.[34]

Both parties used corrupt means: encouraging immigrants to vote illegally, buying votes, dangling government jobs to recruit groups such as the Irish. Corrupt election judges and vote fraud were common in the North. Both parties and their conniving leaders seemed major obstacles to reform. Still, though some Whigs appealed to immigrant Catholics, Democrats seemed the main party blocking moral purification.[35]

Democrats were slaveholders' main shield against reform. Most masters were native-born Protestants, but antislavery reformers saw Catholicism and slavery as linked by more than the Democratic party.[36] Both kept revival from large groups: Catholicism from immigrants, slavery from blacks. The result was two enclaves of sin: urban ghettoes and slave plantations.

Many saw a third enclave of sin: Mormon Utah. As pioneers passed through Utah, reports filtered back East of polygamy, religious coercion, Brigham Young's heavy-handed rule and harassment of non-Mormon federal officials. Mormons used the forms of republicanism in Utah Territory to preserve their religious monopoly. In national politics, though, they were vulnerable. No party sought or needed their votes: they did not have statehood and were not numerous like Southerners or the Irish. In dealing with this out-group, the political courtroom was not deadlocked: both parties and both sections supported President Buchanan when he sent the U.S. Army to replace Young as territorial governor. Young had his own army and conflict seemed imminent. Mediation produced a face-saving compromise: Young stepped down but retained de facto control.[37]

That did not open Utah to revival or reform. Likewise, Democrats and constitutions saved urban ghettos and Southern plantations from similar intervention. Salt Lake City, the Bowery and Alabama's Black Belt were still closed to reform and revival. The Second Great Awakening summer was ending, and America was not saved.

Can politics succeed if preaching fails? Frustrated, some evangelicals called for a return to America's Christian origins. They "demanded that government protect the 'true Christianity' of its people from Catholics, Mormons, infidels and atheists." Others disliked its origins. Noah Webster doubted that a government set up "solely by the aid of *human reason*" could be Christian: "Our constitution recognizes no Supreme Being, and expresses no dependence on Divine aid." The system it set up "can not be a good government."[38]

Rather than dispute origins, others formed third parties to accomplish reform. Evangelicals in the revival-rich Burned-Over District of western New York started the Antimason party in 1826. They charged that Freemasonry was "an infidel society at war with true Christianity." Masonic oaths restricted one's freedom of conscience. Its hierarchy resembled Roman Catholic hierarchy. Antimasonry "was at base a religious crusade against sin," which largely won when many Masons quit the lodges. In the mid-1840s the American Republicans fought to save the Protestant character of public schools.[39]

Also crusaders against sin, abolitionists divided over political action. William Lloyd Garrison's wing opposed it. Evangelicals, many from "the revival-enriched soil of upstate New York," favored it and in 1840 formed the Liberty party ("vote as you pray"), but it won a minuscule vote. Yet the Mexican War, westward expansion, Democratic factionalism and a slave-owning Whig presidential candidate added pieces to the antislavery coalition. Its rallying point became the Wilmot Proviso, a congressional motion (never passed) to keep slavery out of territories acquired from Mexico. In August 1848, the Free Soil party was born in a convention that was like "a protracted revival meeting." Its presidential candidate, Martin Van Buren, won five times as many votes as the Liberty party had in 1844.[40]

Bringing the religious issue of antislavery to politics and expanding the antislavery coalition had consequences. It angered Southern evangelicals and pushed them away from their previous nonpolitical stance. The Free Soil party grew beyond a core of *relatively* idealistic, altruistic, religiously motivated reformers to add thousands of self-interested supporters with strong desires, hatreds, prejudices and fears. A drive to free slaves became a drive to keep Western lands free of blacks. David Wilmot argued, "The negro race already occupy enough of this fair continent; let us keep what remains for ourselves and our children . . . for the free white laborer, who shall desire to hew him out a home of happiness and peace, on the distant shores of the mighty Pacific." That hardly spoke to the conscience.[41] Too little religion remained in such reform to convict or convert. Yet enough of "the spirit of the religious enthusiast" remained to upset the political system.[42] Free Soil goals were still nonnegotiable even if its antislavery was diluted.

Reformers erred in thinking that politics could succeed where preaching had failed. A political courtroom was a profoundly conservative place that resisted reform more than the most hardened sinner. Talk of precedents and constitutionality discouraged innovation. Power was fragmented into several power bases, so reformers had to capture *all* of them for long periods to enact reforms. To safeguard reform from future legislative repeal, they had to amend the Constitution, which was difficult. The Constitution gave antireform groups political confidence. It helped Southerners resist nineteenth-century Christendom's growing antislavery sentiments.[43]

Looking back, we see that reformers could have retained Christian integrity through nonviolent direct action: sending antislavery speakers south until whites' violent response discredited proslavery. But that point is anachronistic. Such tactics were pioneered by the civil rights movement, which knew that Southern politicians would not listen. Antebellum reformers shared the nineteenth-century faith in democracy and could not resist the temptation to try political action.

So the turn to politics distorted Christian faith and practice. Slavery was an entrenched, politically powerful institution. Wrestling with it partially lamed evangelicalism and individual Christians in both North and South. The struggle drove some individuals away from orthodox Christianity, though it's often hard to say which came first, their abolitionism or their heterodoxy.

Abolitionists William Lloyd Garrison and Wendell Phillips harshly attacked orthodoxy and churches for accepting slavery. They and their followers stressed individual conscience above state, Bible or church. One proclaimed, *"Humanity before all things*—before all books and all institutions; and God in the soul is the only authority." For some, "God in the soul" meant that the soul was God. In their human-centered utopianism they assumed that the gospel erased the consequences of the Fall (here, government), or they rejected the gospel if it didn't. Their consciences took extreme positions and then swung to opposite extremes. In the 1830s, many preached personal pacifism, or nonresistance, and denied government's right to use the sword to enforce laws. By the 1850s, men such as Phillips and Theodore Parker felt *they* could use the sword to start slave revolts. There was a "total collapse" of "nonviolent abolitionism in the 1850s" due to events and the barriers to peacefully ending slavery.[44]

Defending slavery distorted Southerners' Christianity too. In the 1830s, Southern ministers argued that slavery was biblical, an argument used against Southern antislavery evangelicals twenty years earlier. They battled unorthodox abolitionists with biblical inerrancy, which the apostles Peter and Paul had not designed to defend slavery. Misusing Scripture discredited scriptural literalism and made ministers politicians' tools. Southern evangelicals dropped their attack on the pagan code of honor. Like the conquistadors' God, the Southerners' God became "an auxiliary rather than a Lord," an aide-de-camp in the proslavery fight. Southern editors and politicians used ministers as shields against Northern reformers. The *Charleston Mercury* noted, "Our most efficient champion against the machinations of the zealot, is the reflecting, prudent, meek Christian."[45]

Political concepts distorted thinking about the church. Methodist *Discipline* and Baptist congregational autonomy gained constitutional status. Copying states' rights talk, the *Alabama Baptist* argued, "There is no such thing as *the Baptist Church*": a local church is "republican, all authority being invested in the people." Politics could stymie the gospel. During the nullification crisis of 1832-1833, one South Carolina church reported, "8 faithful days of preaching and not a single convert . . . nothing but quarreling." Christianity was distorted to sanction the honor code, notes Wyatt-Brown. "No need to make choices between honor and Christianity, between Athens and Jerusalem," for Southerners' God "could be worshiped not only as a saving Christ but as the Ruler of Honor, Pride, and Race."[46] That was not literally biblical!

Northern antislavery evangelicals felt ground "between the upper and nether millstones of a *proslavery* Christianity, and an *anti-Christian* abolitionism." The former withdrew from national denominational bodies; that denied them the chance to use church discipline against slave-owning brothers. The latter forced them to form their own antislavery society. They were angered by some denominations' stress on saving institutions, a "time-serving ecclesiastical policy" that led them to form separate antislavery denominations. They questioned their priorities. Did revival or abolition come first? Proslavery misuse of literalism caused some to overreact and to adopt "a rational and historical approach to the interpretation of Scripture," not a literal one.[47] The struggle distorted their faith too. These were the times that twisted men's souls.

The "Dynamic of Call and Response" Between North and South

Reformers' political action started a pattern: side A's act or deed, which side B perceives as an insult, B's aggrieved response seen by A as an insult, followed by A's aggrieved response, which B sees as an insult. This political liturgy of "call and response" became routine in 1830-1860.[48]

Political historians blame "the true believer convinced of his righteousness" for bringing religion into the political system.[49] There is some truth in this assessment, as we have seen, but these historians downplay the role of the political courtroom in aggravating disputes and overlook the need to deal with slavery. They see the political system as fundamental, faith as optional. Yet Christianity is fundamental and eternal, constitutions and democracies derivative and temporal. Founders and democratic Common Men had discarded a Christian worldview for a constitutional, republican one. In dealing with moral issues, they used the code of honor, not the Christian code. They saw the word *sin* as an insult. True believers cannot be blamed for this proud hardheartedness.

When did the pattern begin? Perhaps in 1819-1820, when Northern congressmen tried to attach antislavery conditions to Missouri's statehood. Certainly, Southerners saw 1830s antislavery pamphlets and petitions as insults. The Southern response, Gag Rules, offended Northerners' republican honor: "If representatives could not discuss their constituents' wishes, representative government was arguably destroyed." Aggrieved, Representative John Quincy

Adams responded with "a petition from 22 persons, declaring themselves to be slaves." Insulted, a South Carolinian demanded that Adams be censured. Adams wryly answered "that the 22 slaves petitioned to remain enslaved!" Innocently, he asked why he should be censured for helping slaves remain slaves! The laughter offended the Southerner.[50]

The pattern continued. Northerners resented the clause in the Constitution counting slaves as three-fifths of a person in determining representation in the House. That gave the South extra House seats for people to whom it denied the vote and violated the principle of fair and equal representation. Northerners resented proposals to annex Texas and divide it into five slave states to insure Southern control of the Senate. When annexation led to the Mexican War, they responded with the Wilmot Proviso, which, fumed one Virginian, "pretends to an insulting exclusiveness or superiority . . . which says in effect to the Southernman, Avaunt! You are not my equal, and hence are to be excluded as carrying a moral taint with you." Southerners such as Calhoun responded with a theory that the Constitution gave Congress no right to restrict slavery in territories. Indignant, Abraham Lincoln at Cooper Institute denied that the Founders intended any such theory.[51] Southerners threatened secession if their rights and theories were not respected.

In the context of the formal code of honor, this exchange of insults and aggrieved responses was highly dangerous. It had to lead to an apology or a duel. To make matters worse, each side had a different concept of honor, and each was offending the other's sense of it. Northerners honored the Founders, their perpetual Union, majority rule, the rule of law. Southerners' theories, threats of secession, demands for minority rights and talk of violence offended Northerners. Southerners' honor focused on family, neighborhood, kin and state. Northerners' attacks on slavery insulted all of them, for all were linked to slavery.

The political system aggravated the pattern, notes historian David Potter. Frequent elections "meant the constant exploitation of sectional tensions for the purpose of arousing the voters." Different rules for representation in the Senate and House encouraged gridlock: the South ruled the Senate, the North the House. In a politics of sectional loyalty, Northern Whigs battled Northern Democrats for the title of best defender of Northern interests. Southern Whigs competed with Southern Democrats to be the first to see insults and to give aggrieved responses.

Constitutional limits on federal power meant that "Congress could do little about slavery except talk about it." Its debates offended both sides. The Constitution steered debate away from "direct and intelligible alternatives of emancipation versus continued servitude" toward "technicalities of legal doctrine" and "constitutional scholasticism"—away from slavery where it existed toward slavery where it could not thrive, the Far West territories.[52]

The heights of absurdity were scaled in the 1846-1848 debate over forming Oregon territory. Both sides admitted that Oregon would be free soil, but in the political courtroom both were afraid of creating a precedent, so they fought for eighteen months over what to give as the reason for Oregon's free-soil status! After "a night of violent speeches, punctuated by one challenge to a duel," the Senate finally passed an Oregon Act in August 1848. Attention shifted to California, New Mexico and Utah, where conditions made slavery very unlikely. "Abstraction, the abstract right of doing what cannot be done," moaned one debater in the political courtroom.[53]

Because they had to appeal to both sections in the quadrennial presidential elections, political parties helped to tie the nation together—but with ambiguity, not answers. In the 1848 election, neither took a clear stand on slavery in the territories. Democrats ran Lewis Cass, who favored popular sovereignty: let settlers decide. But decide immediately, in time to keep slave owners from entering the territory, or later, when applying for statehood and after masters had entered? In the North, Democratic politicians said the former, in the South the latter. Popular sovereignty's "seductive ambiguity" won votes in both sections. Whigs' ambiguity came in adopting no platform at all and nominating an ex-general, Zachary Taylor, who had not taken a public stand on slavery and refused to do so. Taylor won, but a system that rewarded men who made the "territorial issue an object of sophistry, evasion, and constitutional hair-splitting" could not resolve the issue.[54]

The political courtroom rang with threats of disunion in 1849-1850. Southerners vowed to leave if their rights were not preserved. "For three weeks, amid scenes of rancor and incipient violence," the House tried to elect a Speaker. A Southern convention was called, presumably to consider secession. Coming from the Compromise tradition, Clay offered a grand deal, dramatized the risk of disunion and assembled "in awesome array the patriotic images of statesmanship, union, and compromise." In three great speeches Clay, Webster and Calhoun debated compromise and union.[55]

Events seemed to follow the Compromise tradition. The Compromise of 1850 passed Congress and was signed by the president—thanks to the timely death of the anti-Compromise Taylor and successor Millard Fillmore's support for the bill.[56]

Appearances were deceptive. The Compromise was more an armistice: "North and South did not consent to each other's terms." Most Northern congressmen voted against Clay's concessions to the South, and vice versa. Only a few moderates voted for the whole Compromise. Stephen A. Douglas's Northern Democrats gave it the key yes votes. Party men such as Douglas and Fillmore pushed it through Congress after the Great Compromiser, Clay, left to recuperate at Newport's resorts. Before, in 1820 and 1833, statesmen such as Clay used Union-saving rhetoric to forge Union-saving deals which became virtual articles of the Constitution. Now, not relying on oratory, "Douglas's henchmen were busy making real bargains over railroads and Texas bonds" to get a deal passed.

Strong parties were the new factor. During the 1840s the two parties consolidated their control of politics. Events showed that the Democratic party was the Compromise's main prop. Taylor's tilt to antislavery and Northern Whigs' insulting refusal to support Fillmore's Compromise severely hurt Whigs in the South. Only Democrats remained strong North and South. Democrats became the "second," the gentleman-friend seeking a compromise between quarreling gentlemen. Ending insults and responses depended on Democratic strength in both sections.[57]

But a partisan compromise based on back-room deals lacked stability or credibility. Lobbyists for Texas bondholders pushing compromise were only one whiff of a persistent odor of corruption that "damaged the good name of Congress and made its resolution of the sectional conflict less trustworthy." That Democrats such as Douglas now used compromise as "a weapon" for "party warfare" damaged the good name of compromise. Using fear of disunion and hope of reconciliation as partisan tools tarnished these ideas. Voters ceased to respond to them.[58] If the "second" was not trusted, could a duel be long delayed?

After years of Whigs' evasions and two-faced campaigns, Northern voters abandoned them. Nativist, anti-Catholic, antiliquor, antislavery Northerners no longer believed Whig politicians' suggestions of sympathy with these causes. In 1853-1854, nativist Know-Nothings rose to power in some Northern states and stole from the Whigs many of their Northern supporters. That did not damage Democrats, who had never been a home for these causes. But it led to a new Northern party, soon to become an antagonist itself, not a "second."[59]

"What Preparation Have You Made for Eternity?" Steps to a Duel[60]

In 1854 Douglas unintentionally helped create the new party by arousing Northern fury with his Kansas-Nebraska Act, which repealed the Missouri Compromise. Rather than see westward expansion and railroad-building delayed by Missourians unhappy with that Compromise, Douglas discarded it just when the North was to receive its reward from the deal—a free Kansas and Nebraska. Northerners saw repeal as a "gross violation of a sacred pledge," and Northern ministers preached thundering sermons against the Act. By putting popular sovereignty to a practical test in Kansas, the Act also ended its "seductive ambiguity." Fighting over land claims and slavery, Kansas settlers gave the nation a miniature, bloody preview of the Great Duel. In a tragic irony, Christian (Northern) missionaries in Kansas suffered violence at the hands of (Southern) Christians![61]

The Republican party was the North's aggrieved response to the Kansas-Nebraska insult. At first it was unclear whether Republicans or Know-Nothings would replace Northern Whigs—whether antislavery or nativism would be the dominant issue. Many nativist Know-Nothings hated the Kansas-Nebraska Act too, and in many areas Know-Nothings were stronger than Republicans.

In 1856 a burst of insult-and-response gave victory to Republicans and antislavery. A proslavery mob invaded free-soil Lawrence, Kansas; John Brown retaliated by killing five proslavery settlers. Senator Charles Sumner gave a speech ("The Crime Against Kansas") which insulted South Carolina Senator Andrew P. Butler. Congressman Preston Brooks, Butler's cousin, responded by caning Sumner to the point of unconsciousness in the Senate chamber. Northerners were angered by Brooks's insult to rules of democratic debate and by Southern praise for him. Slaveholders were more aggressive and more powerful than other reform-resisting groups and committed more insults against Northern voters, who then stressed their anti-Southern views more than their anti-immigrant, anti-Catholic or antiliquor ones. Negative motives drove them. Anger at Southern insults, not abolitionist idealism, led them to vote Republican.[62]

Republican party managers broadened the antislavery tent far beyond its Free-Soil dimensions to house nativists, anti-Catholics and temperance advocates who could also be anti-Southern. To help attract these newcomers, they changed the emphasis in reform: a slave power threatening to rule free Northerners and insulting their republican honor was now the chief enemy, not the institution enslaving African-Americans. "Tapping the moral energy of evangelical free soilers," they satisfied nativists and temperance folks with state and local proposals while keeping the slave power their national focus. Still, shrewd party managers could not keep evangelicals from giving the new party a decidedly religious, intolerant tone.[63]

Southerners saw a quasi-religious, anti-Southern party as an insult. Angered that Republican John C. Frémont might win the 1856 presidential election, they threatened to secede if he did. He lost, but Republicans became the North's dominant party, a standing insult which could not be washed away, for a majority of Northerners kept on supporting it.[64]

Events raced to a climax. The Supreme Court tried to play final authority on slavery in the territories. Its pro-Southern *Dred Scott* ruling led many Northerners to believe Republican charges of a slave-power conspiracy. Based on vote fraud, Kansas's proslavery Lecompton Constitution offended even Douglas's sense of fairness. It caused a fateful split among Democrats, the party propping up the 1850 Compromise.

In 1857-1858 a great revival spread from New York City to other Northern cities: "It is a great and wonderful day in the [churches] of Christ, and a precursor to some great event," predicted one Northerner. The major evangelical churches added "several hundred thousand new members." The revival's leaders kept politics out of revival meetings and hoped that the outpouring of the Spirit would heal division between classes and between sections. But the revival was "seemingly ineffectual" in the South, and Christianity gave leaders and converts no blueprint for resolving the sectional crisis. Besides, evangelical fervor had helped heat up sectionalism, so how could evangelical revival help end it?[65] It was far too late for revival to reconcile the sections. Christianity does not privilege the status quo no matter how fervently Americans wanted to keep the status quo and avoid the "great event."

John Brown had a blueprint and brought Kansas violence to Virginia by seizing the Harpers Ferry Arsenal to spark a slave revolt in October 1859. Six prominent abolitionists financed his raid. Brown engaged in direct action and, once in the Arsenal, showed the passivity of a civil rights demonstrator—as though awaiting martyrdom—but he had given up the moral high ground by violently seizing it. Abolitionism's distorting effects on Christian faith were visible in Brown, who looked like an Old Testament prophet. New Testament grace seemed a futuristic idea to him. His zeal to unleash slave violence against masters only hardened Southerners' consciences. Worse was the praise Northerners heaped on him. Here was proof of their conspiracy fears: Yankees *were* plotting slave revolts.[66]

Three days after Brown was hanged, the political courtroom reconvened. The House fell into a two-month battle over electing a Speaker. Enough Southern Democrats refused to support the Northern Democratic candidate to deny him victory. They did not mind the long delay; "they were quite willing to paralyze the federal government." Congressmen went armed to the bitter debates. Once "a pistol fell from the pocket of a New York congressman, and other members, thinking that he had drawn it intending to shoot, almost went wild." A Wild West "shootout on the floor of Congress seemed" possible.[67]

The election of Republican Abraham Lincoln sparked the shootout. A South Carolinian asked, "Do you think the people of the South, the Lord Proprietors of the land, would let this low fellow rule for them?" No, "never will he receive the homage of gentlemen." Never would he receive their challenge to a personal duel either. They did not consider him worthy of that honor. So they began the ritualized steps that led to the national duel. They left Washington and Congress to go home and consult with their friends, their fellow Southerners. Secession conventions wrote lists of grievances, duelists' notes justifying the duel to the public. With their former "second," the Democrats, hopelessly split, Virginia and other Middle South states acted as "seconds" for the seceding Deep South. They sought face-saving concessions from the insulters—the incoming Republicans. When Lincoln called for troops to fight secession, they became principals too and prepared to duel.[68]

In the Compromise tradition, a leader now came forward and used the threat of disunion to muster support for a grand deal. But Clay was dead and Douglas discredited. Aggrieved Northerners stood by their honor, ably stated by Lincoln, who refused to reassure the South lest it "make me appear . . . anxious to apologize and beg forgiveness." Northerners honored perpetual Union and majority rule. Secession was an insult to both: losers left rather than accept election results. The North would fight before surrendering majority rule or Union.[69]

Lincoln's First Inaugural was a lawyerly speech to a political courtroom that his foes had left. Point by point, he made his case: Southerners should trust his speeches, the Republican platform and Northern congressmen's oath to uphold the Constitution. (In the suspicion following Harpers Ferry, how could they?) He inferred that the Constitution "implied" a perpetual Union, though it was not "expressed." He denied that the Northern majority had broken any "plainly written provision of the Constitution." He argued, "Plainly, the central idea of secession, is the essence of anarchy." Yet he would oppose anarchy only by holding government property and delivering the mail—unless Southerners "repelled" mail deliveries. This was Constitution talk, carefully worded legal complexities, lawyerly caveats and cautious assertions. Only in the last three paragraphs did Lincoln's speech-writing talents soar.[70]

The Great Duel: Synopsis

Lincoln and the North went to war to save constitutional Union, not to free slaves. It was not an antislavery crusade but a Great Duel of men similarly obsessed with dissimilar concepts of honor. Revealingly, they began by jockeying to see who would bear the public blame for firing first. Both sides' pride was at stake: Southern pride in their republican, genteel states' perpetual rights; Northern pride in a democratic Union's perpetual triumph. Both rejected Christian principles as rules for politics. Both revered inherited constitutional principles, which each understood differently. Slavery and religious antislavery proved impossible for those principles to handle without Christian principles of repentance, redemption and reconciliation. As converted slaves had learned, the cross could redeem suffering. White males—the political participants North and South—would not apply the cross's principles to the slavery issue. So they faced the bloody duel which the principle of honor demanded. The resulting slaughter was hardly inevitable or constructive. It did not yield justice or reconciliation. Perhaps the most apt question in March 1861 was one posed by a church newspaper: *"What preparation have you made for eternity?"*[71]

The Redeemer Lord used war to end slavery. Despite the combatants' unchristian stress on honor, he used it to spark revivals in both armies. He could partially redeem even a Great Duel. Yet he was not "marching on" with either army or with both. In his Second Inaugural, Lincoln said it best: "The prayers of both could not be answered; that of neither has been answered fully. The Almighty has His own purposes." He spoke in Old Testament terms of "the mighty scourge of war" as God's punishment for "American Slavery." That it did become, but he did not address the possibility that if both sides had applied the New Testament gospel to their differences, they might have partly escaped punishment. His Second Inaugural did not mention the Constitution which had so dominated his First. Yet by making punishment sound inevitable, he seemed to absolve the Constitution, political parties, North and South from blame in causing the war. True, the war's *length* might have been God's "scourge," but the *war* they brought on themselves.[72]

7

Exodus
Slaves Freed,
Capitalism Enters
Its Promised Land

R ELIGIOUS, ZEALOUS ABOLITION-
ism offending the honor of participants in the political courtroom caused the
Civil War, not capitalism. (Also, the political courtroom itself—a political
culture focused on legalism and constitutionalism as much as actual issues—
helped cause the war.) In fact, war jeopardized Northern and Southern capital.
Yet the war and related events strengthened capitalism, not churches, reform
societies or political courtrooms. The political-religious project of Reconstruction failed, but a new kind of capitalism succeeded in dominating American
life. No one planned that outcome; it was not directly caused by the war. That
new capitalism started before the war and would have triumphed anyway, but
the war helped it triumph swiftly and completely.

Understanding Reconstruction's failure and industrial capitalism's success
is vital to any understanding of how Christian faith has influenced—or failed
to influence—American history. A 1990s inner-city "underclass" is a legacy of
a failed Reconstruction; the Civil Rights movement of the 1950s and 1960s
sparked a second Reconstruction necessitated by the failure of the first. Were

evangelicals who helped bring on war with their zealous abolitionism guilty of failing to finish the task of emancipating blacks? Reconstruction's failure also raises questions about industrial capitalism and its ability or inability to produce economic development in disadvantaged societies. We must link these two topics also because both were major consequences of the Civil War.

We have looked at Puritanism, the Revolution, westward expansion, and the Civil War with a narrowly focused lens that captures American events only. When looking at post-1865 events, we must remember that the United States was a small corner of Western civilization. If we recall the destructive dynamism of limitless, amoral, individualistic capitalism in fifteenth-century Italian city-states, it is not surprising that the postwar American dynamo was not religious zeal or political idealism but capitalism, aided by a transcontinental market and new transportation networks. Industrial capitalism replaced merchant capitalism in organizing self-centered drives, ambitions, lusts and hatreds. Merchant capitalism organized plantation slavery; industrial capitalism organized a consumer society.

"Sound the Loud Timbrel o'er Egypt's Dark Sea": Emancipation

Emancipation was a drama of near-biblical dimensions. Approximately four million slaves were freed in four years. The prayers of thousands of African-Americans were answered. Prosperous and strong in the 1850s, slave owners rashly removed themselves from the Constitution's protection in 1861. The Almighty used that to bring freedom. In Boston a black preacher led a crowd in singing "Sound the loud timbrel o'er Egypt's dark sea, Jehovah has triumphed, his people are free." A biblical "Year of Jubilee" dawned. A black soldiers' band played that tune in the streets of Richmond.[1] The South was turned upside down.

Freed slaves reacted with understandable emotions and decisions. Many left their home plantations. They traveled to prove that they had this right and to reunite families divided by slave sales. Once families were reunited, black males took patriarchal powers which masters had denied them. Some blacks "took new names that reflected the lofty hopes inspired by emancipation." Many moved to Southern cities. Many withdrew from whites' churches to form their own, and they started their own schools. Slave owners had restricted education for blacks, so freedmen rushed to learn their letters. In these projects they made great initial progress. One black missionary boasted, "We have progressed a century in a year."[2]

Traditionally, a persecuted group progressed by migrating to America, forming a colony around religious-communal values, acquiring land for semisubsistence farming and building its own institutions. It partially withdrew from markets—or arrived before markets were dominant—then entered markets from a position of communal strength. Slavery and racism had similar (greater) effects on blacks as religious persecution had on seventeenth-century European sects. Would migration, colonies, churches and land ownership also forge a strong African-American community?

Emancipation was the first step. It took blacks out of plantation capitalism. It removed this capital "asset" from the planter's account books. It enabled the freed woman and child to quit field work. It reduced the economy's sphere of influence as did other religiously motivated reforms such as Sunday-closing laws. It took a people part way out of the market's calculations and put them in the more humane realms of church, family and school. Many African-Americans also wanted to escape the market by not raising cotton for profit but raising corn for family security.[3] That proved impossible, but by forming churches and schools and re-forming families, they showed that their goals were the same as whites' goals.

New churches meant new steps. Churches and pastors led in politics, in education, in family reunions, in forming new societies. William Montgomery calls them "practically the only black social institutions at the onset of freedom." Another historian, Eric Foner, notes that their "multiple functions testified to [their] centrality in the black community."[4]

That's as far as African-Americans could go on this path. Like Pilgrims, they formed separate churches, but they could not migrate, start colonies, acquire land or even partially withdraw from markets. Timing and racism worked against them. Emancipation came after almost all tillable lands in the Old Southwest (Alabama, Mississippi, Texas, Louisiana and Arkansas) had been claimed. For them, "free" land was no solution. Their exodus to Kansas in 1879-1880 was unlike earlier migrations. They lacked funds, information about Kansas and leaders. When they arrived, the best land was taken, whites would not hire them as farm workers, and except for some old Free Soil party men, whites were prejudiced against them. Except for a few colonies such as Nicodemus, the exodus became a contest between whites to hurry them on to the next village.[5]

In the South, too, racism blocked them. Whites refused to sell them land, threatened the few whites who offered to sell, attacked their schools and churches, shot or intimidated those who voted and retaliated against any who showed disrespect to whites. When the Lord redeemed the Hebrews from Egyptian slavery, he "made the Egyptians favorably disposed toward the people, and they gave them what they asked for." That was not true of blacks and their ex-masters. Rebels gave up armies and slaves, but "surrender did not signify an admission of guilt. . . . Repentance was therefore inappropriate." Honor was kept in "the myth of southern innocence," of the Lost Cause: gallant men had lost to superior might, not to right.[6]

Republicans used Union troops, constitutional amendments, Acts of Congress and patronage to save freedmen from vengeful ex-Confederates. Their Radical Reconstruction with its Civil Rights Act of 1866 and Amendments Thirteen, Fourteen and Fifteen was a "revolution in constitutionalism" that sought to let the national government rule in the political courtroom. Yet veneration of a Constitution limiting federal power and granting states' rights reduced their options. A belief in the sanctity of private property also hamstrung them. All these caused them to deny freedmen's request for land. Unwilling to confiscate ex-Confederates' lands, they had no Southern land to give; prewar wooing of white settlers meant no western land either. Most damaging was their loss of the will to enforce freedmen's rights. By 1873, the revolution was over.[7]

Instead they gave freedmen formal access to the political courtroom: the vote, a Southern Republican party to vote for and the right to file lawsuits to obtain civil rights. Without land, without enough federal troops to enforce laws, without jobs except those offered by planters, access to the political courtroom proved woefully inadequate. In another grand deal, the Compromise of 1877, they took back their gifts. Southern Democrats gave Rutherford B. Hayes the White House and received a free hand to finish taking over state governments and to deny votes, rights and lawsuits to blacks.[8]

This failure was not due to Northern evangelicals' unwillingness to back prewar rhetoric with postwar deeds. They did head south to teach freedmen and to help reconstruct the South. But the Republican party included more than zealous evangelicals. To win, it had diluted the Free-Soil Party's strong antislavery emphasis; Republicanism was more anti-South and anti-slave-power than problack. The Civil War had ended Southerners' seemingly excessive power in Washington, so the average Republican became more concerned with economic issues, especially after the economic downturn of 1873.

African-Americans as the Orphans of Plantation Capitalism

We can better understand the failure of Reconstruction by using a comparative perspective gained from studying other postemancipation societies also shaped by a plantation capitalism growing staple crops for export. African-Americans in the tobacco- and cotton-growing South shared a similar fate with freed blacks in the sugar-growing, coffee-growing West Indies and Brazil. Brought to the New World by merchants' plantation capitalism, they were freed from plantations but not from capitalism. As plantation capitalism died, they became its orphans, soon to be apprenticed to a new master.

For four hundred years, plantations growing staple crops had been capitalism's dynamic growth sector. As more Europeans could afford tobacco, sugar, cotton cloth and coffee, demand for them increased. In England, the cotton textile industry "was the fastest-growing industry of the 1770's and 1780's." Its rapid mechanization helped to trigger England's Industrial Revolution. The Old Southwest had been rapidly settled to meet textile machines' (and world markets') ravenous appetite for cotton. But by the 1870s, "the industrial focus of world capitalism had moved well beyond textiles."[9] Tobacco's seventeenth-century heyday was a more distant memory. Now, industrial capitalism marketed manufactured goods more than staple crops.

Emancipation made staple-crop agriculture less attractive to investors. Freeing gang laborers, it hurt plantations and their economies of scale, which earned profits and dividends. "Postslavery plantation societies faced stagnating output, declining attractiveness to European capital, and a diminished role in the expansion of western capitalism." They became economic backwaters as freedmen left plantations to "replicate their family-sized farms across the vast landscape." Europeans had replaced Native Americans' subsistence, small-scale farms with large-scale plantations. Freedmen went back to the small-scale farms. Yet "emancipation could not possibly square the circle by providing" freedmen with a higher living standard than Indians had had on the same-sized farms. Capitalists with investments in these regions tried to prevent freedmen from growing food instead of staple crops for export.[10]

Emancipation became a battle over what to grow on smaller farms. It deprived planters of human "capital," but they had land, mills, gins and other assets whose value would plummet if freedmen switched to food crops. Southern land owners and Northern capitalists saw blacks as needed laborers who must return to hoeing cotton to save their investments. New York had prospered by financing and organizing cotton exporting. Now, Northern capitalists opposed Radical Reconstruction for fear that it would end large-scale cotton production. Landowners used state laws, federal troops and Freedmen's Bureau agents to force blacks to return to plantations as wage workers.[11]

They did not totally succeed. Gang labor under planters' supervision was a distasteful reminder of slavery. Freedmen resisted it. Planters often lacked the capital to pay monthly wages before harvest, and freedmen disliked waiting for their pay until harvest. A compromise was worked out. Blacks gained the partial independence of working small farms as tenants. Landowners gained a partial transfer of their risk of falling cotton prices to freedmen: the freedman paid his rent and earned his profit in cotton bales; he too would be hurt by falling prices. Northern capitalists were happy: Southerners returned to growing export crops.[12]

Motivating freedmen and whites to grow cotton were high cotton prices in 1864-1865 caused by wartime shortages. The 1864 price was $1.02 per pound. But by 1867 it fell to 32¢. It fell further in the 1870s, but by then farmers were trapped into growing cotton. Their landlord and local merchant insisted they do so. As cotton prices fell and they fell into debt, the cotton crop became the merchants' collateral. So they grew fewer foodstuffs and more cotton, which drove down cotton prices and drove them deeper into debt to merchants for more purchased foodstuffs and supplies. It was a vicious circle.[13]

Capitalism based on free labor did not rebuild the South as many Northerners predicted it would.[14] Capitalism does not create the political, social and moral base it rests upon. It depends on churches, schools and governments to do so. Its prices and markets organize whatever motives, inequalities, social divisions and disorder exist. They don't reform these. They organized a postwar South with its racism, illiteracy, poverty, postwar violence and disorder into a dysfunctional economy: goods and services were bought and sold, but buyers and sellers were worse off after the exchange.

Moral concerns do not set prices and interest rates. Markets abstract price from events without distinguishing between just and unjust events. Questions of morality or justice do not register here. The prewar cotton trade was financed by cotton factors and bankers who offered credit to planters whose lands and slaves were the collateral. From creditors' perspective, emancipation, though an act of social justice, eliminated one form of collateral. Making postwar loans more risky were falling land values and landowners' loss of control over work done on small tenant farms. Factors and bankers stopped financing the trade despite the justice of emancipation.

Northern wholesalers took over the financing of it, though they had no direct interest in the trade. They offered short-term credit to Southern retailers, who extended credit to farmers at extortionate interest rates which averaged 60 percent! Farmers had to buy on credit, and retailers were the only source of credit. Their options limited by the range of a mule-drawn wagon, they had to go to the local country store, which obtained a local monopoly. Falling cotton prices and 60 percent interest caused a debtors' slavery that devastated Southern agriculture for decades. Yet in capitalists' calculus, the system worked. Rural merchants accumulated capital and landholdings. Northern wholesalers prospered. Southern savings were invested in the North, but Yankee dividends looked the same as Dixie's.[15]

Civil War and Peace Lead Northern Capitalism to a Promised Land

The strength of an abstracting capitalism with its strong economic motives meant that industrial capitalism benefited most from the war. Republicans and evangelicals trying to create a South of free labor, civil rights, Yankee-style schools and Yankee industriousness faced obstacles: racism, anti-Yankee resentment and bitter war memories. Northern missionaries who came to teach, convert and help freedmen faced ridicule and threats. Yet Northern wholesalers' capital flowed South, met no barriers it could not flow around and earned them and their retailer-customers large profits. Anti-Yankee bias did not stop the flow of Northern capital.

From 1860 to 1905, Northern industry, retailing and finance entered a Promised Land, a huge national market with a growing population made accessible by innovations in transportation and communication. It was as if Columbus had discovered an incredibly short route to a China teeming with customers with bulging billfolds, eager to buy. The lucrative marketing possibilities inspired new products, new techniques, new technologies and the creation of a new consumer culture. (In part, the South's postwar economic failure was relative—compared to the economic miracle north of the Ohio River.[16])

The North was partway to the Promised Land by 1860. Factories used mass-production methods in some industries. Railroads had crossed the Mississippi, but westward expansion kept delaying a rail-linked national market, which "repeatedly formed, only to be disrupted by population movements, before being restored once again" as more track was laid. Legally "a national market was potential rather than actual," for states licensed and taxed out-of-state firms to protect local ones. Yet states were nurseries of industrial capitalism too. With a Jacksonian national government hostile to national banks and monopolies, capital sheltered under friendly state governments. With democratic politics hostile, capital hired lawyers ("the shock troops of capitalism") to use Constitution and common law to give property, contracts and incorporations almost unlimited rights. With president and Congress sometimes hostile, capital found the Supreme Court friendly.[17]

Capitalists largely blunted churches' hostility to their individualistic, amoral, limitless drive to accumulate. Calvinists encouraged thrift and industry and opposed greed, but Calvinism was under attack. Unitarians were most in tune with "the market mentality," as Sellers notes: "Their God endowed people with enough rationality and prudential morality to win for themselves . . . the salvation of earthly happiness." Evangelical merchants and manufacturers such as Moses Brown and Lewis Tappen used "benevolence" to forge an "evangelical capitalist culture" despite tension between the adjectives.[18]

Exhausted by war and Reconstruction, evangelicals further relaxed their opposition to capitalist ethics. Darwin's *Origin of Species* (1859) undercut the faith of many after the war, when it started to influence the public. By the 1880s, evangelicalism was not the vigorous, crusading force it had been only fifty years earlier. Merchants took advantage of that to convert Americans to a consumerism different from Calvinism.[19]

The economy lost steam during the war: planters' repudiation of debts, high taxes, inflation, an emphasis on armaments and loss of cotton exports all slowed it. Aggregate statistics that economists stress grew sluggishly, if at all.[20]

Those effects ended with the war. For the next forty years, Northern victory led to economic growth and the rule of capital. It ended the secession threat, which had imperiled Union and economy, and the threat that Westerners might copy Southerners' example. Indivisible Union led to an undivided national market. It removed strict constructionists, whose constitutional straitjacket had kept Congress from passing procapitalist legislation or subsidizing projects such as transcontinental railroads.[21] Rebels' departure from Washington in 1861 allowed Congress to enact such laws and subsidies. Secession broke the stalemate in the political system. Other wars gave chances for reform, but never since 1865 have reformers' foes forfeited the game and left town. Once enacted, reforms could not be easily undone: Homestead Act, Morrill Act for land-grant colleges, Pacific Railroad Act subsidizing a transcontinental railroad, the high Morrill tariff and a bill creating the Department of Agriculture. The U.S. government became a key sponsor of economic development.[22]

Essential were the National Banking Acts (1863 and 1864). Before, state-chartered banks issued various bank notes, some redeemable in gold and silver, some not. This wildcat currency was all the country had, except for gold and silver coins. Businesses used checks drawn on bank deposits, but bank failures endangered these too. The Civil War made this system seem especially inadequate. English investors withdrew their capital just when the U.S. government needed to borrow to finance the war, for which American capital seemed inadequate. The two National Banking Acts authorized "national banks," which had to keep a reserve of government securities to back their bank notes and deposits. In turn, they bought U.S. bonds, and their bank notes (plus government Greenbacks) became "a uniform national currency, based on the public credit." This made a national market possible. No longer did merchants in St. Joseph, Missouri, hesitate to accept bank notes from Bangor, Maine.[23]

Capitalism speaks the language of money; its words are prices. When the worth of a bank note is unpredictable and must be discounted, capitalism's words are partly unintelligible and deals are more risky. With U.S. bonds and U.S. rules backing bank notes, words were clear and deals were safer.

Government borrowing raised savings and forced Americans to invest in the war. It created "a new class of finance capitalists" in New York City. They made New York's Stock Exchange and bond market the center of American capitalism. During the war, their options were limited by the government's voracious need for capital. The U.S. Treasury became the four-hundred-pound gorilla on Wall Street. Its hoards of gold or Greenbacks, its enormous bank deposits and its huge loans threatened markets' delicate balances. But after 1865, its rapid repayment of debts owed to them made *them* the four-hundred-pound gorilla with "a dominant position in the coordination and financing of industrial expansion." They financed capitalism's move into the Promised Land, a national mass consumer market.[24]

They were aided by "integrated capital markets" created by wartime borrowing and banking acts. In the abstracting manner of capitalism, capital flowed freely between the bond market, stock market, gold exchange market, Greenback market and a market for bankers' reserve deposits. Everything had its price, and price regulated everything. What could not be abstracted out was the change of seasons—a vital detail in a still very agricultural nation. During spring planting and fall harvest, farmers' need for cash overwhelmed banks that lacked enough Greenbacks.[25] Capitalism could not abstract the pain out of bank failures or end boom-and-bust cycles, but those seemed small prices to pay for a national market.

The war launched the careers of famous entrepreneurs. The Union did not commandeer goods and services but paid private firms for them. It created a huge national army market for uniforms, shoes, foodstuffs, mules and other items. Uncle Sam transported and distributed these goods and guaranteed high sales volumes, which meant low per-unit costs and high profits. The lucrative opportunities attracted men such as John Wanamaker, Andrew Carnegie and John D. Rockefeller.[26]

A New Capitalism's Promised Land Is Canaan, Land of Idolatry

To understand industrial capitalism and consumerism, we must go beyond standard debates focusing on human-centered questions: Did it oppress the poor? Did it exploit labor? Did it waste natural resources? Did it destroy rural life? Did it stress individuals over society, business over politics? These are important questions but not the most important. We must go beyond asking if some other system, socialism for example, could have better met the human-centered criteria that the questions imply. The central issue is not humanity versus nature, rich versus poor, urban versus rural, or capital versus labor. It is humanity against God. By seeing industrial capitalism as an exceedingly efficient Babel project, we see it clearest.

The scriptural account of the original Babel project reveals that "the whole world had one language and a common speech"—and a common ambition: "Come, let us build ourselves a city, with a tower that reaches to the heavens, so that we may make a name for ourselves."[27] Industrial capitalism and its consumer culture were more efficient, more democratic and seemingly more humane than prior human tactics for rebelling against God. It could best build a city, a tower, a name. Using citizens' self-sacrifices, republicanism built a nation that made a name for its Founders; consumer culture offered the citizens self-satisfactions that proved more popular. Merchant capitalism had built an economy on luxuries few could afford; consumer culture "democratized desire" and promised luxury for all. Plantation capitalism had created more slaves than planters; consumerism promised workers luxuries that no wealthy planter enjoyed. Here was a better Babel. [28]

It was built on workers' good intentions. Few had consciously immoral or rebellious goals. At the individual level, where workers' hands touched bricks, they sought to feed families, to improve their children's future, even to honor God by work well done. Most did not intend to build a Babel. Many rebelled against the immorality and exploitation they saw in industrial capitalism. They sought to reform or end it. But capitalism used reforms and opposition to add more bricks: "every popular cultural or political movement . . . arose originally against the market," notes Sellers, but "under the daily pressure" of competition "every such movement eventually became a mode of accommodating to capitalist necessity."[29]

Individual capitalists intended a profit project, not a Babel project. Many had good intentions: to provide employees with decent work and customers with needed products. At industrial capitalism's innovating, expanding margins, its amoral, limitless, acquisitive motives ruled. But this was its cutting edge, and that is what shaped it, not the old family firm's desire for loyalty and stability. A hothouse competition drove it "at a forced clip." Individual capitalists took risks like fifteenth-century seafaring merchants and innovated on land: saving time, eliminating bottlenecks, accumulating expertise, anticipating development far in advance, speculating, gambling on future prices, stripping natural resources, leap-frogging ahead of competitors, externalizing costs, treating people as mere commodities.[30] Markets rewarded innovators, not the old family firm, and forced those who valued loyalty or stability or quality above price or profit to reorder their priorities or else perish. Innovators shaped industries. As rebels, they shaped these around habits of human rebellion against God, around the lusts and drives that rebellion produced.

Capitalism promised to abstract good out of rebellion. Its ideology claimed that selfishness worked a common human good: democratic prosperity. But to get there, many small idols had to be built. Few intended the cumulative effect—a new land of idolatry. This was no conspiracy, but a system that integrated and used human rebellion against God could have no other long-term result than to systematize idolatry.

Why did God allow this system to develop if it was rooted in rebellion against him? He had halted the first Babel project "to give space [and time] for his scheme of salvation to be worked out in the people of God," notes economist Donald Hay.[31] Then there was no Israel, no Messiah, no cross or resurrection, no gospel. By 1865 or 1905, there had been—for more than eighteen hundred years—so there was no need to halt the new Babel project in order to work out the scheme of salvation. The new Babel project seemed certain to culminate in a human claim to be God. Capitalism's attempt to transcend all limits suggested that claim, since only God is limitless. Paul strongly suggests in 2 Thessalonians that the claim to be God will usher in the return of Christ, who will put an end to human rebellion. Meanwhile, capitalism's dynamism would serve as an engine driving this human rebellion through its final stages, and thus accomplishing God's purposes.[32]

The Promised Land: Beyond Man-Made, Natural or Divine Limits

At the core of capitalism was the limitless accumulation and multiplication of capital, the attempt to transcend limits to accumulating capital, whether geographical, natural, individual, mortal, spatial, temporal, moral, political, governmental or technological. Greed was not more expansive and innovative because it was more sinful than lust, political ambition, thirst for fame or other expressions of human rebellion. It was not more sinful, simply more expandable, multipliable, abstractive and efficient.

Lawyers had secured for capital some constitutional and legal exemptions from limits. Incorporation allowed a new company to combine more capital than one individual or family could accumulate and to keep it combined longer than a single lifetime. A corporation had an unlimited life, beyond the human lives that created it but which were not responsible for its debts. Intended to give blacks civil rights, by 1905 the Fourteenth Amendment was used by courts to give corporations rights as "persons." The anticapitalist Ignatius Donnelly joked that the Supreme Court might rule that "corporations have the right to marry and rear children." That was unnecessary, for capital could reproduce much faster than humans.[33]

Railroad and telegraph had begun to eliminate limits of distance, time and climate. By 1840 a railroad could "carry annually per mile more than fifty times the freight carried by a canal" and could operate in winter, when canals and rivers froze. From prerailroad 1830 to postrailroad 1857, travel time from New York to Chicago plummeted from three weeks to one day. One Chicagoan exclaimed, "Railroads are talismanic wands. They have a charming power. They do wonders—they work miracles." Stringing wires along railroad tracks, telegraph companies worked miracles of communication that complemented railroads' wonders. By 1860, some fifty thousand miles of telegraph wire offered "almost instantaneous" communication.[34]

Trains rapidly hauling goods and wires instantly communicating prices revolutionized business. They expanded the national market to hitherto inaccessible places. They ended seasonal inaccessibility due to winter freezing of water routes. By ending this dead time and other delays, they made time more valuable to capitalists. By greatly raising the limits on size of shipments, they made high sales volumes more valuable too. Time became money, and so did higher volume. Rapid turnover of inventory earned higher profits. Before, with lengthy delays in transportation and communication, why should a capitalist speed resource-gathering, manufacturing, selling or decision-making? Why increase volume when ships or wagons could carry only small cargoes? Now, every step was speeded up and done in maximum volume to lower per-unit costs, raise profits and multiply capital.

Grain was carried and stored in bulk bins, not sacks, and stored in grain elevators, not warehouses. Manufacturing was done less in artisans' workshops and more in factories using interchangeable parts assembled in quantity on moving lines by specialized, semiskilled workers. To achieve economies of scale and speed, "multiunit business enterprises" were organized like armies, with a hierarchy of managers who made decisions and communicated them swiftly by telegraph or telephone to obedient employees.[35]

Racing to increase profits, investors and hired managers transcended other limits. Evading one limit always revealed another one. If trains made winter into summer by shipping year-round, their refrigerated cars made summer into winter to enable meat packers to ship dressed beef cross-country. Farmers bred animals to be slaughtered at an earlier age—to save valuable time. When handled in bins, not sacks, each farmer's grain lost its identity. The grain industry could transcend the limits set by sacks of grain with name tags. Elevators gave farmers elevator receipts, which formed the basis for a betting system. In futures markets, traders used the receipts to bet on future price changes. Bets were not limited to stored grain. Often neither buyer nor seller had or wanted grain: "Men who don't own something are selling something to men who don't really want it." This was "a market not in grain but in the *price* of grain." Finally, access to the market (the Chicago Board of Trade) was also a product for sale as "the Board began to conduct a market in the market itself." Capital flowed around limits, even the limit of reality.[36]

Where reality was no barrier, would morality stop anyone? Grain traders cornered markets. Elevator operators bribed the Illinois legislature to prevent state regulation. Railroads corrupted Congress. Firms bribed local and state officials. Chicago wholesalers offered prostitutes and gambling dens to lure retailers to town: "a market in vice and corruption," where "sex was a commodity like any other." One crusader reported that a prominent madam "regards the question from the economic standpoint. Morals no more enter into her business than they do into the business of bulls and bears on the Stock Exchange." Madam and wholesaler externalized the social costs of vice: they were borne by people in vice-plagued neighborhoods or by rural villages whose daughters fell into prostitution. They were off the ledgers of madams and wholesalers. Similarly, industrial capitalism treated labor as a commodity, though the worker was made in the image of God. The social costs—injuries, work-related diseases and deaths, separated families—also were largely off corporate ledgers.[37]

Capital exceeded natural limits of sustainable resource use. Forests, ore deposits, soil fertility, buffalo herds, pasture land were depleted in the industrial process.[38] Science and technology were enlisted to transcend the limits of human skill, animal power, geographical location, weather or the capabilities of prior technology. Science and technology had a cumulative, accelerating logic of their own, which added greatly to the dynamism of industrial capitalism.

Changes were portrayed as "progress" for humanity, made by entrepreneurs, inventors and managers, the heroes of the Industrial Revolution. They did make peoples' lives easier and more enjoyable, yet the motive was not benevolence so much as a limitless desire to multiply capital. Inventor Thomas Edison said, "Anything that won't sell, I don't want to invent." Finance capitalists saw the lucrative potential of selling in a national market. Integrated capital markets cut the price of capital "relative to labor and land," encouraged investments in new technologies and ensured a flow of capital to regions or industries where returns were highest. States and cities feared that regulating business might end the flow, so governmental limits on capital were dropped or never set.[39]

Capitalists even transcended the limits of a competitive market. Competition to achieve economies of scale and speed and to use new technologies resulted in lower per-unit costs. That lowered retail prices, but profit seekers fought that trend by merging firms or by making price-setting deals with competitors. By 1904 the top 318 companies owned 40 percent of U.S. manufacturing assets. In fifty different industries, the largest firm produced 60 percent or more of the output. Financiers such as J. P. Morgan often brokered mergers to end competition that threatened investors' dividends and capital.[40]

Industrial Capitalism Defeats Opponents and Possesses the Land

Industrial capitalism was a marvelous, efficient machine, but destructive aspects of its dynamism aroused opposition. Reformers disgusted at its corruption of politics demanded civil service reform. Turn-of-the-century merger mania aided the antitrust movement in a country fearful of centralized power, economic or political. Making labor a commodity brought exploitation. At Carnegie's Homestead steel plant, unskilled laborers worked eighty-four-hour weeks—twelve hours for seven days. Employers kept wages low, helped by the abundant labor from massive immigration, migration from farm to city and women's entry into the work force.

The Knights of Labor and the American Federation of Labor tried to organize workers despite their ethnic, religious and racial diversity. Having switched to cash crops after railroads made markets accessible, farmers organized Granges and Alliances to protest centralized markets, futures gambling, elevator abuses and rail monopolies. But opponents failed to change industrial capitalism much. Where they reformed it, they only smoothed its rough edges. They discovered the "market's power to bend oppositional forces to its own ends."[41] Several factors aided capitalism.

First, a fragmented, federalist system of government required opponents to control all three branches for extended periods in order to enact structural reforms. But the Supreme Court's tradition of defending the rights of property and corporations meant that the judicial branch was an unlikely takeover prospect. It could block reform all by itself.

Second, capitalists learned to make popular, democratic appeals through their Republican party, "Prosperity's Advance Agent": "free enterprise" promised prosperity to all and created a seemingly democratic consumerism with mass appeal.

Third, opponents' moral points were compromised because many had embraced capitalism's markets only to turn against these after their own economic interest was hurt by the latest economic change. Farmers had hailed railroads, elevators and distant markets, only to attack all three after crop prices fell. Workers had migrated to the United States to take jobs created by industrial capitalism. Some were scabs who replaced striking native-born workers only to face similar tactics when they formed unions. Small-town merchants who preached antimonopoly against Sears, Roebuck or Wards for using railroads and parcel post service to compete against them had themselves profited from the coming of railroads.

Fourth, industrial capitalism had its good side. It lowered prices and invented new products. It created a higher standard of living for more people than any previous system. It generally rewarded hard work and punished sloth in a way that often seemed just, in conformity to Christian ethics. Even its most reviled aspects had some positive effects: middlemen assumed risks of distribution, storage and price changes; futures markets left the latter risk to gamblers who thrived on it; child labor lowered prices for consumers; mergers brought economies of scale and some lower prices.

Fifth, industrial capitalism could accommodate many of its opponents' projects: rural cooperatives, skilled workers' unions, child labor laws, civil service reform, federal income tax, eight-hour workday, government regulation, a toothless antitrust law, immigration restriction, collective bargaining. These were merely changes in the rules, not a different game.

These five factors point to a fundamental, sixth fact: industrial capitalism did not primarily set countryside against city, labor against capital, business against government, rich against poor, native-born against immigrant, or whites against blacks. These fights could be compromised or finessed; goods and services could be redistributed to groups. Fundamentally, it integrated human rebellion against God—rebels who opposed capitalism also opposed God and so were always apt to be co-opted by it, to be enlisted in its Babel project. Opposition to it or reform of it must be religious; it must point to the ultimate conflict between scriptural Christianity and limitless capitalism.

That was conceivable but not achievable after the Civil War. On the early nineteenth-century frontier, evangelicalism had been democratized, acculturated and split into many competing denominations which could not now oppose an industrial capitalism wooing and aweing Americans with new technologies and new products. The denomination that tried would lose the religious competition. By the early 1870s, evangelicals were morally exhausted after a long antislavery struggle and cultural fights over liquor, Sunday closing, anti-Catholicism and the public schools. Most retained their postmillennial belief that the church would usher in God's kingdom before Christ returned. In capitalism's amazing economic and technological progress, they saw evidence that it was a fellow usher, not a foe. Besides, the New Testament did not offer a blueprint for a just economy by which capitalism could be judged deficient. Many did not see that capitalism's battle against limits was not only to subdue the earth and to reduce poverty, disease and isolation. A grandiose Babel project was not yet visible.[42]

A Promised Land for Consumers—the "Land of Desire"

The rise of consumerism was part of that project to remold American society, to distort religious faith itself. Economists picture a product's journey as a line running from raw materials to factory to manufactured product on a wholesaler's shelf to the retail item which consumers buy. The "forward" direction is toward consumers, "backward" toward raw materials. Entrepreneurs who speeded up manufacturing, for example, found that of limited value unless they could also speed up the extraction and transportation of raw materials the factory used. So they innovated backward to speed up their supply. They also had to innovate forward—to speed consumer purchasing—to avoid oversupply and falling prices.

Overproduction threatened the economy, not just one firm or one industry. "After 1875, many economists, merchants, and manufacturers feared that the business economy would be so committed to more and more productivity, so money-mad, that it would cause glutting, overproduction, and economic crisis." Capital did not earn its profit until the consumer bought. Every investor's dividend depended on that sale. Multiplying capital demanded a multiplication of consumers' purchases.[43]

Part of the solution was technical: to speed up the flow of goods to consumers. Railroads and telegraph (later, telephone) wires were essential. Using them, Postmaster General (and merchant) John Wanamaker started "fast mail-train service on a transcontinental basis." Once out of office, he and others lobbied the Post Office to deliver mail and parcels to rural farmsteads. Firms now had a cheap, efficient, dependable way to get goods to every household. Mail-order giants such as Wards and Sears, Roebuck could not have succeeded without that. In urban areas, streetcars brought consumers to the goods and made the downtown department store possible.[44]

Part of the solution was organizational. Wholesale houses, mail-order giants, department stores and chain stores handled transactions efficiently "in-house" with a managerial hierarchy. High volume and rapid turnover helped them cut per-unit costs and retail prices so that more consumers could afford to buy. Low prices multiplied purchases. Well-managed shipping departments handled multiplied orders: from one Chicago building, Sears could fill more than a hundred thousand orders per day.[45]

Part of the solution was tactical: fixed-price and one-price policies, discounts, coupons, cash-and-carry ("no credit and no deliveries"), self-service and frequent "sales." All were meant to reduce the retail price and encourage buying.[46]

Part of the solution had to be cultural. A nation of penny-pinching Puritans would not daily mail a hundred thousand orders for gewgaws, bric-a-brac and superfluities. A nation of Bible readers avoiding greed, luxury and desire was not a retailers' paradise. The Tenth Commandment condemned coveting, and Jesus warned against worrying "about your life, what you will eat or drink; or about your body, what you will wear." Verses about birds gathering food and lilies clothed without cost did not reassure retailers. Nor did the apostle Paul's preaching "godliness with contentment" and warning that those who wanted more fell "into many foolish and harmful desires."[47]

Wanamaker compared innovators to Columbus: "Few had faith that he could ever reach the Land of Desire." Innovating merchants faced a daunting task too. To lure Americans to the Land of Desire, they needed idols and adult fantasies. Historian William Leach notes that they had to create "some imaginative notion of what constitutes the good life"—to "bring to life a set of images, symbols, and signs that stir up interest" and loyalty. They needed "strategies of enticement." Showing goods in store window displays and in visually appealing ads awakened desire. Color and light stirred "the cravings of sinful man, the lust of his eyes."[48]

Female mannequins wearing underwear aroused male sexual desire. Wanamaker's display of women's hats and gloves "was meant to convey the idea of luxury or of abandon to sensual desires." Hiding the humdrum ledger-book side of stores, merchants made them into "adult fantasy environments": French salons, Parisian streets or "Japanese gardens." Very popular was "the oriental theme," which appealed to desire "for a 'sensual' life more 'satisfying' than traditional Christianity could endorse." Oriental scenes suggested distance from Christian faith. Using them, merchants could suggest abandonment of Christian restraint without advocating it directly.[49]

Women were the major buyers in U.S. families, so merchants designed displays to lure them. The fashion industry enticed them to buy new clothes annually before old ones wore out. Buyers returned from Paris with the annual style changes. New styles were paraded at fashion shows, and purses were opened.[50]

That shows that industrial capitalism did not just meet people's needs. It raised middle-class Americans' wants and their standard of living to new heights. It brought more of them into the middle class. Yet it sought to transcend limits. It was not satisfied with limited profits from selling a few more necessities to a growing population. To approach the goal of limitless profits, it had to multiply products and people's wants, convince them to abandon Christian moderation, entice them to buy new goods long before old ones wore out. It had to create a consumer culture, a Canaan, land of idols, luxury and adult fantasy.

The New Canaan Undercuts Christianity and Exalts Humanity

Consumer culture undermined the work ethic capitalism demanded of its workers. It required "people to be pious souls in the workplace, wild pagans at the cash register." At work, self-control was needed, in the store self-indulgence. It undercut the morality and civic virtue on which it rested. It then needed more government powers or its own self-policing to enforce rules that individual consciences had kept before.[51]

It undercut the Christian message so gradually that evangelicals such as Wanamaker failed to notice. They were ill-equipped to fight consumerism when it posed as *progress*. Being postmillennialists, they believed that the church, perhaps aided by secular forces, would create a thousand-year era (millennium) of righteousness, peace and prosperity. Then Christ would return. "Optimistic about the spiritual progress of the culture," they "believed in the compatibility of religion and commerce and that both were moving on a fast track toward progress."

Downplaying conflict between secular and sacred, they could hardly take a strong stand against buying goods. Henry Ward Beecher softened supernaturalism, sanctified "the progress of civilization," equated religion with morality and relieved "the anxieties of his affluent Brooklyn suburbanite audience, who sensed a conflict between their new wealth and the stern Puritan morality" of their parents. He eased them into consumerism.[52]

A more pessimistic rival, premillennialism, appealed to evangelicals disturbed by Beecher's modernizing. It squared off against secularism, Darwinism, higher criticism and materialism. Its harder edge challenged the cultural compromises of postmillennialism. Its appeal cannot be explained away as a product of supposed anxieties in late-nineteenth-century America. It did not first rise amid the shock of World War I but amid Gilded Age optimism. It was ill-suited to U.S. churches, for its "doctrinal rigor" and stress on divine sovereignty were Calvinist, and Americans had mostly forsaken Calvinism decades earlier. Its "authoritarian and ideological character" ill-fit their practical, democratic denominations. It was a Spirit-led strengthening of biblical literalism, belief in prophecy and antimaterialism in an age when the church badly needed such strengthening.

Of course, its forms were shaped by that age's preoccupations: scientific classification, scientism, Hegelian progressions. Premillennialism's view of historical change was too supernatural. It understated God's use of political, cultural and economic change to accomplish his purposes. Still, the Spirit used it to offer an escape from the dead end of celebrating progress.[53]

Premillennialists could not know how much gradual change would occur before Christ's return. American capitalism could not openly start a Babel project when most Americans had a Christian worldview. Yet its consumer culture was gradually undermining Christian belief. Its "cult of the new" worshiped the superiority of innovations over traditions. Strengthened by scientific and technological innovations, this cult subtly undercut faith in a nineteen-hundred-year-old revelation. Faith seemed outmoded, yet consumerism offered nothing specific to replace it. Orientalism was still a motif more than a movement.[54]

Capitalism's potential as a Babel project was stunningly revealed at the World's Columbian Exposition in Chicago from May to October 1893. One year late in celebrating the four-hundredth anniversary of the Columbian encounter, the Great Fair was Chicago's and America's chance to make a name for themselves. Using plaster and jute, architects "used classical motifs to create a Beaux Arts architectural fantasy of domes, arches, fountains, and colonnades." The exhibit buildings formed an encyclopedia of human knowledge and skill: "Agriculture, Machinery, Transportation, Liberal Arts, Electricity, and so on." International exhibits formed "the Parliament of Man, the Federation of the World," said one guidebook. Some twelve million visitors saw breathtaking vistas. One exclaimed, "Turn your eyes to whatever building you please, you see hosts of suns, moons and satellites illuminating this model of an earthly heaven."[55] The Great Fair was an earthly heaven, an adult fantasy to beat them all, a giant window display enticing visitors but hiding Chicago's gritty realities.

World's Congresses met to discuss twenty topics, including labor, education and religion. At each one, "controversy was prohibited and the passing of resolutions of approval or censure was forbidden." The organizer proclaimed, "A new age has dawned. A new leader has taken command. The name of this leader is peace."[56]

Meeting in the Hall of Columbus, the World's Parliament of Religions featured representatives from ten religions. The *Chicago Tribune* reported, "It was a consummate triumph of liberalism; a study of comparative religions by a great university [the audience of four thousand] . . . in the pure light of reason." It was "the crown upon the head of gathered nations." Remarkably, it occurred "in Chicago, the youngest and most materialistic of cities." Americans had their first close look at Oriental religions, including Hinduism. Swami Vivekenanda "electrified his listeners." Yet this "unspoken but sublime protest against materialism" failed to slow the advance of consumerism. Nor did it advance religious cosmopolitanism. America was still too strongly Christian for that. The delegates sang the Hallelujah Chorus at the closing meeting.[57]

As an exercise in globalism, the White City (as the Great Fair was called) was a century ahead of its time. "Rather than stimulating a true cosmopolitanism," it stirred in American visitors "a growing spirit of nationalism." They were not ready for a Federation of the World. Nor did the fair display human, or even American, cultural unity. Henry Adams complained that "since Noah's Ark, no such Babel of loose and ill joined, such vague and ill-defined and unrelated thoughts and half-thoughts and experimental outcries as the Exposition, had ever ruffled the surface of the Lakes." Americans were too preoccupied with hurdling limits to set exact goals. "Chicago asked in 1893 for the first time the question whether the American people knew where they were driving." Adams doubted they did. The White City showed humans rebelling against God but disagreeing on what should symbolize their rebellion.[58]

Migration to the Consumers' Canaan Is Not Always Liberating

Rejecting proposals to show blacks' progress since emancipation, organizers excluded African-American exhibits and kept blacks from responsible posts. Rather than a White City, Frederick Douglass charged, "the World's Fair now in progress is . . . 'a whited sepulcher' " to African-Americans. He quoted Jesus' attack on Pharisees' outward piety and inner impurity. Capitalism's progress could not hide its moral shortcomings.[59]

Its defenders stressed the mobility of labor and capital: labor migrates to areas of labor scarcity and high wages, capital to areas of capital scarcity and high interest rates; migration corrects regional shortages or regional pockets of poverty. The South—with its capital shortages, low wages and African-American poverty—was the regional test case.

Some Northern capital did migrate south from 1875 to 1920. In New England, the cotton textile industry faced irksome postwar limits to growth. Due to its "relative technological stability," it could not use new technologies as a magic wand to reduce its labor costs. Unions blocked other wage-reduction tactics. Laws limited managers' hiring of child and female labor to avoid unionized males' high-priced labor. Competition from other industries helped keep wages high in New England.

In the South, capital faced none of these limits. Few industries competed for wage labor. Unions or restrictive laws were absent. Agriculture's seasonal, low-wage labor pattern helped to keep nonfarm wages low. In the 1890s conservative Democrats squelched an interracial alliance of debtors and passed laws favoring textile mill owners in order to attract Northern capital. By 1939 the Carolina Piedmont "had replaced New England as the center of American cotton textile production." Yet that did not make this low-wage area into a high-wage area, as capitalism's defenders predicted. Racial antagonisms among its lower classes enabled mill owners and landowners to retain political control. Workers remained low-wage and nonunion into the 1980s. Capitalism built on existing social conditions but did not reform them.[60]

Workers also migrated—African-American workers going north to a high-wage, consumer economy that capitalism was creating there. They had the same motives as other migrants—plus a desire to escape segregation and sharecropping. Southern landowners tried to stop them, but freedmen's children saw their parents' plight and wanted out. From 1890 to 1910 some two hundred thousand, mostly young, migrants headed north. As consumers, would they find a freedom they had missed as producers? Could capitalism's Canaan liberate?[61]

New York City was an early destination. A capitalist economy could entice workers with regional wage differences, but it could not ensure individual access to high-wage jobs. Due to racial discrimination, early arrivals took menial jobs and lived in vice-ridden, low-rent areas such as the Tenderloin District. Despite one black preacher's "gospel bombardments" against it, prostitution thrived there as it had in the whites' Bowery. Led by black churches, Southern black communities were formed in some nearly segregated New York neighborhoods.[62]

Suburban housing and consumerism enticed African-Americans to move farther. Elevated railways and subways built into rural Harlem sparked a wave of real-estate speculation as Harlem became Manhattan's first suburb. Real estate values soared only to crash in 1904-1905. Taking advantage of rock-bottom values, black investor-realtor Philip Payton purchased brownstones and rented to blacks "willing to scrimp to live in beautiful apartments in an exclusive section of the city." Prejudiced whites tried to exclude blacks, but Payton's black tenants' presence lowered the rents, as white tenants would no longer accept prior rental terms. When landlords earned more by renting to blacks than to whites, the laws of economics made Harlem an African-American colony.[63]

Religious-communal values came second in forming this "colony." That proved fateful for blacks, as it had for whites. In the 1920s in-migration, intraracial conflict, employers' bias and overpopulation stole Harlem's future. Here was high-cost housing for low-wage workers. Families sublet apartments and took in boarders. Crowded brownstones deteriorated. Families paid 33 percent of their incomes on rent (white New Yorkers paid 20 percent). Unready for urban life, rural blacks fell prey to a consumer culture of vice, as whites had. White liberals romanticized a new Negro in fast-paced, amoral Harlem just as Europeans had the Indians: "They saw Negroes not as people but as symbols of everything America was not." White males flocked to Harlem's cabarets to see scantily clad black women. The 1929 Stock Market Crash ended that. By 1930 Harlem was an "incredible slum" created by high-priced consumerism without high-wage jobs to pay for it.[64]

The Creation of a Consumer Culture: Synopsis

Despite its seemingly democratic nature—one price for all and stores open to all—consumer culture did not liberate blacks. Neither had Reconstruction's free-labor producerism. The religious and political idealism of Reconstruction could not liberate them when it was blocked by laissez-faire ideas, constitutionalism, racism and partisanship. Women's emancipation has been chronologically associated with movements for African-American emancipation, but as we will see, (white) women's much greater freedom to participate in a consumer culture did not truly liberate them either. These failures would have fateful consequences for the nation and its cities. So would the success of wartime nationalist reforms and postwar economic development in freeing capitalism and bringing it to the Promised Land of a national consumer market whose huge potential profits motivated entrepreneurs to create a consumer culture. This Land of Desire partly showed capitalism's true nature, but America's Christian aura partly hid it. The Babel project had not yet risen above obscuring clouds.

8

Women Aim for
Reform & Equality
but End Up
with Consumerism

WE MUST EXAMINE THE HISTORY
of women in America in order to assess current charges that the Christian faith
has served to delay or defeat women's emancipation just as it is alleged
(incorrectly) to have delayed blacks' emancipation. But first we must get past
several confusions.

Current debates between evangelicals and feminists over "family values"
foster the misleading idea that today's feminism is mainly a critique of Christian
beliefs on women and the family. But history shows intermediate steps between
past generations' Christian faith and today's feminism. Few women went
directly from one to the other. Feminism is largely a critique of the Enlightenment's, not Christianity's, failure to keep its promises. To understand nineteenth-century attitudes and the origins of contemporary feminism, therefore,
we must start with the Enlightenment and its rejection of divine revelation as
set forth in Scripture.

The term *feminism* was rarely used before 1914, so we must sort through
changing definitions of women's rights as we go. To make our task harder,

current non-Christian assumptions about gender and family hinder our ability to comprehend nineteenth-century attitudes. Textbooks play off this incomprehension.

For instance, *The American People* reprints an 1848 marriage certificate. In the center is a picture of bride, groom and minister; to the left is fourteen "Requirements of the Husband," to the right twelve "Requirements of the Wife." The two lists are similar, though not identical. The caption asserts that the certificate "makes clear male dominance and female subservience." It does not explain that differences in duties (for example, wives' submission "as unto the Lord") were seen in the context of Christian faith. Later it cites three women reformers and concludes, "The struggle for that kind of liberation continues today." The three are anachronistically enlisted in causes they might prefer to avoid. Describing later changes in women's roles, it gives quotes sure to anger current college students without explaining the nineteenth-century context. It claims, "Many men worried about female independence because it threatened their own masculinity." Such a statement is exceedingly hard to prove.[1]

The Enlightenment and Individual Equality

Scripture portrays human existence as inextricably caught up in a struggle between God and a world rebelling against him. James is most direct: "You adulterous people, don't you know that friendship with the world is hatred toward God? Anyone who chooses to be a friend of the world becomes an enemy of God." Paul notes that "the sinful mind is hostile to God." John warns, "If anyone loves the world, the love of the Father is not in him." This almost unbearably stark conflict was most graphically displayed when the world crucified the Father's Son.[2] Paradoxically, that act allows the Father to forgive rebels and to urge them to be reconciled to him, since Christ's death paid the just penalty for their rebellion.

Today's feminism sees human existence as inextricably caught up in a struggle between men and women for power, rights and freedom. If we take a New Testament view, say that of Christians in Nero's Rome (c. A.D. 64), that idea is almost incomprehensible. A male, Jesus of Nazareth, died for men's *and* women's sins and is worshiped by both. God has given marriage and family to unite women and men. Paul's command to wives to submit to husbands comes in the context of the battle between Father and world—just as he commanded all Christians to "submit to one another out of reverence for Christ." Submission vindicates the Father's creation of male and female in the teeth of the world's rebellion against that gendered creation. It vindicates Christ's position as leader of his church in the face of attempts to rebel against him.[3]

Feminism reverses everything. The wife's relationship to her husband becomes the great dilemma, male-female relations the great battle. The conflict between the Father and the world is trivialized. Lucretia's momentary quarrel with Lucas over yesterday's dinner is made to overshadow the fact that Nero will set them both ablaze tomorrow as Christian martyrs. It is hard to get from one view to the other without taking intermediate steps. The key step was the Enlightenment. Today's feminism remains the child of the Enlightenment.

We have examined the Enlightenment's influence on the American Revolution and Constitution (see chapter four). The Enlightenment was built on the proposition that rationalist man of the eighteenth century achieved a clearer understanding of humanity and nature through reason than was previously possible through divine revelation. Christians define humans as thinking creatures who yet lack God's wisdom or power. Denying divine revelation, Enlightened thinkers ceased to define humanity by reference to God as the "Other." They saw woman as the "other," to which they contrasted "man." Man was not woman.[4] They saw life as a struggle between freedom and tyranny or between individuals and the state, not between the Father and the world. Denying Christ's deity, they stripped the cross of its meaning. The Creator and his human creatures were seen to be in harmony, not conflict. By denying the conflict between Father and world, they aggravated tensions between male and female.

In the United States, with its weak governments, their battle of individual freedom versus state tyranny proved no contest, a sham fight. Gender provoked the real fight. Historian Elizabeth Fox-Genovese notes how their "discourse of individualism," of individual freedom, took "for granted that the individual is male and . . . treated woman, the other, as the problem." Republicanism was more male-centered than Christianity. They assumed that the citizen was male. Citizens' rights were males' rights. One of Thomas Paine's Enlightened works was *The Rights of Man*. But women objected to being ignored. The English writer Mary Wollstonecraft wrote *A Vindication of the Rights of Women* (1792) to protest the devaluing of women's education in Revolutionary France.[5]

Enlightened thinkers did not always intend to devalue women. The key was that they "justified" woman's role "by reference to what was natural for [her] sex, rather than divinely ordained." They debated women's *nature* and the degree to which education could change it. Diderot believed that reproduction virtually determined female behavior. Others thought nurture more important than nature. Some saw Native American societies as a true state of nature where women's true nature was seen. Dropping biblical teachings about women, they poked, prodded, studied and found women emotional, impressionable, imaginative and needing just the right kind of education.[6] Instead of voluntarily submitting to husbands in order to honor Christ, perhaps women necessarily submitted because that was their nature.

The two Enlightened revolutions (in America and France) raised the possibility of "radical changes in the relationship between the sexes." Wollstonecraft's *Vindication* showed that "the language of revolution was beginning to excite speculation about the position of women." Yet, for contemporaries, her ideas were discredited by reports of her "dangerously free [premarital] sexuality."[7] Radical changes remained only possibilities and were not discredited by being put into practice, as was the French Revolution. American feminism has been an ongoing revolution which has never quite seized power or admitted to being accountable for its consequences. Its philosophes always have an ancien régime to critique, rarely a Robespierre to regret.

In the United States radical changes were less likely than in Revolutionary France. There was no American Wollstonecraft, and males controlled republicanism. The idea of equality for males "tore through American society and culture with awesome power." That left women worse off. In colonial, hierarchical society, everyone had superiors. Inequality was part of being human, regardless of gender. A colonial merchant's wife was superior to a working-class male even though she had to accept a position below her husband. But in democratic, egalitarian America "women were transformed into the inferiors not only of same-class men but of all men." This inferior status "became all-encompassing and carried a more negative social connotation" than before. As American males adopted individualism, they defined it as male and excluded women from its freedoms.[8] The thwarting of possible changes and the breaking of implicit promises of equality angered women more than millennia-old scriptural injunctions to submit.

The one clear gain for women was increased educational opportunities, meant to train them in "republican motherhood." A republic needed virtuous citizens, and mothers could teach virtue to the male citizen-to-be if they were first trained themselves. A republic needed educated mothers more than did a monarchy, so women's status was slightly improved, but for the republic's sake more than for theirs. Even this small role lost significance as the male citizen's virtuous battle against state tyranny became a sham affair. When he used the language of liberty for his self-interest, the republic hardly needed a republican mother to teach him a selfishness that came naturally. Virtue lost its meaning for males. It came to mean "enlightened female sociability and affection" and finally "seemed to mean little more than female chastity."[9]

The Creation of Separate Spheres in Antebellum America
The role of rebellion and revivals. Early-nineteenth-century revivals slowly gave back to American women the role of teaching males virtue—this time Christian, not republican, virtue. They were supposed to teach males to stand with the Father against worldly vices. In regions where revival gave women this role, their status improved. Where democratic male individualism reigned unchallenged, their status declined.

More occurred than improved status or changed definitions of virtue. From 1800 to the 1920s, men and women went from performing separate duties in one sphere (farm or home workshop) to separate spheres of home (women) and work (men), and then partially back to one sphere, the factory or office, where both worked. Several causes and ideologies motivated women to make these changes and to help shape them, but industrial capitalism ultimately drew the most benefit from these changes. Women made them while seeking revival and equal rights, but these proved mirages by the 1920s. They arrived in industrial capitalism's Land of Desire instead.

A battle between revival and male rebellion helped to shape the first transition to separate spheres. Rebelling against God meant distancing oneself from home, especially in cities. Changes in work patterns distanced men from the home, but they sought distance as much as economic changes forced it on them.

Consider "sporting male" culture and prostitution in New York City. Visiting a prostitute is a dramatic male rejection of home and marriage. Before 1820 only transient males, such as soldiers and sailors, visited prostitutes, who were present in only two or three neighborhoods. From 1820 to 1865 brothels tripled in number and spread to respectable areas. A sporting male culture that glorified promiscuity multiplied the potential clients. Jacksonian male democracy helped produce the sporting male. With the social hierarchy overthrown, masters no longer supervised the private lives of apprentices and journeymen, who now had lower incomes and less prospect of becoming masters. They formed a permanent sporting class. Individualism freed up married men to visit prostitutes (unbeknownst to their wives). Demand increased, and so did the supply:

servant girls and milliners were freed from employers' control to be part-time prostitutes. With wages low, "many young females choose to prostitute"—5-10 percent of New York's young women.[10]

Entrepreneurs had free reign and government little power in the Jacksonian Age of laissez-faire and free markets. High land values in Manhattan led landlords to look for tenants who could afford high rents. Wealthy men from prominent families recruited madams as high-rent tenants; prostitution "offered windfall profits to the neighborhood landlord." Poorer men and the madams found it "an avenue of upward mobility." Theater owners allowed prostitutes in to boost admissions. Entrepreneurs "rationalized commercial sex, transforming it into a visible commodity of consumption," which they displayed in windows and on street corners to increase demand. As printing improved, pornography was added to a growing sex industry.[11]

The consequences were predictable: "these years also saw increasing abuse of women." Male gangs raided brothels and forced madams to pay protection money to political bosses or to hire pimps for protection. "Commerce preceded Christianity in determining real sexual behavior," and young males looked on every young woman as a potential sexual partner. A relationship meant to be private, exclusive and affectionate became public, promiscuous and exploitative. Hostility between the sexes grew. At the trial of a young male accused of murdering a prostitute, rival groups of sporting males and young women expressed their hostility to each other. Abortions increased, and fortunes were made in that business too.[12]

All this came before Darwin, before secularization, when evangelical religion dominated national life as never before or since. Thus the result was not to bring men and women together into one public sphere of promiscuity. America was too religious for a 1960s-type love-in to prove universally popular. Instead revivalism battled promiscuity, and that helped to shape two separate spheres. Revivalism is "premised on a society polarized between sinners and saved engaged in perpetual battle"—on the conflict between the Father and the world. Men fought for the Father too. Arthur and Lewis Tappan joined other men to fight drunkenness, prostitution and sporting male culture. Yet revival and reform came to be seen as women's job, part of their domestic sphere. The evangelical Female Moral Reform Society fought prostitution, the sexual double standard and "male sexual and economic greed."[13]

Women had prominent roles in the battle as preachers, prophets and exhorters. Their unexpected public words could aid the Spirit in breaking down human conventions, as itinerants did in the First Awakening. Catherine Beecher enlisted them as teachers in the battle to redeem the West. "Female converts outnumbered males by a ratio of three to two" in the Second Awakening. Working for temperance, abolition, prison reform and moral reform gave female converts public roles they were denied in politics. Such roles were extensions of their role to protect home and family. Women had to go public to help the church restrain male greed, intemperance and lust.[14]

Battles between revival and male rebellion (along with the privatization of faith) helped to shape separate spheres—workplace, saloon and political meeting for men; home and church for women—but it did not create the idea. Urbanization and a commercial, industrial economy drove men out of the home, out of self-employment and into wage work. Yet the Puritan father would never have surrendered religious leadership to his wife even if he had worked outside the home. More than economics was involved. Republicanism and rebellion unleashed male individualism, which drove men to seek rewards and pleasures apart from family. Revivalism fought back and drove women to maintain family and morality despite male absence.[15]

Shaped by conflict, separate spheres was not a harmonious ideal but a *modus vivendi* full of tension and latent anger. Sporting males and "long-hunting" patriarchs resented marriage as "female control"; women resented male greed and desertion. Cultural authorities tamed and rationalized the idea into a cultural equivalent of the Constitution's separation of judicial, executive and legislative powers. As courts and legislatures had different functions, men and women had different natures and different spheres of action. Using science and reason, people found gender differences far beyond obvious and scriptural ones. Women were naturally pious, moral, modest, submissive, emotional, caring, sexually pure and domestic; men were unemotional, calculating, self-interested, ambitious, irreligious and sexually impure. An unscriptural dichotomy was set up: male sexuality against female spirituality. Since women were its allies, the Christian message was recast to fit their nature: "the qualities of the reborn Christian" were "quintessentially female," for example, humility, obedience and servanthood.[16]

That was a culture-bound distortion. Jesus of Nazareth, the Son of God, was a humble, obedient servant, so how could those qualities be female? Paul had commanded wives to submit to husbands not because that was their nature but because it honored Christ. Sarah Grimké astutely criticized this distinction between male and female virtues as "one of the anti-Christian 'traditions of men' which are taught instead of the 'commandments of God.' " Another woman writer noted that the distortion discredited the faith: "devotional sentiment" was seen as "suitable to the weakness of the female mind, *and for that reason,* disgraceful to the superior wisdom of man."[17]

They sought to strengthen the faith, not weaken it, but evangelicals' skill at adapting it to a democratic culture led them to distort it—with harmful long-term effects. We cannot blame women. Clergy and laypeople, men and women, adapted for good motives. Conflict often distorts combatants and twists them into the reverse image of their opponents. Fighting male individualism, evangelicals feminized their message. Their message of sin, judgment, the cross and the need for conversion was inherently stern, not sentimental, though it produced traits that could be sentimentalized. Even by Victorian standards, it was not inherently feminine. Assigning it to women subtly changed it, though. As religious leaders in the home, they turned it from "conversion as an individual catastrophic event" toward "a new gradualistic view of conversion within the family" that emphasized a mother's role. She became "the actual agent of conversion" as she taught children. She often did bring her children to Christ, but an overemphasis on her role risked allowing family ties to restrict the Spirit's work in the birth from above.[18]

The role of capitalism and male individualism. Revival and rebellion were not the only forces creating separate spheres. The early pre-Civil War beginnings of industrial capitalism played a part, and separate spheres helped to make its later, spectacular growth possible. It did not cause males' rebellion, but it used it. Industrial capitalism did not cause females to seek to reform males, but it used females' separate sphere to aid its growth. As male rebellion made separate spheres necessary to save family and religion, the separate spheres aided its growth, which then strengthened rebellion and further separated the spheres.[19]

The growth of a national market economy led to regional specialization, larger firms, less self-employment and more men working outside the home for wages. Combined with the aggressively masculine Jacksonian culture, that led to new extremes of male behavior. Having "to compete for elusive manhood in the market," the young male seeking middle-class success had to show "extremes of aggression, calculation, self-control, and unremitting effort." Such "True Men" could best succeed "by wrenching True Women to opposite extremes of altruism and submission," notes historian Charles Sellers.

Women too shaped their opposite pole in order to keep males from wrecking homes. Separate spheres aided industrial capitalism by freeing males to be aggressive and acquisitive without endangering the survival of home and family. The woman managing the home enabled the workaholic man to push industrial capitalism past all limits. Separating out a female sphere meant removing communal-religious values from economics and politics, now free to be fully male-capitalist.[20]

In a way, separate spheres helped industrial capitalism in its attempt to transcend limits—in this case, the limit imposed by its male workers' competing duties to home and family. Industrial capitalism took women out of the market as its ethos was being shaped. They had had an important market role when goods were made at home, but as industrialization meant "the progressive separation of home and work" and the separation of families from farm and land, "the participation of married women in the American economy" declined. In their childbearing years they were kept at home just when income-producing work was leaving the home. True, widows took over businesses, and young, single women in the industrial Northeast worked in factories before marriage. Yet the former were not numerous, and the latter were temporary, young and unmarried in a society where experience, skill, age and married status brought influence.[21] Married women had influence, but separate spheres applied it to revival, reform and family, not to economics.

No group of women were likely to shape emerging industrial capitalism. It was shaped along very masculine lines: tough-minded, ruthless and narrowly concerned with short-term, quantifiable costs. Considerations of long-term stability, sustainability, emotional and moral costs, long-term effects on persons and institutions were outside its decision-making process, partly because women were outside that process. Male rule without a balancing female role added to its destructive dynamism.

Once shaped by males, it used women and their domestic sphere to lower its costs, while denying them an influence on it. Cottage industries or "outwork" flourished in textiles and clothing. The labor of women and children at home was cheap. Using the home as a substitute workshop, capitalists lowered labor and building costs. Advocates of separate spheres attacked this invasion of the home, but lower-class families needed the money. Urban lower-class women also took in boarders. Farm women sold butter, eggs or vegetables. Other women or young girls worked in factories or as domestic servants.[22]

Females' income-earning work differed from men's work. It furthered male interests, not female workers' goals. The money went to pay family expenses or for sons' education and so to give them a better chance for success, not to educate the woman or to accumulate capital so that she could expand her trade. Farm women's sales of eggs and butter paid "living expenses" so that men's income from field crops could "pay for mortgages and the new machinery." Women worked to enable men to expand farming operations. Many farmers would not reverse the cash flow and use crop proceeds to beautify, improve or expand the house. There was a dual family economy: women's was for daily consumption, family-oriented, cash-based, not credit-based; men's was credit-based, market-oriented, capital-accumulating.[23]

Generally, women's work subsidized capitalist development. It enabled farmers to survive on lower crop prices and laborers on lower wages.[24] Whether "outwork" or factory work, cheap female labor lowered the costs of labor, resources and food, so firms could invest more in technology, buildings and inventory. Or they lowered prices to expand consumer markets.

Women's housework aided capitalist development, though it was not bought, sold or recorded in ledger books. The preindustrial household needed the labor of both men and women. Men had to cut and haul wood, harvest and grind grain and do other chores that limited their work outside the home. New technologies such as the stove and new products such as merchant white flour saved labor—mostly, male labor. As head of household, the male did not choose to assume extra duties to replace those he lost to technology. He chose to use his greater household leisure to increase his work outside the home—for wages or at his own shop. He and his wife chose to use technology to increase the family's living standard (more cakes, cleaner rooms, better meals) rather than reduce the wife's labor. Her work increased. Men were freed up for industrial capitalism; women were more tied to the home.[25]

Men used their role for their advantage—to add wealth, to increase their status or living standards—rather than to honor the Lord or to ease their wives' labors. Industrial capitalism transcended limits set by their former duties at home. Separate spheres helped it to take off in America.

Women Protest Men's Use of Separate Spheres to Exploit Them

In 1848, women's rights activist Jane Elisabeth Jones protested: "Sphere! No, 'circle' would be a better name for woman's present walk; for it is round, round, round, like a blind horse on a mill wheel."[26] It was no coincidence that she wrote this in Ohio's *Anti-Slavery Bugle,* no coincidence that women awoke to their condition while working for abolition. By leading women to use secular reasons for their public role in reform, abolitionism helped lead them away from the idea of separate spheres altogether, though that took decades.

Other reform causes sought to turn males back to virtue to create a happy and pious family. In these causes, male vices were not seen as economic but moral: alcoholism, promiscuity, profanity, violence, domestic abuse. This type of reform did not seek female freedom or equality. It accepted male rule in business and politics. It did not show women that men used economic change to advance men's interests more than the family's. (Though some came home sober each night, they still exploited their wives' submission.) Also, causes such as temperance made progress. Frustration did not force women to search for something more than moral reform of males. These causes were rooted in New Testament faith, which did not set female equality or freedom as goals to pursue. Thus these causes could not encourage female individualism or a women's rights movement.

None of that was true of the abolition cause. It sought to help African-American families and to end masters' domestic abuses, but its goals went beyond family or morality. It was partly rooted in Christianity, but it was also grounded in Enlightened individual rights, Revolutionary liberty and democratic equality. It sought to extend the Revolution's promise of liberty and equality to African-Americans. It sought economic justice too, free laborers as well as sober ones. It required government action, not just private repentance. Most important, it was a reform blocked by the Constitution and the political courtroom. Frustrated, abolitionists such as Garrison turned to an extremely moralistic and individualistic politics that rejected Constitution and Christianity. This politics was the seed bed for a new women's rights movement.[27]

With abolition blocked in the 1830s and 1840s, some white women began to see that black males' grievances might apply to them: lack of freedom, the humiliation of inequality, no right to individual self-fulfillment, no right to vote or speak publicly. Soon "the relationship of husband and wife was most frequently compared to that of master and slave on the southern plantation." Abolitionist Lydia Maria Child charged, "Cursed is that system of considering human beings as chattel! Whether it be because they are women, or because they are colored." Male abolitionists' refusal to allow women equal roles in abolition societies or the right to speak before mixed audiences triggered this recognition in some women.[28]

Female abolitionists began to cross over from a Christian to an Enlightened view of family, marriage, society and politics—for the best of causes but with less than ideal effects. In battling slavery, they used a self-righteous, indignant critique ill-suited to other social ills with less clear-cut villains. On the highly charged moral battlefield of 1845-1860, male individualism provoked female individualism. Female reformers "were drawn to the Romantic versions of individualism": the individual was "a bundle of potentialities which required freedom as their essential medium of growth." Liberty was mainly "individualistic": "equal access to all aspects of American life and . . . the career open to talents."[29]

As Fox-Genovese notes, wives were not slaves despite "rhetorically strong analogies." Wives submitted to husbands, but marriage often "offered women protection against the uncertainties of single life—offered them economic support and a social and personal identity that enhanced their self-respect." Mostly middle-class and well educated, female abolitionists embarked on a campaign to gain an equal right to compete in a democratic, capitalist, individualistic society without knowing whether their poorer sisters would be helped or hurt by the competition. They "sought recognition from and status within the world of white males," but could less-educated women find it too? From the start, the women's movement was led by upper- or middle-class white women. It had a hard time crossing class or racial barriers between women.[30]

Like eighteenth-century gentlemen, mid-nineteenth-century gentlewomen cast aside Christianity (especially Calvinism) for Enlightened individualism. Not revivalism but "reform became the main religion for most of them." They "moved consistently away from orthodox Protestantism . . . toward more liberal denominations and beliefs"—partly because evangelicals had failed to take a stronger stand against slavery. Yet they would have exited orthodoxy anyway, for rational religion offered them a greater role. The Unitarian Theodore Parker addressed God as "Father and Mother of us all," which no evangelical minister would do.

Different women exited through different doors: Quakers' individual Inner Light, Garrison's anticlerical abolitionism, Unitarianism and Transcendentalism. But their destination was the same: the rationalist "human rights argument of Enlightenment philosophy and Revolutionary ideology" in the public sphere, an idealistic striving for "universal reform," including equal rights for women and, for many of them, an embrace of spiritualism. Fittingly, their 1848 Seneca Falls conference issued a manifesto echoing the Declaration of Independence.[31]

Unlike many signers of the Declaration, gentlewomen quarreled with Scripture over its prescriptions concerning women more than its supernaturalism.

Like their predecessors, many moved from the moderate stance of reinterpreting the Bible to the skeptical stance of discarding it. In 1895 Matilda Gage and Elizabeth Cady Stanton published the *Woman's Bible,* an irreverent, rationalist "glossary on various biblical selections pertaining to women." It used higher criticism, Darwinian evolution and skeptical rationalism to cast aside scriptural limits on women's roles and rights.[32]

The move away from orthodoxy freed them from the limited reform goals of male virtue and family welfare. They could seek change for their sake, not the family's. They could redefine woman's sphere. One woman's rights advocate insisted that "woman's sphere can not be bounded. Its prescribed orbit is the largest place that in her highest development she can fill." Reason led where revelation never would. Abolitionism led them to seek voting rights for women as well as for African-American males. Black suffrage and its Fourteenth Amendment adding "male" to the Constitution spurred them to create women's suffrage groups. Middle-class white women felt humiliated that illiterate freedmen could vote while they could not.[33]

Creating a women's rights movement had the important effect of organizing hitherto scattered efforts. Previously, as Gerda Lerner notes, "the invisibility of prior women's work to the women successors" meant that women used "their energy to reinvent the wheel, over and over again, generation after generation."[34] This had delayed women's radicalization. Each generation's protesters thought themselves radical but did not go far beyond their predecessors' views. Now, a process of ideological accumulation began, much like the accumulation of scientific knowledge over the centuries. Yet, though feminists would make more radical demands with time, they would not outgrow their Enlightened, individualistic roots.

Separate Spheres Begin to Overlap and Boundaries to Blur

Late-nineteenth-century reform and revival. Events in the late nineteenth century freed many women from the narrow domestic sphere, but that proved less liberating than expected. As industrial capitalism entered its Promised Land, it increasingly brought women together with men into the same sphere of work, whether office or factory. Religion no longer so strongly separated the spheres. As female reformers joined male individualists in departing from Christianity and as the fires of antebellum revival died out, the female domestic sphere lost much of its religious rationale. It became tied to Victorian, middle-class rationales: the family's status shown in the well-dressed, educated, virtuous, leisured wife and daughters in the front parlor. Yet middle-class status was partly a marketable commodity—the right furniture in the front parlor—so industrial capitalism was better able to penetrate *this* domestic sphere than the old one centered on the mother trying to Christianize her husband and children.[35]

Continuities remained. Temperance remained as a moral reform cause, though now "a secular reform with evangelical roots." Francis Willard's Women's Christian Temperance Union (WCTU) had as its motto "Women will bless and brighten every place she enters, and will enter every place." Women, not women bringing the gospel, would reform a male world. In a clash with evangelist Dwight L. Moody, Willard argued that he "emphasize[d] the regeneration of men" too much and help for women and children (and women's suffrage) not enough. Temperance adapted to the more secular postwar world.[36]

Other post-1865 reform groups were even more secular. Middle-class women formed women's clubs as "the late nineteenth-century successor to the earlier women's church societies." Literary, secular, educational, clubs furthered middle-class values more than specifically Christian ones. They performed good deeds, but not for the kingdom. Some groups, such as Boston's Women's Educational and Industrial Union (WEIU), were non-Christian, liberal and Darwinist. Their college-educated founders sympathized with the new social sciences then replacing the gospel as the reform ideology and methodology. Their goals carried them into urban and state politics, largely male turf before. Male Progressives made politics less one-sidedly masculine in tone by turning from political parties to nonpartisan interest groups and reform causes which women often joined.[37]

Encouraged by early gains in Wyoming and Utah, the women's suffrage drive also carried women into this male world of politics. Like abolitionism, women's suffrage proved more threatening and took longer than first anticipated. It too split into rival moderate and radical groups, but that allowed women of many different persuasions to support the cause. Some women joined the Anti-Woman Suffrage Society to oppose it. Like proslavery Southerners, conservatives erred in using Scripture to oppose it and in exaggerating its impact: it would "tear down all the blessed traditions, . . . desolate our homes and firesides, . . . unsex our mothers, wives and sisters, and turn our blessed temples of domestic peace into ward political assembly rooms."[38] That tied Christianity to a cultural status quo. It pushed suffragists toward an anti-Christian stance which some were disposed to take anyway.

Reform brought women into men's sphere of politics, and postwar revival carried men into the female sphere of religion. Premillennialism, which replaced postmillennialism, dropped the latter's sentimentalizing about women's superior piety. A new brand of male revivalist (such as Moody) preached to convert men (nothing new) by using a masculine message. One warned, "The great train of the nineteenth century is rushing down the track of time [and] the young men are running this train. Unless the Lord interferes, they will land us in perdition." Both men and women responded to this tougher message, which was not antiwoman. It was the Spirit's correction of the prior sentimentalizing distortion. Males were not threatened by women, nor fundamentalists by liberals, nor Americans by pessimism in the 1870s when premillennialism came, as one historian claims.[39]

Tough, pessimistic, quasi-Calvinist, premillennialism sounded more masculine, but it was not a reaction against feminism. The term had yet to be introduced, and the women's movement was still embryonic. It was a reaction against antebellum evangelicalism.[40] It sought to refocus the church on the battle lines between the Father and the world, which antebellum reform had blurred. It sharpened them. The women's movement focused on other matters: the failure of democratic, free-market, individualistic America to extend equal rights and roles to women. There was little dialogue between the two.

Women moving into men's sphere and men into women's and the blurring boundaries between them showed that separate spheres had been shaped by the struggle of revival and reform against male individualism. With revival increasingly male, with reformers often not Christian and with females individualistic too, the idea of Christian women protecting homes against male wickedness began to lose credibility. Economic and cultural trends softened boundaries and overlapped spheres at the same time. There was not yet one sphere, but that was on its way.

Overlapping spheres in the workplace. By the late nineteenth century, industrial capitalism had drawn men away from many of their domestic duties and had largely transcended this limit on male workers' single-minded devotion to the firm. It was ready to hire more women at lower wages to save labor costs. Now the firm was large and efficient enough to employ them in offices and factories, not as "outwork" laborers at home. Industrial capitalism's growth was advanced by some overlap in separate spheres—now that separate spheres had accomplished their initial purpose.

This first occurred in the federal bureaucracy during the Civil War, not in a private firm. In 1861 the Treasury Department hired female clerks at one-half the lowest male wage to save money. Other agencies followed suit. Managers reorganized "the work, often subdividing the tasks and creating certain routinized jobs specifically for female employees." Middle-class men and women faced possible loss of face or status in the federal office: men in doing office work instead of more masculine manual or self-employed work, women in working outside the home at all. Yet here women could earn more in a setting cleaner and more respectable than a factory. Here men disabled in the war could earn a decent salary. They created "a neutral zone between two separate spheres—habitable by both middle-class men and women."[41]

In this neutral zone, managers controlled male swearing, drinking, smoking and outbursts of temper. Middle-class women tried to keep these acts out of the home. Keeping them out of the office partially domesticated it, but it could not fully be home. Females had to learn the competitive, individualistic ways of the workplace. Keeping romance and sex out was more difficult. "For Victorians, the exposure of women to strange men in a male environment spelled danger—and that danger was specifically sexual," notes historian Cindy Aron. Fears came true. Supervisors sexually harassed workers. Females flirted to gain promotions. Rumors of "treasury courtesans" tainted females. How could you tell good from bad when they all talked to strange men?

The government clamped down with Christian morality—male or female clerks suspected of adultery or fornication were often dismissed—but it could not restore formal separate spheres. "There seemed to grow up a large gray area where innuendo, flirtation, and bantering became the norm." Lines blurred. Some acts that had been inappropriate no longer were, but some still were. Men and women saw the new lines differently. A neutral zone could be a combat zone.[42]

As technology made brains and quick hands as useful as sheer brawn, manufacturers hired more women, most young and single. They divided skilled crafts into many unskilled tasks for which they often paid young women a piece rate. Education, training or experience counted for little. Productivity was everything. The average male had three times the experience of the average female, whose expected future work life was only 15 percent of his, yet the employer did not greatly discriminate in his favor. Current—not past or future—productivity was rewarded. Strong social norms enforced a strict segregation of men and women in most factory jobs, however. That meant hiring costlier male labor, not cheaper female labor, for some jobs. Here industrial capitalism still showed preindustrial values by favoring the family man over the cheaper female worker even when profit maximization called for cutting labor costs. Yet males knew that employers had used female labor earlier to cut costs and that this sentimental side would not last forever.[43]

They were quite unsentimental in replacing male clerks with female ones. Before, a male clerk worked closely with the owner and hoped for eventual promotion to management. Then in the 1880s and 1890s typewriters, adding machines, telephones and other devices simplified tasks. The firm's greater size multiplied the number of repetitive tasks, which could now be efficiently divided among specialists—stenographer-typist, bookkeeper and cashier. Deskilling and routinizing led to the hiring of cheap female labor. By 1890, 15 percent of clerical workers were female; by 1930 it was 50 percent. Recruiting young women was easy, for clerical jobs paid 150 percent of manufacturing wages in 1890. The workplace was much cleaner, and women with high-school diplomas, office training, dexterity and middle-class manners had a great advantage over many male applicants.[44]

Men and women worked in the office, but not on an equal footing. Wage discrimination exceeded that in factories. In both, it was caused by capitalism's tendency to abstract more than it was caused by male prejudice. In large firms, managers, more than the labor market, set wages and policies. To rationalize employee relations, they created personnel offices, which set wages so as to reduce turnover and motivate workers. They avoided the high information cost of finding out each female worker's career plans. They made "scientific" assumptions and "often used [female] sex as a signal of shorter expected job tenure." Historian Claudia Goldin notes that "firms . . . found it profitable to treat women not as individuals, but as a group": 95 percent would marry, and 80 percent of these would quit work upon marriage. Assuming short female tenure, they put women on a "short job ladder"—short on promotions or raises. The "dictates of profit maximization" lowered female wages, "even in the absence of biases toward female employees."[45]

At first, young single women's move into clerical work was driven by a demand for cheap female labor, not by major changes in women's expectations. Firms needed office workers and paid wages high enough to recruit young women into the office and out of helping their mothers at home. Labor-saving devices in the home made mothers more willing to let them leave. Strong social and religious norms against wage work for married women kept mothers out of the job market, as did the long hours and lack of part-time jobs. Yet these norms steadily weakened. As a new generation of single women with high-school diplomas and work experience married, as their number of children decreased and as their individualistic desire for self-fulfillment grew, they were poised to shatter norms against working wives when labor demand went high enough.[46]

Though the new generation saw this as liberating, it was not and could not be. These changes were driven by economics, not by emancipating ideas. They fit the needs of firms and were controlled by them—by *males'* firms and by a capitalism shaped by males. The new, giant, merged firms of 1900 would prove difficult for female reformers to reform.

The growing influence of consumer culture on women. Capitalism's need for consumers drew women to department stores and other retail outlets. Originally a refuge from the workshop and a religious retreat from the market, the home was now part of the consumer culture. The wife who worked at home was enticed into a "separate world of consumer fantasy." Her power over consumption decisions increased just as she was increasingly separated from the processes of production that determined her family's ability to finance these decisions. She was tempted to buy beyond family income, to attempt upward mobility by purchasing French draperies or furniture. Shopping brought her downtown, into what had been male public space, and created another neutral zone. It was "the most widely visible sign of female emancipation in the modern city," more exciting than the prospect of a trip to the polling place.[47]

Emancipation was an illusion, yet a powerful one tied to the women's rights movement, whose individualism and growing irreligion reduced women's ability to resist consumerism's enticements. Fox-Genovese warns, "The worst nightmare that serious feminists must face is that in a decade or two the women's movement may be seen as having done the dirty work of capitalism" by weakening communities and norms that restrain markets.[48] Trying to persuade women to redefine feminism, Fox-Genovese puts that nightmare in the future, as something which her recommendations will avoid. But it is actually past reality. By 1900 the women's rights movement had already begun to do capitalism's dirty work.

Women came back to a capitalist market whose rules had been shaped by men while they were largely absent. Those rules stressed a tough-minded, bottom-line, cost-conscious outlook, a narrow accounting that counted only what could be quantified in ledger books. The quality of relationships, the strength of church and family, the state of the environment and of public morality—all were external matters, not reflected in prices, irrelevant to markets. The costs of damaging them were externalized; the firm did not bear them. Others did—often women. Part of capitalism's destructive dynamism was due to its one-sidedness: it was secular and paid little heed to God; it was masculine and paid little heed to feminine influences.[49]

Individualistic, middle-class, often anti-Christian, devaluing domesticity, stressing wage work, late-nineteenth-century female reformers did capitalism's dirty work—getting women out of the home and into the market—with no chance of reshaping or restraining capitalism. They could not reshape or restrain a capitalism that had created the middle class, that used individualism and anti-Christian rebellion to expand its sphere, that had devalued domesticity and stressed wage work long before they did. The frustrations of trying only radicalized them.

A New Woman Rebels Against Religion and Separate Spheres

A new generation of women with different experiences and expectations grew up in the late nineteenth century. The New Woman had a high-school diploma and sometimes a college degree. She worked outside the home and associated with men at work. She sought individual fulfillment and had more room to seek it. Many female reformers welcomed her at first. Yet like republican gentlemen aghast at the self-seeking Jacksonian Common Man produced by the Revolution, they came to question the New Woman their reforms and ideas helped to create.[50]

The New Woman often totally rejected Christianity. Going beyond her mother's rejection of the parson's Calvinism, she threw the parson's *and* the Enlightened gentlewoman's ideas overboard. She was so out of touch with evangelicalism that she could not even rebel against it. Rebelling against what was closer at hand, she turned against Victorian morality and against "scientific" views of female nature.

Continuing the Enlightenment's search for female "nature," Victorians, Christians and non-Christians, adopted untenable views on women's nature and role. New Testament instructions to Christian wives to submit to their husbands "so that no one will malign the word of God" were given in the context of the battle between the Father and the world.[51] Scripture did not suggest that women's nature left them little choice but to submit. It did not say that God designed male or female psychology or physiology so as to leave humans little choice but to obey him. Obedience might go *against* both male and female nature.

Rejecting scriptural revelation, Victorian scientists speculated about female nature. Using Darwinian evolutionary theory and Herbert Spencer's adaptation of it, Edward Clarke argued that a taxing Harvard education "would seriously threaten [a woman's] reproductive capacity." Avoiding "ethics or metaphysics," he admitted that women should do whatever they were able to do. But in a scientific light he asked, "What can she do?" He answered with Darwinism: in the nonbiblical, male-designed hierarchy of mental functions, women had less of the top-rated reason and more of the bottom-rated emotion, which showed "her affinity for lower forms of life." Darwin felt that males evolved at a faster rate than females because of their "higher metabolic rate." With physiological determinism, others argued that the "womb . . . dominated a woman's mental as well as physical life, producing a weak, submissive, uncreative, emotional, intuitive, and generally inferior personality."[52]

Just as Jefferson would not trust Scripture that blacks too were created in God's image but had to seek scientific proof of their equality (which he never found), so Victorian scientists would not trust Scripture for women's equality with men but sought a proof that many males among them never found. None of this was at all Christian. Yet when female social scientists attacked it, they did not question Clarke's "evolutionary, hereditarian, and anthropometric" assumptions, which they shared. Instead they tested female college graduates, who turned out to be unharmed by hard studying. Revealing their anti-Christian bias, they blamed the "emotional strain" some female graduates reported on the "introspective, self-accusing spirit" of Puritanism. They were not engaging a Christian view of women but a Darwinian, naturalistic one. They were so distant in time from Sarah Edwards (Jonathan's wife) that they probably meant Victorian fastidiousness, not Sarah's faith, by the term *Puritanism*.[53]

Social science replaced Christianity in other realms too. Robert Crunden shows how many Progressive-era reformers such as Jane Addams and John Dewey came from evangelical homes. They seized on social science and settlement houses as ways to keep the serving, self-sacrificing habits of evangelicalism minus the doctrine. For Dewey and Addams, a more communal, less individualistic, less one-sidedly male view of democracy attained near religious significance: "acceptance of democracy brings a certain life-giving power" (Addams); "the next religious prophet . . . will be the man who succeeds in pointing out the religious meaning of democracy" (Dewey).[54]

Democracy did not encourage prophetic denunciations of sin. Consider social scientists' approach to prostitution. Katherine B. Davis studied "female offenders," many of them prostitutes from New York City. Rather than attack "male sexual and economic greed" like the antebellum Female Moral Reform Society, she gave intelligence tests which "told Davis what she wanted to hear." Psychological tests replaced the gospel tracts and friendly visits of antebellum reformers. They pointed to low IQs, single-parent families and hereditary diseases as causes of prostitution. Ironically, prostitution was declining in New York, partly because relaxed moral standards meant that males could obtain sex free of charge.[55]

Social-scientific reform, the women's rights movement and college education led to an expanded female individualism that regarded fewer acts as sins. It was most fully developed in Greenwich Village by a group of female reformers, writers, journalists, socialists and professionals called Heterodoxy. Members were cosmopolitan, intellectual, unorthodox and individualistic. Novelist-member Rose Young proclaimed, "The freeing of the individuality of woman does not mean original sin; it means the finding of her own soul." But it did demonstrate original sin. Heterosexual immorality and homosexuality spread in the group, in the Village and in feminist circles, though suffragists tried to conceal this lest it damage the cause.[56]

Instead of widening women's sphere, they cast overboard spheres, female piety and women's nature. Heterodoxy members organized two February 1914 meetings at Cooper Union, at which the term *feminist* was first popularized. A leader announced, "We intend simply to be ourselves, not just our little female selves, but our whole, big, human selves." One female socialist elsewhere exclaimed, "Am I the Christian gentlewoman my mother slaved to make me? No indeed. I am a poet, a wine-bibber, a radical; a non-church-goer who will no longer sing in the church choir or lead prayer meeting with a testimonial." Going AWOL from women's role in religion and moral reform, they enlisted on the world's side in its battle against the Father. They thought they were brave rebels battling for autonomy, but they were pawns in that larger battle. "They assumed that free women could meet men as equals on the terrain of sexual desire just as on the terrain of political representation or professional expertise." But intimate relations between the sexes were inherently unequal: men exploited women who defied morality.[57]

Greenwich Village feminists were no more liberated by the resulting sexual consumerism than Harlem's African-Americans were by the consumerism of expensive apartments and cabarets. When their sexual rebellion went mainstream in the 1920s, it did not liberate but produced the "flapper" as sex object.

Women's Suffrage and Reform Efforts: Synopsis

The mingling of young men and women at office, school and factory, and an anti-Christian assault on moral standards, led to a sexual revolution and the flapper. A new lifestyle of female individualism emerged from the changed circumstances and ideas encountered by young working girls and college-educated women. "The glamor of the working girl lay in her proximity to men in the office context." Industrial capitalism gave young women the illusion of emancipation, but the reality was the secretary as "office wife." Not liberated in her productive role as secretary, she sought emancipation as a consumer, spectator and sex object. "In this sexualized consumer economy, young women learned to market themselves as products." They were not liberated but recruited "into the individualistic ethos of a consumer economy."[58]

Feminism did capitalism's dirty work. Its individualism could not restrain the market or keep it out of private life, for entrepreneurs could develop products which they could advertise as essential for female individualists: cosmetics, fashionable clothes, personal hygiene products, movies with "vamp" stars to model the new "female sexual assertiveness."[59] Based on human rebellion itself, capitalism was quite compatible with female rebellion against God's moral commands.

Gentlemen's Enlightened rebellion against Christianity led to male individualism and the "sporting male." Likewise, Victorian gentlewomen's rebellion and their search for an elusive Enlightened equality with men led to female individualism and the flapper. Predictably, women's suffrage did not lead to idealistic, reform-minded, feminist politics, as its backers expected, but to a decade of apolitical self-centered consumerism. Older reformers deplored younger women's "unmistakable tendency to emulate the vices of men"— smoking and illicit sex.[60] But they lacked the moral absolutes to stop it. Social-scientific "norms" lacked power to restrain vices.

The women who best resisted individualism, avoided consumerism and maintained "the Victorian female community" were missionaries. By 1893 more than 60 percent of America's foreign missionaries were women. Men turned to higher-paying work, but women were true to the Great Commission. Feminist historians distort this topic. They focus on the "battle of the sexes": male missionaries' insistence that wives care for home and children; mission work as escape from women's rights battles at home; missionary reports of abuse of women overseas as arguments "for patriarchy" at home.[61] They miss the key fact: these women escaped Victorian domesticity and narrow views of female "nature" without individualistically doing capitalism's dirty work. These women did not fall for the myth that a "battle of the sexes" or the individual's fight for autonomy had superseded the battle between the Father and the world.

Gradually, women won greater control over mission work and established their own mission boards. But chafing at male control did not lead to rebellion against the Father. Where female chafing at male-centered capitalism or democracy led to female rebellion against God, the resulting liberation could only be partial and problematic.

Pure religion was the best restraint on capitalism; irreligious movements which tried to reform capitalism were soon co-opted by it. Feminism was no exception. It further heated the Western "cultural hothouse" and hastened the "forced clip" of Western innovation. A female Renaissance, it too was individualistic, trying to transcend the limits of women's reproductive and nurturing roles. By encouraging rebellion against God, it added to the destructive dynamism of a supposedly Christian civilization rebelling against the Christian God. Thus it too served to accelerate history.

9

History's Accelerator
America Abroad,
for Pious
& Impious Ends

ON FEW SUBJECTS ARE OPINIONS SO
passionately held and dispassionate analyses so rare as U.S. foreign policy.
Anger over the Vietnam War and other Cold War projects continues to distort
historians' accounts of century-old U.S. policies. Take Julie Roy Jeffrey and
Peter J. Frederick's section "Becoming a World Power" in *The American
People*.[1]

They begin with Winthrop's "City upon a Hill," which set Americans on a
"special mission" to "spread the exemplary American model to an imperfect
world." That "implied a more aggressive foreign policy." "Implied" is right, for
in the next three pages they fail to prove that it was aggressive from 1865 to
1895. Instead it proves to be scenes from Gilbert and Sullivan: a dreaming,
ridiculed secretary of state (Seward); a rejected treaty to acquire Santo Do-
mingo; a delayed diplomatic conference; a sailors' barroom brawl in Chile; a
coup and a failed annexation attempt in Hawaii; a typhoon sinking U.S. and
German warships set to do battle off Samoa; and a brief spat with Britain over
Venezuela's border. They admit U.S. weakness—its army "ranked thirteenth in

the world, behind that of Bulgaria"—but write of "aspirations of an emerging world power . . . whose rise to power had come so quickly."[2] Did it have aspirations, and can they be blamed on the Puritans?

They continue to distort the post-1895 picture too. The 3-4 percent of U.S. exports going to China and Japan, the 3.6 percent of U.S. overseas investments going to Central America and a few men meeting with Theodore Roosevelt do mighty things abroad. Missionaries spread not the gospel but moralizing Anglo-Saxon values. America's "holy war" against Spain and Roosevelt's vigorous foreign policy—ten years of America abroad—sprawl across twenty-one pages of text. Taft's four years of quiet diplomacy get no coverage; Wilson's four years devoted to undoing Roosevelt's policy gets two pages. A recent CD-ROM textbook calls an apolitical ragtime tune "an ode to expansionism" because it is about a sailor-pianist on board the cruiser *Alabama*.[3]

Four Problems in Describing and Assessing America Abroad

There are many obstacles to a fair, balanced analysis of U.S. foreign policy. Four questions help us focus on the problem areas: How do we define that pejorative term *imperialism?* How do we assess charges of hypocrisy? When does an idea or proposal become official and thus evidence of U.S. policy? Is it fair when historians focus on U.S. acts and omit the acts of other nations?

Historians often use *imperialism* to mean little more than Americans going to new places to trade or preach. A better definition, however, is "the policy of extending a nation's authority by territorial acquisition or by the establishment of economic and political hegemony over other nations."[4] But was hegemony (domination) always achieved through force? If it came by selling goods or preaching, was it really domination?

Historians have stretched imperialism to cover cases where non-Western peoples preferred Western goods, religion or culture. That privileges the status quo that existed in these locales before European contact and implicitly criticizes any cultural, religious or economic change after that, even if desired by the peoples concerned. To be meaningful, *imperialistic* must have an opposite, an antonym—*nonimperialistic*—so that Europeans either act imperialistically or do not. If *imperialistic* merely describes what Europeans (and Americans) do when away from home, it lacks precise meaning. It merely means European-ness overseas or American-ness abroad, a self-contradiction. To be meaningful, *imperialism* must connote effective political or economic control, not just effective marketing or preaching.[5]

Second, how do we assess charges of hypocrisy? Frederick and Jeffrey state that the war against Filipino guerrillas "exposed the hypocrisies of" overseas expansion. Howard Zinn implies that American profit seekers in postwar Havana exposed the hypocrisy of U.S. idealism in supporting the Cuban rebellion.[6] But did Americans vote on the policy? No, they voted on candidates who often were silent on their foreign-policy intentions. In fact, foreign policy was made by presidents, subject to Senate approval, and was often not a major campaign issue. Often politicians saw it as their preserve and did not consult voters' uninformed opinions—except when war seemed imminent. Unelected officials in the State and Navy departments might initiate policy without much consulting with elected officials. Finally, with a change in administration, a warlike act might be approved by an official who had no hand in the previous, peaceful policy. Thus it is hard to prove that Americans or U.S. officials were hypocrites.

Third, when does an idea or proposal become official and thus evidence of U.S. policy? Historians cite ideas proposed by subordinates but rejected by higher-ups as evidence of U.S. policy. Is bureaucrats' talk about ideas incriminating behavior now that historians can read their correspondence? What about failed or dropped ideas? Americans in Hawaii seized power and asked the United States to annex Hawaii. Outgoing President Harrison proposed, but incoming President Cleveland vetoed, the idea. Does that prove U.S. imperialism?[7]

Fourth, is it fair when historians focus on U.S. acts and omit the acts of other nations? Though an understandable emphasis when writing U.S. history, this can seriously distort the picture. It is like aiming a video camera at only one boxer in a heavyweight fight. By editing out the other boxer and *his* blows, we can make the one boxer look ridiculously aggressive. Jeffrey and Frederick portray an aggressive United States largely by omitting the actions of European powers from 1865 to 1895. Foreign policy should be seen from a cosmopolitan perspective, with other peoples' acts as essential parts of the story.

Distortions matter. Using the "City upon a Hill" idea, many historians set the United States up as a Christian nation and charge it with aggression, imperialism and hypocrisy. Christianity gets the blame too. Jeffrey and Frederick portray Americans as busybodies seeking "to do good in a world that does wrong." Winthrop's warning that "the eyes of all people are upon us," so Puritans better not fail, becomes in their hands an arrogant demand that others copy the American model, which "became a permanent goal of American" foreign policy. Some Americans' goal of spreading the gospel becomes "American missionary expansionism" that rationalized imperialism.[8] We have seen that Winthrop was not a utopian, that many Founders were not Christians and that charges of hypocrisy and imperialism are difficult to prove and are often distortions of the evidence.

Failures of U.S. Officialdom Abroad

We must briefly assess U.S. foreign policy, even though the U.S. government did not represent Christianity. Compared to Britain, France and Germany, the United States was a failure at imperialism. Brother Jonathan was a Johnny-come-lately and played the imperialist game poorly. From 1820 to 1875, he was preoccupied with westward expansion, slavery, Civil War and Reconstruction, and from 1875 to 1890 with building railroads and a national market. U.S. technology, capital, political will and labor went into those projects more than into overseas ones.[9]

After the Civil War, the U.S. government's power overseas declined. Reliant on clipper sailing ships, the U.S. merchant marine fell behind "steam-powered British, Dutch, and French fleets." The United States largely dismantled its wartime six-hundred-ship Navy. By 1878 the U.S. Navy was the world's twelfth largest, smaller than Denmark's. It had few overseas naval coaling stations to fuel steam-powered ships, so it required its ships to have backup sails. The U.S. Army ranked behind Bulgaria's. The State Department was inadequate. Outside major European capitals, the U.S. diplomatic corps was "above all else amateur and unstable." Low-paid and transient, U.S. diplomats were often political hacks rewarded for party loyalty—or missionaries serving until the next political appointee arrived.[10]

With these tools the United States could not conduct a consistent worldwide foreign policy. It had different foreign policies for different continents. It had to be opportunistic: here taking advantage of British naval power to assert the Monroe Doctrine in Latin America, there recognizing its inferiority to major European powers by staying out of European affairs. In China it followed British forces and claimed privileges they won. Hypocritically, it denied any aggressive intentions toward China while it reaped fruits of British aggression.[11]

Weakness began at home. Imperialist Alfred T. Mahan grumbled, "Any project of extending the sphere of the United States . . . is met by the constitutional lion in the path." In a political courtroom of constitutionalism, power fragmented; debates centered on constitutional quibbles, not on overseas conditions; decisions were reversed or avoided; decision-makers were not reelected; diplomats were loyal to senators, not to presidents or secretaries of state. Reformers trying to alter an old foreign policy had to control for an extended time the Senate, Supreme Court and presidency.[12]

The brief ten-year period (1898-1908) of clear U.S. imperialism proves the government's usual weakness abroad. In these ten years the United States acquired its major overseas colonies and territories—Hawaii, Puerto Rico, the Philippines and other islands, such as Wake Island and Guam—and rights to build the Panama Canal. The Open Door Notes on China, the de facto protectorate over Cuba, Theodore Roosevelt's arbitration ending the Russo-Japanese War (1905), and a role in a Western force ending China's Boxer Rebellion all occurred in this ten-year window of opportunity, as did the first U.S. interventions in several Central American nations. The Supreme Court gave its Solomonic ruling on a question asked in the political courtroom: Did the Constitution apply in conquered territories? Yes and no. Secretary of State Elihu Root paraphrased the Court's answer, "Ye-es, as near as I can make out the Constitution follows the flag—but doesn't quite catch up with it."[13]

Much was done in ten years, but the key point is that it was a brief period. Americans' support for adventures abroad was ephemeral. Before anti-Spanish jingoism erupted in March-April 1898, the Senate failed to approve a treaty with a Hawaiian government "begging to be annexed" by the U.S. That, historian Charles Campbell notes, "is impossible to reconcile with the imperialistic mood that is often supposed to have engulfed the American people in the mid-1890s." Right up to Dewey's victory at Manila Bay, "the old-fashioned repugnance for anything smacking of territorial expansion overseas remained remarkably strong."[14] Patriotic fervor aroused by the war and Dewey's victory opened the window of opportunity. Roosevelt's free-wheeling policy was a stick keeping it open. Briefly, Americans supported acquiring overseas lands as a military necessity or as a reward for soldiers' sacrifices. They had not supported it earlier and would not later.

Ten years were brief compared to the half-century heyday of Europe's "new imperialism" from 1858 to 1914; the United States' forty-eight-year rule over Filipinos was short compared to Britain's 190-year rule of India. A few U.S. colonies were minuscule compared to a British Empire which in 1900 "included a quarter of the people of the world and nearly a quarter of its lands." Britain's Empire was largely complete in 1897, but the U.S. had not begun to assemble its empire—if its few island possessions can be dignified with that name.[15]

The window was closed by Taft's political vulnerability and by the anti-imperialism of the Democrats, winners in 1912 with Woodrow Wilson. He appointed 1900 anti-imperialist candidate William Jennings Bryan as the new secretary of state and largely undid Taft's dollar diplomacy. Before 1908 the United States had installed an elected legislature in its major colony, the Philippines, and by 1916 it had promised the islands eventual independence. Small comfort to Filipino nationalists, those moves were still a rebuke to ardent U.S. imperialists. Roosevelt was angered by these moves, yet historians like Jeffrey and Frederick devote scant space to this rebuke.[16]

That is not to argue that Americans abandoned imperialism because of their Christian faith (though that was a factor for Bryan). Americans' traditional republicanism discouraged the taking of colonies, but, more important, these proposed colonies held out few opportunities for the masses of self-interested male citizens. Individualistic males would not sacrifice only to build an empire for the State. Westward expansion had opened up new lands for *them* to settle. Where enough peoples of other races lived at a great enough distance from the United States to make removal impractical, Americans would not sacrifice for a conquest that would benefit a few plantation owners or corporations. The U.S. government followed those few citizens who had personal interests abroad and who asked a senator, representative or president for government help.[17] It rarely staked out its own interests and then successfully insisted that Americans sacrifice just to maintain these.

So in asking what America's impact was on the world—Christianizing or secularizing, good or bad—we must examine the individual American citizen or company abroad. Americans sought profits abroad. Motivated by the profits possible in a national market, U.S. firms had developed appealing consumer goods and a consumer culture that broke down cultural barriers to no-holds-barred shopping. As sixteenth-century European consumer goods disrupted indigenous New World societies, so American consumer goods disrupted Asian and Pacific societies in the nineteenth and twentieth centuries. Firms that used railroads, the telegraph, refrigerated cars and other technologies to transcend natural limits in the United States sought to transcend the artificial limits of a nation's borders.

American missionaries went abroad to preach the gospel. They came early to a number of lands and cities: Bombay (1813), Burma (1813), Hawaii (1820), China (1830), Thailand (1831), Turkey (1831), the Punjab (1833), Indonesia (1834), Egypt (1854), Japan (1859) and Korea (1884). They were part of a global movement. It is hard to say what percent of missionaries at any one time were Americans. In 1890 Americans were 36 percent of ordained Protestant missionaries (Britons were 38 percent), but that omits lay and female missionaries. The percent of Protestant missionaries to China who were Americans increased from 35 percent (1900) to 43 percent (1910) to 47 percent (1935-1936).[18]

Citizens, their institutions, their mission boards and their corporations went overseas and dragged a reluctant government along to protect their ventures. Their forte was not imperialism (effective political or economic *control*) but effective marketing or preaching *(influence)*. They did not cause U.S. dominance but joined a "world revolution of Westernization" led by Britain. Lord Lytton abandoned English understatement to claim that Britain led "a gradual but gigantic revolution—the greatest and most momentous social, moral, and religious, as well as political revolution which, perhaps, the world has ever witnessed."[19]

If not the greatest, this Westernizing revolution greatly accelerated history. It is provincial to claim that the United States had a leading role in it then, but many historians write as if the United States did. Walter LaFeber, for example, correctly notes "that Americans . . . acted as catalysts for revolution as they searched for economic and missionary opportunities around the world." Yet he does not place Americans' role within the context of the West's destructive dynamism.[20] That was the catalyst for global change.

We must assess this Westernizing revolution and its relationship to Christianity. Was Christianization the same as Westernization? We must examine the activities of American citizens abroad to answer that.

Males, Markets and Missions in the Pacific

America abroad proved a mix of opposites, a self-contradiction. The good and the undesirable were strewn overseas as Americans arrived in ports, plantations, islands and interior villages across the globe. Wheat and tares grew together, as in Jesus' parable. Other nations were unsure which was the true America. In the parable the landowner sowed only good seed; an enemy secretly sowed weed seeds.[21] The United States was not so free of responsibility for what later was called the Ugly American abroad. A democracy partly shapes its citizens as it is shaped by them. Catering to voters' whims and wishes, nineteenth-century U.S. governments lacked will or means to keep tares at home or control their conduct abroad. After the Second Awakening, Americans were one of the most pious peoples, yet democratic individualism and anti-Christian rebellion made them one of the most profane too. Westering Americans entered the Pacific world in ways that showed the paradoxes of America abroad.

Like trade winds, the motives that drove them across the continent drove them across the Pacific to various islands and coastlines. Like mountain men trapping beaver for European markets, Americans gathered "sea-otter pelts, seal skins, and furs and hides" in the Pacific for sale to China. Like hunters shooting buffalo nearly to extinction, whalers harpooned sperm whales till they were scarce. Forty-niners headed for a gold rush in Australia. Seafarers' need for recreation and supplies created new island economies; merchants and plantation owners followed seafarers as they had the pioneers. Like Columbus or Cortés, where these Americans landed they left "a lurid trail of demoralization, dissipation, and disease."[22]

We see *this* America abroad when we pick up the trail in Hawaii. We also see the trail left by missionaries. Here two Americas collided abroad. Historians subsume both under the category of "Expanding America." But differences between whaling crews and missionaries outweigh the similarity in citizenship. Both groups came from New England. Entrepreneurs who financed, captains who led whaling expeditions, crew members (at first) and missionaries were mostly Yankees. After months at sea, sailors were ready to exchange steady Yankee habits for some carousing. Male rebellion against church and parson had helped motivate them to join whaling crews. Stories of beautiful, willing South Seas women circulated in New England taverns. Early experiences in Hawaii tended to confirm the stories.[23]

Enter Yankee missionaries. They made slow progress, but a Great Revival (1839-1842) brought twenty thousand converts. Winning influence over Hawaii's king, they became his advisers. They brought the parson's morality to Hawaii, persuaded native women to withhold sexual favors from sailors and the king to issue Puritan-style blue laws. Imagine a sailor's "frustration [at] fleeing Puritanism in America only to arrive in paradise and find his more righteous brothers there ahead of him."

Cultural influence is a two-way street. Missionaries brought Christianity to Hawaii; writers brought immorality, not indigenous innocence, to the United States. Travel writers and novelists such as Herman Melville *(Typee, Omoo)* popularized Hawaii and other islands as paradise. What the New World had been to Europeans—an idyllic land of innocent, property-free, masterless peoples—South Seas islands became for many Americans. In Nuku Hiva

(Typee), Melville found "an absence of commerce, finance, and poverty." Beachcombing males jumped ship to quit the rat race of competitive individualism and rebel against Christian morality. Unlike the Bowery, the South Seas gave them sexual services for free. Popularizing and marketing this tempting vision, writers undercut Christian morality back home and recruited more beachcombers to come to paradise.[24]

Writing South Seas novels became a cottage industry that Hollywood used to create a consumer's Land of Desire. "Writer after writer departed for the Pacific using the books and novels of their predecessors as guide and inspiration": Robert Louis Stevenson, Jack London, Charles Nordhoff and James Hall *(Mutiny on the Bounty)*, Robert Dean Frisbie, James Michener *(Tales of the South Pacific; Hawaii)*. Starting with Melville, most despised missionaries for ruining paradise.[25]

These Americans cannot be subsumed under one heading. They showed Westernization's contradictions, but American beachcombers and missionaries in a few Pacific islands did not greatly affect the course of history. When it hit continents such as Africa and Asia, Westernization had a greater world-historical impact. So we will focus on Asia first, specifically China.

Western Imperialism, Capitalism and Missions in China

An enormous country in population and land mass, farther from the United States, China forced marketer and missionary to be more organized and persistent. It offered greater potential rewards as market and mission field, but only large firms and mission agencies could reap them. Missionaries' quick influence and beachcombers' liberty—so easy in Hawaii—were unlikely in the world's oldest extant empire and proud center of Confucian culture. China's rulers did not ask missionaries for advice or permit foreigners to wander at will among their people.[26]

Influence went both ways: Chinese came to America as well as Americans to China; Chinese had opinions about Americans as well as Americans opinions about the Chinese. Both Chinese and Americans had feelings of cultural superiority.

Trade between the two nations began in 1784 when the U.S. ship *Empress of China* sailed to Canton. For the next seventy years, merchant capitalism ruled the China trade: long, slow voyages, factors in Canton, trade in luxury goods, amoral U.S. merchants carrying illegal opium to China. Confucian writers and governments did not esteem merchants or foreigners. They lumped Americans with other Westerners as "ocean barbarians." In Chinese, Westerners were depicted by "the character for sheep with the sign for water added alongside." Their names were "transliterated or translated . . . in ways intended to demean and give unsavory connotations."[27]

Informed Chinese, mainly government officials, regarded the "flowery flag country" more favorably than other Western nations. Their main enemy was Britain, and America's two sucessful wars against Britain seemed like models China might copy. A series of mid-nineteenth-century books written by Chinese officials such as Wei Yüan and Hsü Chi-yü admiringly described the United States as a technologically advanced, prosperous, well-governed, well-educated society. As part of "barbarian management," Chinese officials hoped to use the less aggressive U.S. government to restrain more aggressive Europeans, who sought special trading privileges and treaty rights. The books gave policy-makers needed information on this possible ally, the United States.

They praised George Washington but criticized Christians. Wei quoted from anti-Christian works: one doubted that Christians would revere the cross if their Savior had really died on one. In a second edition, he added popular anti-Christian myths: for example, that pastors removed the eyes from Chinese corpses and mixed these with lead to make silver. Hsü retold the old tale that Christianity was "an offshoot of Buddhism."[28]

When Wei and Hsü wrote their books, few Chinese had had direct contact with American missionaries, who were still confined to a few treaty ports. Unlike opium merchants, early missionaries faced daunting barriers, including the culture and language. The *shen-shih* (Chinese gentry) owed their social role, and the government its legitimacy, to Confucianism, "a state ideology"-cum-religion. Christianity was *tso-tao,* the "wrong path," a religious "heterodoxy" causing political and social anarchy. In light of Chinese-Confucian cultural superiority, to say that truth could come from outside China seemed folly. Missionaries often waited seven to ten years for their first convert, and the death toll among missionaries was high. Due to "an unfavorable climate and constant toil in the midst of anxiety," 20 percent of the first Protestant missionaries to China "died in the field."[29]

Textbooks discuss American missions to China (and other places) at this initial, unsuccessful phase and in connection with the antimissionary Boxer Rebellion. But they are silent about ongoing twentieth-century missions or the estimated twenty million Chinese Protestants in 1990—an impressive fruit of American (and other) missionary efforts.[30] Short-term failure is noted, whereas long-range success is a taboo subject. Yet missionaries adjusted to conditions and found effective ways to evangelize by 1900. Some "began to diversify into education, care for foundlings, and medical assistance." Americans joined China Inland Mission, a new kind of agency which recruited less-educated Christians to work as itinerant evangelists, wear Chinese clothes and preach in unreached interior regions. Americans formed colleges to reach youth. The YMCA began new programs for urban Chinese students in the late 1890s. By 1900 there were 250,000 Protestant Chinese and almost 750,000 Catholics. A good foundation had been laid.[31]

At the same time, U.S. firms switched from merchant to industrial capitalism, from trading luxury goods in ports to marketing mass-produced consumer goods in the interior. Singer Sewing Machine Company pioneered in this global transition. Frustrated at fluctuating domestic demand, it sought foreign markets. Selling on installment with low down payments through local agents, Singer achieved great success abroad. It offered a democratic product, affordable, practical and profitable as a tool for home-based business. "By 1900 Singer had 60,000 sales agents" around the world, "and its name had entered some foreign languages as the word for sewing machine." Like missionaries, Singer encountered barriers: opposition from Chinese tailors and an unfamiliar retail system. In 1904-1914, about 1 percent of exported U.S. sewing machines went to China.[32]

Standard Oil marketed kerosene to Chinese consumers who were looking for better lighting. Other firms sold tobacco and cotton textiles. New technologies such as steamships, telegraph and railroads made this new industrial marketing possible. Yet trade with China was only 2 percent of U.S. foreign trade in 1900. The fabled "China market" was a mirage. Japan captured the cotton textile market, and the British monopolized markets for other goods. The average Chinese did not buy many U.S. goods: "many lived in the inaccessible interior and few had much purchasing power."[33] Modern transportation could get goods to them but not provide money to buy them. Jobs could, but they were in the United States.

Shaking Paradigms of Superiority: Missionaries and Migrants

Steamships brought Chinese laborers to U.S. job markets more than U.S. goods to Chinese markets. Labor was a commodity too. U.S. goods were not cheap enough for Chinese markets, but Chinese labor was cheap enough for U.S. markets. After 1850, "a flood" of Chinese sought "the new opportunities which

Western trade, capital, and technology had created in the mines, railways, and commercialized agriculture" in the United States and Latin America. Industrial capitalism had ironic results. No sooner had Americans conquered a continent than their transcontinental economy drew half a million Chinese immigrants. Not religiously motivated, permanent or family-centered, this migration was economically motivated, male-centered and often temporary. In Confucian eyes, it had the same result as conversion to Christianity: "an unfilial abandonment of family." Chinese males came to earn money, to send much of it back to their families and to return in ten years or so. Economic motives led to unbalanced communities. Less than 8 percent of migrants were females; prostitution became nineteenth-century "Chinatown's most prosperous industry," employing 50 percent of Chinese-American women in 1870. Like sporting males, Chinese males distant from home sought temporary female companions.[34]

Industrial capitalism was more disruptive than Christian proselytizing in China and America. Emigration was a business with steamship agents, emigration brokers in Hong Kong and emigration bankers among San Francisco's Chinese-American merchants.[35] They profited from the new global labor market. But like some Old Testament judgment, the effects of westward expansion, industrialization and new technologies came down upon Americans' own heads. Their westward expansion turned out to be part of a broader global Westernization. Chinese immigration soon, but only partially, undid the project they thought they had furthered, the westward advance of Anglo-Saxon peoples, for their westering caused Asian peoples to advance east.[36] Their little project propelled God's larger project of connecting peoples and accelerating history.

Many were furious, especially in California, where most Chinese-Americans first settled. By 1870 Chinese composed about 8 percent of California's population and 25 percent of its labor force. There were many reasons for anger. Workers saw that firms welcomed Chinese migrants as cheap labor and externalized the social costs. Whites felt, often correctly, that Chinese laborers undercut wage rates, lived in their own communities, refused "to assimilate by becoming a good Christian and citizen," formed secret societies that often became criminal gangs, sent much of their wages back to China ("a constant drain on the national wealth") and spent the rest on Chinese, not American, goods. Yet whites did not protest employers' exploitation of Chinese workers, and their anger was partly racial prejudice against the Chinese. To be fair, we must recognize that anti-Chinese prejudice also erupted in the Philippines, Thailand and elsewhere—wherever the Chinese emigrated.[37]

Americans were especially angered by the shaking of their paradigm of racial superiority, a worldview that saw Anglo-Saxons as the world's most skilled people. "Even Sinophobes" had to admire the Chinese for "their wonderful manual skill, their highly developed and intelligent imitative faculties, their tireless industry, and their abnormal frugality." In the Social Darwinian battle for survival of the fittest, Chinese laborers proved fitter, and whites reacted with violence. One Chinese-American editor recalled being "spat upon, kicked, stoned, and forced to run for my life time and again just because I was Chinese." Whites called for laws to end Chinese immigration. Congress responded with a series of such laws (1882, 1888, 1892) despite protests from China.[38]

A similar but reverse process occurred in China, where missionaries and Westernization shook the Chinese paradigm of cultural superiority. Historians often criticize missionaries for disrupting indigenous cultures, for being culture-bound, unable to distinguish Christianity from Western culture. In some cases, they are correct. Missionaries made mistakes. Yet in advanced, literate cultures such as China's, non-Christian hearers could be more culture-bound than Christian preachers. Confucian religion was inextricably linked to the Chinese state and society—more than Christianity was to European or American states and societies. The Enlightenment and later secularizing trends had partially decoupled them there. In China, they stayed linked. Cultural prejudice, family pressure, social stigma and governmental hostility toward the new faith impeded Chinese listeners from hearing the gospel with an open mind. Confucianism linked individual, family, town, government and empire to block the gospel.[39]

Before the gospel could be heard, this paradigm of Chinese cultural superiority had to be shaken by the clear fact of Western military, commercial and technological superiority. Despite Westerners' impious goals, God used Western imperialism and capitalism in a redemptive way as tools to increase the gospel's credibility in China. That did not justify imperialism or economic exploitation; he quickly dropped those tools and did not allow his use of them to justify Westerners' use of them. World War I, partly caused by imperial rivalries, was a case of the West reaping the harsh fruits of militaristic imperialism.[40] It started the process of decolonization. Imperialism was a short-term paradigm-shaker, global evangelization the enduring long-term phenomenon.

Many Chinese reacted with anger to this paradigm shaking, just as Californians had. "The complaints of Chinese nativists bore an embarrassing resemblance to those of their American counterparts." Missionaries and Chinese converts bore the brunt of the anger. In Foochow, as two American missionaries "were walking in the suburb south of the river, they had trouble with some Chinese boys, who struck them, kicked them, and threw things at them." Later, a mob torched a missions college building.

After 1860 China "was deluged with a growing torrent of violently anti-Christian pamphlets and tracts." Best known was *Pi-hsieh-chi-shih* ("A Record of Facts to Ward Off Heterodoxy"). Not a collection of facts, notes historian Paul Cohen, it was "a curious patchwork of Christian history and practices, tales of the lascivious behavior of priests and converts, weird and obscene barbarian customs, and esoteric terminology." Exploiting the average Chinese reader's ignorance of the West, it cleverly made "it difficult for him to judge just where fact ends and falsehood begins." Such pamphlets sparked anti-Christian riots on days when students gathered in cities to take the Confucian classical exams.[41]

By the late nineteenth century, Cohen adds, some anti-Christian Chinese realized that "there were forces in the West itself which were hostile to Christianity, or, if not to Christianity, at least to the Christian missionary enterprise." Yang Hsiang-chi "attacked Christianity from the viewpoint of modern Western science," Wang T'ao from the viewpoint of positivism. Interactions were complex. Orientalism appealed to Westerners tired of Christianity. Their anti-Christian ideas went East to help Asians oppose Western missionaries. Last, the Western *tso-tao* of Marxism, a wrong path wreaking serious political and religious damage, also went East to block the gospel.[42]

Rather than anti-Christian ideas, many historians blame an "irritating and sometimes provocative foreign missionary presence" for the anger and the riots. Their presuppositions privilege the religious status quo before missions: peoples should be left undisturbed in their ancestral beliefs, safe from Christian missionaries. Yet, in a rapidly interconnecting world, preserving the status quo is impossible. They also do not protest Eastern religions' impact on American society.

They reinterpret China's most violent anti-Christian event, the so-called Boxer Rebellion of 1899-1900, which was not a rebellion against the authorities. The Qing dynasty and the Empress Dowager supported the Boxers against the foreigners. The Boxer slogan was "Xing-Qing mie-yang" ("Revive the Qing, destroy the foreign"). Thus Joseph W. Esherick grabs quotes to portray negatively "this alliance of Christian proselytizing and Western imperialism."

He downplays or omits Boxer atrocities: they killed 32 Americans, 157 Europeans, and untold thousands of Chinese Christians. He mostly blames foreign troops hastening to Beijing to relieve the legations.[43]

Many historians' paradigm is this: Christian proselytizers disturb other cultures, fail to make converts and largely deserve the anger and violence they receive. The evidence shatters that paradigm. In the 1990s, some twenty million Chinese Christians worship Christ (many in house churches). They are most numerous in areas of extensive nineteenth-century mission work: Zhejiang and Fujian provinces. Historians rarely note the post-1920s survival of Christianity in China. In a 1974 book on China missions, John K. Fairbank noted that "few of the Chinese people were likely to become Christians"; "missionaries' long-continued effort, if measured in numbers of converts, had failed." Still, American missions to China were interesting, as one source for "the Maoist message of today," a possible source of U.S. policy in Vietnam, an influence on U.S. churches, a partner in U.S. imperialism—as a cause of everything but the one thing they were meant to cause and *did cause,* vibrant Chinese churches. Fairbank's 1986 book *The Great Chinese Revolution* and Jack Gray's 1990 book *Rebellions and Revolutions* ignore Chinese churches. Similarly, feminist historians reduce the world-historical to the personal: missions are just ways for women to show their abilities. Chinese churches prove that missions did not fail, were not steps to self-fulfillment and are not interesting only for extraneous reasons. They succeeded in what they set out to do: bringing the gospel to China.[44]

Maoism is gone. U.S. imperialism is largely gone. The Vietnam War is over. Women have other outlets for their abilities. But the gospel lives and thrives in China. In spring 1995, some one thousand Chinese evangelists went out from Henan province to preach throughout China, a 1990s indigenous version of the old China Inland Mission.[45]

From the vantage point of today's Chinese churches, the American missionary experience in China fulfills this psalm:
Those who sow in tears
   will reap with songs of joy.
He who goes out weeping,
   carrying seed to sow,
will return with songs of joy,
   carrying sheaves with him.
Some have lived to sing the songs of joy. The daughter of Dr. Nelson Bell, a

medical missionary in Jiangsu province, Ruth Bell Graham returned in 1980, and again in 1988, with her husband Billy Graham. In 1980 one Chinese friend of the family told her, "Your father led me to Christ and I am still a Christian. . . . The seed your father sowed is bearing fruit." Later, unconfirmed reports had two hundred thousand Christians living in that part of Jiangsu.[46] Most missionaries did not live to see this fruit, but they planted seeds, and the church rejoiced to see them grow and ripen.

Japan: U.S. Government Experts Go Abroad More Than the Gospel

In Japan, America abroad was markedly different from China. Japan's Westernization was markedly different from China's too. Japan was the exception to the East Asian rule. Here the U.S. government, via Commodore Matthew C. Perry, took the initiative, not missionaries or merchants. Here scientific, enlightened, expert Americans seized the opportunity Japan offered more than did evangelicals. The Japanese seized on Westernization as a tool to remake their nation. They controlled the process and filtered out Christianity as a Western idea they did not find useful for nation-building.

Japan under Tokugawa rule was an argument against historians' view that foreign cultures should not be disrupted by proselytizers. After a brief sixteenth-century flirtation with Christianity, Japanese shoguns like Iemitsu ruthlessly exterminated the Catholic faith. Partly to prevent any Christian resurgence, they built "an eerily modern form of totalitarianism," writes Peter Booth Wiley, with cell groups, informers, a "spy system," the "surreptitious entry of homes," frequent executions and censorship. Cell groups mobilized the people "for periodic tramplings on the cross to prevent the revival of Christianity." Heavily taxed peasants supported an unproductive *samurai* class. Feudal warlords, or *daimyo,* built mansions in Edo (Tokyo), "a city of resplendent decadence." Shoguns kept Japanese from traveling overseas and foreigners from visiting Japan. This partly Confucian system—and a worldview picturing Japan as "the Divine Land" and the emperor as a virtual god—combined to shut the door on the gospel.[47]

The U.S. government wanted to "open" Japan in order to obtain coal and harbors for steamships, not to preach the gospel. Also, a treaty could secure better treatment for U.S. sailors shipwrecked off Japan. Missionary and profit motives were secondary, and U.S. firms were more interested in the China market. "To whet the appetites of the Japanese" for trade, Commodore Perry collected consumer goods to take to Japan: "a case of Colt arms, a daguerreotype camera, a telegraph, clocks, stoves, farm implements, two folios" by James Audubon "and a quarter-sized steam locomotive with tender, cars, and track." Yet trade was a carrot, not the main goal.[48]

Samuel Wells Williams, American missionary to China, went along to interpret. Williams correctly saw Perry's little project as part of a larger one: "I am sure that the Japanese policy of seclusion is not according to God's plan of bringing the nations of the earth to a knowledge of his truth."[49]

Perry's success in entering Edo Bay demonstrated the shogun's military incompetence and broke the popular illusion, sustained by government secrecy, of Japan's military strength. What good was military dictatorship if it could not militarily defend Japan? By 1868, after attempts "at expelling the barbarians" failed, "young samurai reformers" realized that they must copy barbarian methods to strengthen Japan. They ended the Tokugawa shogunate, restored power to the Meiji emperor and began a series of partially Westernizing reforms. The paradigm of Japanese superiority was only partially, temporarily shaken. They saw no need for Christianity. They rebuilt the paradigm with Western experts and technology.[50]

They selected experts and technologies from many Western nations. They valued American practicality, public education and agriculture. But to retain U.S. experts, they had to repeal laws declaring Christianity "a prohibited religion, punishable by death." Yet they filtered out Americans' Christian beliefs and absorbed only the enlightened, scientific advice. On a monument to American agricultural expert William S. Clark, they shortened "his terse parting advice" to his Japanese students—"Boys, be ambitious in the service of the Lord"—to the more terse, more secular "Boys, be ambitious."[51]

That was the official editing and filtering, but Clark's "enthusiastic" Christianity had "exercised such an influence" that every student in his first and second classes converted to Christ. Other American experts gave out the gospel with their advice. By 1888, there were 451 Protestant missionaries in Japan, and some twenty-five thousand Japanese Christians, who had already formed their own national churches. The "most notable" missionary was a Japanese who had studied in the United States, Shimeta Niishima, whose Christian school in Kyoto had a "storm of revival" in 1884. That was unusual. Cultural resistance and a mission focus on elites yielded a small "Japanese Christianity that was intellectual and individual," notes historian Stephen Neill, not "a mass movement" reaching the lower classes.[52]

America abroad produced startling resemblances to America at home. U.S.

experts aided in the agricultural development of Hokkaido. Its capital Sapporo was "laid out in a rectilinear" grid like an American Midwestern town. Its rural "landscape, laced with stone walls and dotted with dairy cows, red barns, and silos, is reminiscent of Wisconsin."[53]

Influence goes both ways. If some Japanese converted to Christianity, some Americans converted to Buddhism. One Yankee, Ernest Fenollosa, after years in Japan, advocated "a coming cultural fusion of East and West." His friend William S. Bigelow adopted Buddhism after traveling in Japan and promoted it to others at "his epicurean summer retreat" near Nantucket. Japan's greatest export to the United States was silk, used for luxury clothing. By 1913 Elizabeth Gurley Flynn exaggerated, "Every woman wanted a silk gown, and the more flimsy it was the more she wanted it." Silk gowns and stockings helped merchants create a consumer Land of Desire. "By World War I, American silk mills were each year using more raw fiber than all of Europe combined," and they exploited labor worse than any other industry to make silk affordable to more consumers. Using silk, merchants staged Japanese fashion displays to sell goods with suggested sensuality.[54]

Less popular were Japanese immigrants to America. Like the Chinese, they were mostly single male laborers who came to the West Coast, where they faced hostility and discrimination. Unlike the Chinese, "they came with the approval of their government"—much stronger than China's. They were part of a Japanese program of "commercial and human expansion" in the Pacific which shook the paradigm of Anglo-Saxons' westward advance. Japanese moving east to Hawaii drew their government's attention to it as Americans moving west drew *theirs* into its affairs. A collision threatened. Americans overthrew Queen Liliuokalani, restricted Japanese immigration and sought U.S. annexation. Japan sent the warship *Naniwa* to Honolulu and talked of war, but negotiations ended the threat. One reason for U.S. annexation was to prevent Japanese annexation. In 1907, West Coast race riots and anti-Asian laws "sparked anti-American outcries in Japan" and another crisis. Roosevelt had to mollify Japan through diplomacy.[55]

A Nationalist Paradigm Shaken, Koreans Accept a Christian One

Japan's strength alarmed the United States but emboldened the Japanese to reject Christianity. The opposite occurred in Korea. That nation's political weakness led many Koreans to embrace Christianity as a way to strengthen their nation. Like Japan, Korea was "opened" to Western trade and influence by a U.S. naval officer who signed a treaty with Korea in 1882.[56] Korea could not control its Westernization, however, for it was caught between Japan and China.

In culture and religion, Korea was close to China. Its upper classes adhered to "neo-Confucian orthodoxy." It was a satellite of China before the Qing succumbed to European and, later, Japanese aggression. Its lower classes practiced an animistic religion. The first American missionary, the Methodist Dr. Horace Allen, came in 1884. He used medicine and education to appeal discretely to the elite. Presbyterians brought a different tactic: direct preaching to the lower classes. Different methods worked in tandem to give Koreans a choice, but the gospel was not widely accepted until mid-1890s events shook Koreans' religious paradigms. A new nationalist faith, Tonghak, was discredited by its defeat in an 1894-1895 revolt. Confucianism lost credibility because of Japan's humiliating defeat of Qing China in 1895. Buddhism was "suffering a serious loss of morale" partly due to "allegations of sexual immorality and financial misconduct by monks and nuns at this time."[57]

Missionaries "contrasted the weakness of Korean [neo-Confucian] orthodoxy with the vibrancy of the Western 'Christian' nations," notes historian Kenneth Wells. Fighting back, the Confucian minister of education called Christianity the barbarians' religion. Korean Christians replied in the newspaper *Tongnip Sinmun:* "Western nations flourished because they were not above abiding by a religion that was not their own but had come from the East." Christ was neither European nor Korean, but available to both. Some Korean Confucian scholars converted to Christ. Korean reformers turned to Protestants to help improve education. After the reformers and *Tongnip Sinmun* were repressed by the rulers, the Seoul YMCA and its newspaper led the cause.

Some reformers were inspired by U.S. political and economic ideas, which they did not distinguish clearly from Christianity. Korean Christian leader Yun Ch'iho returned from years of study in the United States with a critique of Confucian tradition that was part American, part Christian. He contrasted American public virtue with Confucian privatism and familism and U.S. capitalism's rapid exchange of goods with Korean hoarding for family security.[58] U.S. influence on Korea was complex, but individuals, not government, took the lead. Confidence in Korea's future was shaken when Japan defeated Korea in 1905. Occupying troops repressed Korean nationalism and tried to make Korea part of Japan. That was one factor causing the Great Revival of 1907-1908. U.S. missions were clearly another.

Premillennial and fundamentalist, Korean Protestantism showed marks of American preaching. Yet the Holy Spirit shaped revival so that it was not political, nationalist or Westernizing but showed "a desperate desire for holiness and renewal." The "indigenisation of Christianity" was God's work in the revival, which "had a particularly Korean flavour about it and, as their own unique experience," showed them that "the faith belonged to their race and nation. No longer could Christianity be described as a Western religion." Revival recurred in 1910 and 1914. In 1895 only 528 Koreans were baptized church members; by 1910 two hundred thousand Koreans (1.5 percent) were Protestants.[59]

Korea had been partly Christianized, not Americanized, and Japan controlled its government, economy and culture. Protestant churches were secret or potential allies of Korean nationalism, not Americanization. Like Puritans in the Bay colony, Koreans looked to Old Testament Israel (not the United States) as their model of an oppressed people surviving. A Korean woman who played Queen Esther in a drama recalled, "When I pleaded with King Ahasuerus to save the Hebrews, the words became a plea for Korea. And the meaning of my lines ... was clearly understood by the audience."[60] The paradigm of the Hermit Kingdom, Confucian and independent, was shattered, but that worked to scatter the seeds of the gospel. They bore fruit. Today about 25 percent of South Korea's population is Christian, and they are sending out missionaries to other nations.

Philippines: Short-term Imperialism Fails, the Gospel Succeeds

The Philippines were different. Catholicism had ruled there since the sixteenth-century Spanish conquest. Its influence "was more pervasive than profound," and "the indigenous tribal structure and its values" endured, but most modern Filipinos can recall "no background of an ancient non-Christian culture." Spanish rule partly Westernized the islands—more in cities and among elites. Plantation capitalists raised sugar cane. Sparking anti-Chinese feelings among Filipinos, many Chinese migrants came and prospered as shopkeepers and merchants, but they had to adapt to Catholicism and Western values. When the United States seized the islands, "the Filipinos were easier to co-opt than other Asians" but not easy to conquer. They lacked a strong national identity (their history "was colonial history"), but they fought hard against U.S. forces.[61] Protestant missionaries came in 1899 with U.S. troops and administrators. That had mixed results for missions. Korea showed missions succeeding with little help from government, the Philippines how they succeeded despite too much "help."

Evangelicalism and imperialism were intertwined during the imperialist window of opportunity. In 1898 an evangelical president, William McKinley, decided to keep the Philippines, newly seized from Spain. Converted at the age of ten, he was a sincere Christian whose care for his "semi-invalid" wife assumed "the character of lifelong martyrdom." In the White House (1897-1901) he "often entertained guests with Sunday evening hymn sings." Agonizing over whether to keep the islands, he understandably turned to his God for guidance. Unfortunately, but also understandably, he stated his imperial vision in Christian terms. And in a sermon at McKinley's church with the president in attendance, Methodist bishop Frank Bristol conflated the nation and Christianity, the United States and Israel: "If God ever had a peculiar people He has them now."[62]

Events soon showed that nations do not turn the other cheek or meekly rule or use troops to teach Sunday school. Evangelicalism and imperialism slowly parted company, though close political ties between evangelicals and the Republican party and between evangelicalism and patriotism meant they never split completely over U.S. policy in the Philippines.

U.S. rule in the Philippines was milder than Japan's rule in Korea—once the Filipino revolt had been crushed. The United States fought a most un-Christian four-year war against guerrillas. Atrocities were committed by both sides, but American ones helped shake McKinley's paradigm of a Christian nation Christianizing others. Once they won, Americans "were uniquely benign, almost sentimental imperialists." Congress kept "American individuals and corporations from acquiring large land holdings in the Philippines." It gave Filipinos "a national legislature, the first in Asia, as early as 1907" and promised them independence in 1916. Americans brought change: land redistribution, public works, legal reforms, education, higher literacy rates and a public health campaign. Education was the showpiece. More than a thousand American teachers came. "Guided by" them, "Filipinos rapidly attained the highest literacy rate in Southeast Asia"—literacy in English, which helped unite a "far-flung archipelago" with numerous indigenous languages.[63]

Patriotic Protestant missionaries sympathized with U.S. troops, though some were critical. Protected by colonial officials, uncertain of their fate if Filipinos won self-rule, they feared Filipino nationalism, which distracted hearers from the gospel. Continuing the tradition of Christians in U.S. politics and U.S.

politicians' wooing of Christians, some of them unwisely opposed a Filipino legislature while Governor (later president) William H. Taft solicited their support.[64]

Colonial rulers did not stay unequally yoked to gospel preachers. Events and attitudes divided them. Missionaries acted as "the conscience of the American experiment." Officials saw them as nuisances. By "sometimes heated, sometimes telling criticisms of the government," they tried "to purify American colonialism," notes historian Kenneth Clymer. They criticized U.S. soldiers' drinking and sexual immorality and the licensing of opium sales and gambling. A Baptist noted, "Our own countrymen need the Gospel quite as much as the natives." A Presbyterian feared that the war's end and the start of economic development would "turn loose upon us a vast horde of the moral scum of America, coming in search of money at any price." They attacked a "sleazy side of American commercial interests" and a "condescending, unsympathetic attitude toward Filipinos." They did not silently coexist with U.S. military, political and economic policies, though they were not fully divorced from other Americans on the islands.

Gradually they showed enough cultural tolerance, support for Filipino aspirations, acquiescence in Filipino control of churches and distance from U.S. colonialism to win "striking" numbers of Filipinos to Christ. By 1925, 105,000 Filipinos were Protestant church members. In the early 1980s about one million traced their religious roots to Protestant missions.[65] The gospel bore fruit despite negative aspects of imperialism.

Missionaries, Historians and Eschatology

Historians' negative portrait of missionaries is a clear reason we cannot leave history to secular specialists but must have a Christian interpretation. Can we expect objective and comprehensive accounts from them when a major event such as global evangelization, in which Americans played a major role, is unreported or distorted? History texts focus on the early, difficult years of missions and are silent on the post-1920s world Christian movement. They use historicism—the belief that historical origins explain (or explain *away)* ideas—to discredit missions by associating them with nineteenth-century European imperialism. Origins are not destiny. National churches in Africa, Asia and Oceania thrive today after having outgrown their European origins. They are prophetic witnesses to Western churches declining in zeal and piety.

Historians fit individual missionaries to the Procrustean bed of an antimissionary paradigm. Take Lysle E. Meyer on Thomas Jefferson Bowen, white Georgian and Baptist missionary to central Africa in the mid-nineteenth century. Like bookends, his introduction and summary give the paradigm: Bowen is "astonishingly ill-prepared," racially prejudiced, resisted by African leaders and unsuccessful. In between, the evidence paints a different picture. Bowen corrected his initial mistake of thinking that the Muslim Fulani would be receptive. He preached to the Yoruba with the support of their leaders and African-Americans. For an antebellum white Southerner, he had surprisingly little racial prejudice toward Africans. Though he left Africa, other Baptists continued his successful mission to the Yoruba. Meyer's facts do not fit his paradigm.[66]

Historians place missionaries in impossible dilemmas. They are often condemned no matter what they do. If they offer practical assistance, they are changing the culture. If they just preach the gospel, they are ignoring human needs. If they teach in English, they are altering the culture. If they teach in the native language, they are denying people the advantage of a command of English. The historian creates an artificial dichotomy between helping people and saving souls. He or she emphasizes missionaries' bickering and gives quotes expressing their dislike of native customs—quotes sure to anger 1990s armchair readers who have never served far from home under primitive living conditions. He or she examines them as part of some other subject and ignores their reason for being.[67]

One 1890s observer noted in India, "It seems, however, to be the correct thing for the ordinary tourist to speak with unutterable contempt of missionaries, and then, to avoid being prejudiced in any way, carefully to refrain from ever going within ten miles of them and their work."[68] Why contempt? Missionaries challenge modern relativism and cultural pluralism. They proclaim a universal truth for all peoples. Having non-Western peoples accept Christ as Lord and become Christian, not Western, seems to shake the modern paradigm of cultural relativism. His universal appeal supports his claim to be Lord and shows the folly of privileging a religious status quo. Rather than this result, moderns prefer a secular idea of progress—history leads to the victory of democratic capitalism. If they cannot believe that, they prefer postmodern disillusionment, skepticism about secular progress, Eastern cyclical reincarnation—anything but relentlessly advancing religious progress.

Christianity has its own idea of progress: the gospel will be preached to more and more peoples, and when all have heard it the Lord's second coming will be at hand (Matthew 24:14; Mark 13:10). Two hundred years of mission history shows *that* progress is on schedule—an alarming idea many prefer not to consider. They comfort themselves with tales of 1840s missionaries woefully ignorant and ineffectual, rather than confront the reality of 1990s global Christianity. Many Americans celebrate secular change—in technology, fashion, ideas, science or recreation. But when faced with God directing change to achieve his goals, they prefer myths of stability. They rebel at *this* Change Agent. They say, "Where is this 'coming' he promised? Ever since our fathers died, everything goes on as it has since the beginning of creation."[69] History's recent acceleration shows that events do not go on as always.

History's Accelerator: Synopsis

Other Americans besides missionaries accelerated history: beachcombers, sex-obsessed novelists on South Sea islands, Bostonians converting to Buddhism, capitalists marketing sewing machines and cigarettes in China and U.S. naval officers "opening" Japan or Korea. They were all used by God to advance the gospel around the Pacific, to shatter American and Asian paradigms, to speed a Westernization that united the globe economically, politically and (almost) culturally by the 1920s. One global market and improved communications and transportation made worldwide evangelization possible, a process culminating in Billy Graham's 1995 Global Mission crusade. Whether abroad for pious or impious ends, Americans were instruments in God's hands.

The spread of the gospel demonstrated that Christian eschatology—the doctrine of last things, of history's end and Christ's reign—was increasingly more plausible than secular views of history's future course. Yet most Americans were slow to recognize that. America became more secular as history became more eschatological, even apocalyptic. In the last three chapters we will examine this growing disjuncture.

10

Getting Real
The U.S. Adjusts to Reality to Fight Totalitarianism

IN THE 1920S MOST AMERICANS HAD not given up hope in secular progress. They hailed advances in fashion, ideas, science, technology and recreation. Hard as they tried to return to normalcy, though, they could not say "everything goes on as it has since the beginning of creation."[1] World War I had been too great a cataclysm, too terrible a surprise, showing that history was not going in the expected direction. If the old goal of unending secular progress was unrealistic, were former means—values, activities, beliefs, norms—also outmoded now? Americans would spend the next forty years adjusting to changed realities wrought by World War I.

This pragmatic response would prove inadequate. It was not based on an eschatology, an understanding of where history was going. World War I showed that it was not going where Americans had thought it was, but they avoided the question of where it *was* headed and merely adjusted to each new twist and turn. This was known as pragmatic realism.

The theologian of political realism, Reinhold Niebuhr, defined *realism* as "the disposition to take all factors in a social and political situation, which offer resistance to established norms, into account, particularly the factors of self-interest and power." He contrasted realism with a naive idealism that did not take realities into account.[2] The war showed that Western nations' thirst for power did "offer resistance to established norms" of nineteenth-century ideal-ism. The deaths of nearly nine million combatants and almost as many civilians showed ideas of Western moral superiority to be folly.

Americans looked back fondly on that nineteenth-century world of ideals as a Golden Age. It wasn't. Yet it seemed an age of fixed principles: the gold standard, European world hegemony led by Britain, Victorian moral values (fraying at the edges), material progress, peace between European nations and, when war came, no attacks on civilians. Specific peoples added specific principles: Britons and Americans—the superiority of Anglo-Saxons and par-liamentary democracies; Americans—"no entangling alliances," no part in Europe's wars and national security on a conquered continent. None of the norms was fully Christian; America's came from republicanism, Enlightenment and Jacksonian males' rifles. All flourished in an age when Darwin, German higher criticism, positivism and Marxism undermined faith. Yet post-Christian societies clung to the norms as secular fundamentals more necessary after they had let gospel fundamentals go. Apostasy may not end but, rather, intensify the need for norms and ideals.

The war undercut these norms and ideals, but, instead of turning to a Christian faith that is realistic about humanity, many Americans turned to a pragmatic realism that is realistic but lacks an eschatology. They tried to live in an apocalyptic age with no doctrine to explain apocalypse. Like Yankee tinkerers, they tried by trial and error to defuse a live bomb.

They first had to adjust the fixed principle of no alliances and no entry into European wars, a norm in U.S. foreign-policy fundamentalism unchanged for 130 years. The 1915-1917 debate over U.S. entry into World War I sounded uncannily like the 1805-1812 debate over the U.S. response to the Napoleonic Wars. Neutrals' rights to sail the seas and to trade with belligerents had been the key issues then too. U.S. entry broke the fixed principles, but it is more surprising how long Americans continued to cling to them.[3]

World War I and the War Mobilization of the American People

Mixing a realism about post-1812 changes with an idealism soaring beyond the Founders', President Wilson took the United States into the Great War. He was too much the "typical son of the manse" to be a pure, hard-headed realist. He mixed the two. He encouraged U.S. bankers to loan to Britain and France in order to boost U.S. exports, then idealistically discouraged the bankers in an effort to force the Allies to negotiate an end to the conflict. After Germany's sinking of the *Lusitania* showed Americans the brutality of twentieth-century total warfare, he first compared the United States to "a man . . . too proud to fight," then recanted that idealism and sought a German apology. When Germany resumed unlimited U-boat warfare, he realized that only the United States could end the carnage but idealized the postwar peace he imagined it could create. His speech asking Congress to declare war admitted that war would be "terrible and disastrous," yet it would make the world "safe for democracy." He would drop the Founders' foreign policy, but only to save the world.[4]

War meant dropping much else: a weak army, an ineffectual government abroad and a political courtroom fragmenting power and quarreling over constitutional minutiae. The United States was woefully unprepared. Its army numbered only about one hundred thousand men, and its citizens disliked a military draft. It lacked a munitions industry like Germany's or Britain's to manufacture tanks or advanced artillery. It lacked ethnic unity. Groups fresh from Europe and loyal to the Old Country might Balkanize the war effort. German-Americans and Irish-Americans opposed it.[5]

This "social and political situation" meant that Wilson had to mobilize the nation for war. The United States was far from the front, fought a shorter war, sent far fewer men into combat and suffered much less than European belligerents. Yet domestic weaknesses meant that its war mobilization was closer to Germany's all-out "war socialism" than those fortunate facts might indicate. This was more of a total mobilization than ever before: Wilson's rhetoric more intensely idealistic, patriots' demand for loyalty more insistent, government propaganda more shrill, Washington bureaucrats' power more pervasive, vigilantes' nighttime raids more vicious. German militarism was seen as something like what might today be called totalitarianism; American socialists' dissent was seen as treason, the Allies' cause as the only hope for humanity.[6]

Mobilization changed realities. "War socialism" was a model later used by the New Deal. A War Industries Board (WIB) led by "Dr. Facts" (Bernard Baruch) and staffed with "dollar-a-year" businessmen set prices and production quotas. Herbert Hoover's Food Administration decreed "Wheatless Mondays, Meatless Tuesdays, and Porkless Thursdays and Saturdays" so that more food could go to troops and Allies. The war was mostly paid for by consumers' cutting their consumption due to inflation, wheatless days and Liberty Loan drives. Uncle Sam did the consuming and ran the railroads too. The Committee on Public Information (CPI) mobilized salesmen, history professors, movie stars and artists to persuade citizens to loan, volunteer, sacrifice and hate Germany and dissenters.[7] The ideal of limited government had to be discarded.

By mutual consent, the political courtroom was largely adjourned for the war. Most Americans agreed that potentially unconstitutional agencies or laws were only temporary and that dissenters who sought shelter in the Bill of Rights were only traitors. There was no "states' rights" dissent, and both parties favored the war. Narrow legalism was suspended. Women's suffrage and prohibition were put in the Constitution.[8]

Adjournment meant less gridlock but more threats to civil liberties and public order, which lasted into the 1920s. In 1915, an Atlanta salesman revived the Reconstruction-era Ku Klux Klan (KKK) as a fraternal lodge, but its wartime role in chasing draft dodgers and marching in parades gave it a taste for more thrilling, clandestine, coercive rituals. Anarchists retaliated for wartime repression with postwar bombings, which in turn helped produce a Red Scare and more repression. Wartime suspicion of Germans was extended to other groups. Wartime 100 percent Americanism was an old stock, patriotic Protestant norm to which others were expected to conform.[9]

Abroad, Wilson headed for the Paris Peace Conference armed with idealism and a study of international realities made by his "Dr. Facts" experts, "The Inquiry." Editor William Allen White described them as a "desperate group of college professors in horn-rim glasses" loaded with books and charts "and all sorts of literary crowbars with which to pry up the boundaries of Europe" to suit Wilson's idealism. Awaiting him, writes a French historian, were Allies who saw his idealism "as naiveté."

Paris greeted him as a near messiah. Children threw flowers at his feet in England. Yet his hope for a just peace foundered on postwar hostilities and Great Power self-interest. Partly, he failed to use U.S. financial clout and his Allies' need for loans to extract concessions. Partly, his eschatology was skewed: a U.S. president was not going to bring the history of war to an end. He could not shape the future to his facts. Partly, wrote Niebuhr, he was a "typical son of the manse" who believed "too much in words." His League of Nations became little more than words.[10]

The Senate rejected the words. The political courtroom was back in session. Senators argued over the treaty's fine print as Anti-Federalists did over the

Constitution's. Some feared that the treaty was unconstitutional, others that it would give Wilson a third term. Republican leader Henry Cabot Lodge hated Wilson. As *The Federalist* predicted, ambition counteracted ambition; one branch checked another. A treaty supporter complained about "the spectacle . . . of a branch of the Congress of the United States—the Senate—being in apparent hostility to executive head of this Government."[11]

By his rhetoric, Wilson had so linked Progressivism to the war effort and his subsequent treaty that the treaty's defeat brought disillusionment with the war and the Progressives who ran it. The failure of Wilson's ends was seen as proof that his means, his moralistic internationalism, were unrealistic. Overreaching idealism bred cynicism.[12] Idealism needed realistic goals; it needed Christianity's realism about humanity and sure sense of history's direction if its morals were to survive.

World War I Leads to the Rise of Totalitarianism in Europe

Cynicism and amorality grew rapidly in postwar Europe. Americans who had battled German militarism found that war bred worse systems. In the war's ashes, many Europeans ditched Victorian liberals' idea that history progressed toward their ideals. In defeated Russia and Germany and in disillusioned Italy, so-called totalitarian movements offered new visions of history that could motivate poor, devastated peoples to catch up with the victorious West (United States, Britain and France). Marxism saw "history as an economic struggle of classes." Anti-Marxist, German Nazism and Italian fascism saw "history as a natural fight of races." These and Soviet Russia rejected Christian and enlightened views of history. All had new fundamental principles to replace those lost in 1914-1918. All rejected liberal restraints on state power, outlawed other parties, suppressed human rights, used violence freely and mobilized their peoples like the KKK, CPI and WIB rolled into one. Realists, they used any means to reach their ends.[13]

Distorting the Enlightenment with their pseudoscientific theories of economics or race, Marxists and fascists benefited from the failure of the Enlightenment's overreaching idealism. By weakening the belief that human equality and freedom are grounded in God's creative act, by grounding them in nature and natural law instead, the Enlightenment paved the way for cynical realism that pointed to actual inequality and formed pseudoscientific theories to explain it. By weakening confidence in Christian eschatology, it paved the way for Marxist utopianism and the Nazi Thousand-Year Reich. World War I was the cataclysm that exposed the Enlightenment's folly.

Europe's cultured elite felt that it exposed the folly of bourgeois morality, with its "fake security, fake culture, and fake life." They celebrated, recalled Hannah Arendt, as the mob and its leaders destroyed respectability. "History, which was a forgery anyway, might as well be the playground of crackpots." Why not "admit cruelty, disregard of human values, and general amorality, because this at least destroyed the duplicity," the contrast between ideal and real "upon which the existing society seemed to rest"? Instead of a "fake" morality that made virtue a means to middle-class status, they admired totalitarians willing to sacrifice their lives for the cause. Here was a hard-edged virtue, not a "fake security."[14]

Having escaped war damage and defeat, Americans were less disillusioned or cynical. Yet their confidence in democracy's triumph was shaken. Was history going Marxists' or fascists' way? "War socialism" indicated that it might be. Marxism was most alarming. Like Asians moving east to challenge Americans' westward paradigm, Marxists claiming that *theirs* was the world's model society challenged Americans' paradigm that their capitalist democracy was the model. "Lenin's ideological arrow had hit the heart of their universalist aspirations, implanting a permanent sense of insecurity."

Russia's Marxists formed the Communist International (Comintern) in March 1919 "to fight by all available means, including armed struggle," to depose the world's property-owning class and to set up "an international Soviet republic as a transitional stage to the complete abolition of the State." For more than twenty years, a strong Japan and Great Britain and a rising Germany separated the United States from the Soviet Union and kept their universalist aspirations from directly colliding. A 1920s temporary withdrawal of the United States from global duties also delayed the danger of collision.[15]

Still, Americans feared the U.S. Communist Party. In the Red Scare of 1919-1920 their fear led them to exaggerate its strength, to confuse it with anarchist and syndicalist groups and to ignore its tendency toward fatal sectarianism. Though they had abandoned Christianity, U.S. communists kept the imprint of Western, quasi-Christian thought patterns. They had not become communal, Pueblo-like revolutionaries consumed by unity and selflessness. They divided into factions, accused each other of heresy, argued over doctrine, hated the group *closest* to them in ideas, divided history into dispensations and looked forward to the stateless millennium.[16] They kept the idea of eschatology as they greatly changed its contents. Anarchist bombings in 1919 and communist cell groups raised the question of how an open, democratic society could combat terrorism and totalitarianism.

The Land of Desire Everywhere Threatens Victorian Values

There were other domestic enemies besides communists. The 1920s saw renewed anxiety over immorality. Some Americans linked the two threats by equating Bolshevism with "free love." Americans tried to revive old fundamental principles: the gold standard, limited government, isolationism, Anglo-Saxon supremacy and Victorian morality. Temporarily if partially reviving the first three, they failed to renew the last two.

New technologies and techniques worked against them. The Land of Desire created by Wanamaker and others had been confined to downtown—to department stores, specialty shops and theaters inaccessible to many Americans. Now the Model T, movie theater, radio, chain store, telephone and Rural Free Delivery brought it to remote hamlets. A rural pastor had to worry that his people might be seduced. New delivery systems made consumerism powerful, ubiquitous, threatening. Feminism loosened the moral role of women and their resistance to new products. Immoral behavior emerged from Greenwich Village, Chicago and Harlem into the mainstream. A flapper made a prostitute unnecessary, though one might be found at the local roadhouse. Immigrant culture was a pawn in an attack on old Anglo-Saxon morality. Capitalism discredited tradition to sell new goods. Youth used new goods to shape "a new lifestyle" hostile to "the pious idealism of the Wilsonian era." Using realism to ridicule this pious idealism was a multiplying class of intellectuals whose revolt against Victorianism achieved critical mass in the 1920s.[17]

It all came together in the film industry. When movies arrived, Europeans had already rejected Victorian morality, but Americans had not. Movies helped them do so. Popular with immigrants, the first films shown in nickelodeons were often foreign-made films that "ridiculed Victorian values." That was a limited market. To break into the large middle-class, old stock American market, filmmakers and theater owners accepted censorship to get "a seal of approval." Old stock filmmaker D. W. Griffith achieved great, temporary popularity with films favoring Victorian values. Like anticapitalist reformers strengthening capitalism, antivice reformers such as Griffith strengthened the film industry so that it could convert Americans to a newer model of morality more in line with consumerism.[18]

That was done gradually. Films evolved from (1) those whose characters overcame temptation to (2) those whose comic characters did not to (3) those which got the audience laughing "at the Victorian standards themselves." The "subversive ideals first came into view . . . in comedies," where they could be laughed off. The "star" helped: people accepted new ideas from a familiar personality whom they liked. Mary Pickford and Douglas Fairbanks were the main stars whose films showed audiences that through youthful play they could have more fun and buy more goods than their ancestors, yet retain the discipline and respectability needed to maintain job and family.

This "morality" served self-interest, not Christ. One needed just enough of it to avoid being a "fallen" woman or unemployed man, but not so much that one stopped having fun. The man confined his pleasure to his leisure time so that he would earn enough at work to buy consumer goods for his ideal woman. The single woman might fall for sex, but she then married and limited her fun to home and husband—and consumer goods.[19]

Other factors made films powerful persuaders. Cars brought Americans to thousands of movie theaters where a darkened room and dreamlike environment created "a passive but receptive imagination." Theaters were opulent palaces symbolizing the Land of Desire—pagan temples such as New York's Roxy, which opened in 1926 to "pealing chimes" and "a man dressed like a monk" blasphemously shouting "Let there be light!" A *New Yorker* cartoon showed a small girl asking (of the Roxy), "Does God live here?" In the 1920s more people went to the movies than to church on Sunday in Muncie, Indiana, according to Robert and Helen Lynd's famous study. By going to Hollywood, they could see stars prove the reality of the dream life in a Southern California that made a visual break with the Anglo-Saxon, Victorian past.[20] Dreams were realities in Hollywood.

Movies advanced consumerism. As an "essentially passive consumer," an American woman imitated celebrities more than the European upper classes and bought goods "for personal gratification" more than increased social status. Her ideal kitchen "combined the attributes of a sitting room, a boudoir, and a laboratory." American couples had more goods to buy: refrigerators, cars on the installment plan, radios and electric appliances. Their buying helped fuel the 1920s boom that caused many to see depression as a thing of the past.[21]

Consumerism triumphed. Capitalists who sold the idea of history as progress to ever greater consumption were rewarded when that seemed to be a reality. Their capital multiplied: from 1923 to 1929 corporate profits increased 62 percent, dividends 65 percent; from 1925 to 1929 the value of stocks traded on the New York Stock Exchange tripled. Capitalism's hothouse competition led to a "race to erect the loftiest skyscraper." New industries emerged. New car sales stimulated highway construction and sales of suburban homes. Americans praised the businessmen and reelected the Republicans who brought material progress.[22]

Four Groups Try to Oppose or Limit Capitalist Consumerism

But Marxists and many intellectuals abhorred businessmen's reign—not because of immorality (they dropped cultural issues in disgust after wartime witch-hunting) but for ideological reasons. Its membership falling from fifteen thousand in 1923 to ninety-three hundred in 1929, the Communist Party was so small that it gained only a few moral victories such as the one in Gastonia, North Carolina (1929), which cost-cutting, labor-exploiting textile mill owners handed to it.

Tired of soft, self-seeking, security-first consumerism, intellectuals admired tough, self-sacrificing communists who braved violence to help strikers or blacks. They found heroes in the strikers and blacks, victims of the WASP mentality they hated. Children of Progressives, or disillusioned Progressives themselves, they sought something with a harder edge than John Dewey's faith in democracy or Methodist ministers' hope in the Social Gospel.[23]

This first group had no clear theory of where history was headed and were too few to direct its course anyway. They were swayed by appearances, by a plausible victim story: Nicola Sacco and Bartolomeo Vanzetti, two Italian-American anarchists found guilty at a biased trial of committing murder during a holdup. Intellectuals protested the scheduled execution. Anglo-Saxon bigots and antiradical zealots in the old Puritan town of Dedham, Massachusetts, had condemned two foreigners. Here was a chance to blast the WASP mentality. After the execution, Malcolm Cowley wrote a poem—"March on, oh dago Christs." Christs they weren't—though they may have been innocent of the holdup charges. They weren't "innocent dreamers," writes historian Paul Avrich, but bomb-throwing Galleanist anarchists "almost certainly" involved in the 1919 bombings. An anarchist comrade probably planted a bomb that killed thirty-three people on Wall Street in September 1919 to retaliate for their arrest.[24]

A rule of opposites is no way to assess character. Sacco and Vanzetti were the opposites of Judge Webster Thayer, "a cadaverous old Yankee with a hearty dislike of radicals."[25] Being his antitheses did not make them innocent. Nor did polarizing trials develop a true theory to fight consumerism.

Writing a year before the execution, Lewis Mumford, representing a second group, praised antebellum Yankeedom as a "thriving regional culture." He and other regionalists found their fundamental principles in American folk culture. Here was a reality to use against false genteel culture and Hollywood's homogenizing, make-believe mass culture. Here, in the reality of place, the American folk and regionalists could stand against capitalism's abstracting logic that denied the uniqueness of places. Regionalism's strength was in diversity. It was a sort of geographical New Age movement: each region—New England, the rural (white) South, the Native American Southwest—had its own truth as true as any other. Together they stood against New York, urban life, highbrow culture and the Sears, Roebuck catalog that tried to define one national culture. Regionalists tried to make "regionalism into a democratic civic religion, a utopian ideology, and a radical politics."[26]

Yet a few artists and writers, a few handicrafters and musicians, could not restrain capitalism's dynamism. As it transcended limits, "places lost their particularity and became abstractions on organizational charts." Regionalists offered cultural sectionalism, but few politicians or investors signed up—not surprisingly, given the failure of political sectionalism. Regionalists missed the broader history: Western civilization as "cultural hothouse."[27] They could not slow history's accelerating pace. They could not convince regional folk to refuse Sears goods, pay higher prices for local ones instead and drop out of the national consumer market. Religiously motivated Puritan colonizers of Dedham might have made those sacrifices, but regionalists had no motive to offer as strong as the religious one.[28] Neither could they offer a future millennium, for they did not know where history was headed.

Liberal Protestants, the third group, opposed aspects of capitalist consumerism and had religious motives. Believers in the Social Gospel of Walter Rauschenbusch and Washington Gladden, they fought the "fundamental heresy of the industrial world"—that capitalism has its laws apart from Christianity. In 1919 they were at their strongest and most optimistic. Wartime mobilization and Prohibition showed the possibilities of social reform. Mainline denominations were at peak strength, and their leaders saw "the social spectrum not as capital-bourgeois-labor, or as upper-middle-lower, but as capital-church-labor." Their Federal Council of Churches' report on industrial capitalism anticipated many New Deal reforms.[29]

They were strong yet weak. They recruited few workers to their churches. Their membership lists were misleading. The modernist-fundamentalist controversy of the 1920s meant that many members did not support liberal ministers or denominational committees. They personalized issues: "unconverted" capitalist Elbert Gary faced off against "converted" John D. Rockefeller Jr. in their view. Their critique of industrial capitalism as "proud, self-conscious, selfish" was eighty years too late. Males had shaped it already. Huge investments had been made in the belief that it would not change no matter what ministers said. Many mainline members succumbed to consumerism: their Social Gospel ministers' "discipline and denial" could not compete with Pickford and Fairbanks for their loyalty. "Protestantism had never been more profoundly out of touch with the cultural vanguards" than in the Jazz Age, notes Donald Meyer.[30]

In 1927 realist Reinhold Niebuhr attacked this liberal Protestantism as "a religious optimism which is true to the facts of neither the world of nature nor the world of history." More to the point, it had no fundamentals on which to stand and endure these facts. It had abandoned Christian fundamentals: Christ's divinity, his atoning death, his resurrection, his return. It disbelieved their literal truth but used them as symbols of love's suffering and triumph. In it, "the content of salvation tended to become the values of social life."

Lacking transcendent truth, it offered only "discipline and denial" and symbols to counter consumerism's attractive new values. Without a clear vision of where history was headed, religious liberals could be either Pollyannas or Niebuhrian realists—fatuous optimists or camp-followers of whatever facts were victorious. Niebuhr's realism was just religious liberalism with a harder edge but with no clearer eschatology. A kind of "Dr. Facts," he went from Wilsonian idealism to mild socialism to near revolutionary Marxism to Cold War anticommunism.[31] Realism could mean that facts shaped you.

Liberal Protestants fanned out in all directions. Bruce Barton used their vagueness about Jesus of Nazareth to redesign Jesus for capitalist consumerism. In *The Man Nobody Knows* Jesus became "a prototype of the hardworking American executive." An ad executive, Barton showed how liberal Protestants' Jesus "began to look more and more like" them. Their social message(s) produced their view(s) of Jesus, not the other way around. Methodist Harry Ward drifted into proto-New Age talk and pro-Bolshevism. Dewey called for a natural religion of pure idealism. Rebelling against his father's Methodist orthodoxy, William Dudley Pelley went through Wilsonian and Social Gospel stages, joined Hollywood as a screenwriter and went into a trance that converted him to spiritualism. Later he drew on fascist anti-Semitism to attack Hollywood immorality![32]

Fundamentalists, the fourth group, were not amorphous or vague in their view of Jesus Christ and history, but they often failed to see the threat capitalist consumerism posed. Some did. Arno C. Gaebelein warned that Barton's distorted view of Jesus struck "at the very heart of Christianity." In *The Signs of the Times* (1910), Isaac Haldeman had warned, "Commerce is becoming a universal kingdom, a sign that the Coming of the Lord draweth nigh." Fundamentalism too had its strengths going into the 1920s. World War I confirmed its premillennial pessimism, the Balfour Declaration its belief that a Jewish nation would regain Palestine. "The Reverend A. B. Simpson . . . wept as he read the Balfour Declaration to his congregation." It had a clear idea where history was headed—an idea that seemed increasingly true to the facts.[33]

Yet it had little idea where American history had been or what anti-Christian strains had filled that history. It could hardly tell its Americanism from its Christianity. Confronted with disturbing trends—consumerism, liberal theology, movies, Bolshevism, urbanization, feminism, violations of Prohibition—it could hardly distinguish mere threats to American tradition from serious threats to the gospel.

Even in its exposition of biblical prophecy, it sometimes made the God-centered Word a human-centered tool by demanding that God fulfill literal prophecies in the way and at the time that suited fundamentalists' interests. Or it insisted that humanity's inevitable decline not touch too close to home. It sometimes seemed to rejoice in others' declension instead of weeping over them. But we must not accuse a whole group of inconsistency, for many individuals were consistent. Hindsight is easy. In the 1920s fundamentalists felt on the defensive, more out of touch with the cultural vanguards than liberal Protestants. Defensiveness led to bitterness, extremism and un-Christian behavior. Yet they did the essential task—they saved a literal gospel for contemporaries and the future.

However, some of them allied with the KKK to save Anglo-Saxon supremacy and Victorian morality—to fight a decline touching too close to home. The Klan recruited ministers by giving them free memberships and lecturing fees. Ministers allowed Klansmen to march into church in full regalia, to give talks and to march out singing "Onward, Christian Soldiers." The Klan sold itself as the defender of morality, protector of women, enforcer of Prohibition and enemy of radicalism and modernism. "The Klan organizer was told to find out what was worrying a community and to offer the Klan as a solution."

To the minister, the male KKK (with women's auxiliary) seemed a solution to a century-old worry: how to get the rebellious American male into church and on the right side in revival's battle against rebellion. The KKK seemed "the only hope of bringing Christians back into the fold"—male ones, that is. A minister's masculinity was affirmed when KKK males affirmed the church's importance by marching into it en masse.[34]

In the mid-1920s the KKK was "an important force in local and national politics." It persecuted old stock "black sheep" more than blacks, Catholics or Jews: battling bootleggers, flogging adulterers, chastising young girls and boys "caught riding together in cars" and raiding roadhouses. Yet this self-proclaimed friend to Americanism and morality was no true friend to Christianity. In it male rebellion was thinly disguised by a hypocritical moralistic vigilantism. The Klan was fraternal lodge, sales gimmick, slush fund, lynch mob and stag party rolled into one. Many Klansmen privately violated the morals they publicly defended. The Indiana Klan leader's home was "one of the bastions of high life in the state." His Military Machine, police force and "block-by-block" spy network would have made any totalitarian regime proud.

"The godly came more and more to realize that the Klan was not" godly.[35] By using the Klan to enforce morality, the godly seemed to be tempering their idealism with 1920s realism. But an idealistic cause was hurt most by crude, "realistic" means. Christianity could not be advanced by that kind of realism.[36]

None of the four groups made headway against capitalist consumerism. Prosperity and property ownership made Marxism unattractive. With no real Marxist threat, property owners had no reason to empower a fascist Klan to crush Reds. The Klan lacked a credible national leader and was too spoils-minded and undisciplined. Regionalists could not undo a national market that railroads and telegraph had created. Liberals and fundamentalists did not blame capitalist consumerism as such—only its immoral products. Their battle with each other weakened each one's limited critique. Americans were satisfied with symbolic traditionalism: Henry Ford's "homespun ways," Lindbergh's shy modesty, Coolidge's "parsimony, restraint, and laconic behavior." Capitalists and traditionalists stayed in one party, the GOP. Americans, wrote Walter Lippmann, wanted "a Puritanism deluxe . . . to praise the classic virtues, while continuing to enjoy all the modern conveniences."[37]

Capitalist Fundamentalism Leads to Capitalist Apocalypse

Americans were generally satisfied with their pragmatic 1920s adjustments to postwar realities, but the 1920s policies could not succeed. They did not fully adjust to reality, and they held on to too many outdated fundamental principles: limited government, balanced budgets, laissez-faire, the gold standard. Twenties capitalism enriched investors, not consumers. Capital multiplied, but workers' buying power rose slowly. That undercut an economy now reliant on consumer spending. There was an air of unreality about the twenties' economy.

Encouraged by advertisers, consumers looked beyond a product's function and bought it for the "status, power, sex appeal, peace of mind" the ads linked it to. Investors looked beyond a stock share's functional worth—based on the firm's earnings—and bought it expecting its value to soar and never fall. Speculation was nothing new. Yet land speculation was based on *some* future owner's actual use of land. Values rose because more lucrative, intensive uses were anticipated. In the 1920s stocks became "commodities valued for their own sake, with seemingly little relation to the companies that issued them."

From January 1 to October 1, 1929, total share values on the New York Stock Exchange soared from $67 to $87 billion. Firms loaned money to speculators rather than build more plants. A corporation "could make less money by using its surplus funds in production than it could by lending the money to purchasers of stocks, the value of which was supposed to be determined by the profit on that production." That didn't make sense in commonsense terms.[38] But it made sense in the "logic of capital," where limitless accumulation and multiplication of capital were the rule. If capitalists had to make actual goods to do that, fine. If they could multiply capital without making anything—by cashing in on other people's expectations of economic growth—nothing in capitalism's logic stopped them. It encouraged them.

The main disconnection from reality came when faith in capitalists led to acceptance of their fundamental principle—a return to the gold standard, suspended during World War I. Capitalists' fundamentalism centered on the gold standard, which involved several assumptions: "a free flow of gold" between nations; the value of national currencies fixed in terms of gold; no international body to regulate flows or values; no penalty for nations accumulating gold; a penalty (devaluation or deflation) for one's losing gold. Here was an Invisible Hand regulating the world economy through gold flows. Here was real value, an honest dollar and full repayment of debts. Capitalism accepted immorality or dishonesty in goods, movies, deals or labor relations, but not in money. Prices were its language. Here dishonesty meant gibberish, a Babel-like dispersal of national economies.[39]

During the 1920s, nations slowly returned to the gold standard, but financial policymakers failed to see the extent of postwar change. London was no longer the world's financial center, adjusting gold flows and currency rates; New York was the new center, but the United States refused to assume the duties of global leadership. It maximized its exports, set tariffs high to cut imports and insisted that Europeans repay war debts, but (by tariffs) it denied them dollars with which to do so. The gold standard norm no longer fit reality. Humpty Dumpty, the Victorian gold standard, could not be put back together.

This capitalist fundamentalism came falling down in the Stock Market Crash of October 1929. It "reduced private wealth by about 10 percent." Consumer spending plummeted in 1930. President Hoover stuck to the orthodoxy of a balanced budget, the Federal Reserve to that of the gold standard. Both policies helped make a recession into a depression. Instead of lowering interest rates to boost the economy, the Fed raised rates in September 1931 to keep the United States on the gold standard, a fundamentalist step out of touch with reality. Depression dealt a fatal blow to the Versailles world order too, as the international economic cooperation needed to sustain it sank beneath a tide of economic nationalism.[40]

The Great Depression was a cataclysm which ought to have convinced pragmatic Americans that they were woefully ignorant of where history was headed, but they kept on tinkering. It did not shake our first group, Marxists and intellectuals. They hailed it as proof that capitalism was finished. Writer Edmund Wilson recalled, "One couldn't help being exhilarated at this sudden, unexpected collapse of that stupid gigantic fraud." It gave "writers and artists . . . a new sense of power to find ourselves still carrying on, while the bankers, for a change, were taking a beating."[41]

Ordinary Americans were shaken. More than thirty years had passed since the last depression. Many Americans believed that the problem of business cycles had been solved. October 1929 shook their paradigm of unending progress, just as August 1914 had. Yet they turned to further pragmatic tinkering. They rejected capitalist fundamentalism with its gold-standard certainties and Marxism with its secular eschatology. They struck out on an unknown path; their leaders disclaimed any knowledge of where history was headed. They would find out as they went.

New Deal Pragmatism Replaces 1920s Faith in Fixed Laws
The bank failures and the devastated economy led people to demand change even if it meant ditching old orthodoxies. Franklin D. Roosevelt obliged them.

After breaking one norm by flying to Chicago to accept the Democratic nomination, he promised, "We will break foolish traditions." Once sworn in on March 4, 1933, he kept his word. Prohibition was ended. The United States went off the gold standard. An "alphabet soup" of new federal agencies broke the traditions of a limited federal government, a balanced budget and laissez-faire. The U.S. government administered relief, planned giant public works projects, set wages and hours of employment, tried to set farm prices and became the nation's largest employer. It recognized the Soviet Union.[42]

FDR was a pragmatist experimenting to see what would work. He refused to make his advisers' ideas into new orthodoxies. He adjusted slowly: the First New Deal (1933-1934), then a Second (1935-1936) and then the Third (1937-1938).[43] Experimenters are carried along by events.

Pragmatic realists saw that America had to adjust to realities if democratic values were to survive. Anglo-Saxon moral rule through Prohibition had to be discarded: massive immigration and numerous ethnic groups made it impossible. Individual workers and consumers did not bargain as equals with corporate employers, retailers and manufacturers. The government could not let markets determine how many consumers would be employed now that the economy depended on consumer spending. Jeffersonian limited government did not fit with firms that were nearly unlimited in size. *A Visible Hand had to run things*. The Enlightenment search for natural laws had failed. A watchmaker *government* would have to tinker, repair and monitor the mechanism.

Pragmatism was the New Deal's norm. It was "America's one original contribution to the world of philosophy," according to historian John P. Diggins. It broke "the deductive chains of nineteenth-century conservative ideology" and replaced fundamental rules with experimentation. John Dewey was its main advocate. He denied absolute truth or preexisting values: "values evolved naturally out of the processes of action." He held to "a morality of consequences": means would be judged by their consequences, not by "traditional moral authority."[44] FDR was Dewey's disciple—if unknowingly.

Four 1920s Groups' Reactions to New Deal Domestic Realism

Marxists and intellectuals wavered, depending on where they thought history was headed and how fast. In 1933 capitalism seemed to be collapsing, so FDR was a reactionary for trying to save it. As the Nazis gained power in Germany, the Comintern switched to an Anti-Fascist Popular Front and welcomed New Dealers into it. In 1937-1941 history's goal meant the Soviet Union's survival.

New Dealers who helped the Soviet Union were supported. Some liberal intellectuals supported the New Deal from the start. Its focus on economic tinkering fit their postwar move from irrational cultural and moral issues to rational economic ones. Events caused these pragmatists to take wild swings from one "rational" issue to another.[45]

Some liberal Protestants, such as Niebuhr, attacked New Deal inadequacies and talked of violent class struggle. But most welcomed the New Deal as a needed reform of capitalism. FDR was an Episcopalian whose humanitarian politics were shaped by the Social Gospel. The mainline *Christian Century* supported him in 1932. A key adviser, Adolf A. Berle Jr., "the son of a Congregationalist minister," was intent on putting "some of the teachings of the Social Gospel into practice."[46] Yet the Social Gospel was secularized. New Dealers used ideas because they were realistic, not because they were religious. The New Deal was a triumph for the Social more than the Gospel.

It seemed a triumph for the Regional too. The Depression slowed the homogenizing advance of national urban consumerism. Some people moved back to the land. Shaken Americans searched their history for roots that would hold. New Dealers had an "apparent commonality of interests with the regionalist movement": regional planning, a new Native American policy, cultural preservation by the WPA's "federal writers, arts, and theater projects" and the National Folk Festival. Depression led regionalists to view the folk more realistically. They rewrote U.S. history to critique westward expansion and the treatment of blacks and Indians. But their hoped-for rural renaissance failed to occur. After Pearl Harbor, regionalism "was largely wiped out by the *nationalizing* requirements of wartime." Americans turned to internationalism, not regionalism, which was "a ghost dance which attracted few converts."[47]

To fundamentalists, the New Deal did not even seem their triumph. Reacting to FDR's realism in hiring Jewish advisers, dropping orthodoxies and recognizing the Soviet Union, some, such as Kansas minister Gerald Winrod, took a sharp turn rightward to anti-Semitism and neofascism. Winrod was an exception, a young prodigy whose career advanced faster than his judgment. Many fundamentalists voted for FDR at first. Yet as the New Deal polarized the United States into liberal and conservative parties, there could be little doubt which side they would support. The liberal camp included too many of their opponents: Social Gospelers, urban Catholics, secular and Jewish intellectuals.[48]

While debating the New Deal, Americans were reading about Europe's totalitarian regimes and trying to decide if the New Deal was neofascist or neocommunist. Totalitarianism might come to the United States, and if Americans were to stop it they had to spot its advance agents. In 1935 there was little sign that totalitarian regimes were totally evil. Perhaps they would prove appealing to Americans if liberals did not watch out. Who knew how history would turn out?

Red scares and Red hopes were nothing new. Since 1917, Americans had studied the Soviet Union. Liberals could not take too negative a view of the Soviet Experiment lest opponents use it to argue against an American Experiment. Conservatives had argued "that collectivism must fail," so they had to find Russian failure lest liberals be encouraged.

Liberals scanned America for potential fascists. Some saw fascism as "a revolt by frightened members of the middle classes"—perhaps fundamentalists, Elks, the American Legion or the Catholic Church. Sinclair Lewis saw it in the small-town narrow-mindedness he had criticized in *Main Street*. With both extremes under attack, the safe place to be was in the center. The "militant centrism that would dominate the 1950s already existed in embryo" by 1939, observes historian Leo Ribuffo.[49]

Foreign Policy Realism: The Fight Against Totalitarians Abroad

Isolationism was one backward-looking orthodoxy that temporarily survived New Deal realism to become part of "militant centrism." FDR had to repudiate his Wilsonian internationalism when he ran for president in 1932. A militant isolationism was written into law in the 1930s. Seeing U.S. entry into World War I as a mistake, Congress passed and FDR signed three Neutrality Acts that barred U.S. arms exports, loans and travel to warring nations.[50]

Pragmatist Dewey's strong support for isolationism revealed a weakness in pragmatism. When studying realities and experimenting did not produce rules to guide decision-making, he turned to history for absolutes. Pointing to 1917, he formed a foreign-policy morality of historical analogy which proved misplaced. A look forward through Christian eschatology might give guidance, but not a look backward. Hitler was not the Kaiser. German, Italian and Japanese aggression showed that World War I had been only the first stage in a modern Thirty Years' War. The Allies' 1918 victory and 1919 treaty would not go uncontested.[51] U.S. soldiers made the victory and Wilson shaped the treaty, so how could the United States escape the coming rematch? Pragmatists like to believe that something can be done to influence events, but fascist politics was preparation for and glorification of war, and no finely tuned American or British policies could have changed that fact or averted a rematch.[52]

Also looking back, French and British leaders saw Nazis as German nationalists only correcting problems in the treaty. Privately Roosevelt thought their appeasement of Hitler at Munich disastrous, but publicly he did nothing. FDR was "tied down by isolationist chains that he had helped to forge." He had to break them before he was free to act. Events forced the pragmatic experimenter to reverse course again.[53]

Pearl Harbor circumvented isolationists' preventive measures. They had legislated to keep the United States out of another war like World War I, but their laws could not keep it from responding to an attack. They had guarded the European door to war, but war came via the Pacific. U.S. expansion into the Pacific finally came into conflict with Japan's Pacific imperialism.

War was a new reality that adjusted thinking on domestic issues too. Military spending and unbalanced budgets brought the nation out of the Depression. Prosperity and businessmen's service in wartime government agencies improved capitalism's tarnished image. That further changed a New Deal which had begun with attacks on capitalists as "economic royalists." Now New Dealers followed realities around till they were advocating a New Era consumerism, which they had attacked in 1933. New Deal economist Alvin Hansen asserted, "Consumption is the frontier of the future." Mass consumption had been a means; now it became the end. Rather than advocate federal spending to do needed projects, FDR now advocated it "to promote mass consumption." Like prior anticapitalist reformers, New Dealers too ended up strengthening capitalism.[54]

Shocks of 1945: Pragmatists Stumble into an Apocalyptic Age

World War II also led pragmatic Americans on a zigzag course toward foreign-policy views they hated in 1939. During the war they reconverted to idealistic Wilsonian internationalism by reading Wendell Willkie's *One World* and supporting Cordell Hull's campaign for a postwar international organization like the League. Popular enthusiasm caused a skeptical FDR to endorse this pacific, idealistic internationalism. This was not realists' internationalism of alliances, spheres of interest and U.S. troops overseas protecting the balance of power. Idealistic Americans had *not* converted to that notion.[55]

They were shocked by 1945. On both European and Pacific fronts, the joy of victory was tempered with anguish. The liberation of Nazi concentration camps confirmed Hitler's genocide of Europe's Jews. American audiences reacted "with an appalled solemnity" in April-May 1945 to film footage of the death camps. Here was total evil. Yet their Army Air Force by February 1945 was pragmatically dropping the principle of not bombing civilians. Conventional bombing of Berlin, Dresden and Tokyo preceded the devastation caused by atomic bombs dropped on Hiroshima and Nagasaki, which showed total war and the total weapon.[56] Americans reached out for victory only to touch apocalypse. The year 1914 had brought them a near-apocalyptic conflict, but the end of the modern Thirty Years' War did not end that danger. The Bomb only made the danger more realistic.

How could pragmatic realists account for these realities? Total evil and the total weapon were factors which did more than "offer resistance to established norms." They threatened apocalypse. They made historical analogies nearly useless as future guides. How could realists calmly consider "factors of self-interest and power"? Didn't atomic bombs make some realities final ones? Didn't the Holocaust prove that *realpolitik* would not limit itself to a few murders or a few conquests? Would these factors combine to destroy humanity? Pragmatic realists lacked an eschatology to assure them that apocalypse would not occur. They were catapulted into an apocalyptic age after they had lost their Protestant ancestors' eschatology.

The other shock was the end of the wartime alliance between the United States, the Soviet Union and Britain. Fascists, Nazis and Japanese militarists separating American from Russian universalism were now removed. Two universalisms stood face-to-face and did not like what they saw in each other. By fall 1945, Soviet actions in Eastern Europe and at the United Nations had alienated many Americans. A House committee was "appalled by the police state atmosphere they found in the USSR." On February 9, 1946, Stalin warned that "contradictions" in capitalism would continue to produce wars. On February 22, George Kennan's famous Long Telegram from Moscow warned against an idealistic "one worldism" and urged a realistic assessment of Soviet expansionism. On March 5, Winston Churchill gave his "Iron Curtain" speech.[57]

Americans did not want a Cold War right after wartime sacrifices. They "wanted to enjoy the fruits of victory, but events would not let them." They "still longed for isolation from the vicissitudes of European politics." In 1943-1944, they had signed on to a "talking" internationalism, not to U.S. troops stationed in Europe, A-bomb threats and perpetual tension. Britain played a key role in nudging the United States toward a long-term role in setting up a new European balance of power and containing Soviet expansionism. British and U.S. officials learned that if they used the United Nations as a forum for opposing the Soviets, Americans were oddly reassured and more willing to back them. The British saw that U.S. leaders could "practice *realpolitik* only within the context of an international collective security organization." That reassured Americans who recalled the idealistic hopes of 1943-1944.[58]

Chasing One's Tail: Americans Become Realists, but Too Late

Much revisionist criticism of U.S. Cold War policy misses the point. The problem was not a lack of realism. The United States was not paranoid, ignorant of communism or overzealous in reacting to Stalin's moves. Nor did it use immoral means out of all proportion to the threat.[59] Americans were realists learning from past mistakes, avoiding the fateful appeasement of Munich and the 1920s withdrawal from world affairs. If anything, they were too idealistic and slow to see that Stalin would advance as far as they would let him into the power vacuum of central Europe. The British were total realists before Americans were.

By the time Americans learned their lessons, the hour was late for realism. Reality had shifted to the total evil of a totalitarian enemy, a total U.S. commitment to defend any nation threatened by it and defense with a total weapon. These totalities compromised any attempt to combine morality and realism. Allied bombings of Dresden and Tokyo had shown that defeating Hitler and Tojo was seen as so moral that it justified bombing civilians—a morality of consequences.[60] Hiroshima and Nagasaki continued that belief.

Truman dropped the A-bomb to end the war with Japan, but he saw "intimidation of the Soviet Union as a valuable by-product." Pressure built to internationalize the A-bomb under U.N. auspices—an idealistic Wilsonian notion—but a U.S. monopoly (temporary) tempted Congress, public and president to keep other nations from learning the A-bomb's technical details. Truman decided to "appear to be internationalizing the bomb while retaining its monopoly." The result was an arms race, not a monopoly. After the Soviets' first atomic explosion in September 1949, Truman ordered development of a hydrogen bomb. Some scientists argued that it not be developed and disarmament be tried instead. Realists scoffed at that. Disarming was hard to monitor. Mutually assured destruction (MAD) was a more realistic peacekeeper.[61] Niebuhr called MAD a "final revelation of the incongruity of human existence."[62]

Human existence without direct divine rule was what had become incongruous. MAD did not reveal a uniquely American incapacity. No nation could have done better than the United States against the undeniable evil of Stalinism. No nation could completely fulfill such a total role—seeming to hold humanity's future in its hands and deciding what hostile move meant the end. The nation that tried was sure to be corrupted by such power. CIA plots to topple governments and assassinate foreign leaders, support for right-wing dictators, public lying, corporations profiteering from the Cold War, wild talk of "nuking" enemies, demonizing opponents—these were inevitable corruptions, not signs of a uniquely American perfidy or inability.

Who could hold such power and not be corrupted by it? Only the promised Davidic King, the Messiah, God's Anointed. More than the fanciful wish of Puritan divines, the Christian millennium became a logical necessity, the only way out. There was no way to reverse the scientific advances that led to the bomb and the arms race. No way to uninvent technologies. No way to purify a nation's leaders so that they could responsibly use such power. Realists knew that. Niebuhr noted, "The ironic tendency of virtues to turn into vices when too complacently relied upon" leads to "a frantic anti-Communism" that is "similar in its temper of hatefulness to Communism itself." He had to hope that identifying a tendency would teach leaders to avoid it. But his "christological symbols" could not rise up from the page to take the global burden or to stop amoral leaders.[63]

Only a literal Christ could. Yet realists scoffed at his literal return. Niebuhr admitted "our present nuclear dilemma" in 1960, but he doubted an eschatological end to it: "The symbol of Christ and anti-Christ for this dilemma of history may be archaic, but still it is closer to the facts than a simple idea of historical progress." That was faint praise—to be more realistic than folly. He and fellow realists balanced on the knife's edge of paradox: the bomb as "our ultimate insecurity and our immediate security."[64] Many Americans could not bear to balance for long on a knife's edge.

Realism could not stay moral for long; symbols could not mediate between moral goals and immoral means. With Cold War stakes so high, U.S. leaders found it realistic and pragmatic to use immoral means to stave off the greater evil of a communist victory. They used Dewey's morality of consequences. They lacked a morality of certainties—that good will triumph, that the messianic rule will come. Eschatological certainties are both realistic and idealistic. They do not rest on human action, so they do not encourage us to use immoral means. *Who* is coming is more important than *when*. Christ's moral nature determines which acts are rewarded and which punished. He allows no plea of innocence based on intended consequences.

Heights of Realism: 1950s America and the Suburban Consensus

From 1946 to 1960, Americans perfected their adaptation to post-1917 realities. That period is often seen as one of conformity, but it was a conformity to perceived realities. Realism is the key to understanding it. Americans showed they had learned the lesson of 1920s escapism (they shouldered enormous global duties), of 1920s laissez-faire speculation (the government regulated banks, firms and Wall Street), of 1930s appeasement (they refused to surrender Berlin), of 1940s wartime prosperity (consumerism was vital to America's way of life and its crusade against communism).[65]

Suburban life with its consumerism and familism was their key realistic adaptation. Postwar housing developments were realistic solutions to a serious housing crisis. The instant suburb combined many small solutions: mass-produced houses, affordable financing (low down payments, twenty- and thirty-year mortgages, FHA or VA financing), standard sizes for kitchen appliances and cabinets. It made home ownership and middle-class status affordable for millions. That reduced class antagonisms. In a consumers' democracy, many Americans could consume some luxuries. That made them more committed to the Cold War battle. Suburbs built democracy: suburbanites were "joiners"; they were "more tolerant and democratic." Suburban living solidified a national culture that realistically accepted a national market, unlike regionalism.[66]

The suburb perfected industrial capitalism, as shaped by democratic male individualism. Except when men were away at work, it was a male-ruled community. It was built on the car, the 1950s symbol of democratic male individualism. "At home a domesticated male, the car owner behind his steering wheel was king of the road, flying free in imagination even as he crawled through traffic." In a highly rational, functionalist society, women did not fly free but were given roles based on biology: sexual partner, mother, child-care provider. After the Depression's poverty and postponed dreams, after wartime anxieties, women were willing to do these duties. They agreed to focus on homemaking and child rearing; men "agreed to get ahead and take good care of them." Suburbs seemed better than early-nineteenth-century churches at reducing male rebellion. There still was some, but male-female bargains were often kept.[67]

Christianity was partly domesticated too, stripped of its supernatural, exclusivist zeal and enlisted as realism's helpmate. In Eisenhower's famous words,

"Our government makes no sense unless it is founded on a deeply felt religious belief—and I don't care what it is." Faith was important for its social function, not for its object or its eschatology. "The American Way of Life, not Christianity, was the real religion of the country." Christian beliefs were private values. Americanism was the public fact. Privatizing belief reduced religious intolerance and increased social harmony so needed for the Cold War.[68] Yet the "American Way of Life" could give no certain hope that it—or any good—would triumph. A Christianity enlisted in the Cold War could not easily critique U.S. Cold War tactics or give this certain hope.

Suburban living harnessed morality to individual (and national) self-interest. With his own house, car, kids and loving wife, it was in a male's interest to be conventionally, outwardly moral. So many pleasures were now available at home that he need not rebel or go elsewhere. The strong profamily consensus of the 1950s pulled him back home if he did stray. It seemed in women's self-interest to perform their roles. Teenagers were reconciled to adult society by a "conformist" youth culture of cars, movies, soda fountains and moon-in-June pop hits. Consumerism was reconciled with morality by centering it in home and family. Pickford and Fairbanks were right: a cult of youth, sports and suburban family life allowed one to have fun, a corporate job and a moral family life. A functional morality better suited than Victorianism to a consumer culture had apparently been found. Suburbia seemed a realistic adaptation to decades-old consumerism.[69]

Anticommunism gave consumerism a moral purpose: winning the Cold War. Satisfied in consumerism, Americans would not mind their Cold War sacrifices. So U.S. leaders hoped, anyway.

The usual criticisms of the fifties are misdirected to tensions between individual freedom and social order, to a mass conformity stifling individual dissent or creativity.[70] That is a backward-looking view—the fifties seen through the distorting lens of the sixties. It ignores the historical context of 1917-1945. The fifties were the culmination of a thirty-year process of pragmatic tinkering. America had been fine-tuned and road-tested. The faults of the fifties lie in pragmatic realism itself. Abroad, it sought to bear Cold War burdens that could not be morally borne. At home, it sought morality for self-interested reasons more than to glorify God.

Heights of Realism: The Kennedys and the Cuban Missile Crisis
The fifties' realist consensus did not end in 1960. John F. Kennedy's election

is often seen as a key turning point, but it was not. The postwar period from 1945 to 1965 was ruled by realism, whether of the Democratic or Republican kind. The range of acceptable political beliefs had steadily narrowed. Debate over totalitarianism ended fascism and communism as allowable opinions. Henry Wallace's 1948 defeat marginalized Popular Front liberals. Eisenhower's refusal to undo New Deal programs cut out die-hard anti-New-Dealers. His rebuke of Senator Joseph McCarthy further narrowed the spectrum.[71]

Historians are mistaken in seeing 1960 as the triumph of liberalism, the sixties as a revolt against liberalism. The Cold War liberals whom Kennedy led were liberal *realists*. They differed from conservative realists such as Eisenhower mostly in mood, not substance. They too were Cold Warriors, Niebuhrian realists who hated blind ideology of the Right or Left. They too were friends of capitalism, which the New Deal had humanized. Critical of some aspects of consumerism, they mainly opposed the self-satisfied mood of Ike's America. Their candidate pledged to "get the country moving again."[72]

Born in 1917, the key turning point, John F. Kennedy was a tough Niebuhrian realist and master of the "cool style"—"detached, ironic, self-mocking, graceful under pressure." His New Frontiersmen were "brash, arrogant" realists. He took realism to the heights of global involvement and sacrificial spirit. His Inaugural Address demanded that Americans sacrifice: "We shall pay any price, bear any burden, meet any hardship, support any friend, oppose any foe to assure the survival and the success of liberty." In the Cuban Missile Crisis, he nearly carried through on his promise to pay any price.[73]

On Tuesday, October 16, 1962, the CIA informed him that the Russians were installing medium- and long-range missiles in Cuba. It was assumed that these were armed with nuclear warheads. Kennedy had cause to be alarmed. He was caught in a chain of historical events. Republicans had charged Truman with being "soft on Communism." If they made the same charge against him with regard to Cuba, he was vulnerable, for in 1960 he had flailed them for allowing Castro's communist regime. In April 1961, Kennedy was stung by the failed Bay of Pigs invasion. In September and early October 1962, Republican Senator Kenneth Keating claimed that the Soviets were installing missiles in Cuba. Kennedy denied it, but he could not appear weak now, for he felt that Soviet leader Nikita Khrushchev had browbeaten him at the June 1961 summit.[74]

More distant history was also being considered in the White House. Kennedy had read Barbara Tuchman's *Guns of August,* a new book on statesmen's miscalculations leading to World War I. Thirties appeasement was also on his mind that week. His Harvard senior thesis, published as *Why England Slept* (1940), was "a stunning indictment of . . . the policy of appeasement." In his TV address announcing the discovery of the missiles, he stated, "The 1930's taught us a clear lesson: aggressive conduct, if allowed to go unchecked and unchallenged, ultimately leads to war."[75] Christians turn to Scripture for clear lessons; pragmatists turn to history. But which was the right historical analogy, August 1914 or Munich?

President Kennedy did not want to miscalculate and start a nuclear war, but appeasement or the appearance of weakness was more dangerous now than in 1938. Now appearances were everything. A nuclear deterrent was useless if the Soviets reasonably doubted that the United States would use it. The Soviets could advance step by step, challenging the United States, as Henry Kissinger warned, "whether we are willing to commit suicide to prevent encroachments" which did not "threaten our existence directly, but which may be a step on the road to our ultimate destruction." Were the Soviets pragmatists setting up experiments such that the rational U.S. response was always to back down?[76]

When Kennedy's task force on the crisis, the ExComm, met later that week, two options were quickly discarded: doing nothing and seeking removal of the missiles through diplomacy. These two were thought to make the United States and Kennedy look weak. Another option, air strikes against the missile sites, gave the Soviets little choice but to respond militarily and the United States little choice but to follow up with an invasion of Cuba. Pragmatic realists wanted flexibility, not necessity. They wanted to learn from early results of the ongoing experiment before having to choose later moves.

On Saturday, October 20, the president chose a two-step approach: (1) a naval blockade, or "naval quarantine," which would send a tough message and test Moscow's position but would not remove any missiles, and (2) an ultimatum for removal of the missiles, which implied an invasion or air strikes if they were not removed. On Monday, JFK announced the quarantine in a televised speech. The quarantine was the experimental phase. It would begin Wednesday.[77] The ultimatum hinted at finality.

On Wednesday there was considerable tension as Russian ships approached U.S. ships in the quarantine zone. Realists did not control events but "would have to wait" for the results of their experiment. A message came that the Russian ships had stopped. Dean Rusk reportedly said, "We're eyeball to eyeball and I think the other fellow just blinked." But it was not over so soon.

A successful blockade did not remove missiles. Echoing (unintentionally?) the words of Jesus in Gethsemane, Robert Kennedy recalled, "The feeling grew that this cup was not going to pass and that a direct military confrontation between the two great military powers was inevitable." His account in *Thirteen Days* gives no hint that American leaders humbly appealed to God during this near-apocalyptic crisis. They seemed ready to go to nuclear war. As Khrushchev said, "The smell of burning hung in the air."[78]

Saturday, October 27, was the worst day. "War seemed near," and the missiles were nearly operational. The United States would have to invade by Tuesday if they were not removed. According to Robert, his brother "was deciding, for the U.S., the Soviet Union, Turkey, NATO, and really for all mankind." That left no room for God's sovereignty or Christian eschatology. On Sunday, after two Soviet messages eased tensions, the brothers talked in the Oval Office. JFK felt that he was deciding for all space (the globe) and for all time (would there be a future?). Children might "never have a chance to make a decision, to vote in an election, to run for office, to lead a revolution, to determine their own destinies."[79] That was hubris; he was not Christ at Gethsemane deciding humanity's fate.

He and his ExComm were not even who they claimed to be—cool, pragmatic leaders controlling the military, rationally assessing the crisis and capably resolving it. Declassified ExComm transcripts and recently released Soviet and Cuban records reveal a different reality. ExComm members, including JFK, were distracted, emotional, irrational: "Thoughts ramble . . . options ooze into the ether." Some gave advice while JFK kept important facts from them. Even those in the inner circle were not in full control. They were mistaken as to why the Soviet Union deployed the missiles, about its troop strength and tactical nuclear weapons in Cuba, about who ordered an American U-2 plane shot down, about who authorized a Soviet official to negotiate (no one!). They did not know of potentially serious moves made by a U.S. military they claimed to control. Their thinking was clouded by the "actor-observer" fallacy: I act defensively, you act provocatively. The president's thinking may have been clouded by "bolstering"—exaggerating the likely effects of inaction to make action a necessity, not a choice.[80]

Misinformation was just as prevalent on the Soviet side. Two pragmatists probed at each other in the dark. Political scientist Laurence Chang concludes that this new evidence "makes the crisis seem a far more dangerous incident than earlier believed."[81] Actually the new evidence shows divine sovereignty at work. There's no reason why the two stumbling superpowers did not collide in the dark, except that God's ancient promises of a coming Messiah's earthly rule made it impossible for human space and time to be destroyed in 1962.

Pragmatic Realism: Synopsis

That does not excuse Kennedy (or Khrushchev) for seeming to risk it. To Kennedy the end was possible, even likely. Yet the fault lies in pragmatic realism too. October 1962 showed that pragmatic realism's hour had passed. With such stakes, one could not *responsibly* experiment and then justify it by a morality of consequences. Only in retrospect did the consequences, the lack of a nuclear war and the missiles' removal, *seem* to justify the risk. Time and space survived. JFK soared in the polls. Yet pragmatic realism was found wanting. It lacked any clear sense of where it led, any certainty that it would get there and any moral justification for the risks it asked Americans (and others) to assume along the way.

Most Americans did not see that nuclear brinkmanship called into question several assumptions: unlimited global involvement (the credibility of U.S. guarantees to defend West Berlin was seemingly at stake in the Cuban Missile Crisis) to save a global balance of power, their Cold War sacrifices and hence the consumerism that rewarded them for sacrifices and the self-interested morality that motivated them to sacrifice. Some Americans did see this. They rebelled at a policy of balancing on a knife's edge, and rebellion against pragmatic realism would fracture the national consensus.

11

"At Sixes & Sevens" *A Revolt Against Realism Splinters America*

THE SIXTIES AND SEVENTIES SHOWED that a *people* who had abandoned belief in Christian eschatology were as dangerous as *leaders* who had abandoned it. After the Kennedy brothers came student radicals who believed that future time and global space were theirs to preserve. The Cuban Missile Crisis risked a catastrophe that never came; the sixties caused some smaller yet real ones. The Crisis was a two-week affair that did not discredit realism with a long stalemate. It was a quick win that confirmed it in realists' eyes. The sixties, however, was a series of crises that discredited realism in many Americans' eyes. (For a definition of pragmatic realism, see the beginning of chapter ten.)

To understand America in the nineties, we must come to terms with the sixties (and seventies), and we must do so in a fair and balanced way. Many 1990s issues and problems were first mainstreamed in the 1960s: drug use, street crime, abortion rights, gay rights, culture wars, teen pregnancy, out-of-wedlock births, rising divorce rates and so on. Some writers who try to be fair and balanced on 1990s issues omit the 1960s—perhaps because Republican

candidates have blamed liberal Democrats for sixties problems.[1] The sixties
have become a partisan issue, but we cannot afford to give up the historical
context just because it has been misused. A fair, nonpartisan look at the sixties
is needed for a fair look at the present.

We must be wary of some current accounts of the 1960s. Sixties activists
often ended up in history and sociology departments, but they have biases on
their formative decade. Influential accounts of sixties protests come from
participants: Todd Gitlin, James Miller, Richard Flacks, Mary King. Though
honest about failure, they paint the sixties with a background glow of youthful
idealism that softens failure.[2]

We must understand that conservatives too are implicated in sixties failures.
They too were part of a fifties realist consensus that unraveled in the sixties.
We must also be fair about the strengths of that consensus, which is often
incorrectly portrayed as mindless conformity certain to collapse. With realism
a weak reed, some accounts make Kennedy liberals the protagonists and the
sixties the time of liberalism's fall.[3] That's the memory of sixties radicals, who
were mainly arguing with liberals. That view makes the Nixon presidency
Nixon's personal triumph when it was really the repeat triumph of a resilient
realism. That makes the sixties debate one of the Left versus the further Left,
when the Right was responsible too. That view understates the importance of
the black church to the civil rights movement and of the evangelical revival to
America's recovery from the sixties. It understates the damage caused by
society's splintering in the sixties.

The sixties were a time of revolt against realism, against the narrow political
spectrum, industrial capitalism, consumer culture and Cold War consensus. For
many Americans, realism was discredited, delegitimized by its failure to end
Southern segregation, its reliance on nuclear deterrence and its Vietnam War.
Before examining delegitimizing messages, we must look at the critics who
developed them, the audiences who listened to them and the messengers who
brought them.

The Delegitimizing Critics

Their messengers and audience. Critics had attacked the realist consensus in
the 1950s. They focused on its cultural weaknesses more than its economic and
antitotalitarian strengths. The fifties had what Gitlin calls "zones of negativity":
beatniks, the folk music scene, intellectuals such as C. Wright Mills and Paul
Goodman, rock 'n' roll, *Mad* magazine, Hollywood rebels such as James Dean

and the Old Left. The 1960s New Left critique of suburbia, Cold War, conformity and capitalism came from these sources.

The realist consensus had glaring weaknesses. It had little idea how the Cold War might end. It had no eschatology. It had few if any absolutes: values were prized for their usefulness, not their absolute truth. Thus its authority figures "were *proprietors* without a cause," argues Gitlin. After its parents had adopted consumerism, how could they keep marketers from profiting from a young consumers' subculture? What began as a middle-class, college-fraternity, conformist subculture in the 1920s was becoming, by 1960, a working-class, rebellious one that was more threatening to adults' realist consensus.[4]

College students were a potential audience for critics. Their numbers were growing. In 1946 only about two million students attended college. That nearly doubled to 3.8 million by 1960 and doubled again to 7.8 million by 1969, when the United States had "more college students than farmers, construction workers, miners, or transportation workers."[5] The United States was probably the first society in human history for which that was true. The students' parents' post-1917 success in adjusting capitalism to make middle-class aspirations—here a college education for one's children—possible for more Americans created this huge potential audience for anti-middle-class rhetoric.

In 1960 it was only a potential one. College students were preoccupied with "the rules of fraternity and pantie raid and the Big Game." (High-schoolers mimicked collegians.) Yet they listened to the critique of realism. They were not tied to society's real institutions: they did not have their own families, work for corporations or government, belong to unions, serve in the armed forces or participate in voluntary associations. Temporarily, they were not in the "real world" but only preparing for it. They were unaware of the series of tradeoffs, compromises and adjustments which institutions had made to new post-1917 realities. The one institution they knew, the university, was slow to adjust to their increased numbers. They had grievances: overcrowded classes, impersonal instruction, unapproachable faculty, outdated courses.[6]

Still, a few complaints about Economics 101 would hardly make a revolution. A stronger critique was needed—and go-betweens or messengers to communicate it to this audience. Activists in groups such as Students for a Democratic Society (SDS) played that role. Early SDS activists were heirs of the Old Left, even of realism, though they tried to escape or ignore this history. Many were children of liberal, socialist or communist parents who raised them in an egalitarian, nonauthoritarian manner. Like feminism in 1913, sixties radicalism was not an argument with Christianity—it came out of very secular ideas—but an argument with liberalism and socialism, with the inability of enlightened science and democracy to fulfill their promises.[7]

They were thrown into an apocalyptic age without a faith in Christian eschatology. They inherited a democratic ideology which put the burden of preventing apocalypse on citizens' shoulders. At Madison, Wisconsin, during a National Student Association Congress in August 1961, SDS leader Tom Hayden had an impromptu argument with conservative William F. Buckley. Hayden charged that capitalists exploited workers. "Buckley said, 'The trouble with you liberals is that you have no eschatology.' " The activist who recalled this added, "I went running around trying to figure out what an eschatology was."[8]

We need not accept Buckley's eschatology (what was it?) or blame New Leftists whose parents left them none, but we can see the consequences of lacking one. With no idea of where history was going, with the idea that citizens had to steer it, they went from liberal to radical to bizarre as they pushed, only to discover that realism was too strong to overthrow.

Intellectual origins: New Left and the Port Huron Statement. The New Left started out not far removed from fifties realism. Though it critiqued that consensus, it owed a great debt to what Mills called "crackpot realism." Its founding document, SDS's Port Huron Statement (1962), grounded idealism in a detailed "Dr. Facts" analysis of society. It charged the consensus with a lack of realism: terms such as " 'free world' . . . reflect realities poorly, if at all, and seem to function more as ruling myths than as descriptive principles." Realists "act out a defeatism that is labelled realistic." Realism came out of concrete events of the 1930s and 1940s, not out of a philosophical theory, but New Leftists minimized that. "Ignorant of history many of them defiantly remained."[9]

The Port Huron Statement was a very American document, which drew on pragmatism and the ideology of democracy. Its main author, Tom Hayden, had read Dewey and accepted Dewey's pragmatism and faith in democracy. "Participatory democracy" was Port Huron's (and the New Left's) main theme. It connoted an experimental "effort to test the limits of democracy in modern life." It sought to rescue the democratic idea from post-1917 realist compromises with capitalism, consumerism, antitotalitarian struggle and the national security state. It tried vainly to rescue it from two hundred years of secularization. It contained some of the "face-to-face community" of the Puritan town meeting and the Quakers' "redemptive community."[10]

Without the devout motives of Puritans and Quakers, how could their warm, loving communities be recreated? How could secular New Leftists recreate their religious spirit? Port Huron reflected the agnosticism of New Leftists' parents and the existentialism of intellectuals who survived the crises of the 1930s and 1940s. The New Left's descent into antirealism can be partly blamed on realists who used existentialism to steel Americans to endure Cold War tensions and the absurdity of mutually assured destruction. Diggins calls existentialism "a crisis philosophy in which each individual must decide although there is no assurance of being right." Small wonder realist existentialism became Hayden's "reckless existentialism," a "leap of faith," "a kind of anarchism," a stab at commitment "without the aid of eternal values." Not knowing what was right or where history was headed, one still had to choose.[11]

As James Miller notes, "participatory democracy" was riddled with ambiguities. Did it require a new Constitution or a socialist economy? Was it compatible with representation? Was it quasi-religious or ruthlessly secular? Was it C. Wright Mills's "politics of theatrical fury and mythomanic fervor, of high moral seriousness, savage social criticism and peculiarly blinkered self-righteousness"? It was sold as both traditionally American and daringly innovative. But which was it?[12]

Could one revitalize democracy in an apocalyptic age of global forces which citizens could not alter? Walter Lippmann observed forty years earlier, "If democracy cannot direct affairs, then a philosophy which expects it to direct them will encourage the people to attempt the impossible."[13] Won't they get frustrated, and where will frustration lead them? That occurred as New Leftists wrestled with the issues of civil rights, nuclear threats and the Vietnam War. All three delegitimized a realist consensus yet were hard to resolve. Frustrated, the New Left moved from a moderate critique to an outright rejection of realism.

The Delegitimizing of Realism: The Civil Rights Movement

Brown and the white backlash. The civil rights movement too had its roots in the ideas and events of the post-1917 period. Indeed, it could not have focused the nation's attention on the one problem of Southern segregation if the realist consensus had not (seemingly or temporarily) solved other problems. TV and other media helped it reach a national market which consensus had solidified. If Americans were *not* prosperous, content with consumerism and united on an antitotalitarian foreign policy, they would be too preoccupied with economic and foreign issues to focus on segregation. They had been too preoccupied before 1947. Realists' narrowing of the political spectrum, the exclusion of communists and Popular Fronters, made "possible the reemergence of a social movement critical of the racial status quo."[14] Opponents could not credibly paint it as communist.

Realism's successes made the movement possible. Its failures made the movement necessary. It had rarely paused after 1917 to ponder the injustices of Southern segregation.

Some historians argue that industrialization, urbanization, defense plants in the 1940s South, blacks' wartime service, the mechanization of cotton picking, Truman's civil rights moves and 1940s court decisions all undercut segregation before the movement took off in the mid-1950s. Their arguments are not persuasive. Sociologist Aldon Morris notes, "The idea that urbanization created a 'New Negro' eager to change his status in American society is not borne out by the evidence." The fierce white backlash after *Brown* v. *Board of Education* (1954) suggests that segregation did not rest on ruralism or sharecropping or a lack of court decisions.[15]

Stressing socioeconomic causes is one way historians downplay the role of Christianity and the African-American church in the civil rights movement. In many texts it advances through the fifties and early sixties like a train without an engine. It passes important stations—Montgomery, Little Rock, Greensboro, Birmingham and Selma—with no indication what is driving it except Supreme Court decisions and the simultaneous advance of liberalism. Dr. Martin Luther King's pastorate at Dexter Avenue Baptist Church is mentioned as a biographical fact, but little is said of the African-American church generally or of African-Americans' faith. The role of more secular NAACP lawyers is stressed instead.[16]

None of the suggested causes seems strong enough to have driven it. From 1940 to 1954, Southern white liberals won some elections, but many abandoned their mild prointegration views when segregationists raised the race issue. Secular liberalism did not motivate many to risk their political careers or to go to jail to end Jim Crow. The legal work of Thurgood Marshall and others was admirable, but even their great victory, the *Brown* decision, had little immediate effect in ending school segregation. By 1960 under 1 percent of Southern black children attended integrated schools. At that rate, someone calculated, it would take 7,288 years to integrate Southern schools! *Brown*'s inspirational effect on the movement has been greatly overstated too.[17]

The *Brown* ruling was entangled in the political courtroom as Southern states and school districts stalled, closed schools and passed laws they knew were unconstitutional but would take courts years to adjudicate. One Southern columnist urged, "Let us pledge ourselves to litigate this thing for fifty years." In 1956, more than one hundred Southern congressmen and senators signed a states' rights declaration opposing *Brown.* In a replay of the 1850s political courtroom, constitutionalism and strict construction were debated, not segregation, and a president was clearly reluctant to enforce the ruling.[18]

Angrier encounters occurred on Southern streets and back roads. The KKK and White Citizens Councils used violence, economic pressure and ballots to intimidate blacks and pressure white politicians. Massive resistance to *Brown* "propelled politics in virtually every southern state several notches to the right on racial issues." Far from improving race relations, *Brown* sparked a white backlash that worsened them. Democratic elections rewarded white extremism.[19]

Neither urbanization, liberalism, Supreme Court cases nor democracy beat segregation. Nor did the white backlash defeat itself. Without African-Americans willing to stand up to it and expose it to Northern public opinion, it would have won. Those African-Americans at first came overwhelmingly from the black church. Urbanization had not secularized them; it made their urban churches stronger than their rural ones. In the mid-1950s more than 98 percent of the members of the two main civil rights organizations in Montgomery and Birmingham were church members. This was "foremost a religious movement . . . a moral drama played to a people who understood the awful and wonderful implications of evangelical Christianity." The black church had a "central and overpowering role" in that drama.[20]

The civil rights movement could not succeed through political processes; it bypassed them to make a moral appeal. That was true at the state and local level in the South, where blacks were harassed and barred from voting, and in Washington, where Southern Democrats chaired congressional committees and Senate filibusters gave minorities veto power. Not finding the political courtroom sympathetic, civil rights leaders used the media to put external pressure on it. Their main tactic of nonviolent direct action had its roots partly in a Christian refusal to obey unjust laws.[21]

Martin Luther King fuses Social Gospel, realism and faith. That's not to argue that evangelicalism or fundamentalism defeated segregation. Almost all Southern white evangelicals and fundamentalists supported segregation. A vast chasm yawned between their pocket New Testaments and their prejudices. Fundamentalist black ministers were often "other-worldly," content to "describe the furniture in heaven," not attack the injustice on earth. Both white and black ministers were expected not to attack the racial status quo. Still, the gospel's underlying universalism offered blacks and whites potential liberation from the "stifling localism" of Southern racial norms. More than theoretical universalism was needed. White churches had to compete for members in a racist society; black churches were vulnerable to violent threats; both had a gospel that prescribed saints' individual behavior in detail but that lacked an exact blueprint of a just society.[22]

The Social Gospel and Northern liberalism were the needed help that nudged Southerners, black and white, to see the gospel's practical implications. A key factor was that the movement united theological conservatives and liberals within the black church and brought white Social Gospelers to aid the black church. No fundamentalist-modernist split here, but a temporarily fruitful union of liberals' passion for social justice and fundamentalists' fervent faith. In Southern blacks, Social Gospelers finally found a proletariat that attended Protestant churches—one whose poverty, race, piety and regional identity kept them free from a national consumer culture. Their moral cause and their direct action tactics revived a moribund Social Gospel tradition in mainline Northern churches and moved it off its faith in mere words.[23]

Martin Luther King Jr. was the key figure in forging this fruitful union. He could communicate with both groups. The son of a fundamentalist minister, he rebelled against his father's beliefs. At Atlanta's Morehouse College, he recalled, "the shackles of fundamentalism were removed from my body." He received a Social Gospel education at liberal Crozer Theological Seminary and tempered that by studying Niebuhrian realism at Boston University. In his sermons at Montgomery's liberal, elite Dexter Avenue Baptist Church, he was " 'not a God man,' meaning that he did not dwell on salvation or describe the furniture in heaven." Like Niebuhr in his Detroit church, King communicated Christian symbols to those who took them literally. As a black in a racist society, he had closer ties to his conservative listeners than Niebuhr had to his.[24]

King was an ally of Northern liberals, but he had to lead his followers against violent forces. A literal faith moved them to march better than did a symbolic one. His followers made the movement more pious than liberals intended. Editors at *Time* protested when the draft for a cover story on King noted that " 'Onward Christian Soldiers' was sung at MIA [Montgomery Improvement

Association] mass meetings." They objected to its "warlike spirit" and, likely, to its Christian spirit. That "clashed with *Time*'s Gandhian slant on King." Blacks in the MIA prayed and sang for three hours before meetings. Before facing police on Selma's bridge, they met in church to sing:

Be not dismayed whate'er betide,

God will take care of you.

Faith steeled people to face violence, disciplined them to avoid resentment and helped to solve the "free rider" problem (it was in one's self-interest to let others pay the price of ending segregation, then reap the benefits oneself).[25]

A church-based movement led by the aptly named Southern Christian Leadership Conference (SCLC) subtly transformed the black church, notes Morris. Boycotts, people ceasing to participate in an evil system, were not far removed from fundamentalism's come-outer spirit. But a change in emphasis was needed. King noted, "Our church is becoming militant, stressing a social gospel as well as a gospel of personal salvation." As a black minister, King could credibly call for this change. A Northern secular liberal could not. Anchored in Southern culture, the black church and its Christian eschatology, the SCLC-led movement generally kept its discipline, its faith and its nonviolent principles. These were not transferred to its offshoot, the Student Non-violent Coordinating Committee (SNCC), to SNCC's white volunteers or to Northern ghettos.[26]

Secularizing civil rights and diffusing grievances: SNCC and SDS. SNCC grew out of the spring 1960 sit-ins. Morris observes, "The black church was the chief institutional force behind the sit-ins." It provided a meeting place and training site, ministers to lead students and financial support. SCLC's Ella Baker helped organize SNCC, but it departed from black church culture. The causes were many: impatience, egalitarian anger at SCLC's celebrities, the radicalizing effect of the violence SNCC activists encountered, the U.S. government's refusal to protect them or to enforce its own laws. SNCC organized blacks in rural areas of Mississippi and Alabama where white violence was worse than in the large cities, which were organized by the SCLC. By the mid-1960s SNCC recruits were less influenced by "southern Christianity" than by "the increasing vogue of Third World radicalism," and SNCC veterans had been radicalized.[27]

White volunteers from the North went south to help SNCC. Hayden went to Atlanta in the fall of 1961 as "the official SDS liaison to the Southern civil rights movement." Helping in SNCC's rural Mississippi voter registration project, he

was beaten in McComb, wrote a report titled "Revolution in Mississippi" and
became convinced that SNCC activists were "the moral vanguard." Gitlin
observes that for SDS "no inspiration was more important than the civil rights
surge"; "SNCC moved us"; "SNCC-SDS connections were thick." In the 1964
Mississippi Freedom Summer campaign, more than a thousand white volunteers worked on SNCC's voter registration drive.[28]

As a rule, these were above-average white students from middle-class to
upper-middle-class liberal families. They shared their parents' values. They
"held to an enormously idealistic and optimistic view of the world," writes
Doug McAdam. They knew of social problems, but they were ill-prepared for
the hatred and violence they saw in Mississippi. Big Business did not shoot
people. They could not recall the 1920s Klan. They were unprepared for the
depths of poverty in rural Mississippi. The middle-class, career-seeking, play-
it-safe consensus of fifties realism left them ill-prepared to cope with virtue
too—the self-sacrificing courage of SNCC staffers and the "honesty, insight
and leadership of rural Negroes." Liberalism and the Social Gospel did not
prepare them for utter contrasts between good and evil. They lacked a clear idea
of how to oppose evil or when (or if) good would finally win. They lacked an
eschatology to explain the battle of good and evil.[29]

In a time warp, as it were, they left the fifties, where some thought it in their
interest to be moderately moral and some to be moderately wicked, and headed
into a South that resembled first-century Rome: the contrast between evil Nero
torching Christians and saintly Christians facing martyrdom was impossibly
intense. In a stark moral drama, "good guys' " pure idealism was as disorienting
as "bad guys' " violent hate.

For the students, the experience delegitimized realism, their parents' middle-class world and the American Way of Life. Here's the full quote from Tom
Hayden: "The honesty, insight and leadership of rural Negroes demonstrated
to the students that their upbringing had been based on a framework of lies."
Middle-class society seemed the enemy that was oppressing blacks as much as
were rural whites. It too had to be flatly opposed, while the noble, idealistic
lives of SNCC staffers had to be fully embraced. One volunteer recalled, "Lots
of the volunteers sort of sat at the feet of the SNCC guys. . . . It was sort of
pathetic, everybody trying to out SNCC each other. . . . Some of the others
almost become [sic] like groupies." Like rock groupies, female volunteers had
sexual relations with the SNCC staffers. A rebellion against middle-class
morality led them to adopt four elements that would form the counterculture—

"communal living, a more liberated sexuality, interracial relationships, and a distinctive style of speech and dress."[30]

Volunteers returned north with a desire to rediscover the community, self-sacrifice, idealism, sexual liberation and nonconformity they had found in Mississippi. They sought a chosen people as honest, good and oppressed as rural blacks were. Understandably, due to the sexual exploitation that was part of Freedom Summer, women saw themselves as an oppressed class. Others saw the Vietnamese, Cubans and other Third World peoples as the innocent oppressed and romantically identified with their causes. Returning volunteers were themselves seen on the campus "as conquering heroes" who radicalized campus audiences with stories of their experiences. At Berkeley, volunteer Mario Savio led the Free Speech Movement and improbably equated university authorities with Mississippi's.[31]

This was all wildly overblown. African-American honesty and insight came out of African-American Christianity, yet some volunteers (illogically) suffered a crisis of faith. Further, rural Alabama and Mississippi were not even typical of the South, let alone of America. Beatings in McComb could not prove that an upbringing in Detroit or an education in Ann Arbor was "based on a framework of lies." Being expelled from the university was not like being beaten in Mississippi.[32] Women weren't shot at like blacks in the rural South. Vietcong guerrillas were not nonviolent saints like the blacks who sang a hymn before leaving the Selma church. Mississippi's poverty was greater than that in most regions, where capitalist consumerism brought Americans unprecedented prosperity.

With the searing emotions from summer volunteer work, white college students attacked the fifties realist consensus. At first a reasoned attack on its excesses, New Left radicalism became an all-out assault on its successes as well as its failures.

The Delegitimizing of Realism: The Cuban Missile Crisis

Nuclear threat and the Cuban Missile Crisis. Perhaps because it was an underlying condition and not an event, such as the Vietnam War or Freedom Summer, the nuclear threat has been underemphasized as a delegitimizing force. Yet Hayden criticized the world the fifties left behind as one "strained by the nearness of total war." SDS's Al Haber called this "a heritage of absurdity." Gitlin recalls fifties kids hiding under school desks during air-raid drills: "We could never take for granted that the world we had been born into was destined to endure." Nuclear bombs "drew a knife-edge line between the generations." To parents the bomb was past reality that ended World War II; to their children it was a threat that might end the future.[33]

Much planning for nuclear war was considered immoral. Academics and consultants devised nuclear war scenarios at think tanks such as Herman Kahn's Hudson Institute. One critic called Kahn's *On Thermonuclear War* "a nuclear version of pornography" for using words such as "wargasm." Hudson's Five-Year Plan showed realists' hubris: "The first year we would put down on paper everything a good secretary of defense would want to know; the next year a good secretary of state; the next year a good president; . . . and the fifth year a good God. And then we'd quit."[34]

MAD made realism absurd. The United States could not show doubts about using the bomb lest the deterrent lose effect. It had to convince the Soviet Union that it would meet a Soviet attack, even a conventional one in Europe, with a nuclear response, which would in turn bring Soviet nuclear retaliation. That "required the United States to risk national suicide for interests not inherently vital to American security," writes historian H. W. Brand. Americans' future was a hostage to "the good behavior of the country they had identified as their mortal enemy." With MAD and the arms race, the United States seemed less secure.[35]

By the late 1950s the arms race and nuclear testing provoked opposition from groups such as SANE (the National Committee for a Sane Nuclear Policy). Activists such as Gitlin came to the New Left through such groups, which adopted the tactics of the SCLC. Khrushchev's and Kennedy's saber-rattling in 1961-1962 led to an antitesting march on Washington in February 1962. Protesters still spoke realists' language then and urged practical objections to get officials to listen. Realist McGeorge Bundy advised them, "Politics is the art of the possible." The nuclear threat was often cited in SDS's Port Huron Statement (June 1962). That added to its tone of urgency, but it was still tough-minded, realistic idealism.[36]

The Cuban Missile Crisis radicalized peace activists away from pragmatic protest. SDS's Ann Arbor chapter led the "first major campus demonstration against the Cuban blockade." Gitlin led one at Harvard. Historical sociologist Barrington Moore argued here that to "make practical proposals, constructive proposals, moderate and realistic proposals, is the most unrealistic thing you can do at this point." In the short term, "Leave the constructive alternatives to Bundy. . . . He has an interest in surviving that is probably at least as strong as ours." The long-term need was for "simultaneous revolutions in the United States and the Soviet Union."[37]

Moore's speech pushed Gitlin and others from realist protest to radicalism: "With humanity hanging in the balance, Moore seemed to be bringing us fresh Old Testament truth."[38] The following week, activists held a "hastily organized" rally in Washington on Saturday, October 27, the bleakest day. Journalist I. F. Stone gave the latest update—Kennedy had called up the Air Force Reserve—and warned, "Six thousand years of human history is about to come to an end." (Did he accept Bishop James Ussher's dating of creation?) As he spoke, Hayden felt, "I was marked for death and what I wanted to do was to be together with my closest friends who were there."[39]

The New Frontiersmen's success in the showdown with Khrushchev did not reassure activists. Hayden recalled that the crisis "alienated us from the Kennedys, the idea that we should all die, people all over the world should be killed over this kind of question." "The week of madness," wrote Hayden soon after, taught activists that they had to "penetrate the political process." In 1962, Cold War fervor made that impossible. Ann Arbor's peace Democrat, running for Congress with some SDS support, made only "a feeble gesture" that October and did not attack Kennedy. He lost. Superpowers would not heed a few students and their "tongue-tied" candidate.[40]

The democratic dogma said they must try: the world's fate rested on them and their candidate. Dogma "will encourage them to attempt the impossible," Lippmann had predicted. The resulting frustration radicalized them: the Cuban Missile Crisis and MAD delegitimized a realism that based national security on the bomb. Radicalization went beyond politics. Blockades and nuclear scenarios were government policies, but they decided human destiny—and thus had religious meaning if you lacked an eschatology to tell you that the Kennedys did not decide humanity's fate. The nuclear threat drove activists beyond personal liberation to seek a new religion. SDSer Jeffry Shero explained, "We are the first generation that grew up with the idea of annihilation. In a situation like this, you have to go out and form your own religion."[41]

The Delegitimizing of Realism: The Vietnam War
The pragmatic war effort. To discredit realism, SNCC activists pointed to realists' ignoring Southern segregation. Cuban crisis protesters pointed to realists' risky foreign policy. Antiwar activists pointed to realists' failures in Vietnam. Here policymakers' pragmatism was the main cause of their failure.

Here the disaster was actual, painful, drawn out and humiliating.

Historian James W. Gibson calls the usual postmortem views on Vietnam "the liberal Vietnam-as-mistake position and the conservative criticism of self-imposed restraint."[42] Both are inadequate. Neither criticizes pragmatic realism. Both use its assumptions: pragmatic realists should know not to make mistakes or not to restrain their own armed forces.

There are other explanations. New Leftists saw the United States as an immoral imperialist power propping up its puppet in a civil war and suppressing the legitimate voice of the Vietnamese people, the National Liberation Front (NLF). That view romanticized the often-murderous NLF forces, downplayed the armed aggression from North Vietnam and ignored the (few) achievements of South Vietnam's leaders. Gibson's postmodern view—that rationalist, managerial "technowar" failed—is better than the New Left one, but it too falls short, as we will see.

Nothing in the situation in South Vietnam made it impossible for the United States to wage a moral yet successful war to help that nation defend itself. That is clear even in George Herring's liberal account. Though "no mere tool of the Soviet Union," Ho Chi Minh was a communist who would have brought one-party rule, repression and confiscation of private property to the South if the United States had not supported Ngo Dinh Diem's anticommunist government. Building South Vietnam "tapped the wellsprings of American idealism" and was not inherently immoral. Diem achieved much in the South by 1959-1960, when North Vietnam decided strongly to support the NLF. Its infiltration of troops into the South and its control of the NLF meant that this was no ordinary civil war. NLF cadres were often assassins; fighting them was not inherently immoral.[43]

Liberals' view that Vietnam was a mistake represents a pragmatic critique: Diem was the wrong man, South Vietnam the wrong place, bombing and GIs and helicopters the wrong tactics; the domino theory was simply wrong. That is a hindsight that is mistaken on many points. Diem was not so unlikely a leader: he was a trained administrator who made progress before the North intervened. South Vietnam "appeared to be flourishing" in the late 1950s. It had a sizable Catholic population which "would provide a counterforce" to the NLF. Its Buddhists feared the NLF. U.S. advisers and helicopters scored impressive gains in 1962, before the North sent regular troops south. By 1967, GIs "had staved off what had appeared to be certain defeat in 1965." They won battles and inflicted high casualties on the enemy. The February 1968 Tet Offensive was a severe defeat for the NLF and the North. Not all dominos fell, but Laos and Cambodia (Kampuchea) did.[44]

The problem was not in the situation but in policymakers' pragmatic realism. Without an absolute morality, they could not handle the moral problems of making policy in a global, potentially apocalyptic, highly technological age. Without an eschatology, they lacked confidence that they would win the Cold War. Their doubts tempted them to go anywhere and do anything to make sure they would. The entire noncommunist world seemed vital: President Kennedy admitted, "I don't know where the non-essential areas are."[45] Any tactic seemed necessary, even assassinating foreign leaders. Policymakers seemed immoral, and given pragmatism's lack of an absolute morality, they often were. In an age of global competition with communism, they took the United States into a war thousands of miles off its Pacific coast. Distance deprived them of war's normal rationale: a threat to U.S. security. That Americans fought Asians (but on behalf of other Asians) added to the perception that the United States was the aggressor—going across the globe to fight another race.

The semblance of an unjust war could have been overcome. Harder to erase was the sight of American military technology, developed in world wars for use against other Western powers, pounding a small non-Western power (North Vietnam) lacking similar technology. Scientific, efficient technology was the ideal means for pragmatists, but it too seemed amoral. In 1967 Secretary of Defense Robert McNamara told LBJ, "The picture of the world's greatest superpower killing or seriously injuring 1,000 noncombatants a week, while trying to pound a tiny, backward nation into submission on an issue whose merits are hotly disputed, is not a pretty one." The "technowar" of massive B-52 bombing raids delegitimized the U.S. war effort in the eyes of New Leftists and people around the world. The raids were limited to avoid Soviet or Chinese intervention, but that prolonged the agony. They could not end the war: a primitive peasant economy like Vietnam's offered few targets.[46]

They showed that the war was mainly a moral struggle, a battle for Vietnamese "hearts and minds" that dated back to the late nineteenth century, when the swift decline of Confucianism left a vacuum in French Indochina, as in Korea and China. Unlike Korea, Vietnam's ex-Confucian scholar-gentry converted to Marxism more than to Christianity. Vietnamese nationalism was mostly Marxist.[47] The Diem regime failed to end corruption or to institute land reform. It failed to reverse the trend toward Marxism. American missionaries or Peace Corps workers might have helped, but the moral battle was largely lost by the

1950s. Moral battles were not pragmatists' priority, and they were ill-equipped to wage them. Western culture was not morally ill-equipped compared to Vietnamese communism. Vietnam showed the moral failure of pragmatic realism, not of the West.

In a postmodern critique, Gibson quotes Henry Kissinger: Western superiority comes from its "notion that the real world is external to the observer"; in other cultures "the real world is almost entirely internal to the observer." In Gibson's view, the West's managerial, scientific view of reality led to managed "technowar" and defeat because U.S. officials ignored stubborn social and cultural realities.[48] That's partly correct. Yet the problem lay not in the idea of an external real world but in the rejection of the God who is external to the real world and the observer, and thus a rejection of his absolute morality that could limit the managerial, scientific, experimental war which Gibson attacks.

Pragmatic realism had "a morality of consequences," notes Diggins: "The rightness of a political action depends on its intended consequences." Here, "pragmatism and Marxism stood" together "in their common opposition to traditional moral authority" and in their experimental approach to history. U.S. intentions were good, so its means were right. Scientific experimentation was pragmatists' method in Vietnam, where "Dr. Facts" McNamara used available technology to raise the Vietcong "body count," the statistical output of the U.S. war machine. Pragmatists sought the maximum output with the least "input" in U.S. casualties. Experiments had managers who used body counts, ratios, charts and so on to assess commanders and technologies for their effectiveness. Managers set the terms of the debate. Critics such as George Ball had to argue that bombing did not achieve its objectives, that it was not pragmatic. Its morality depended on whether or not it worked.[49]

The Vietnam War was an open-ended experiment. That caused problems. Dewey "assumed that values evolved naturally out of" activity; officials assumed that goals, strategies and rationales would evolve out of war. Arthur J. Lovejoy summarized pragmatism: "I am about to have known." Experimenters would know someday; officials would figure out their war aims and means next year. Meanwhile, they experimented without knowing: what was an objection to bombing the North (the South's government was weak) later became a reason for bombing the North (to make it stronger).

Taking the middle way was another means to put off making real choices: Kennedy sent advisers and helicopters but did not withdraw or send combat troops; Lyndon Johnson escalated but did not withdraw or wage all-out war;

Richard Nixon Vietnamized but did not withdraw or keep the status quo. The Cuban Missile Crisis gave pragmatists faith in experimental middle ways—a blockade, not diplomacy or air strikes. It became their historical analogy: gradual escalation could cleverly combine the strengths of force and diplomacy. But Vietnam was unlike Cuba: choosing the *via media* only got the United States into and out of a quagmire slowly.[50]

Pragmatists might lie when it was impolitic to admit that an action was experimental. A president could not admit that he acted only to show resolve or to see what might happen next. Such an admission would rob his acts of their intended effect on opponents. Publicizing the experiment ruined it by distorting the results. So presidents oversold pragmatic steps in a rhetoric of moral certainty which led to "credibility gaps."[51]

Finding absolutes in history, not Scripture, pragmatists used the historical analogy when they wanted moral certainty. History often gave inappropriate analogies: Dewey saw Hitler and 1939-1941 as repeats of Kaiser Wilhelm and 1914-1917; Kennedy, Johnson and McNamara saw South Vietnam in light of Munich. As Santayana said, "Experience abounds, and teaches nothing."[52]

Without Christian morality, pragmatists lost the moral war—in Vietnam, on the campuses, in world public opinion. B-52s, defoliants and high-tech weaponry used against an enemy hidden in a peasant society angered the world and the campus. U.S. and South Vietnamese forces assassinated some twenty thousand "suspected Vietcong" under the Phoenix program. Lower-level managers falsified key data (body counts). Managers' ratings led commanders to use U.S. troops as "bait" to lure Vietcong into the open. GIs were demoralized by that, by guerrilla war in a strange land, by how blacks and working-class whites did most of the fighting. Drug use and "fragging" of officers rose. Amoral pragmatists flooded in to corrupt South Vietnam: bribes, rampant prostitution, drug dealing and a booming consumerism without real economic development.[53]

In the end, American pragmatists resembled communists in their willingness to use any means to win. The differences were that the United States had greater means but lacked North Vietnam's absolute will to win and absolute (coerced) domestic support.

The United States could have fought a perfectly moral war in Vietnam. Yet low-tech tactics, patience, the vulnerability of winning "hearts and minds" one by one in remote villages and slow nation-building would have cost many more casualties and lost domestic support faster than the pragmatists' strategy.

Pragmatic realism had enlisted Americans in Cold War anticommunism by downplaying sacrifices and highlighting consumerism's rewards. Appealing to self-interest eroded the absolute patriotism shown in World Wars I and II. But it was only partially eroded: many Americans made great sacrifices in Korea, Vietnam and elsewhere. They showed a greater willingness to sacrifice than Americans would later show—in the 1990s, for example. But to understand why the Cold War ended, we must admit that in this supreme test, American and Vietnamese anticommunists did not, on the whole, display a greater willingness to lay down their lives for the cause than did Vietnamese communists. We must seek the ultimate explanation for the anticommunist victory in the Cold War in other factors.

Antiwar protest. New Left critics cited immoral aspects of a pragmatists' war to delegitimize the realist consensus, as they had used nuclear absurdity and Southern segregation. Coming later, in the mid-sixties, the antiwar movement inherited the momentum from the civil rights, antinuclear and student rights movements. It shared their stark moralism: Vietnamese peasants, rural black sharecroppers, student demonstrators and children drinking milk contaminated by strontium 90 were virtuous; governments that oppressed them were not. It took antirealist moralism from intellectual circles on the coasts and mainstreamed that to Midwest campuses and to less bookish students.[54]

Radicals identified with the Vietnamese: first with the peasants, later with NLF guerrillas. They came to abhor U.S. "technowar." In April 1965, SDS's president equated U.S. radicals with Vietnamese peasants: "In both countries there are people struggling to build a movement that has the power to change their condition." That equation had to be vague, for the two shared few specific traits or conditions. At the same rally, SNCC's Robert Parris (Moses) equated the GIs' killing of Vietnamese peasants with segregationists killing civil rights workers. (Shooting NLF cadres who used violence too was not the same as shooting nonviolent SNCC volunteers.)

Hayden went to Hanoi looking for a people who could "overcome the raw mechanical firepower of advanced technology." He romanticized them in a book. He took activists to Czechoslovakia and Hanoi to meet them. Rennie Davis "flew out of Hanoi clutching an anti-personnel bomb, which he carried with him everywhere and which he showed to everyone," Hayden recalled. The antiwar message was simplistic: good people versus an evil superpower's technology.[55]

Campus audiences accepted the message's "oversimplified logic." The draft made young males receptive. Yet protest went beyond them and was motivated by more than refusal to serve. Prior sixties causes, fifties critiques, rock and youth culture had prepared students to see America as evil. Leaders conducting nuclear tests, appointing racist judges, denying students' free speech and risking nuclear war over missiles in Cuba were now raining napalm and defoliants on villagers in Vietnam. A "legitimacy crisis" hit the realist authorities. "Death-of-God" theology hit divine authority. (It was illogical to link the two authorities.) "Authority had been knit together. . . . The bureaucrats and generals and fathers had rested their legitimacy on a single 'American way,' so that when the rationales of the Pentagon and the University of California" collapsed, it all seemed to "unravel," argues Todd Gitlin.[56]

Like the idea of equality during the American Revolution, the attack on authority tore through American society with awesome power during the sixties and early seventies.[57] Trying to stop the war, protesters proved hardly more moral than policymakers. Without an absolute morality or a Christian eschatology of eventual victory, they too adopted a pragmatic "morality of consequences." Since their intent to end the war seemed moral to them, so did most any means: burning draft cards, disrupting military bases, battling police, waving the NLF flag, hoping for an NLF win. But for the technicality that Congress had not declared war, many committed treason ("adhering to [the nation's] enemies, giving them aid and comfort"). They corrupted their allies as policymakers did the South Vietnamese: pacifists dropped an absolute morality of peacefully opposing all war and now sanctioned antiwar violence and NLF warmaking. They went, notes Gunter Lewy, from realism's "obsession with communism as totally bad to a preoccupation with American society as totally bad." Hayden talked of "bringing the war back home," of guerrilla war in the United States. Many left the political courtroom for the streets. In democracy's name they sought to overturn policy set by representatives elected by a majority.[58]

Like policymakers, they looked to history for absolutes, but their historical analogies were just as misplaced: U.S. officials as new Hitlers committing genocide in South Vietnam, soldiers who obeyed as "good Germans" following criminals' orders.[59] That was overblown. However questionable its means might often be, the United States was defending a Vietnamese government against a massive infiltration of troops from its neighbor.

Pragmatic policymakers had no Christian eschatology. Instead of certain victory, they offered Americans Cold War stalemate and eternal anticommunist vigilance. Existentialism had been their philosophy too: staying on a knife's edge and acting even if results were uncertain and the future unknown. For many sixties students, that was intolerable after Vietnam showed what a stalemate looked like, and the Cuban crisis what the alternative to stalemate was—nuclear war. For some antiwar protesters, despair led to suicide: the husband of one protester who burned herself to death explained, she "couldn't stand to live any longer under this thing."[60] Suicide might be done as an act of protest, but its futility as a tactic makes one suspect that despair motivated it as much as anger or resolve. Almost all protesters chose to cobble together their own future hope rather than commit suicide.

The Countercultural Revolt Against Realism

Its religion. Rock expressed these apocalyptic fears and millennial hopes. In the summer of 1965 Barry McGuire's "Eve of Destruction," "the fastest-rising song in rock history," angered fundamentalists, though its apocalyptic message was not unlike the one from their pulpits. Bob Dylan's "Mr. Tambourine Man" and the San Francisco Sound offered drugs and mysticism as escapes from the demands of existential action and democratic duty. Going beyond teen dreams and moon-in-June lyrics, rock became an art form heralding new utopias of mind and body. Its height was the Beatles' *Sgt. Pepper's Lonely Hearts Club Band.*[61]

Utopian hope took several forms: Revolution Now, war on ghetto streets, a counterculture of sexual liberation and hallucinogenic drugs and a return to nature. The forms were not mutually exclusive. One could believe in them all. Together they had something for everyone. Here was a substitute pagan religion offering salvation and social justice. Here "the world's good guys formed a solid front" to limit capitalism and governments but not their individualistic selves. They heeded Herbert Marcuse's call to reject the self-discipline of a "scarcity society" and to embrace self-indulgence. In his "Freudian focus," repression was psychological: students were as oppressed as rural blacks. He turned the world upside down: tolerance was totalitarian, affluence domination, politics therapy. This religion promised love in "a surrogate family" of rapidly switching sexual partners. Its drugs gave visions. Its antimaterialism offered a form of asceticism. Its back-to-nature doctrines provided a form of purity and primitivism.[62]

It had its own sense of time. Hayden argued, "The coming of repression will speed up time making a revolutionary situation . . . more likely. . . . If we look at the last ten years we see that history is moving faster and calling us to become a new generation of American revolutionaries."[63] Revolution was its main hope. Gitlin recalls, "The Revolution was an eschatological certainty, a given, a future already unfolding—History cresting the flotsam and jetsam of mere history." It didn't seem to be happening, but it must be. Radicals told themselves that it "had already begun, and proceeded to conjure up . . . allies either nonexistent (revolutionary white youth, industrial workers) or unreliable (Black Panthers) or remote (Vietnamese, Chinese)." They read Chairman Mao's Little Red Book and hailed his bloody Cultural Revolution. *The New York Review of Books* (Molotov cocktail on its cover) spread guerrilla-war chic to "the mainstream of America's intellectual culture." Words begat deeds. From September 1969 to May 1970, about 250 bombings or attempted bombings occurred at ROTC buildings, draft offices and other federal facilities. "The Revolution had to be; there was no one to make it; therefore it had to be forced." That was the syllogism used by the Weathermen and other violent groups.[64]

The frustrations of changing a democracy's mind led others to peaceful, quixotic acts of protest. One SDS chapter sponsored "Gentle Thursday," an annual antirealist fair with no contests, no products for sale, no entry fee and no practical function. In a meaningless self-parody, a SNCC-style sit-in with no purpose, students sat on the grass, blew soap bubbles, drew with chalk and did other "symbolic acts," writes Glenn Jones, to "prefigure, through perform-ance, a postrevolutionary utopia."[65] Nonviolent direct action had lost its senses. Why should campus authorities suppress it?

For the more serious, Marxism offered the eschatological certainty of future revolution. A New Left that began by disowning Marxist shibboleths ended up embracing them. Pragmatic radicalism brought them full circle. SDS's last convention saw rival Marxist factions shouting slogans at each other in a scene out of *Animal Farm*.[66]

Its competition: The revival of evangelical eschatology. Radicals had it all wrong. Christ's return and the final judgment were the eschatological certainties, not revolution or nuclear war. They came slowly with plenty of warning to encourage repentance, not instantaneously to terrorize people. Their certainty encouraged a return to an old religion and an old morality, not the creation of new ones. To the repentant, they offered salvation of one's personality and a new body, not a drug-induced personality change and damaged body. They could not be started or forestalled by human action, so they placed no world-saving democratic duty on the young. They were not acts of government: citizens were not to disobey authority in order to stop them or to make them happen. When they came, they would be seen to be just, not unjust like pragmatists' napalm on Vietnam's villages or realists' risk of nuclear war over Soviet missiles in Cuba. They ushered in Messiah's reign, not humanity's end. They were meaningful, not meaningless; the hope of millennia past, not a modern nightmare.

Many turned to this eschatology. Historian Paul Goodman thought sixties youth were "in a religious crisis." Many turned to evangelicalism and fundamentalism. A revival reached some fifty million Americans ("highbrow critics refused even to acknowledge" it till the late 1970s). "The new evangelicalism actually benefited from the upheavals of the sixties in paradoxical ways," notes one sociologist. The counterculture's attack on the rational, scientific worldview discredited an old critic of Christianity; countercultural sexual immorality discredited this new critic of Christian morals. Campus ministries such as Campus Crusade and InterVarsity Christian Fellowship engaged youth culture and won converts. Groups such as the Christian World Liberation Front engaged the counterculture. Evangelicalism became less rigidly legalistic and more appealing to youth.[67]

Revival was not surprising. The sixties revolt was not against Christianity per se, but against a realism that made faith functional and morality self-interest. Many in the New Left were several steps removed from Christianity. Many came from Old Left homes that had long since rejected it. For those returning to their parents' faith, changes in evangelicalism made it less a return and more their own new adventure.

Old doctrines and theological camps proved adaptable to a new time. Dispensational premillennialist Hal Lindsey was Campus Crusade director at UCLA in the mid-sixties until he tired of the bureaucracy and formed his own campus ministry, Jesus Christ Light and Power Company. Lindsey's dispensational critique of "the institutional church" fit with the Jesus People's critique. He popularized dispensational eschatology in *The Late Great Planet Earth,* the bestselling nonfiction book of the 1970s.[68] A faith that adapted to the frontier could adapt to Berkeley or Haight-Ashbury. God could find redeeming uses even for rebellion, though he would not erase all its consequences.

Its failure: The splintering of society. Revival was not its main or its intended consequence. Its intention was to overthrow realism, but post-1917 adjustments were too strongly entrenched: capitalist consumerism, anticommunism, New Deal programs, suburban familism. These succeeded so well in creating prosperity, a social safety net, national security and family security that they ironically made rebels secure enough to rebel against realism, and realism too secure to be overthrown. By discrediting realism (for some) and creating alternatives, the rebels only cleared space for many subcultures. They did not take power but fragmented it: a nation divided into states was now split into ethnic, age, gender and lifestyle subcultures. A "cultural civil war" broke out and continued for decades. Frustrated by the rational, pragmatic durability of realism, the rebels took an irrational turn that damaged U.S. society.[69]

They went for realism's jugular vein: reason itself. Mood-altering drugs, bizarre clothing, sexual promiscuity, Eastern mysticism—"all were ways of defying the rationalized world" of bureaucracy and technology. Rebels labeled this world as the real insanity: inmates of mental hospitals were sane compared to their guards. In another reversal, "the Cold War distinction between liberal systems and totalitarianism was no longer" accepted, for liberals were corrupt too. Christianity was no longer the only acceptable religion for Americans, nor heterosexuality the only sexual choice, nor marriage the only basis for sexuality and family.

Critics such as Susan Sontag denied the difference between art and pornography. Others denied any sure link between words and the external reality they described. Newly popular on campus in the 1960s, deconstructionism "was relativism run amok. . . . It seemed to mock religion, metaphysics, and art in about equal measure," and its books sounded "like bad translations from the French," writes historian Robert Crunden, mockingly.[70]

In this "new culture," mind was not confined to reason, logic was irrational, and antiheroes such as the Hell's Angels were preferred over heroes. Men were not always men and did not always mate with women, and, when they did, they did not always want kids or a family. Art was not beautiful, and words did not describe reality.[71] Nothing worked as intended. Rebellion against God was carried to an extreme not publicly or widely practiced before in the United States. It became rebellion against the Creator's very rationality. It went far beyond pragmatists' rebellious stress on function and neglect of the Creator.

Its effects were disastrous. "With too few distinctions between what was healthy and what was not, between reason and irrationality, the new culture had no way to ward off the worst elements of human behavior" except "well-intentioned but ineffectual pleas for people to love one another," observes historian Steigerwald. As the American Revolution's idea of equality did not produce virtue but unleashed male individualism, so the sixties attack on authority and realism did not produce community but unleashed male egotism. No longer "repressed" by the old morality, males in SDS and SNCC sexually exploited women. Women thought of shouting out during the trial of the Chicago Eight, "These men are being tried for the wrong reasons!" Women understandably applied New Left rhetoric about oppressed groups to themselves and called for a revolution against male rule. They invented an eschatology that promised the "Last Days of Patriarchy." As "radical feminism attacked heterosexual male dominance," homosexual males seized the chance to do the same. Imitating the NLF, the Gay Liberation Front used the same rhetoric about oppressed groups.[72]

American society splintered into various groups that saw themselves as victims, nursing grievances (some real enough) and withdrawing into separatism. Revolt against the fifties realist consensus widened the gap between parents and youth: issues went from curfews to cohabitation; youth rebellion went from teen problem to political cause; youth gangs went from a temporary delinquency to a permanent urban subculture. Rock sociologist Simon Frith contrasts 1920s youth who formed a middle-class peer culture not hostile to adult culture with sixties rebels who adopted "lower-class values and styles" in "an explicit opposition to both peer-group and adult middle-class norms." Now the gap was wider, the rejection of adults greater, the resulting problems—teen pregnancy, drug use, teen runaways, street violence—deeper than before.[73]

Splintering went far beyond youth. After Black Power advocates in SNCC tried to replace King's integrationism with black nationalism, the separatist style stressing racial or ethnic identity spread to Hispanics, Native Americans and white ethnics. In a "rebirth of native American culture," native religions revived and Native Americans too moved to "cultural isolation." In 1979 a psychiatrist wrote, "Like women and blacks, Vietnam vets are emerging and demanding dignity." More groups arose: Gray Panthers, environmentalists, followers of the "veritable alphabet soup of therapeutic movements"—est, Gestalt, TM, Zen. The New Left fragmented, and that led other Americans to form their own subgroups too. The national culture of 1950s sitcoms and suburbia split up.[74] That was a consequence of lacking a Christian eschatology—and other resources.

The Revolt Against Realism: Synopsis
Historians, journalists and social scientists have correctly pointed to the harmful effects when a few individuals become unbalanced and fanatical about prophecy. But such observers do not see that when a society and its leaders face an

apocalyptic age without faith in Christian eschatology, they become unbalanced too—not about prophecy but about events. The damage is multiplied many times over. The entire society, not just a cult, is damaged by the despair, frustration, escapism, amoral experimentation and social chaos that result. It happened in the sixties.

12

Splinter-New
Media-Driven, Networked, Niched, New Age America

WHERE IS AMERICA HEADED IN THE late 1990s? To begin to answer that, we must look at trends that have continued the social fragmentation begun in the 1960s. The Danes have a word that fits here: *splinterny,* totally new. A splinter of wood newly broken off has that delightful smell of birch or ash or whatever, but each new splinter reduces the block of wood. So Americans enjoy creating new fads, music, lifestyles, technologies and market niches—yet each subdividing of our society tends to weaken its coherence. Thus splintering leads to a demand for some new unifying idea to restore coherence. It is almost axiomatic that Christianity will not be the idea that people demand, for it is not new, it does not place humans at the center of reality, and its revivals tend to create disunity more than unity. But what will they demand?

We are getting ahead of the story. We have to begin by examining the process of splintering. The sixties revolt mainstreamed many issues and problems: drug use, street crime, teen pregnancy, abortion rights, gay rights, divorce and family breakdown. It is not liberal bashing to point that out. The sixties revolt was against liberal *and* conservative realism. To ignore the sixties as a turning point is to analyze issues and problems without any historical context.[1] It leads to accusing media of inciting immorality, governments of defying a fifties consensus that no longer exists, technology of changing culture by itself and the Religious Right of making up these "social issues." It's to play the "blame game" instead of thoughtfully analyzing problems.

Splintering was continued and rendered irreversible by economic, media, technological and political trends. In 1979, President Jimmy Carter warned that "we face centrifugal forces in our society and in our political system—forces of regionalism, forces of ethnicity, of narrow economic interest, of single issue politics—[that] are testing the resiliency of American pluralism and our ability to govern."[2] A splinter-new society tested Americans' resiliency and their politics.

That was obvious. More subtly, splintering deepened their society's move away from fundamental principles, already begun by pragmatists. The pragmatists denied that such principles could reveal truth *before* events and experiments, but they believed in some objective criteria for judging outcomes *after* events and experiments. Even sixties rebels had protested on behalf of values such as peace, love and justice. As society splintered, so many perspectives were created that there were no longer agreed-on criteria for judging outcomes.[3] Pragmatism went to seed. Whatever sold, whatever gained an audience or votes, was deemed a success, even if it had no relation to reality whatsoever, even if it was not sustainable, even if it didn't work after it was sold or elected.

Splintering: Technology and Marketing

Technology and marketing contributed to splintering. Like Italian city-state merchants, capitalist innovators benefited from splintering and lack of social integration. Small firms and new entrepreneurs took advantage of it, of lower costs, technological advances, a switch from manufacturing to the service sector and the downsizing of large corporations.[4] They lacked the capital to penetrate the one national market, dominated by a few large firms that spent heavily on TV ads, that existed for many products: Chevys with tailfins, Johnson & Johnson health-care products, Clairol cosmetics. Sixties changes opened up new niche markets of people who rebelled against this consumer culture—though not against shopping.

Older sectors of the economy stagnated in the seventies, but these newer niche markets partly filled the slack. Daniel Yankelovich wrote of the decade,

"In a matter of a few years we have moved from an uptight culture set in a dynamic economy to a dynamic culture set in an uptight economy."[5]

Cultural, economic and technological change intersected in the entertainment media. They splintered the one national TV-network-dominated market into many niche markets based on lifestyle choices. Even before the changes, network dominance forced many radio stations to abandon the adult market and to appeal to teenagers by playing rock 'n' roll, often in a Top 40 format. Gradually TV eliminated national, general-interest magazines: *Life, Look* and *Saturday Evening Post.* Network shows were cautious. They avoided offending Southern whites or small-town folks who were part of the one national audience. Broadcasters could not select the viewers they wanted.[6]

This began to change in the 1960s. With "the increasingly sophisticated use of 'demographics' " and the rise of FM sound, radio stations that had sought "huge heterogeneous audiences now concentrated on exploring the differences between small homogeneous ones or servicing precisely the musical (and consumer) tastes of specific age, ethnic, or local groups." By the 1970s, FM stations specialized in rock, country and western, Top 40 or rhythm and blues. FM's superior quality drove AM stations back to seek adult audiences with talk radio in "drive time." In the 1980s rock fragmented into punk rock, hard rock and Album Oriented Rock (AOR).[7]

Fragmentation was not due just to new technologies or new marketing techniques. The sixties rebellion against realism popularized and creatively fragmented the rock music scene. The young wanted to separate themselves from parents and parents' uptight realism—and from other youth—by their musical taste. Once the tight suburban consensus of self-interested morality was broken, a hundred cultural flowers bloomed—and each bore the fruit of marketable music or marketable products.

That altered the way the networks and Hollywood competed. NBC switched to relevant "programs that appealed to audiences having superior 'demographics' "—urban and suburban younger adults with higher incomes. CBS dropped its small-town lineup (*The Beverly Hillbillies, The Andy Griffith Show* and so on) to seek the same viewers. Network dominance of a general audience led Hollywood to target "younger or better-educated moviegoers [who] wanted a realism about sex or violence absent on TV" but present in sixties youth culture. Prohibitions against nudity and obscenity were eased starting in the mid-1960s. The market had fragmented into small-town Andy Griffith fans, suburban fans of Dick Van Dyke, young-adult viewers of R-rated films and children flocking to see *The Sound of Music.*[8]

Fragmentation occurred before the technological revolution of the eighties—before cable TV, videocassette recorders (VCRs), Nintendo or personal computers—but they accelerated it. Fragmentation in media aided the entrepreneurs' selling to niche markets. Advertising was more affordable on an FM station than on a network show. For consumer goods, advertising was everything, and the many small lifestyle-niche markets were cheaper to reach than the fifties national market had been. In turn, small firms making products designed for older rock fans who listened to AOR, for example, helped to build and maintain that subgroup. Fans highlighted their identity by what they wore or ate—and by what they listened to. Marketers and lifestyle enclaves reinforced each other.[9]

The personal was political, said feminists. If so, it was public and marketable. One's lifestyle, sexual preference and musical tastes went public. Entrepreneurs seized on people's eagerness to advertise their identity, to wear "T-shirts with slogans, political statements, personal messages, brand names," notes historian Peter Carroll. "As free-floating billboards, they expressed the most blatant invasion of American capitalism into the private sphere." Shopping malls became the new public square, where individuals could purchase goods to forge an identity and could display it in a lifestyle performance.[10] This was partly the unintended result of anticapitalist movements: the New Left, radical feminism and the counterculture.

Discrediting traditional morality and authority meant allowing popular culture and consumerism to enter more areas of American life. Everything seemed open to public discussion; every view seemed to be tolerated; the supporters of every viewpoint seemed to have organized; every such subgroup seemed a niche for marketers to cultivate; there were more media through which to reach niche markets. Governments were not doing this to us. We capitalists and consumers were.

Filmmakers, TV producers and ad agencies appeal to media-saturated Baby Boomers with self-referential films and commercials referring to previous films and commercials. Media history is linear—earlier deceptions make later tactical revisions necessary. Thus "commercials openly admit that they are commercials," Michael Dunne notes, and use "self-references . . . with an audience grown jaded through long exposure to advertising that tried to conceal its designs." Films such as Mel Brooks's *Blazing Saddles* spoof earlier films and TV Westerns. Sitcoms parody earlier sitcoms. This flatters those hip enough to get the joke. Rock and country stars sing about their lives, not real life. The swirl of words, notes and visuals refers to prior words, notes and visuals—not to reality. Show business is the only thing signified.[11]

Begun in 1981, the Music Television (MTV) channel on cable TV is another example of postmodern self-referentiality and circularity, but carried a step further. The rock videos it plays defy all modern rules: they often have no story line, refer back to films or TV shows and are self-referential; sometimes they are videos about making videos; many blur the lines between male and female, past and present, spectator and spectacle. Advertising triumphs over reality: each rock video is a promotional ad for a CD or tape, and the real ads between videos "are increasingly themselves extremely short rock videos." The result is that "MTV functions like one continuous ad." Though videos mock social norms, they do not connect to radical politics. They only give the young consumer a choice of rebellious poses he or she can assume by buying the CD or the jeans. MTV is "about consumption" above all else.[12]

This is more than a human-centered world. It's a media-icon-centered one. A person has to be a celebrity to exist in it. All that exists in it is made equal—the trivial and the earthshaking. TV especially "is an equivalizing medium . . . that establishe[s] equality among otherwise disparate forms of experience." A presidential talk might be interrupted on the evening news by a commercial on bad breath. Here's equality of opportunity, not equality of condition: films and commercials are judged by viewers—not by whether they are true or false but by whether they are entertaining or boring. Dunne cites comical films and shows. He omits the despair of seeking hope only to find that nothing in media *connects* to reality or hope.[13]

A battle rages between conservative and liberal critics of popular culture— and between its supporters and all its critics. Do liberal media spread a subversive popular culture attacking traditional values and denigrating Western culture, as conservatives charge? Do corporate-controlled media sell citizens' leisure back to them as a commodity, creating a "society of the spectacle," a "hyper-reality," which so befuddles them that they cannot tell true from false, as leftist critics charge? Defenders of popular culture charge both sets of critics with elitism: people choose what they want and do not blindly accept what liberal producers or conservative corporations give them.[14]

By focusing on the Father versus the world, we see that these arguments miss the point. Circular, self-referential media hinder people from connecting with the God who exists. They encourage people to believe that God is just a human-created symbol used to sell products or worldviews, that he is inside the circle, not outside. The transcendent reality of God is denied. Circularity leads people to disconnect from real issues that might drive them to the real God. Producers and corporations do not force-feed them; their rebellion against God is sufficient cause. They shape popular culture so that it better fits their rebellion. That does not excuse its peddlers and producers, who are not uniformly liberal or conservative but are usually capitalists who are liberal on social issues. A highbrow-lowbrow dichotomy is not the issue either. An evangelical critique of popular culture need not be elitist. A nonelitist, understandable gospel is the alternative here, not opera. It is preached to people in several popular styles, but many of them reject it.

As David Wells points out, this postmodern, media-driven world is just the "final stages" of modernity starting "to consume its own innards"—not a totally new age. Consumption is still the obsession. Excluding God and "moral and religious values" is not antimodern or postmodern but "quintessentially modern."[15] Rebels saturating themselves in self-referential media try to banish God and reality in vain: off-screen, history keeps happening—unedited, linear, live, unsponsored—and God makes relentless progress pursuing his goals.

Splintering: Failure to Reconstruct a Political Consensus

Politics can be circular, self-referential and evasive too. Political history still happened, and no leader could reconstruct the realist consensus, even on such noncultural issues as the energy crisis, tax reform and the budget.

The Constitution upended Nixon's attempt. Americans accepted realpolitik when aimed at foreign enemies but not when aimed at domestic ones. Or the political courtroom and its Constitution would not accept it. Once Judge John J. Sirica refused to treat the Watergate break-in as mere burglary, the Constitution seemed like some Invisible Hand working inexorably through Senate hearings, grand jury proceedings, a Supreme Court decision on the Nixon tapes and House impeachment hearings to bring an out-of-control White House into line. The press played its role well. Yet it was the negative triumph that courtrooms produce: a guilty verdict, not a new policy consensus.[16]

Nixon's successor, Gerald Ford, lost his chance at consensus-building when he pardoned Nixon. Feelings about the former president were too strong, and Ford's political-courtroom pardon of Nixon overshadowed his try at governing.

A slim majority elected Jimmy Carter in a bid to unite around traditional morality and realism—as adjusted to civil rights, cultural pluralism and a limited post-Vietnam foreign policy. Carter was ideally suited to bridging barriers and creating consensus: a white Southerner, he supported civil rights and could "connect" to black audiences; a born-again Baptist, he understood secularism and sixties rebellion; a fiscal conservative, he was a moderate on social issues and opposed the Vietnam War. Carter was evangelical revival, civil rights movement and sixties revolt come to Washington. As a politician, he used a comprehensive policy approach to build a "public goods" consensus to beat fragmenting interest groups. Bicentennial patriotism created the mood suited to that approach.[17]

No wonder the Reverend Martin Luther King Sr. intoned in his benediction at the 1976 Democratic National Convention, "Surely the Lord sent Jimmy Carter to come on out and bring America back where she belongs." Carter considered using 2 Chronicles 7:14 as the text for his inaugural address but was told that it sounded self-righteous. So he chose Micah 6:8 instead.[18] Yet the United States was not and never could be Israel. Nor would it humble itself or turn from rebellion and be healed.

The energy crisis caused by U.S. dependence on OPEC oil was a perfect test for Carter's comprehensive approach, suggests political scientist Erwin C. Hargrove, because "it pitted the national interest, and a public good, against regional and economic interests." Carter put forward a comprehensive energy plan before interest groups could fragment it in-the-making, but Congress balked. "It was too liberal for conservatives"—it regulated prices—"and too conservative for liberals"—it raised them. Americans did not rally around it. As energy consumers, they would not pay more (energy taxes) or use less (conservation). It went against the grain of their consumerism and "threatened corporate profits." Energy-producing states such as Oklahoma and Texas fought it. A modified plan was passed by late 1978, but the debate showed that Americans could not unite to limit consumerism. In a splintered society divided by culture, history, regions and media, one subgroup feared that others would benefit or avoid the sacrifices.[19]

That was the basic cause of the high inflation of the Carter years. Carter's energy policy was inflationary, and so were OPEC's oil price increases—from less than five dollars a barrel in 1973 to thirty-five dollars a barrel in 1981. Americans could have accepted the resulting one-cause, one-time decline in their real income and living standards, but they would not. Instead everyone's rush to protect *their* real income—unions seeking wage hikes above Carter's guidelines, seniors getting social security and other entitlements indexed to the

CPI, married women and teens entering the job market and farmers seeking higher farm price supports—all pushed the inflation rate to 13.5 percent by 1980 (briefly it hit 17 percent).[20] The 1950s consensus had been built on the guarantee of higher living standards. Carter could not build another one without that guarantee. The second round of OPEC increases accompanied the Iranian Revolution—itself the fatal blow to Carter's presidency.

Carter combined Wilsonian idealism with a minimum of Cold War realism. A moral realist, he would defend the Free World while reforming it. An evangelical familiar with Christian eschatology, he had to work with secular assumptions and through bureaucrats used to a "process," says Gary Sick, that was "incremental, goal-oriented, competitive and fundamentally rational," a "chess game" suited to pragmatic players. Iran's Revolution confronted them with the opposite. Experts grossly underestimated the strength and will of the revolt's clerical leader, Ayatollah Khomeini. A State Department official later admitted, "Whoever took religion seriously?"[21]

As the Ayatollah's followers staged street demonstrations at forty-day intervals and risked death to defy the Shah's soldiers, American officials looked "for points of leverage and control" and found none. They were pragmatists facing an eschatological event: many Shiite Moslems believed that Khomeini was a ninth-century *imam* who had "miraculously disappeared" in A.D. 873 but now, "when the world was in dire trouble," was reappearing "as the Mahdi, or Messiah." Khomeini did not deny it, but "allowed himself to be addressed as 'imam' " —"which had obvious messianic implications for Iranians." When he did return to Iran from exile on February 1, 1979 (the year 1400 in the lunar calendar), millions thronged the streets of Tehran.[22] Carter's chess players faced a second coming!

Here was the irony: a born-again president who had to govern in the style of American pragmatism faced a religious fundamentalism and a (false) messianic return. His only "point of leverage" was to urge the Shah to unleash the military on street demonstrators, but the *moral* realist rejected that option.[23] Helpless to stop Khomeini or to join him, then to free the U.S. hostages or to forget them, Carter looked weak, but it was pragmatism that was weak when faced with would-be martyrs and eschatological events. If Reagan had been president, he might have unleashed the Shah's soldiers on street mobs, but that too would have failed against a supposed messianic return.

A final factor in Carter's failure to build consensus—a factor Hargrove says little about—was the culture war over ERA, abortion, school prayer and other issues. Carter was a Democratic Calvin Coolidge in that his personal religiosity and morality partly masked the nation's ongoing moral fragmentation but did nothing to stop it. Nor did he take a conservative stand on moral issues unleashed by the sixties revolt—especially abortion. The renewed feminism of the late sixties sought legalized abortion as a step to giving women full equality with men. The natural process of pregnancy and childbirth was a choice, feminists argued. By choosing not to deliver, women could avoid interrupting careers and enduring other consequences men never had to face.[24]

At the start of Nixon's second term, the Supreme Court had tried to forestall the issue with its *Roe* v. *Wade* decision (January 1973), which struck down a Texas law that restricted abortions—and thus all similar state laws.[25] But the Court failed to construct a national consensus. That is not because abortion is a moral issue on which there are only two possible, antagonistic, uncompromisable views, as is commonly supposed. As sociologist James Davison Hunter points out, the issue produces ambivalence among Americans, most of whom "land somewhere in the middle of this debate." A decision that allowed variations between states, that prohibited abortion past the first trimester, and that required a reason such as rape, incest, serious deformity or risk to the mother's life would have won broad support. It would have been politically acceptable to most Americans. Many Americans support *Roe* in the mistaken belief that it is such a compromise decision.[26]

An absolute constitutionalism prevents the Court from making the compromises made in Western Europe on abortion (or on gun control—absolutism comes from both the political Right and Left). A right is in the Constitution or it isn't. The document and the justices who interpret it are more absolutist than are moralists. Even its defenders saw *Roe* v. *Wade* as a questionably reasoned ruling that found an abortion right no one had seen in an 186-year-old document. Yet "subsequent decisions not only reaffirmed *Roe* but extended its interpretation," writes Hunter, until the Court provided "a foundation for the practice of abortion on demand for the full nine months."

Justices appointed by Reagan and Bush doubted *Roe*'s constitutional logic, but the Court in 1992 (*Casey* v. *Pennsylvania Planned Parenthood*) stood on precedent and affirmed *Roe* to protect the Court's "legitimacy." Instead a "crisis in legitimacy" has spread to the entire government: prolifers judge a government that allows abortion to be partly illegitimate; prochoice advocates' fears that government might disallow abortion lead them to judge it potentially illegitimate.[27]

The failure of the Court to forge a consensus on the abortion issue—and on other issues in the culture war doomed efforts to construct a broad political consensus. It doomed the efforts of Democrats, the majority party since 1932. Even before *Roe,* its 1972 nominee, George McGovern, lost votes among Democratic blue-collar and Catholic voters due to his liberal stand on cultural issues such as abortion. After winning over fellow evangelicals (especially Southern ones) in 1976 with a moderate stand, Jimmy Carter lost them in 1980. Michael Barone concludes, "The cultural segment of America which" saw "Jimmy Carter as its kind of American had decided he was not" and now felt "disappointed" or "betrayed" by him.[28]

A Consensus That Isn't: Laissez-Faire Tax-Cutting Deregulation

Ronald Reagan's two popular terms appeared to forge an eighties realism: renewed anticommunism, reliance on "free enterprise" for economic growth, profamily policies, nostalgia for the WASP small-town values of Reagan's boyhood in Illinois. Yet this was a pseudorealism upheld by a pseudoconsensus—the only one possible in a fragmented society.

The Reagan revolution demanded little of voters, so they had little invested in his program. It asked them to grant themselves a 30 percent tax cut (reduced to 25 percent) and promised to get government off their backs (by deregulating *firms*). "Proposed tax cuts provided an essential common ground for the right-of-center coalition" at "the core of the Reagan revolution." It did not demand that Americans sacrifice to *do* something. Its proposed budget cuts were greatly reduced by Congress. The increase in defense spending was mostly paid for with borrowed money, much of it from foreign investors. Fifties realism eased sacrifices with consumer goods, but it required some pain: the Korean War and nearly balanced budgets. Never tested, eighties patriotism never grew strong but only grew fat on easy wins such as Grenada and symbolic ones such as the 1984 Summer Olympics.[29]

When inflation fell rapidly in the eighties, federal (and state) revenues declined far more than projected, and Reagan's 1981 plan "proved to be the most wildly inaccurate economic forecast in American history." The tax cut combined with inadequate budget cuts to produce budget deficits which soared to more than $200 billion. The political courtroom could not address them, much less reduce them.[30]

A surrealist politics came to resemble media-centered pop culture. Like competing media, the Republican president and Democratic Congress peddled their products to niche markets of media-saturated voters used to commercials that appealed to their subconscious mind but did not connect to rational ideas.

An entertaining commercial cannot be proven false. Social critic Neil Postman analyzed why people ignored Reagan's misstatements: in a Media Age, talk is decontextualized, contradictions do not exist, and reports about them are seen as boring. Neither Democrats nor Republicans proposed a balanced budget or connected to fiscal reality. They used direct mail loaded with partisan rhetoric to appeal to their core support groups and soothing sound bites and commercials to appeal to the general voter. Celebrity endorsements became a key tactic. Reagan rose to power as a famous former actor. Politics became circular and self-referential: Reagan acted like FDR, and his would-be Democratic challengers like JFK.[31]

A few relics of the age of print, such as Senators Robert Dole and Pete Domenici, protested that the numbers didn't add up, but media-savvy pols knew that it didn't matter.[32] Surreal media culture contributed to this surreal outcome: democracy functioned—votes were cast and candidates won or lost—but it failed that basic test of any government, namely, balancing revenues and expenses. Reagan's budgets were "dead on arrival" on Capitol Hill. Budget-makers cooked the numbers. Budgets were just signs, political responses to other budget-signs. They did not signify fiscal reality. Politics was the signified. It differed little from show business. Citizens half-knew that politicians were insulting their intelligence, but they kept watching the Reagan-Tip O'Neill show anyway.

The disconnect went beyond the budget. Deregulation of S&Ls and eighties greed led to the S&L debacle. As antinuclear forces won support for a "freeze," Reagan proposed his Strategic Defense Initiative (SDI), an expensive high-tech escape from MAD: "zapping incoming missiles with laser beams." Scientists doubted it could be built, economists that it could be financed. Congress approved it as a bargaining chip in arms talks: SDI was a sign to the Soviets and did not signify an actual defense system. Reagan's profamily campaign talk of restoring small-town values was a sign to his support groups that he was with them, but talk was never turned into deeds by the divorced, nonchurchgoing president. Tolerance for and practice of "alternative" lifestyles increased in the eighties. As in Coolidge's day, Americans wanted the symbol of an old-fashioned leader but the reality of wide-open, market-driven innovation in business and morals.[33]

The Nation with No Government and the Soul of a Supermarket
Here was the old American faith in markets and technology and the old distrust

of government. The latter had not failed, as Reaganites charged; Americans just could not agree on what it should do. Old industries were deregulated and new ones partly or belatedly regulated as new technologies revolutionized business and society. Capitalism was free to transcend limits. A capitalism that organized human rebellion—not government—was splintering American society.

Capitalism is often most amoral at its leading edge, at its innovative margins. In the late 1970s, X-rated movies drove the growth of a market for prerecorded videocassettes. In the 1980s, mergers and acquisitions financed with leveraged buyouts and junk bonds swept corporate America, left companies with huge debt loads and threatened workers with layoffs. New, unregulated, computer buy-and-sell programs and the federal deficit (and other factors) caused a stock market crash in October 1987 that nearly closed the New York Stock Exchange. But the Fed's intervention saved the day, and the moral lesson was never learned. The computer revolution linked world financial markets into one global network difficult to monitor or regulate. U.S. firms moved jobs "offshore" to low-wage sites in Singapore or Taiwan. Computer hackers and programmers created a global computer network, the Internet, that might greatly limit the nation's control of its own house—and they did it with government funds. The nation paid no attention, in the faith that markets and technology must be bringing progress.[34]

As in medieval Europe, government performed few of its God-given tasks. Did Americans even want their government to govern? They did not agree on its proper tasks, except that it should aid the two things they did agree on: markets and technology. Its courts enforced contracts. Its schools and universities educated a future work force and enough scientists, engineers and programmers to ensure a future flow of new technologies. Its candidates talked of free markets, better education and new technologies. It controlled crime and kept law and order where factories, farms and offices were located, where goods were transported and where workers and managers lived and commuted—but not elsewhere. It made gestures at controlling its budget and trade deficits when it had to reassure Wall Street and foreign investors. It did not dare slow transfer payments and foreign goods flowing to consumers. Lest it disrupt markets or U.S. competitiveness, it did little to prevent U.S. firms from sending jobs overseas, from busting unions or from being acquired by foreign firms. Hamstrung by constitutionalism, it did little to control an abortion industry that sold to women the "right" to end lives, little to control a stream of sex and violence which the media broadcast to children and adults or the high-tech weapons which citizens carried or their new extralegal militias. It could not enforce its own immigration laws: firms and citizens wanted cheap labor.[35]

In the nation with the soul of a supermarket, buying, selling and inventing things to buy and sell were everything. Faith became a marketable commodity. Entrepreneurs sold near-death experiences, recoveries, new techniques and a New Age.

When communism fell in the Soviet Union and Eastern Europe, this Cold War victory seemed to validate Americans' emphasis on markets and technology. It was not Americans' self-sacrifices or government efficiency that toppled Marx and Lenin but capitalism's markets and new technologies that left Soviet central planners hopelessly behind. Underlying problems in U.S. society had not prevented victory, so the incentive for addressing them was lessened.[36]

Splinter-New America: An Underclass but No Culture

But to let markets and technology work was to let them further subdivide society. Using the new technologies of cable TV, VCRs, satellite dishes, personal computers (PCs), compact discs (CDs) and video games, the entertainment industry further developed niche markets that reflected and deepened society's fragmentation: MTV's youth niche, ESPN's male sports fans, Nintendo's preteen market. To attract consumers, sellers added more sex and violence. Heading the opposite way, a Christian "infotainment" industry had fifteen hundred religious radio and TV stations, eighty publishers, more than six thousand bookstores, a religious music market and its own clean-cut Las Vegas at Branson, Missouri.

Rich and poor went in opposite ways too as global capitalism widened class divisions. In the 1980s "earnings dropped 8 percent for the poorest 20 percent and rose 9 percent for the top 20 percent" of Americans. New immigrants added to the ethnic diversity but also to ethnic tensions, as some groups prospered more than others.[37]

Some groups joined the "underclass." The word became a subject of controversy, but the existence of a permanently unemployed, welfare-dependent, crime-beset, poverty-stricken class in the nation's inner cities could not be denied. It was primarily African-American, with some East Coast Puerto Ricans and West Coast Hispanics included. Postindustrial, global capitalism was hard on the urban poor. Jobs required greater skill and more education; those that did not moved to East Asia. Factory jobs left inner-city areas and moved to the suburbs. Office jobs came, but the unskilled could not fill them. High-wage union jobs decreased. Residential segregation increased. Jobless young males turned to drug dealing and street crime, and they abandoned young women to single-parent child rearing. Formerly ethnic job niches meant, for example, that early Italian immigrants helped Italian latecomers get jobs in construction. Now the need for formal credentials and formal hiring procedures reduced this ethnic self-help. Affirmative action helped those few who had credentials, but when they left the ghetto their positive example left too.[38]

The result, historian Thomas J. Sugrue writes, is that "American cityscapes today are eerily apocalyptic." In inner-city Detroit, he adds, "empty hulks of abandoned factories loom over acres of rubble. Whole rows of storefronts are boarded up. Abandoned houses . . . are surrounded by fields overgrown with prairie grass and ragweed. Sixty thousand vacant lots lay strewn throughout the city."[39] And that does not describe the damage to human beings made in God's image but effectively written off by postindustrial capitalism as if they were unusable, unsalvable assets or bad debts.

Capitalism is not altruistic, though individual investors or managers may be. There is little chance to accumulate capital in the inner city except in illegal trades such as drug dealing. Capitalism integrates and prospers societies which have law and order, the work ethic and some social harmony. It does not bridge racial barriers or rebuild societies that lose these essentials (its own consumerism erodes these). So U.S. firms send unskilled manufacturing jobs abroad or hire illegal immigrants to do them here or hire legal ones who have not yet lost their culture, cohesion and work ethic to an Americanizing consumerism. Several sociologists report that now Americanization is a ticket to the underclass for Asian-American and Hispanic youth. Those whose families have been here the longest do the worst in school. "It's dating, it's pregnancy, it's gangs, all the bad Americanization stuff," says one professor of education. African-Americans have been here the longest, are most Americanized and most at risk.[40]

The nation fails to pass on its traditional culture to youth or to immigrants but succeeds only too well in passing on a mass consumer culture that is partly self-destructive and antisocial. The nation retains its traditional culture only in regional pockets and demographic niches. It has no real national culture. Pop culture has long since ridiculed and undermined the old Anglo-Saxon, small-town culture.

The underclass's inner city is a colony whose output is not goods and services but culture—rap music, gun-toting machismo, drugs, antisocial hipness and street gangs. Understandably angry at being written off by society, inner-city males develop a culture of anger that is marketed to white suburban youths, to Asian or Hispanic immigrants and to other parts of the globe through American media exports. A few inner-city entrepreneurs profit. A few become celebrities. Most inner-city residents get nothing but violence and social breakdown. Society largely tolerates this breakdown unless 'hood culture threatens markets, as it did in the L.A. riots. What do we think will happen to antisocial, self-destructive behavior in a market-oriented society? It will be marketed.[41]

Attempts to Forge a New Cultural and Moral Consensus

In the mid-nineties many Americans were very concerned about family break-down, crime, violence as entertainment, a corrupting popular culture and failures in socializing and educating youth. Several movements have attempted to restore civic morality.

Non-Christian attempts. One recycles American history as nostalgia with an uplifting moral message, especially at major celebrations: the Bicentennial, the centennial of the Statue of Liberty, the Constitution's bicentennial. It appears at national spectacles such as the 1984 Summer Olympics in Los Angeles and the 1996 Summer Olympics in Atlanta. Presidents and candidates evoke it: Bill Clinton did with his acceptance speech praising the middle class and his old-time bus tour of Midwestern small towns in July 1992.[42]

Yet morality cannot be restored with historical memories. Christopher Lasch notes, "Nostalgia evokes the past only to bury it alive." The nostalgic moralizer does not dispute the innovator's claim that rapid change makes old norms outdated. He only regrets it. This nostalgic view of U.S. history is under attack by revisionist historians. In high schools and colleges, the U.S. History course is no refuge from the culture wars. Quite the opposite: it is a chief site where they occur. Though often mistaken, revisionists have enough facts right to prove that U.S. history was too amoral to serve as a guide to civic morality.[43]

Another answer, to re-create a civic discourse in American public life, was partly inspired by historians' new emphasis on republicanism as America's shaping ideology. Republicanism stressed citizens' duties, not individuals' rights. After conquering the historical profession in the 1970s and early 1980s, it appeared in political scientists' and sociologists' works such as the 1985 bestseller by Robert Bellah and associates, *Habits of the Heart.* If Americans would drop their individualism, drop their Sheilaism ("Just try to love yourself and be gentle with yourself"), pick up the old republican and biblical languages of community and talk to "our friends, our fellow citizens," then we might reforge a "culture of coherence." (Recently Todd Gitlin has urged the Left to pick up the old language of the Enlightenment, drop identity politics and forge unity.) Clinton's 1992 campaign theme of a "New Covenant" stressing citizens' responsibilities as well as rights fits this theme of civic engagement.[44]

Hunter's analysis of our culture wars, especially the abortion one, fits it too. His analysis is accurate, but with it comes a hope that somehow Americans in the middle will pay attention and seize the debate from the extremists—the special agenda groups that have distorted it. In an odd reversal of Spiro Agnew's praise for the silent majority, academic experts now hope Middle America will prevail! They stress process, discourse, debate and not specific values or truths. "Cultures are dramatic conversations" between people speaking "languages" and reflecting different traditions.[45]

Focusing on process cannot soften the hard reality that the conversationalists hold diametrically opposed views. A focus on process is pragmatic: you deal with process because you cannot change beliefs. Yet merely pragmatic arguments cannot convince debaters of the paramount importance of the process. You cannot tell angry rap singers, militia members or street gangs to please stop interrupting the conversation and expect that you will be heeded. The hothouse pace of cultural and technological change rapidly erodes "communities of memory" and traditional "languages," and a pragmatic warning about heeding cultural speed limits will not slow it. Even after excluding the religious and corporate Right, Gitlin can find no common rules by which leftists are likely to return to talking civilly to each other, despite their common memories. Even those who agree on the sixties often cannot stand to stay in the same room with each other.[46] What hope is there that those split by the sixties can do so?

A third answer is to downplay cultural issues and stress the economy and its rewards. Democrats and Republicans, liberals and conservatives, use this approach. Clinton aide James Carville in 1992 used the internal campaign motto "The Economy, Stupid." Other Democrats campaign on the issues of "jobs, jobs, jobs"—as if more fifteen-dollar-per-hour union jobs was all the nation needed. A more conservative take comes from Francis Fukuyama, who argues that liberal democracy with its free markets, freedoms and widely distributed prosperity will make Americans contented bourgeois consumers who will have no other ideology to turn to if they do grow restless. The contented consumer will become "the Last Man"; the dialectical struggle for freedom and honor that drives history will end.[47]

Yet, Fukuyama admits, capitalism undermines the community and family life that is needed for capitalism and a capitalist work ethic. His stress on the individual's hunger for recognition comes from German philosopher G. W. F. Hegel, who saw Christianity as the ideology of slaves. Agreeing with that, Fukuyama ignores the battle of the world against the Father, which supplies history with a dialectical struggle and every human society with an internal contradiction, even if people manage to resolve lesser contradictions. After democratic, capitalist people have granted each other equal recognition and equal opportunity, their rebellion against their Creator will drive history until that rebellion ends.[48]

Christian attempts. Christians present a fourth answer, a new moral consensus much like the old fifties consensus and Victorian norms. The U.S. Catholic bishops advocate a consistent policy of social justice and an end to legalized abortions, but the Vatican's unpopular stands on birth control and women's rights have undercut their support among Catholics. And they have no clear political home: most Democrats' strong prochoice position deprives them of their traditional one, whereas prolife Republicans often do not accept their views on social justice.

Evangelicals accommodate themselves to Republicans' probusiness platforms in exchange for the GOP's support for their profamily views on social issues: prolife, anti-gay rights and support for school prayer and private-school vouchers. Since the late seventies, through groups such as Jerry Falwell's Moral Majority, James Dobson's Focus on the Family, the Family Research Council and the Christian Coalition, they have played a major role in reinvigorating the GOP. In May 1995 the Christian Coalition had "1.6 million active supporters and [a] $25 million budget," reported *Time*. Best of all, in a media- and market-driven nation, it benefits from the momentum generated by a vast, growing Christian "infotainment" sector. In this subculture, consumerism recruits people to politics more than it distracts them from it. Purchasing books, CDs, tapes and magazines motivates and reinforces political activity. "The Christians are close to winning the whole war; they might do it by '96," predicts one Republican pollster.[49]

That is surely too optimistic a view, unless beating Bill Clinton is seen as "the whole war." To endorse and influence a winning presidential candidate is not to forge a new moral consensus or to win the culture wars. We have already had one born-again president who failed at consensus-building. The nation would be better off with an evangelical consensus that limited consumerism's inroads into family life, motivated altruistic attempts to help the underclass and tamed the antisocial, violent pop culture. Yet that outcome is unlikely for seven practical reasons, plus one theological one.

First, the constitutional fragmentation of power requires Christians to control all three branches of the federal government for years—plus many state governments. That is highly unlikely.

Second, the Constitution, the Supreme Court and the legal culture are profoundly secular and committed to upholding precedent, as *Casey* showed. Despite the growing number of evangelical lawyers and legal advocacy groups, the legal system would strictly limit "profamily," proreligion or prolife policies of presidency, Congress or the states. Like Pickett's charge, *Casey* may have been the high-water mark of prolifers' attempt to overthrow *Roe*. They were thrown back and are unlikely to get as close again.[50]

Third, as Hunter notes, "the secular knowledge sector is a crucial influence in determining the outcome of our cultural conflict." Like the legal profession, its influence weighs against evangelicals. It is linked to the state, whose "*very ethos* . . . is unsupportive of a broad cultural system" such as evangelicalism that promotes "transcendent ideals." Those who see the state as a few elected officials and ignore its bureaucrats, its academic auxiliaries and its secular ethos underestimate its virtual immunity from Christian influence.[51]

Fourth, this secular state seems to fit a society that is religiously diverse. Besides Protestants, Catholics and Jews, it has Muslims, Hindus, various New Age groups, Buddhists and innumerable cults. As new religions grow and religious entrepreneurs cultivate niche markets, a secular state seems more needed to handle diversity and soothe potential friction.

Fifth, given evangelicals' ideas on acceptable behavior, their coming to power would reverse postsixties splintering into lifestyle enclaves. That would be strongly resisted. Small firms, alternative media, computer services, whole industries and many entrepreneurs have a financial stake in the continued existence of these lifestyle enclaves, which are niche markets for them. They oppose a return to a highly moral exclusivist consensus that denounces these niches. Firms that market vices co-opt other firms, the media and individuals into defending their right to market, notes John C. Burnham.[52]

It rarely works in reverse. Markets rarely co-opt sinners into outlawing vice. Fundamentally, worshiping and obeying God are free of charge, like inhaling air. Marketers do market these, but they cannot co-opt society into outlawing impiety and disobedience in order to increase the market share for worship and obedience.

Marketing tends to corrupt worship and obedience by replacing pious motives with profit motives. The Christian infotainment industry is lucrative: "the total annual income of Christian adults" in the United States is estimated at nearly a trillion dollars. Secular marketers enter this vast niche market, and Christian ones become more profit-minded. The apostle Paul could write, "Unlike so many, we do not peddle the word of God for profit," but unlike him, many do in the 1990s. The potential profits tempt even the most sincere Christian writer, preacher or musician. The result is less "speak[ing] before God with sincerity"—and more of what David Wells calls "secular evangelicalism," whose "marketing" matches that of a postmodern world unoffended by a self-help gospel that is "just one more commodity in a crowded marketplace."[53]

Sixth, as the evangelical army marches toward the heights of political power, its ranks are thinned, its ardor cooled and its motives corrupted—not by the enemy ahead, that is seen commanding the heights, but by a largely unseen one off to the side, a secularizing consumerism. It can hardly defend against or even recognize that enemy. To work within the GOP is to accept the consumerism that party has always advanced and its definition of the enemy: big government, "new class" liberals on campus and in the media, and minorities seeking special treatment. These can express anti-Christian biases. But GOP coalition-building leads many evangelicals to accept what Lasch calls "the fundamental contradiction . . . of the new right": its claim that moral decay results from the new class's "concerted attack on business" and is not "the cultural expression of consumer capitalism." Actually, marketers selling video games, cyberporn, dating services, lottery tickets or "crack" prove more popular and more subversive than neo-Marxist professors lecturing on "world systems" theory.[54]

Seventh, "new class" intellectuals pull some evangelicals away from the faith. Hunter cites Antonio Gramsci's theory that progressive intellectuals assimilate traditional ones and his own observation of this process at work "among the younger cohorts of elites" in evangelicalism. In a pluralist society, you can choose between several exit doors out of exclusivist faith into tolerant secularism. "Accommodation to the spirit of the times" is one. Consumerism is another. Compromising on theology to hold political coalitions together is a third. (God's commands become "family values" to make them salable.) A multitude of exit doors is implied in Jesus' saying about the narrow road to life and the broad road to destruction.[55]

Theologically, the problem with a Christian attempt at cultural consensus is that Christianity is divine revelation. With its exclusive truths, it must be privileged above human belief systems. Yet evangelical theologian Alister McGrath writes, "We just need to realize that it is now bad tactics to major on the truth question." The "truth question" offends people in an age of pluralism and multiculturalism, so some evangelicals sidestep it. Wells notes that evangelicals seeking to market evangelicalism are stressing "greater self-discovery," downplaying "divine transcendence" and moral absolutes in ways that yield "a New Age kind of spirituality, even if it retains the patina of evangelical rhetoric." Marketable evangelicalism proves false to a transcendent God.[56]

True evangelical faith will not be marketable. It is past revelation that is unalterable. That offends in an age of novelty and innovation. It is a faith of the cross calling on individuals to limit or sacrifice themselves, to give up greed, lust and ambition. That offends in a new Renaissance of limitless, acquisitive individualism, where Everyperson is his or her own merchant sailing the World Wide Web. It places God at the center of reality. That provokes human rebellion. How can it win a cultural election in this or any other age?

"Neutron Rebellion": God's Commands Fall, People Left Standing

A new technological revolution is facilitating a quantum leap in human rebellion against God. Renaissance artists and merchants used classical writings and business techniques to perfect their rebellion; the enlightened gentry used human deductive reasoning to attack divine revelation. A New Age uses a computerized consciousness more spiritual, instantaneous, global, yet individualized, than the old clunky "Dr. Facts" rationality. It is decentralized: Internet, interactive TV, video conferencing and VCRs "narrow-cast," not broadcast. People narrowcast to each other. Or they select and edit the broadcasts they view. Here is Peter Schwartz's 1995 futurist's hype: "We have moved from the atomized disconnected hierarchical civilization to the networked interconnected globalized civilization, literally in this year."[57]

This move makes even less likely a Christian cultural consensus. Its underlying spirit is not conducive to Christian worship and obedience. Part of the Western cultural hothouse's "forced clip," it seeks a human-centered consciousness apart from Christianity. David Wells warns, "We Westerners, once the custodians of a stable moral order, have become like loosed bats whose silent, unpredictable flight in the new civilization is an omen of something gone dreadfully wrong."[58] Without forgetting the unpredictability of loosed bats, let's try to analyze its underlying principles.

The cultural hothouse expands globally and technically at an accelerating pace. Few nations dare to restrict or regulate the new computer technologies for fear of being left behind economically and militarily. Scientific and technological progress is seen as inherently good. Its appeal crosses racial and cultural lines. That makes history linear, "directional" and "universal," as Fukuyama observes. There's no going back. Neil Postman claims, "Once a technology is admitted, it plays out its hand; it does what it is designed to do." That is too deterministic. People profit from allowing it to play out its hand. Investors finance and companies develop new technologies lest they be left behind. Enormous profits reward them if their innovations become new standards for the industry, such as Microsoft's Windows: Bill Gates is worth at least ten billion dollars. Here is limitless capital accumulation with a vengeance.[59]

The usual criticisms of this new civilization fall short. It is not true, as Postman charges, "that the computer has increased the power of large-scale organizations" but is of little "advantage to the masses of people." Old sixties activists, hackers and academics have created a "computerized counterculture" of Power to the People—power to communicate with each other, to copy software at will, to discuss any subject without censorship, to form innumerable lifestyle enclaves on BBSs, chat channels and news groups. But, critics correctly charge, their empowering Internet has obscenity, tirades, harassment, pornography, violent games such as Doom and MUDs, identity fraud, addicted users and gambling dens. Hackers can steal your credit-card number. Firms can monitor your purchases, governments your on-line activities. Netheads are as alarmed as their critics about censorship, though they ridicule police computer illiteracy just as sixties potheads laughed at "pigs" trying to enforce antimarijuana laws.[60]

Computers can be misused off the Internet. Wall Street "quants" (quantitative analysts) devise a complex computer-calculated "parallel universe of side bets and speculative mutations" called derivatives. These can be high-risk bets: for instance, a twenty-eight-year-old trader bankrupted Barings by betting hundreds of millions of dollars on a simple one, the Nikkei 225 index.[61]

Computer video games with their "MTV-blaring, schoolyard-taunting, testosterone-burning spirit" reach a "core audience" of "boys ages 8 to 14." Games such as "Hell: A Cyberpunk Thriller" and "Mortal Kombat" and "Night Trap" feature sickening, realistic violence and fast-paced action. Do they lead to violent behavior? They apparently do make kids more aggressive. Hollywood and Silicon Valley compete to make interactive games for adults such as "Voyeur, a kinky murder mystery" that empowers you to be both Peeping Tom and Sherlock Holmes. Interactivity makes sex and violence more salable.[62]

Another criticism is that millions of people in the Third World and in the inner city will be left totally out of this new computerized world. In the United States in 1993, "white families [were] three times as likely as blacks or Hispanics to have computers at home." In June 1995 "more than half the people on the planet [had] yet to place their first telephone call," and "many African countries" were "out of the loop of the global economy." That was when global marketing over Internet was a novelty. Imagine how out of the loop they will be when it is a necessity. Before they were exploited but needed. Now city planner Manuel Castells warns, "They are not exploited; they are ignored. . . . That's much worse."[63]

New technologies and new forms of social control may end many of these criticisms. Already parents can buy "SurfWatch" or "Net Nanny" to keep cyberporn away from Net-surfing kids. Women are exploited in the making and viewing of cyberporn, but computers could create sex scenes for which no women need disrobe. Hackers can use encryption to stop governments from monitoring on-line activities, "cancelbots" to erase mass-e-mailed ads and video channels to expose false sexual identities on-line. Governments can use computers to regulate computer-calculated and computer-marketed derivatives. Capitalism does not make technologies for the penniless, but mass distribution of computers and modems to hooked-up Third World countries is conceivable. Schools could get inner-city kids hooked up too.[64]

It is possible to refine technology to make vices such as pornography, gambling, on-screen murder or virtual sex seemingly victimless. Confine them to consenting adults. Keep them away from kids. Ensure that there's no deception. Keep them virtual. There would still be negative consequences for participants—jaded, depraved minds numbed by lesser evils and hungry for greater, more vivid ones—but society may cease to define those as negative. In the 1980s controversy raged over deploying the neutron bomb, which killed people but left buildings standing. The Information Age makes possible a "neutron rebellion" that violates God's commands but seems to leave people unharmed. (Neutron is a misnomer for an electronic age.) With no negative feedback, people have no reason to moderate rebellion, so it rages out of control.

This new age may even hurt capitalism, the traditional integrator of human rebellion, and place the people in power. Technology may integrate rebellion instead. Like sixteenth-century Europeans seeing New World societies as propertyless, masterless utopias with no idea of sin, Netheads make the Net free of property, masters or sin. No one controls it, you copy much of the software for free, and you bring your lusts and hatreds to it. Everyperson is his or her own merchant fetching desired data from Hong Kong at little cost. With digital infotainment, everyone can be amoral, innovative and limitlessly acquisitive.[65]

That will not bring technological utopia. Property and rulers are not the sources of human misery. Ignoring depravity does not eliminate it. Obtaining the consent of other adults does not secure God's consent. Violating God's commands cannot leave people unharmed. To commit acts only in cyberspace—where they are thoughts more than acts—is still to violate God's commands. Jesus said, "For out of the heart come evil thoughts, murder, adultery, sexual immorality, theft, false testimony, slander. These are what make a man 'unclean' "—even if they come out only in cyberspace, in virtual reality.[66]

Here, sinful (often, male) individualism runs rampant. The individual projects himself (Netheads are mostly males) into cyberspace and transcends the limits of geography, of sexual or personal identity, of personal accountability and of his minority or loner status. He finds someone somewhere to listen or interact with him. Interacting with him is voluntary, so community and self-centeredness seem compatible. "People in virtual communities do just about everything people do in real life, but we leave our bodies behind," Rheingold notes.[67]

Babel Project: Omnipresent, Omniscient, Unilingual Humanity

Though they leave their bodies behind, they don't leave sin behind. Condemning even lustful thoughts, Christianity will not be their spirituality of choice—though it offers forgiveness to repentant believers.

The Digital, or Information, Age represents a new Babel project, a new Renaissance, which seeks to transcend limits that Christianity and primitive tools have placed on humanity. Global networks gather the humanity which God scattered at Babel. Software that translates from one language to another in real time will undo the post-Babel confusion of language. Internet empowers an individual (1) to be innumerable places at once—"publishing" information to millions simultaneously, (2) to send data-seeking "knowbots" into "the vast pools of online databases" to acquire all knowledge, and (3) to do something five thousand miles away that was impossible before. These are fledgling steps to (1) omnipresence, (2) omniscience and (3) omnipotence—three traditional attributes of God.[68] In a recent book on computers, Stephen Talbott writes, "Images of a global, electronically mediated collective consciousness, of Teilhard de Chardin's omega point, and of machines crossing over into a new and superior form of personhood are rife on the Net."[69]

Of course people have good, worthwhile uses for these new capabilities, which can transmit scriptural teachings to Hong Kong or warn Israelis of the start of the Gulf War. We cannot imagine that they can be uninvented. A new technology is more than a tool, though people first see it as only that. It subtly changes our way of perceiving and thinking about the world and ourselves, but Postman is too deterministic: human users have power to shape it. When this technology offers "omni" attributes, humans are unlikely to reject or limit it. And it is unlikely to produce humility. Its output—digitized information—is abstract, virtual, nonmaterial.[70] It is likely to affect consciousness and spirituality to a greater extent than the more physical, material outputs of previous technologies. It can speed halfway across the globe as fast as a prayer.

Rheingold gives an interesting anecdote about the WELL (Whole Earth 'Lectronic Link) virtual community. A member went to the Himalayas for a month-long study of Dzogchen, Tibetan Zen Buddhism. In American, individualistic style—"I really feel it's the right move for me"—she became a Buddhist nun. But like nineteenth-century missionaries, she succumbed to a local amoeba and contracted hepatitis. Like a foreign mission board, WELLites used the Net to gather information on her condition and to arrange treatment in New Delhi—none had to go there. The American abroad recovered, e-mailed her thanks and, in mixed eco-New-Age-Buddhist-Hinduism, attributed her recovery to "contributions of green energy . . . beams, prayers, and pujas [Hindu prayer rituals]." America abroad had changed indeed![71]

At Babel "they said, 'Come, let us build ourselves a city, with a tower that reaches to the heavens, so that we may make a name for ourselves.' " Not intentionally referring back to Babel, information technologies reporter Peter Leyden asks, "What kind of synergy will be created this time around, as all the minds on the planet become wired together through the Net?" Some believers in the Gaia thesis—that earth is a living organism—believe what will be created is nothing less than the Gaia-organism's brain. The earth will think![72]

Earth does not show signs of getting the "big head," but Information Age humans do show signs of overweening pride, partly caused by the "omni" attributes. It shows up in global superstars such as Michael Jackson (whose 1995 CD *HIStory, Past, Present & Future—Book I* seems grandiosely titled) and in common consumers accustomed to getting the "omni" attributes when and how they want them.[73] Hubris is most likely to get out of control in the generation that grows up with video games, interactive TV and the World Wide Web. Their grandparents, who were shaped by radio, and their Boomer parents, who were shaped by TV, carry residual attitudes from more primitive times. They will not be limited by residual attitudes. Fundamental cultural change comes slowly, but it does come.

That pride in being more places, knowing more facts and doing more things than any humans before already shows up in futurists' and computer advocates' hype about the Digital Age. The experts have an eschatology. They claim to know where history is going. Like cartoon prophets carrying the sign "Repent, the End Is Near," they warn the old-fashioned of the need to change. Alvin and Heidi Toffler wrote in January 1995, "Those that fail to do so will swirl down the storm drain of history." Their message coincides with consumerism's love of novelty and a new generation's disdain for a primitive past.[74]

This new Babel project will most likely not aim to build a city that reaches to the heavens but will aim to raise humanity to the status of divinity. Global networks make one city seem too parochial and too limited a goal. Democracy and individualism demand that accomplishments not be limited to an elite but be spread to all humanity. Acquiring "omni" attributes previously seen as God's alone suggests that humans' goal is to claim to be gods or godlike. That is the goal of the New Age movement (though it is hazardous to generalize about "a movement which scorns systematic thought and welcomes paradoxes, contradictions and even outright irrationality").[75] Some similarities between Digital Age and New Age suggest a "harmonic convergence" of the two, though perhaps not until changes are made to both.

The constellation of beliefs and hopes known as the New Age movement is quite old—millennia old in Eastern religions and a century old in the United States. They were first mainstreamed and widely publicized in the United States in the late 1960s. Vishal Mangalwadi identifies several strands in New Age thinking: Teilhard de Chardin's evolutionary philosophy, Indian gurus and Zen masters of the sixties and seventies, paranormal psychology, Age of Aquarius hype, a "youth culture susceptible to cults" and "a growing interest in the mystical experience of sex," psychedelic drugs and rock music. They produced a mix of Eastern immanence, occult explorations of the spirit world, postmodern rejection of Enlightenment rationality, individualist self-fulfillment and the old consumer wish for a sensuality beyond what Christianity allows. The pessimism, anti-individualism and obedience to gurus which characterized many Eastern religions have been changed to a New Age optimistic individualism more attractive in the West.[76]

New Age thought will likely be further altered to fit the new globalized, supra-Western individualism of the Digital Age—or to fit some future quantum leap in technology—but it already forms the likely basis for a new cultural consensus. In its syncretism, it incorporates nearly every lifestyle enclave and subgroup: feminists, animal rights activists, environmentalists, homosexuals, the human potential groups, the men's movement, *Playboy* readers and advocates of the new physics. It is a kind of Parliament of World Religions and Lifestyles. The human ambition to be God is its basic principle, and that unifies all human rebellions, since the rejection of God's authority lies at the heart of them all.[77]

It is a suprareligion, but it has most of the factors that sociologist Rodney Stark identifies as necessary for the success of a new religion. Rosemary Ruether and Matthew Fox "ask Christians to add to their religious culture" the above-listed lifestyle values, "not to discard" their Scriptures. They (falsely) claim continuity with historic Christianity. New Age thinking differs from consumer culture, but not too much. It thrives in the free religious market in the United States and the West. David Wells notes its ability to market itself to postmoderns. Its spirit-channeling and mysticism differ from materialism enough to be attractive but are individualistic enough to fit a consumer culture. It seems to have some factors of failure too, such as a lack of centralized leadership or organization, but these factors may not apply to an umbrella suprareligion or they may be overcome in the future.[78]

Though he critiques "New Ageism," Matthew Fox in his *The Coming of the Cosmic Christ* demonstrates many elements in its appeal. He defines the "Cosmic Christ" as "the *divine* pattern that connects in the person of Jesus Christ (but by no means is limited to that person). . . . [It] might be living next door or even inside one's deepest and truest self. The reign of God may well be among us after all." Cosmic Christ is "Revealer of the Divine 'I Am' in Every Creature." This pattern so like ourselves will accept Native American religions, save Mother Earth, let youth culture flourish, glorify sexual love and the phallus (like the Hindu god Shiva), get us "to embrace diversity," including homosexuality, and bring peace and social justice to the globe.[79]

Fox's creation spirituality is only one possible form a new global, pluralist consensus might take. It lacks the work ethic needed in even computerized capitalism, but it shows the general outlines of a new consensus that fits a global, high-tech, multilifestyle society. It is not as antithetical to capitalism as is Christianity, which critiques limitless, amoral, acquisitive capitalism. Computerized capitalism with its niche markets and global reach will be no barrier to a New Age consensus, nor the consensus any barrier to it.

Fox's vision is a blasphemous culmination of the West's centuries-old rebellion against the Christianity it claims as its own. To use the name of the holy Christ for this unholy "pattern" is astonishing effrontery. Here's an open invitation for Antichrist to come, offer divinity to all, show respect for every lifestyle and personify a New Age. The apostle Paul wrote of "the rebellion" which would come when "the man of lawlessness is revealed" and succeeds in convincing humanity to believe "the lie," namely, that he is God. They would believe it because they "have not believed the truth but have delighted in wickedness." Here is one blueprint for The Rebellion, though it will likely be rejected for some other plan. Here is one model of The Lie.[80]

Postmodern, media-driven confusions over personal identity, fantasy and reality, marketability and reliability will leave postmodern humans ready to believe The Lie. The Rebellion, the Man of Lawlessness and The Lie serve God's purpose, for they usher in the Lord's return. He is the "Last Man," whose coming means history's end. The liberal, capitalist democrat is not the Last Man whose triumph means the end of history (defined as dialectical struggle of ideologies), as Fukuyama claims. That man will not be last and thus assign a final meaning to all of human history. Jesus Christ is "the Alpha and the Omega, the First and the Last, the Beginning and the End."[81] He will assign final meaning.

Predictions made by prophecy writers of the imminent return of Jesus Christ are ridiculed by historians such as Paul Boyer—often for good reason. They guess wildly at the identity of the antichrist, point to every new development as a sign of the end and make money off prophecy books that exploit the latest world events. Yet Boyer does not compare their predictions with secular or other religious ones. Matthew Fox has a millennial vision for the year 2000.[82] Futurists have also been known to make wild guesses. Predictions must be compared to other predictions, not to hindsight.

The truth of Christ's return rests on his credibility and not on the character of prophecy writers. Their overhyped current events are just links in a chain of final events and no human can know how long the chain is, but Christ's return is basic to Christianity, part of the Nicene Creed, implied in the Lord's Prayer, a necessary result of God's becoming man at Bethlehem and a necessary vindication of a crucified Messiah. As Wells argues, the cross of Christ "is the shadow of the executioner's ax" soon to fall in God's righteous judgment of rebellious human societies. If the Father judged sin imputed to the obedient Son, he will not hesitate to judge sins committed by the rebellious world.[83] And, when the Judge is the Son who died for sin and offered a pardon that was spurned, there can be no complaint that the sentence is unjust. The one person missing in Boyer's account of prophecy is Jesus Christ.

Eschatology and a Christian Interpretation of U.S. History: Synopsis

Why examine Christian eschatology when interpreting American history? How can we use the unknown future to learn about the (better-)known past? To interpret is to explain the meaning of something. Meanings change as later events occur. That is one reason historians are reluctant to interpret the recent past. Later events give a fuller meaning to prior ones. There can be no later perspective, no more complete hindsight, than at the end. We must use Christian eschatology to interpret when Fukuyama uses capitalist eschatology and the Tofflers Third Wave eschatology to interpret U.S. history as, respectively, a capitalist triumph and an agrarian-industrial prologue to the postindustrial future. Those meanings can only be seen to be false in light of Christian eschatology.

American exceptionalism can only, finally, be seen to be false in light of Christian eschatology. We have no reason to believe that this diverse, individualistic, technology-worshiping society will not join The Rebellion. Unlike the old Cold War, the United States will not be the good empire that battles Antichrist's evil empire. Now two rival cosmopolitanisms battle: a secular one united by global computerized capitalism and a Christian one created by the global preaching of the gospel. Later Christ will battle Antichrist. American unbelievers will be no less wicked and American Christians no more saved than people of other nations. There may not even be a U.S. government. It may dissolve and flee to the history books to escape its creditors, as Daniel Boone fled to the woods to escape his. Its Founders may lose the immortal fame they sought. Instead the ancient prophecy will be fully fulfilled: "the stone the builders rejected has become the capstone."[84] The Christ whom many of them rejected will be the final meaning of the history that they looked to for immortality.

We cannot use American ideals of liberty, democracy, free enterprise and tolerance as yardsticks by which to evaluate U.S. history. Their meaning changes, so how can they measure accurately?[85] They will be superseded by specifically Christian ideals, so how can they provide final meaning? Even the one Christian interpretation (others are possible) offered here will be superseded. Christ's return is the one sure, final, unchangeable event which alone provides that final meaning. That is why this interpretation has used Christian truth, Christian eschatology and Christ's return to find a truer meaning for American history from Columbus to Clinton, and beyond.

Notes

Chapter 1: 1492

[1]Here and above, *Diario of Christopher Columbus's First Voyage to America, 1492-1493,* trans. Oliver Dunn and James E. Kelley Jr. (Norman: University of Oklahoma Press, 1989), pp. 63, 65; Kirkpatrick Sale, *The Conquest of Paradise: Christopher Columbus and the Columbian Legacy* (New York: Knopf, 1990), pp. 92-94, 96-97, 106-8, 110-11. For the significance of planting crosses and naming places, see Luis N. Rivera, *A Violent Evangelism: The Political and Religious Conquest of the Americas* (Louisville, Ky.: Westminster/John Knox Press, 1992), pp. 7-8, 10-11.

[2]Sale, *Conquest of Paradise,* p. 103.

[3]See, for example, "Whose America?" in *Time,* July 8, 1991, pp. 12-21. See also the debate over the *National Standards for United States History,* for example, *Time,* November 7, 1994, p. 64.

[4]Zavala, quoted in Rivera, *Violent Evangelism,* p. 18. On pp. 14-18 Rivera discusses the problem of what to call it. For the problem of population estimates, see John D. Daniels, "The Indian Population of North America in 1492," *William and Mary Quarterly,* 3rd ser., 49, no. 2 (April 1992): 298-320; David Henige, "On the Contact Population of Hispaniola: History as Higher Mathematics," *Hispanic American Historical Review* 58, no. 2 (1978): 217-37; R. A. Zambardino's "Critique" of Henige in *Hispanic American Historical Review* 58, no. 4 (1978): 700-708, and Henige's reply (pp. 709-12). The quote is from Henige, p. 236 (who is quoting from Jonathan Swift's *Gulliver's Travels*).

[5]Sale, *Conquest of Paradise,* pp. 80-81, 288; David E. Stannard, *American Holocaust: Columbus and the Conquest of the New World* (New York: Oxford University Press, 1992), pp. 154-93, 246, quotes from pp. 154, 190, 246. Calvin Luther Martin (*In the Spirit of the Earth: Rethinking History and Time* [Baltimore: Johns Hopkins University Press, 1992], pp. 58-59) calls Jehovah "a frank and virulently potent icon of a newly emerging historical consciousness." His love of nature and study of the fur trade convinced him of the folly of his father's Protestant Christianity (pp. 109-30).

[6]Gary B. Nash et al., *The American People: Creating a Nation and a Society,* 3rd ed. (New York: HarperCollins, 1994), pp. 5, 14; James Kirby Martin et al., *America and Its People*

(Glenview, Ill.: Scott, Foresman, 1989), pp. 10, 33.

[7]Stannard, *American Holocaust,* pp. 51-52, 79-80; *William and Mary Quarterly,* 3rd ser., 49, no. 2 (April 1992): 384-87. Columnist Otis Pike ("Say What You Will, Columbus Is a Hero" [October 1992], clipping of Minneapolis *Star Tribune* in author's possession) objects that given Aztec and Inca brutalities, it is unfair to blame Columbus "for all the evils that have befallen the true natives since" 1492. For a review of revisionist books on the Columbian encounter, see Ida Altman and Reginald D. Butler, "The Contact of Cultures: Perspectives on the Quincentenary," *American Historical Review* 99, no. 2 (April 1994): 478-503.

[8]David B. Quinn, *North America From Earliest Discovery to First Settlements: The Norse Voyages to 1612* (New York: Harper & Row, 1977), pp. 2-14; Henry Bowden, *American Indians and Christian Missions: Studies in Cultural Conflict* (Chicago: University of Chicago Press, 1981), pp. 15-17, 23.

[9]Geoffrey Conrad and Arthur A. Demarest, *Religion and Empire: The Dynamics of Aztec and Inca Expansionism* (New York: Cambridge University Press, 1984), pp. 98, 100, 102, 107, 113-14; Brian M. Fagan, *Kingdoms of Gold, Kingdoms of Jade: The Americas Before Columbus* (New York: Thames & Hudson, 1991), pp. 48-49.

[10]Bowden, *American Indians and Christian Missions,* pp. 29-35, 69-70; William Brandon, *New Worlds for Old: Reports from the New World and Their Effects on the Development of Social Thought in Europe, 1500-1800* (Athens: Ohio University Press, 1986), pp. 57-59.

[11]Isaiah 1:2-3; 29:13. Numerous New Testament passages on false teachers, human rebellion, the world's hatred of God and human hypocrisy could also be cited. See, for example, the apostle Paul's warning in Romans 8:6-8. For "worldliness" as a "system of values" with "the fallen sinner at its center" in contrast to Christianity, see David F. Wells, *No Place for Truth: Or, Whatever Happened to Evangelical Theology?* (Grand Rapids, Mich.: Eerdmans, 1993), pp. 215-16.

[12]Tzvetan Todorov, *The Conquest of America: The Question of the Other,* trans. Richard Howard (New York: Harper & Row, 1984), pp. 107-8. For a nuanced view of the state of religion in medieval Europe and an analysis of the revisionist view that medieval folk were barely Christianized, see John Van Engen, "The Christian Middle Ages as an Historiographical Problem," *American Historical Review* 91, no. 3 (June 1986): 519-52.

[13]Sale, *Conquest of Paradise,* p. 90; Stannard, *American Holocaust,* p. 57.

[14]Van Engen, "Christian Middle Ages," pp. 532-33; Todorov, *Conquest of America,* p. 108.

[15]A. G. Dickens, *Reformation and Society in Sixteenth-Century Europe* (London: Thames & Hudson, 1966), pp. 34-38, 41, 61; William R. Estep, *Renaissance and Reformation* (Grand Rapids, Mich.: Eerdmans, 1986), pp. 28-30.

[16]Euan Cameron, *The European Reformation* (Oxford: Clarendon, 1991), pp. 10-11, 13, 16, 18-19. Van Engen ("Christian Middle Ages," pp. 543, 549-50) stresses the Christianization of the popular religiosity of relics and rituals, but he too focuses on outward ritual behavior, not inward belief and ethical practice.

[17]J. van Herwaarden and R. de Keyser, quoted in Van Engen, "Christian Middle Ages," p. 520.

[18]Estep, *Renaissance and Reformation,* pp. 28-30, 90; Dickens, *Reformation and Society,* pp. 24-25, 34-35; Peter Laven, *A Comprehensive History of Renaissance Italy, 1464-1534* (New York: Capricorn, 1967), pp. 25, 81-82; Cameron, *European Reformation,* pp. 20-24. Cameron calls these " 'secondary' tasks" of the church and suggests that, burdened with these unwanted tasks, the church had to neglect its spiritual functions. Yet surely there were political and monetary reasons that the church kept these functions even "as society became

more sophisticated" and laypeople became capable of handling them.

[19]Cameron, *European Reformation,* pp. 18-20, 26-28.

[20]This brief sketch of feudalism is based on Norman Cantor, *Medieval History: The Life and Death of a Civilization,* 2nd ed. (New York: Macmillan, 1969), pp. 214-23; and Guy Fourquin, *Lordship and Feudalism in the Middle Ages,* trans. Iris and A. L. Lytton Sells (New York: Pica, 1976), pp. 11-13, 68-71, 99. The quotes are from Cantor. See also Denys Hay, *Europe in the Fourteenth and Fifteenth Centuries* (New York: Holt, Rinehart & Winston, 1966), pp. 63-70. For purposes of this generalized argument, I have avoided the complicated questions of interpretation of medieval European history.

[21]Hay, *Europe,* pp. 129, 130, 131, 158; David Harris Wilson, *A History of England* (New York: Holt, Rinehart & Winston, 1967), pp. 169-74.

[22]Hay, *Europe,* pp. 102-4; Brandon, *New Worlds for Old,* p. 75; Fernand Braudel, *The Wheels of Commerce,* trans. Siân Reynolds (New York: Harper & Row, 1982), pp. 537-41. Although not fully developed, this system was in the process of development in the fifteenth and sixteenth centuries.

[23]Conrad and Demarest, *Religion and Empire,* pp. 118-21. It should be emphasized that the Incas were perhaps the most centralized, statist society in the Americas before Spanish control. See Brandon, *New Worlds for Old,* p. 55. Most indigenous societies did not have taxation systematized and centralized in this way.

[24]Dickens, *Reformation and Society,* p. 61; Estep, *Reformation and Renaissance,* p. 118; Braudel, *Wheels of Commerce,* pp. 154, 186, 378, 559-66; Laven, *Renaissance Italy,* pp. 94, 106; John Day, *The Medieval Market Economy* (Oxford: Basil Blackwell, 1987), pp. 150, 152, 155-57, 174. There were some tax-farmers in Milan and Lombardy, however (see Braudel, *Wheels of Commerce,* p. 399). Richard Goldthwaite (*The Building of Renaissance Florence: An Economic and Social History* [Baltimore: Johns Hopkins University Press, 1980], pp. 34-35, 56-59) argues that city-state taxation and public debts were not so burdensome in Florence, but he does confirm the importance to bankers of papal financing.

[25]Day, *Medieval Market Economy,* p. 157; Braudel, *Wheels of Commerce,* p. 372.

[26]Here and above, Johannes Sløk, *Da mennesket tog magten* (Copenhagen: Centrum, 1989), pp. 7-8, 19-22, 23-24, 29-30, 34-35.

[27]Many Renaissance thinkers and artists remained as religious as other Europeans. See Charles Trinkaus, *The Scope of Renaissance Humanism* (Ann Arbor: University of Michigan Press, 1983), pp. 238-39.

[28]Quinn, *North America from Earliest Discovery,* pp. 72-84, 98; Stannard, *American Holocaust,* pp. 85-87; Karen Ordahl Kupperman, *Settling with the Indians: The Meeting of English and Indian Cultures in America, 1580-1640* (Totowa, N.J.: Rowman & Little-field, 1980), pp. 5-6; Neal Salisbury, *Manitou and Providence: Indians, Europeans and the Making of New England* (New York: Oxford University Press, 1984), p. 29. See also Bowden, *American Indians and Christian Missions,* pp. 77, 91, 98.

[29]James Axtell, *Beyond 1492: Encounters in Colonial North America* (New York: Oxford University Press, 1992), pp. 261-63; Bowden, *American Indians and Christian Missions,* pp. 91-92. For the contrary argument, see Stannard, *American Holocaust,* especially pp. 269-81.

[30]Stannard, *American Holocaust,* pp. 69-71, 76-77, 83-85; Kenneth R. Andrews, N. P. Canny and P. E. H. Hair, eds., *The Westward Enterprise* (Liverpool: Liverpool University Press, 1978), p. 2; Axtell, *Beyond 1492,* pp. 82-83, 84, 87, 89, 96.

[31]Wendy Rose, quoted in Axtell, *Beyond 1492,* pp. 249-51; Altman and Butler, "Contact of

Cultures," pp. 486-87. I have taken the general idea of "the Englishman away from home" from Wendell Berry, *The Unsettling of America: Culture and Agriculture* (San Francisco: Sierra Club, 1977), pp. 3-14.

[32]Here and above, Axtell, *Beyond 1492,* pp. 79-82, 90-91; Altman and Butler, "Contact of Cultures," p. 489; Salisbury, *Manitou and Providence,* p. 37; Todorov, *Conquest of America,* pp. 75-76, 80, 111.

[33]Axtell, *Beyond 1492,* pp. 139-40, 143-44.

[34]Here and above, Todorov, *Conquest of America,* pp. 66-69, 84-87, 94, 107-8. Cortés quoted from Rivera, *Violent Evangelism,* p. 262.

[35]Kenneth R. Andrews, *Trade, Plunder and Settlement: Maritime Enterprise and the Genesis of the British Empire, 1480-1630* (Cambridge: Cambridge University Press, 1984), pp. 31-34, 38, 50-56; Axtell, *Beyond 1492,* pp. 91-92, 245-47, 249-51; Bowden, *American Indians and Christian Missions,* pp. 50-51.

[36]De Las Casas quoted in Rivera, *Violent Evangelism,* p. 37; Mark 14:47; John 18:10; Bowden, *American Indians and Christian Missions,* pp. 51-53, 56-57.

[37]Quinn, *North America from Earliest Discovery,* pp. 100-101; Rivera, *Violent Evangelism,* p. 30; Bowden, *American Indians and Christian Missions,* pp. 87-89.

[38]Bowden, *American Indians and Christian Missions,* pp. 112, 114, 116, 118, 124-25, 129-30.

[39]Brandon, *New Worlds for Old,* pp. ix, 6-19, 23-28, 47-48.

[40]Ibid., pp. 6, 13, 47-48, 66, 83-84, 101-5, 108-11.

[41]Steven Ozment, *Protestants: The Birth of a Revolution* (New York: Doubleday, 1992), p. 215; Cameron, *European Reformation,* p. 417.

[42]Cameron, *European Reformation,* p. 112. Cameron summarizes the Reformers' message on pp. 111-67. He wisely refutes arguments that the Reformation succeeded by appealing to economic, political and class motives or laypeople's dissatisfaction with the "penitential cycle." Yet he rejects the "most face-value explanation of all"—that the Reformers' argument was "more plausible and more biblical"—in favor of his own hypothesis that Reformers "flattered" laypeople "by treating them as fit to hear and to judge the most arcane doctrines of the religious élite" (see pp. 293-313, quotes from p. 311). The Reformers' message of human depravity and inability to contribute to their own salvation was hardly flattering—nor do people risk martyrdom in order to be flattered.

[43]Dickens, *Reformation and Society,* pp. 56-58.

[44]Stephen Innes, *Creating the Commonwealth: The Economic Culture of Puritan New England* (New York: Norton, 1995), pp. 7, 11, 29, 37, 40, 101, 113-18, 123, 127, quotes from pp. 117, 123. The literature on Weber's thesis is too voluminous to cite here; it is summarized in Innes's endnotes.

[45]Ibid., pp. 7, 56, quote from p. 7; Peter L. Berger, ed., *The Capitalist Spirit: Toward a Religious Ethic of Wealth Creation* (San Francisco: ICS Press [Institute for Contemporary Studies], 1990), pp. 7-9, 12, 15-16.

[46]Braudel, *Wheels of Commerce,* pp. 231, 242; see also pp. 231-49. I am also incorporating the definition used by Peter F. Kosloski in his article "The Ethics of Capitalism," in *Philosophical and Economic Foundations of Capitalism,* ed. Svetozar Pejovich (Lexington, Mass.: Heath, 1983), p. 35.

[47]Hay, *Europe,* pp. 117-19, 121, 122-23; Braudel, *Wheels of Commerce,* pp. 36-40. Braudel points out that town governments did most of the regulating, not distant princes. For the greater profitability of the secondary and tertiary sectors (not agriculture, a primary sector), see Fernand Braudel, *The Perspective of the World,* trans. Siân Reynolds (New York:

Harper & Row, 1984), pp. 48, 108.

[48]Braudel, *Wheels of Commerce,* pp. 372, 403-8. See also the sections on Venice and Genoa in Braudel, *Perspective of the World,* pp. 116-38, 157-73.

[49]Amos 8:4-6.

[50]Laven, *Renaissance Italy,* pp. 91-92; Braudel, *Wheels of Commerce,* pp. 90, 142-47, 563-66; Day, *Medieval Market Economy,* pp. 142-44; Braudel, *Perspective of the World,* pp. 66-67.

[51]Laven, *Renaissance Italy,* p. 94. For a complete account of "the quarrel over usury," see Braudel, *Wheels of Commerce,* pp. 559-66.

[52]Braudel, *Perspective of the World,* pp. 66-67.

[53]Braudel, *Wheels of Commerce,* pp. 377-79; Day, *Medieval Market Economy,* pp. 179, 180. The Scripture quotation is from Amos 8:6.

[54]Here and above, Laven, *Renaissance Italy,* pp. 63-64; Braudel, *Wheels of Commerce,* pp. 272-73, 277-79. Genoa is a good example of a city "operating by remote control" and investing much of its capital in faraway places. See Braudel, *Perspective of the World,* pp. 159, 162-69.

[55]Braudel, *Wheels of Commerce,* pp. 586-89.

[56]For Confucianism and Christianity, see Paul A. Cohen, *China and Christianity: The Missionary Movement and the Growth of Chinese Antiforeignism, 1860-1870* (Cambridge, Mass.: Harvard University Press, 1963), pp. 18-19.

[57]He argues that this "Christendom" was effectively Christian in its practices, but Van Engen's point about a self-critical debate within the medieval church does fit with my interpretation here. See Van Engen, "Christian Middle Ages," pp. 539-41, 546-47, 552.

[58]Theodore Von Laue, *The World Revolution of Westernization: The Twentieth Century in Global Perspective* (New York: Oxford University Press, 1987), p. 19.

[59]Sale, *Conquest of Paradise,* pp. 90-91.

[60]J. H. Elliott, quoted in David Brion Davis, *Slavery and Human Progress* (New York: Oxford University Press, 1984), p. 69.

[61]Delno C. West and August Kling, trans. and eds., *Libro de las profecías of Christopher Columbus* (Gainesville: University of Florida Press, 1991), pp. 29-30, 49-50, 68, 109, 111; Pauline Moffitt Watts, "Prophecy and Discovery: On the Spiritual Origins of Christopher Columbus's 'Enterprise of the Indies,' " *American Historical Review* 90 (1985): 74.

Chapter 2: Africa Comes to the Americas, Christ Comes to the Slaves

[1]Philip Curtin's estimate is given in J. D. Fage, *A History of West Africa* (New York: Knopf, 1978), p. 255.

[2]Gary B. Nash et al., *The American People: Creating a Nation and a Society,* 3rd ed. (New York: HarperCollins, 1994), p. 76; Howard Zinn, *A People's History of the United States* (New York: Harper & Row, 1980), p. 35; James K. Martin et al., *America and Its People,* 2nd ed. (New York: HarperCollins College, 1993), p. 38; Gary A. Puckrein, *Little England: Plantation Society and Anglo-Barbadian Politics, 1627-1700* (New York: New York University Press, 1984), pp. 80-81.

[3]First Corinthians 4:12; 1 Thessalonians 4:11; 2 Thessalonians 3:10; Matthew 20:26; Luke 22:26. First Timothy 1:10 and Revelation 18:13 are quoted. For an eloquent attack on "slaveholding religion" as opposed to "the Christianity of Christ," see the appendix to Frederick Douglass, *Narrative of the Life of Frederick Douglass, an American Slave* (New York: Penguin, 1982), pp. 153-59.

[4]David Brion Davis, *Slavery and Human Progress* (New York: Oxford University Press,

1984), pp. 15, 27, 29, 30, 33; Orlando Patterson, *Slavery and Social Death* (Cambridge, Mass.: Harvard University Press, 1982), pp. 88-92. Patterson notes, however, that Romans did not accord honor to Greek slaves who tutored their children.

[5]Peter L. Berger, ed., *The Capitalist Spirit: Toward a Religious Ethic of Wealth Creation* (San Francisco: ICS Press [Institute for Contemporary Studies], 1990), pp. 12, 17.

[6]Richard John Neuhaus, "Wealth and Whimsy: Being Rich, Producing Riches," in *Capitalist Spirit,* ed. Berger, pp. 132-33; 2 Corinthians 4:6. Philemon 16 could be read as an appeal to emancipate Onesimus, to treat him "no longer as a slave, but . . . as a dear brother."

[7]Davis, *Slavery and Human Progress,* pp. xiii, xvi-xvii, 24-26, 53; Fernand Braudel, *The Perspective of the World,* trans. Siân Reynolds (New York: Harper & Row, 1984), pp. 157-66; Philip D. Curtin, *The Rise and Fall of the Plantation Complex: Essays in Atlantic History* (Cambridge: Cambridge University Press, 1990), pp. 8-10. Venice engaged in the Mediterranean slave trade also.

[8]For the debate over slavery's importance to the rise of European capitalism, see J. M. Blaut, *1492: The Debate on Colonialism, Eurocentrism and History* (Trenton, N.J.: Africa World Press, 1992), pp. 41-43; John J. McCusker and Russell R. Menard, *The Economy of British America, 1607-1789* (Chapel Hill: University of North Carolina Press, 1985), pp. 39-45; Franklin W. Knight, "Slavery and Lagging Capitalism in the Spanish and Portuguese American Empires, 1492-1713," in *Slavery and the Rise of the Atlantic System,* ed. Barbara Solow (Cambridge: Cambridge University Press, 1991), pp. 62-74; Braudel, *Perspective of the World,* p. 429; Davis, *Slavery and Human Progress,* p. 73. Knight argues that plantation slavery and the slave trade were major catalysts in the rise of European capitalism. The debate started with Eric Williams's *Capitalism and Slavery* (Chapel Hill: University of North Carolina Press, 1943).

[9]William D. Phillips Jr., "The Old World Background of Slavery in the Americas," in *Atlantic System,* ed. Solow, pp. 43-44, 45-46; Barbara Solow, "Slavery and Colonization," in *Atlantic System,* pp. 21-22, 24-27.

[10]Kenneth R. Andrews, *Trade, Plunder and Settlement: Maritime Enterprise and the Genesis of the British Empire, 1480-1630* (Cambridge: Cambridge University Press, 1984), pp. 7-9, 50-56; Solow, "Slavery and Colonization," pp. 22-23.

[11]For discussions and explanations of this hypothesis, most fully elaborated by E. D. Domar in 1970, see Solow, "Slavery and Colonization," pp. 32-38, and McCusker and Menard, *Economy of British America,* p. 239.

[12]Here and above, Solow, "Slavery and Colonization," pp. 33-35; McCusker and Menard, *Economy of British America,* p. 239.

[13]Solow, "Slavery and Colonization," p. 23; Nash et al., *American People,* p. 71; Andrews et al., *Westward Enterprise,* p. 5; David Hackett Fischer, *Albion's Seed: Four British Folkways in America* (New York: Oxford University Press, 1989), pp. 52-54. Fischer does note that slavery "was fundamentally hostile to the Puritan ethos of New England." He attributes the compact settlement there to soil conditions, to inaccessibility to ocean-going ships and to East Anglian custom (see pp. 53, 181, 183). That ignores the greater temptation to "hive out" in New England than in settled East Anglia. Religious communalism resisted that temptation.

[14]For the numbers of African-American slaves in the North, see, for example, Edgar J. McManus, *Black Bondage in the North* (Syracuse, N.Y.: Syracuse University Press, 1973), pp. 14-17.

[15]Karen Ordahl Kupperman, *Providence Island, 1630-1641: The Other Puritan Colony* (New York: Cambridge University Press, 1993), pp. ix-x, 1-4, 16-17, 21, 113-14, 116, 166,

320-22. Stephen Innes notes the differences in *Creating the Commonwealth: The Economic Culture of Puritan New England* (New York: Norton, 1995), pp. 205, 206-7, 308.

[16]Betty Wood, *Slavery in Colonial Georgia, 1730-1775* (Athens: University of Georgia Press, 1984), pp. 5-9, 20-22; Joyce E. Chaplin, *An Anxious Pursuit: Agricultural Innovation and Modernity in the Lower South* (Chapel Hill: University of North Carolina Press), pp. 38-39, 40-41. The Trustees did not know of the "free land" hypothesis, but they acted to avoid the fate of other colonies.

[17]D. W. Meinig, *Atlantic America, 1492-1800,* vol. 1 of *The Shaping of America: A Geographical Perspective on Five Hundred Years of History* (New Haven, Conn.: Yale University Press, 1986), p. 182; Wood, *Slavery in Colonial Georgia,* pp. 36, 44, 48, 53, 57, 59-71, 83; Chaplin, *Anxious Pursuit,* pp. 40-41.

[18]Wood, *Slavery in Colonial Georgia,* pp. 36, 57. For the concepts of a broad ("external") and narrow ("internal") accounting, I am indebted to Wendell Berry, *Standing by Words* (San Francisco: North Point, 1983), pp. 24-25, 38-52.

[19]Phillips, "Old World Background," p. 52; Puckrein, *Little England,* pp. 40, 53-54; Edmund S. Morgan, *American Slavery, American Freedom: The Ordeal of Colonial Virginia* (New York: Norton, 1975), pp. 63, 83-84, 85-86, 108-10. For a warning against determinism (the assumption that "the transfer" of black slavery "to the various colonies of the New World" was "inevitable"), see Davis, *Slavery and Human Progress,* p. 67. For an extended discussion of how the idea of progress was related to plantation slavery, see Chaplin, *Anxious Pursuit,* pp. 23-65. David Hackett Fischer has some regional-origins determinism in his discussion of Virginia's post-1650 settlers (he largely ignores its first settlers) in *Albion's Seed,* pp. 207-14 and following.

[20]Curtin, *Rise and Fall of the Plantation Complex,* p. 114. Curtin notes, however, that "contemporaries rarely considered [this alternative] or even knew that it existed."

[21]Of course the picture is more complicated. Some supply had to exist to enable demand to take off. Africans were first transported to the Cape Verde and Canary islands and to São Tomé, where slave-worked sugar plantations were found feasible. Then the whole system was carried to the Americas. See, for example, Phillips, "Old World Background," pp. 49-52.

[22]Here and above, see David Eltis, "Europeans and the Rise and Fall of African Slavery in the Americas: An Interpretation," *American Historical Review* 98, no. 5 (December 1993): 1399-1423, quote from p. 1414. Eltis does not stress Christianity's role, and there I disagree with him.

[23]Mechal Sobel, *The World They Made Together: Black and White Values in Eighteenth-Century Virginia* (Princeton, N.J.: Princeton University Press, 1987), pp. 18-20, 71-72, 96-98; J. D. Fage, *A History of Africa* (New York: Knopf, 1978), pp. 58-60, 60-61, 74. Eugene Genovese (*Roll, Jordan, Roll: The World the Slaves Made* [New York: Pantheon, 1972], p. 210) notes, "Traditional West African religion provided an integrated worldview."

[24]This and the following paragraph are based on Fage, *History of Africa,* pp. 46-48, 52, 59, 69, 70-71, 71-72, 72-74, 79, 84, 86, 89-90, 94-96, 101. See also Curtin, *Rise and Fall of the Plantation Complex,* pp. 31-38.

[25]Fage, *History of Africa,* pp. 266-70; Curtin, *Rise and Fall of the Plantation Complex,* pp. 40-42. For a warning against romanticizing slavery in West Africa, see Frederick Cooper, "The Problem of Slavery in African Studies," *Journal of African History* 20, no. 1 (1979): 117.

[26]Braudel, *Wheels of Commerce,* pp. 272-80; Meinig, *Atlantic America,* pp. 164-68 (describ-

ing Barbados, an island with some of the worst consequences). Braudel uses the phrase "capitalism away from home" to refer to activities such as production, which were not merchants' preferred activities.

[27]James A. Rawley, *The Transatlantic Slave Trade: A History* (New York: Norton, 1981), pp. 152-54, 156, 157, 158, 258, 260.

[28]Ibid., pp. 260, 264-65; Herbert S. Klein, "Economic Aspects of the Eighteenth-Century Atlantic Slave Trade," in *The Rise of Merchant Empires: Long-Distance Trade in the Early Modern World, 1350-1750,* ed. James D. Tracy (Cambridge: Cambridge University Press, 1990), p. 299.

[29]Franklin W. Knight, "Slavery and Lagging Capitalism in the Spanish and Portuguese American Empires, 1492-1713," in *Atlantic System,* ed. Solow, pp. 65-66, 72-73; Rawley, *Transatlantic Slave Trade,* pp. 154-55; Fage, *History of Africa,* pp. 248-50. For narrow accounting and externalizing, see Berry, *Standing by Words,* pp. 24-25, 45-51.

[30]Quoted in Rawley, *Transatlantic Slave Trade,* pp. 247-48.

[31]Fage, *History of Africa,* pp. 250-51, 260-62, 265-66, 270, 272-80, 286-88; Rawley, *Transatlantic Slave Trade,* pp. 272-76; Vincent Bakpetu Thompson, *The Making of the African Diaspora in the Americas, 1441-1900* (New York: Longman, 1987), pp. 49, 50-52, 85-91; David Eltis, "Precolonial Western Africa and the Atlantic Economy," in *Atlantic System,* ed. Solow, pp. 97-119; Curtin, *Rise and Fall of the Plantation Complex,* pp. 126-28. For an analysis of the interpretations of African slavery, see Cooper, "Problem of Slavery in African Studies," pp. 103-25.

[32]Morgan, *American Slavery, American Freedom,* pp. 64-68, 69-70, 83-84, 108-10, 112-18, 123, 126-29.

[33]For this and the following two paragraphs, see Puckrein, *Little England,* pp. 32-33, 34, 36-37, 43, 59-62, 63, 66-70, 80-87; Richard S. Dunn, *Sugar and Slaves: The Rise of the Planter Class in the English West Indies, 1624-1713* (Chapel Hill: University of North Carolina Press, 1972), pp. 300-301, 325-26.

[34]Albert J. Raboteau, *Slave Religion: The "Invisible Institution" in the Antebellum South* (New York: Oxford University Press, 1978), pp. 98-101, 105-6, quotes from p. 98; Sobel, *World They Made Together,* pp. 178-79; James D. Essig, *The Bonds of Wickedness: American Evangelicals Against Slavery, 1770-1808* (Philadelphia: Temple University Press, 1982), pp. 10-12. Jon Butler ("Enlarging the Bonds of Christ: Slavery, Evangelism and the Christianization of the White South, 1690-1790," in *The Evangelical Tradition in America,* ed. Leonard I. Sweet [Macon, Ga.: Mercer University Press, 1984], pp. 87-112) sets up a weak Anglican church growth program as "Christianization," then cites its occurrence at the same time as slavery's institutionalization to prove a link between Christianity and the institutionalizing of slavery. This is making a straw man into a murder suspect.

[35]Raboteau, *Slave Religion,* pp. 98-99, 103, 106-7, 115, 121-22.

[36]Quoted in Genovese, *Roll, Jordan, Roll,* p. 214. For the evangelical attack on the sinful lives of slaveholders, see Essig, *Bonds of Wickedness,* pp. 53-56.

[37]Alan Kulikoff, *Tobacco and Slaves: The Development of Southern Cultures in the Chesapeake, 1680-1800* (Chapel Hill: University of North Carolina Press, 1986), pp. 232-34, 237, 238-40; Raboteau, *Slave Religion,* 103; Sobel, *World They Made Together,* pp. 178-79.

[38]Andrews, *Trade, Plunder and Settlement,* pp. 37-38. The literature on the origins of racism and slavery in the Thirteen Colonies is extensive. See, for example, Winthrop D. Jordan, *White over Black: American Attitudes Toward the Negro, 1550-1812* (Chapel Hill: Uni-

versity of North Carolina Press, 1968), especially pp. 3-98.

[39]Sobel, *World They Made Together,* pp. 182-84, 187; Raboteau, *Slave Religion,* pp. 128-30, 134-36. See also Mechal Sobel, *Trabelin' On: The Slave Journey to an Afro-Baptist Faith* (Westport, Conn.: Greenwood, 1979), pp. 79-108; Essig, *Bonds of Wickedness,* pp. 10-12.

[40]Sobel, *World They Made Together,* pp. 188-98; Raboteau, *Slave Religion,* pp. 130-34, 148; Essig, *Bonds of Wickedness,* pp. 26-34. Essig (pp. 20-22) claims, however, that evangelical attacks on slavery did not begin until 1770, in the period of American self-examination preceding the American Revolution.

[41]Raboteau, *Slave Religion,* pp. 127, 148-49; Albert J. Raboteau, "Black Experience in American Evangelicalism: The Meaning of Slavery," in *Evangelical Tradition,* ed. Sweet, p. 183; Patterson, *Slavery and Social Death,* p. 75; Sobel, *World They Made Together,* pp. 180-82; Genovese, *Roll, Jordan, Roll,* pp. 211, 240-55.

[42]Patterson, *Slavery and Social Death,* p. 75; Genovese, *Roll, Jordan, Roll,* p. 253 (quoting Julius Lester). I do not agree with Patterson's attempt to find a great dualism in Pauline theology and its fundamentalist reincarnation, which somehow fitted them to appeal to both masters and slaves.

[43]First Peter 3:8-14; 4:1-2, 12-19. For Sambo, see Stanley Elkins, *Slavery: A Problem in American Institutional and Intellectual Life* (Chicago: University of Chicago Press, 1959). For a summary of the debate on slave resistance, families and culture, see Robert W. Fogel, *Without Consent or Contract: The Rise and Fall of American Slavery* (New York: Norton, 1989), pp. 154-98. The best-known example of an economic analysis is Robert W. Fogel and Stanley W. Engerman's *Time on the Cross: The Economics of American Negro Slavery* (Boston: Little, Brown, 1974). For an implicit hope that slaves would rebel, see Zinn, *People's History,* pp. 33-38. See also William Freehling's flippant description of Nat Turner's Revolt in *Secessionists at Bay,* vol. 1 of *The Road to Disunion: 1776-1854* (New York: Oxford University Press, 1990), pp. 179-84.

[44]John 12:32; Galatians 3:28; Ephesians 2:14-16; see also Colossians 3:11.

[45]Surprised by "the clear evidence of extensive racial interaction" during the Great Awakening, Sobel concludes that it must have been present all along. That seems an unwarranted assumption. See Sobel, *World They Made Together,* p. 3.

[46]For the attacks on antislavery preachers, see, for example, Raboteau, *Slave Religion,* pp. 144-45; Nathan O. Hatch, *The Democratization of American Christianity* (New Haven, Conn.: Yale University Press, 1989), pp. 102-3; Sobel, *Trabelin' On,* pp. 85-89; Essig, *Bonds of Wickedness,* pp. 45-46. For an interesting interfamily quarrel over the revival, with a born-again mother, hostile gentleman-father and hostile Anglican minister uncle, see Henry Mayer, *A Son of Thunder: Patrick Henry and the American Republic* (Charlottesville: University of Virginia Press, 1991), pp. 32-40.

[47]Raboteau, *Slave Religion,* p. 145; T. H. Breen, *Tobacco Culture: The Mentality of the Great Tidewater Planters on the Eve of Revolution* (Princeton, N.J.: Princeton University Press, 1985), pp. 22-23, 26, 29-30, 36-37, 60. Breen (pp. 27-29) disputes Rhys Isaac's argument that Virginia's Baptists posed a threat to wealthy Anglican tobacco planters. For an argument that gentry's *joining* the Baptists and Methodists in the 1790s led to both a falling away from antislavery and, in some preachers, a renewed emphasis on it, see Essig, *Bonds of Wickedness,* pp. 60-65.

[48]McManus, *Black Bondage in the North,* pp. 15-17, 199-214; Gary B. Nash and Jean R. Soderlund, *Freedom by Degrees: Emancipation in Pennsylvania and Its Aftermath* (New York: Oxford University Press, 1991), pp. 8-9, 14-21, 33-36. I consider Delaware to be a Southern colony.

[49]Nash and Soderlund, *Freedom by Degrees,* pp. 47-48, 52-53, 63-66, 71-72. See also David E. Shi, *The Simple Life: Plain Living and High Thinking in American Culture* (New York: Oxford University Press, 1985), pp. 28-49.

[50]Fogel, *Without Consent or Contract,* pp. 169-71; Peter Wood, *Black Majority: Negroes in Colonial South Carolina from 1670 Through the Stono Rebellion* (New York: Norton, 1974), pp. 56-62; Sobel, *World They Made Together,* pp. 46-47, 119-26.

[51]Christine Leigh Heyrman in James W. Davidson et al., *Nation of Nations: A Narrative History of the American Republic* (New York: McGraw-Hill, 1990), pp. 136-40; Nash et al., *American People,* pp. 75-77. The same criticisms apply to Genovese's *Roll, Jordan, Roll,* which stresses the continuity of African religion in black Christianity and says little about Christianity's role in African-Americans' family loyalties (see pp. 209-20, 482-501).

[52]See, for example, Davidson et al., *Nation of Nations,* pp. 62-64; and Martin et al., *America and Its People,* pp. 55, 58, 60-61. Christine Leigh Heyrman (in the former) and Steven Mintz (in the latter) tie slaveholding patriarchalism with domination of females by the use of a provocative picture (Heyrman) and by quoting William Byrd's sexual braggadocio (Mintz). Kulikoff (*Tobacco and Slaves,* pp. 7-8, 166-67) distinguishes between Southern "domestic patriarchalism" and Northern "bourgeois family government."

Chapter 3: Born from Above

[1]For the utopian myth, see James Kirby Martin et al., *America and Its People* (Glenview, Ill.: Scott, Foresman, 1989), pp. 48-49; and Gary B. Nash et al., *The American People: Creating a Nation and a Society,* 3rd ed. (New York: HarperCollins, 1994), pp. 47-48. Martin devotes nine pages to New England and only five and a half pages to New York, New Jersey and Pennsylvania. Christine Leigh Heyrman (in James W. Davidson et al., *Nation of Nations: A Narrative History of the American Republic* [New York: McGraw, 1990]) has sixteen pages on the former and only eight on the latter. Quoted passages are as follows: "a determined band," Davidson et al., *Nation of Nations,* pp. 84, 88; "a people charged," Nash et al., *American People,* pp. 48, 51, 52; and "proud and driving," Bernard Bailyn et al., *The Great Republic: A History of the American People* (Lexington, Mass.: Heath, 1985), 1:47.

[2]Nash et al., *American People,* pp. 46-58, 91-92; Davidson et al., *Nation of Nations,* pp. 84-85, 87-100. In the latter book, Heyrman incorrectly argues that "predestination was the engine driving their social and political activism." Nash (pp. 86-87) and Davidson (pp. 90-91) have sections on Puritans and death, which are based on David E. Stannard, *The Puritan Way of Death: A Study in Religion, Culture and Social Change* (New York: Oxford University Press, 1977). David Hackett Fischer (*Albion's Seed: Four British Folkways in America* [New York: Oxford University Press, 1989], pp. 35-36, 39, 42-49, 151, 155, 181, 183) seems to attribute New England's successes largely to the East Anglian origins of many of its inhabitants.

[3]Charles E. Hambrick-Stowe, *The Practice of Piety: Puritan Devotional Discipline in Seventeenth-Century New England* (Chapel Hill: University of North Carolina Press, 1982), pp. 26, 64-69. For Eliot's work, see Henry Bowden, *American Indians and Christian Missions: Studies in Cultural Conflict* (Chicago: University of Chicago Press, 1981), pp. 118-30. Of course King Philip's War (1675-1676) largely destroyed Eliot's work. Both Stephen Innes's *Creating the Commonwealth: The Economic Culture of Puritan New England* (New York: Norton, 1995) and Fischer's *Albion's Seed* show how successful New England was in terms of demographics, morality, economics, civic institutions and other factors.

[4]Edmund S. Morgan, ed., *Puritan Political Ideas, 1558-1794* (Indianapolis: Bobbs-Merrill, 1965), pp. 76-93, quote from p. 93 (spelling modernized); Theodore Dwight Bozeman, *To Live Ancient Lives: The Primitivist Dimension in Puritanism* (Chapel Hill: University of North Carolina Press, 1988), pp. 92-93, 114-16, 120.

[5]Bozeman, *To Live Ancient Lives,* pp. 82-90, 98-119, 122-23, 194. For the mistaken quotations on utopian mission, see Nash et al., *American People,* pp. 47, 51.

[6]Hambrick-Stowe, *Practice of Piety,* pp. 23-25, 26-30, 38; Stephen Foster, *The Long Argument: English Puritanism and the Shaping of New England Culture* (Chapel Hill: University of North Carolina Press, 1991), pp. 16-19, 27-32.

[7]Hambrick-Stowe, *Practice of Piety,* pp. 21-22; Foster, *Long Argument,* pp. 75-76. Innes correctly notes Max Weber's error in thinking that Puritans worked hard "to *prove* their election"—for they believed in justification by faith alone—but his *Creating the Commonwealth* is full of supposed paradoxes, dichotomies, inner tensions and talk of "an inscrutable God" (p. 311). God's self-revelation in Scripture is not riven with conundrums and contradictions as secular historians suppose.

[8]Foster, *Long Argument,* p. 13; Euan Cameron, *The European Reformation* (Oxford: Clarendon, 1991), pp. 111-21, 132-40. For *sola Scriptura* ("the Word of God alone"), see Harry S. Stout, *The New England Soul: Preaching and Religious Culture in Colonial New England* (New York: Oxford University Press, 1986), pp. 14-15, 149-50; and Bozeman, *To Live Ancient Lives,* pp. 25-29.

[9]For Bozeman's stress on the chronological dimension, see *To Live Ancient Lives,* pp. 15-23, 34, 72. Writing from a historicist viewpoint, he critiques Puritans' "anachronistic" view that the biblical "realm of sacred pattern was closed, all-sufficient, timeless; it was not relative to the times, places, and changes of history" (pp. 17, 34). Yet truth revealed by an immutable, changeless, eternal God would necessarily be "closed, all-sufficient, timeless."

[10]Foster, *Long Argument,* pp. 5-6.

[11]Bozeman, *To Live Ancient Lives,* pp. 139-50, 254-56.

[12]Foster, *Long Argument,* pp. xiii, 5-6, 9, 13, 49-50.

[13]Ibid., pp. 114, 118-20, 137; Bozeman, *To Live Ancient Lives,* pp. 98-114.

[14]Foster, *Long Argument,* pp. 151-54; David Cressy, *Coming Over: Migration and Communication Between England and New England in the Seventeenth Century* (New York: Cambridge University Press, 1987), pp. 45-49; Bailyn et al., *Great Republic,* 1:50-51; Morgan, ed., *Puritan Political Ideas,* pp. xxix-xxx.

[15]Bozeman, *To Live Ancient Lives,* pp. 162, 164-65, 168, 174, 178-79, 182-84, 267-73.

[16]Ibid., pp. 153-60, 254-55, 311; Stout, *New England Soul,* pp. 166-74.

[17]Timothy H. Breen and Stephen Foster, "The Puritans' Greatest Achievement: A Study of Social Cohesion in Seventeenth-Century Massachusetts," in *Puritan New England: Essays on Religion, Society, and Culture,* ed. Alden T. Vaughan and Francis J. Bremer (New York: St. Martin's, 1977), pp. 110-18; Innes, *Creating the Commonwealth,* pp. 284-86. The quote is from the Reforming Synod of 1679, in Hambrick-Stowe, *Practice of Piety,* p. 244.

[18]Carla Gardina Pestana, "The Quaker Executions as Myth and History," *Journal of American History* 80 (September 1993): 441-42, 445, 447, 449; Patricia U. Bonomi, *Under the Cope of Heaven: Religion, Society and Politics in Colonial America* (New York: Oxford University Press, 1986), pp. 27-29.

[19]Innes, *Creating the Commonwealth,* pp. 26, 309, 310. Innes would not exactly agree with my interpretation, but his "communal capitalism" in Massachusetts Bay (see pp. 39, 92) seems an oxymoron. What he describes is the making of a healthy society and an economy that was suited to capitalism once partly secularized. His book is also short on comparisons

with the more capitalist economies of colonial Virginia, South Carolina and even Rhode Island. Charles Sellers, in his *Market Revolution: Jacksonian America, 1815-1846* (New York: Oxford University Press, 1991), notes that anticapitalist movements strengthen capitalism (see chapter five, below).

[20]This is a brief summary of Innes's description of the underlying conditions for Massachusetts Bay's prosperity, especially in chapters 1, 3, and 5.

[21]Christine Leigh Heyrman, *Commerce and Culture: The Maritime Communities of Colonial Massachusetts, 1690-1750* (New York: Norton, 1984), pp. 29, 31-38, 40-41, 209-20, 222-24; Stephen Innes, *Labor in a New Land: Economy and Society in Seventeenth-Century Springfield* (Princeton, N.J.: Princeton University Press, 1983), pp. xvii-xx, 4-6, 9-11, 147-48, 180.

[22]See Heyrman, *Commerce and Culture,* especially pp. 43-46, 47-48, 62-64, 67-69, 74-77, 226-27, 273-303, 330-31, 336-37, 340, 347-52, quote from p. 74. The stress on the churches' role in integration and stability is mine, not Heyrman's. In both towns, Congregationalists' quarrels with Quakers and Anglicans helped cause the conflict. In Gloucester the Quakers' "counter-community" with its "anti-localistic" loyalty to quarterly and yearly meetings in distant cities threatened the town's unity and "social identity," both built on Congregationalism (Heyrman, *Commerce and Culture,* pp. 96-99, 135, 138-40, 273-303).

[23]Bruce C. Daniels, *Dissent and Conformity on Narragansett Bay: The Colonial Rhode Island Town* (Middletown, Conn.: Wesleyan University Press, 1983), p. 22. Innes's failure to compare and contrast Rhode Island and Massachusetts Bay is a major weakness in his *Creating the Commonwealth.*

[24]Bozeman, *To Live Ancient Lives,* pp. 156-57; Sydney V. James, *Colonial Rhode Island: A History* (New York: Scribner's, 1975), pp. 25, 26, 30-31, 37-38, 39, 41-44.

[25]Here and above, see James, *Colonial Rhode Island,* pp. 65-68, 71-72, 76-87, 102-3, 114, 119-20, 135-36, 138-39, 153, 156-58; Daniels, *Dissent and Conformity,* pp. 13-14, 16-20, 87-90; Carl Bridenbaugh, *Fat Mutton and Liberty of Conscience: Society in Rhode Island, 1636-1690* (Providence, R.I.: Brown University Press, 1974), pp. 9-10, 12, 16-19, 27, 39, 49; Lynne Withey, *Urban Growth in Colonial Rhode Island: Newport and Providence in the Eighteenth Century* (Albany: State University of New York Press, 1984), pp. 18-19, 21-23, 24-27.

[26]Daniels, *Dissent and Conformity,* pp. 16-20, 25, 79-81, 87-90, 94-95; James, *Colonial Rhode Island,* pp. 156-58, 163, 172-80; Withey, *Urban Growth,* pp. 24-27. For Massachusetts towns' economic regulation, see, for example, Heyrman, *Commerce and Culture,* p. 57.

[27]James, *Colonial Rhode Island,* pp. 93-99, 172-80; Daniels, *Dissent and Conformity,* p. 79; Jay Coughtry, *The Notorious Triangle: Rhode Island and the African Slave Trade, 1700-1807* (Philadelphia: Temple University Press, 1981).

[28]James, *Colonial Rhode Island,* pp. 189-92, 198-202.

[29]John 3:3; "born from above" is the NIV alternate reading.

[30]Foster, *Long Argument,* pp. 180-82.

[31]Here and above, see Bozeman, *To Live Ancient Lives,* pp. 313-16, 319-23, 328-29, 331; Foster, *Long Argument,* pp. 217-18, 229-30, 250-51; Stout, *New England Soul,* pp. 56, 58.

[32]Robert G. Pope, *The Half-Way Covenant: Church Membership in Puritan New England* (Princeton, N.J.: Princeton University Press, 1969), especially pp. 6-8; Foster, *Long Argument,* pp. 176-77, 186-87, 197, 225-29; Hambrick-Stowe, *Practice of Piety,* pp. 127, 131-32, 249-53; Stout, *New England Soul,* pp. 96-98.

[33]Quoted in Stout, *New England Soul,* p. 97.

[34]Stout, *New England Soul,* pp. 97-98. Citing continued preaching on conversion, Stout disputes Perry Miller's contention that the emphasis on covenant renewal meant dry legalism. However, coming from the same pulpit and the same minister, the message of human responsibility to keep the covenant must have vitiated the doctrine of human inability to please God short of being "born from above" by divine grace.

[35]Bozeman, *To Live Ancient Lives,* pp. 308-9, 328-29; Hambrick-Stowe, *Practice of Piety,* pp. 131-35; Foster, *Long Argument,* pp. 214-18. Of course the "pietist saga of the soul" continued in sermons and private devotions, but the "public concerns" tended to overshadow it or to confuse the plot.

[36]Stout, *New England Soul,* p. 96.

[37]Bozeman, *To Live Ancient Lives,* p. 312; Stout, *New England Soul,* pp. 111-14, 177-79.

[38]Foster, *Long Argument,* pp. 230, 233-37; Stout, *New England Soul,* pp. 166-67, 169-74.

[39]Foster, *Long Argument,* pp. 237, 240-43; Stout, *New England Soul,* pp. 111-14.

[40]Foster, *Long Argument,* pp. 237-39, 248-51.

[41]Stout, *New England Soul,* pp. 141, 144-45, 148-55, 166-67, 169-74; Foster, *Long Argument,* pp. 237-39, 274.

[42]Foster, *Long Argument,* pp. 281-83.

[43]Patricia J. Tracy, *Jonathan Edwards, Pastor: Religion and Society in Eighteenth-Century Northampton* (New York: Hill & Wang, 1980), p. 28.

[44]This account is based on disputes in Gloucester and Northampton as outlined in Heyrman, *Commerce and Culture,* pp. 143-72; and Tracy, *Jonathan Edwards, Pastor,* pp. 125-30. The quotes are from Heyrman (p. 170) and Tracy (p. 126). The Northampton dispute occurred in 1737, eight years after Stoddard's death, but it indicates the kind of forces Stoddard was opposing. His near-dictatorial control assured that the dispute would not break out until after his death.

[45]Tracy, *Jonathan Edwards, Pastor,* pp. 125-28, 148-53; Heyrman, *Commerce and Culture,* pp. 143-81. Quoted passages are from Tracy (pp. 126, 128).

[46]Tracy, *Jonathan Edwards, Pastor,* pp. 22-26, 28, 29-37, 47-48, 128; Stout, *New England Soul,* pp. 99-101; John 3:8. Tracy's statement about unprotected hearts (p. 128) comes during her discussion of Edwards's ministry, but it aptly describes Stoddard's earlier goal.

[47]Tracy, *Jonathan Edwards, Pastor,* pp. 76-80. Tracy tries to show that socioeconomic change and generational conflict led to this 1734-1735 revival, but her argument is unconvincing (see pp. 92-106, 110-12). Marilyn J. Westerkamp (*Triumph of the Laity: Scots-Irish Piety and the Great Awakening, 1625-1760* [New York: Oxford University Press, 1988], pp. 5-6) points out that this model of social change or conflict tends "to remove the revival from the [religious] circumstances within which the contemporary participants experienced it." I am indebted to John Piper's discussion of Edwards in his *The Supremacy of God in Preaching* (Grand Rapids, Mich.: Baker Book House, 1990), pp. 47-49, 65-105.

[48]Tracy, *Jonathan Edwards, Pastor,* pp. 79-83, quotes from p. 80; and Jonathan Edwards, *Narrative of Surprising Conversions, 1735,* excerpted in Marvin Meyers, John Cawelti and Alexander Kern, eds., *Sources of the American Republic: A Documentary History of Politics, Society and Thought* (Glenview, Ill.: Scott, Foresman, 1967), 1:91. See also *The Great Awakening,* ed. C. C. Goen, vol. 4 of *The Works of Jonathan Edwards* (New Haven, Conn.: Yale University Press, 1972), pp. 104, 149.

[49]Tracy, *Jonathan Edwards, Pastor,* pp. 131-34; Meyers et al., *Sources of the American Republic,* p. 89.

[50]Tracy, *Jonathan Edwards, Pastor,* pp. 136-37; Stout, *New England Soul,* pp. 193-95,

197-201. For Edwards's comments on itineracy, see *Great Awakening,* pp. 533-34.

[51]Stout, *New England Soul,* pp. 190-92.

[52]Westerkamp, *Triumph of the Laity,* pp. 20-21, 23-25, 52-73.

[53]Paul K. Conkin, *Cane Ridge: America's Pentecost* (Madison: University of Wisconsin Press, 1990), pp. 20-22. For arguments on the democratizing effect of the Great Awakening, see Stout, *New England Soul,* pp. 207-11; and Westerkamp, *Triumph of the Laity,* p. 4. Westerkamp argues against such a position.

[54]Heyrman, *Commerce and Culture,* pp. 182-83, 197, 369-70. See also Stout, *New England Soul,* pp. 210-11, 217. For an argument stressing the radical, individualistic effects of the Great Awakening in the colonies, see Bonomi, *Under the Cope of Heaven,* pp. 152-60, 161-68, 181-86. For the opposite argument, see Jon Butler, *Awash in a Sea of Faith: Christianizing the American People* (Cambridge, Mass.: Harvard University Press, 1990), pp. 179-82.

[55]Foster, *Long Argument,* pp. 293-305; Susan O'Brien, "A Transatlantic Community of Saints: The Great Awakening and the First Evangelical Network, 1735-1755," *American Historical Review* 91 (1986): 811-32; Butler, *Awash in a Sea of Faith,* pp. 176-77. For an interesting description of the tension within one Connecticut church and the resulting split, see Joy Day Buel and Richard Buel Jr., *The Way of Duty: A Woman and Her Family in Revolutionary America* (New York: Norton, 1984), pp. 9-18.

[56]Stout, *New England Soul,* pp. 198-200; O'Brien, "Transatlantic Community of Saints," pp. 814, 827. Of course, New England Puritans had never totally disconnected from the international Protestant movement.

[57]Westerkamp, *Triumph of the Laity,* p. 199; F. Ernest Stoeffler, ed., *Continental Pietism and Early American Christianity* (Grand Rapids, Mich.: Eerdmans, 1976), pp. 8-10, 14-22, 49, 52-65, 203-6. For New Light criticisms of Moravians' alleged antinomianism, see Westerkamp, *Triumph of the Laity,* pp. 207-8. For an argument that Quaker theology differed from Reformed theology by downplaying the historical Christ and emphasizing a spiritualized "eternal" Christ, see Melvin B. Endy Jr., "Puritanism, Spiritualism and Quakerism: An Historiographical Essay," in *The World of William Penn,* ed. Richard S. Dunn and Mary Maples Dunn (Philadelphia: University of Pennsylvania Press, 1986), pp. 281-301.

[58]Here and above, see Richard W. Pointer, *Protestant Pluralism and the New York Experience: A Study of Eighteenth-Century Religious Diversity* (Bloomington: Indiana University Press, 1988), pp. 40-51; and Stout, *New England Soul,* pp. 203-5, 207, 212, 222-25, 241-42.

[59]Pointer, *Protestant Pluralism,* pp. 48-51.

[60]Stout, *New England Soul,* pp. 223-25, 240-43; Morgan, ed., *Puritan Political Ideas,* pp. 304-30.

[61]Adams quoted in Foster, *Long Argument,* p. 311; Bonomi, *Under the Cope of Heaven,* pp. 102-4.

[62]For the nature of republicanism, see Gordon S. Wood, *The Radicalism of the American Revolution: How a Revolution Transformed a Monarchical Society into a Democratic One Unlike Any That Had Ever Existed* (New York: Knopf, 1992), pp. 95-97, 100-101. The stress on refusers' turn to republicanism is my own, however.

Chapter 4: Gentlemen Think Up a Revolution, a Republic & a Constitution

[1]This and the two preceding paragraphs are based on Gordon S. Wood's brilliant analysis in *The Radicalism of the American Revolution: How a Revolution Transformed a Monarchical Society into a Democratic One Unlike Any That Had Ever Existed* (New York:

Knopf, 1992), pp. 11-92, quotes from pp. 11, 91. Perhaps the best description of gentle-men's political leadership in colonial America is Charles S. Sydnor, *American Revolution-aries in the Making: Political Practices in Washington's Virginia* (New York: Free Press, 1965). Wood's book was raked over the coals in a special "forum" in the *William and Mary Quarterly* (October 1994, pp. 677-716) for stressing ideas and white gentlemen too much, and minorities, the working class and slavery too little. Wood (pp. 703-16) persuasively defends his analysis. I look very critically at white gentlemen, not in a celebratory way, but their dominant political role in the 1770s seems indisputable.

[2]Wood outlines some of the consequences of familylike relationships in *Radicalism of the American Revolution,* pp. 43-77.

[3]Ibid., pp. 17-18, 34-42. The apostle Paul is quoted from 1 Timothy 6:6-8.

[4]Ralph Lerner ("The Thinking Revolutionary," in *Beyond Confederation: Origins of the Constitution and American National Identity,* ed. Richard Beeman, Stephen Botein and Edward C. Carter II [Chapel Hill: University of North Carolina Press, 1987], pp. 38-68, quote from pp. 42, 44) makes this point of taking ideas seriously in his rebuttal to the "ideological school" of historians (Bernard Bailyn, Gordon Wood, J. G. A. Pocock et al.), whose interpretations stress the "relative insignificance of individual thought and individual actors."

[5]Henry F. May, *The Enlightenment in America* (New York: Oxford University Press, 1976), p. xiv. Gay is quoted in Wood, *Radicalism of the American Revolution,* p. 100.

[6]May, *Enlightenment in America,* pp. 5-8, 8-13, 13-15, 20-22; William Brandon, *New Worlds for Old: Reports from the New World and Their Effects on the Development of Social Thought in Europe, 1500-1800* (Athens: Ohio University Press, 1986), pp. 66, 83-84, 87-95, 101-5, 107-10. See also Bernard Bailyn et al., *The Great Republic: A History of the American People* (Lexington, Mass.: Heath, 1985), 1:199-204.

[7]May, *Enlightenment in America,* pp. 133-49, 197-222, 279-80, 293-96; Esmond Wright, *Franklin of Philadelphia* (Cambridge, Mass.: Harvard University Press, 1986), pp. 24-25, 47-50; Jon Butler, *Awash in a Sea of Faith: Christianizing the American People* (Cambridge, Mass.: Harvard University Press, 1990), pp. 214-15; Forrest McDonald, *Novus Ordo Seclorum: The Intellectual Origins of the Constitution* (Lawrence: University Press of Kansas, 1985), pp. 192-93; Garry Wills, *Cincinnatus: George Washington and the Enlightenment* (Garden City, N.Y.: Doubleday, 1984), pp. 23-25. Though Adams made this comment in 1825, it reflected his antiorthodox views throughout his life. Today's evan-gelicals are mistaken on the "faith of the Founders"—partly because they note Founders' references to God and do not carefully note the absence of references to Christ, partly because some Founders were Christians and few were openly anti-Christian. For an analysis of the Revolution as a revolt against arbitrary paternal authority—that of a Calvinist Jehovah and a British king—see Jay Fliegelman, *Prodigals and Pilgrims: The American Revolution Against Patriarchal Authority, 1750-1800* (New York: Cambridge University Press, 1982).

[8]May, *Enlightenment in America,* pp. 26-27 36-40, 118, 121-22, 123-32. For two of Jefferson's private letters on Christianity and Christ's divinity, see Jefferson to Peter Carr, August 10, 1787, and Jefferson to Dr. Joseph Priestley, April 9, 1803, both in *Thomas Jefferson: Writings,* Library of America ed. (New York: Library Classics of the United States, 1984), pp. 900-906, 1120-22.

[9]May, *Enlightenment in America,* pp. 36-41; Meyer Reinhold, *The Classick Pages: Clas-sical Reading of Eighteenth-Century Americans* (University Park, Penn.: American Phil-ological Association, 1975), pp. 1-3, 8-16, 39, 99; Gordon S. Wood, *The Creation of the*

American Republic, 1776-1787 (New York: Norton, 1969), pp. 51-53. May (p. xvi) divides the Enlightenment into four parts: the Moderate Enlightenment (mostly British), the Revolutionary Enlightenment, the Skeptical Enlightenment (British and French) and the Didactic Enlightenment (mostly Scottish). Americans preferred the moderate British Enlightenment.

[10]These ideas are summarized in Bernard Bailyn, *The Ideological Origins of the American Revolution* (Cambridge, Mass.: Harvard University Press, 1967), pp. 34-54, and in his chapter "Power and Liberty," pp. 55-93.

[11]Wood, *Radicalism of the American Revolution,* pp. 95-100. Republicanism is a concept that has been greatly overused by recent historians, many of them New Leftists who used it to project a more participatory, anticommercial, unliberal kind of democracy back into U.S. history. In Daniel T. Rodger's phrase, it was "a word passed through too many hands and made to do too many things" ("Republicanism: The Career of a Concept," *Journal of American History* 79, no. 1 [June 1992]: 11-38, quote from p. 34). Since I am not idealizing participatory democracy, I have tried not to extend the term *republicanism* too far past 1800.

[12]Bailyn, *Ideological Origins,* pp. 25, 35-36, 39, 40-43, 45; Reinhold, *Classick Pages,* pp. 39, 99, 147.

[13]Wood, *Creation,* pp. 16-17; Bailyn, *Ideological Origins,* pp. 51-54; Wood, *Radicalism of the American Revolution,* pp. 109-24.

[14]For the term "political Protestant" I am indebted, believe it or not, to a speech given on the Centennial, July 4, 1876, by future U.S. Senator Knute Nelson at Alexandria, Minnesota. See *Alexandria Post,* July 14, 1876, p. 1.

[15]Robert Kelley, *The Cultural Pattern in American Politics: The First Century,* paperback ed. (Lanham, Md.: University Press of America, 1979), pp. 83-84.

[16]For the classic analysis of this interpretation, see Bailyn, *Ideological Origins,* pp. 94-143 ("Logic of Rebellion") and pp. 144-59 ("A Note on Conspiracy"). The classic account of the Stamp Act protests is Edmund S. Morgan and Helen M. Morgan, *Stamp Act Crisis: Prologue to Revolution,* rev. ed. (New York: Collier, 1963).

[17]Wallace Brown, *The Good Americans: The Loyalists in the American Revolution* (New York: William Morrow, 1969), pp. 30-33, 44-81. Brown emphasized that most Loyalists did not approve of British measures. Most were Whigs but not radical enough to countenance Radical Whiggery in action.

[18]Kelley, *Cultural Pattern,* pp. 40-42, 45, 46-47, 50-58, 64-75; Brown, *Good Americans,* pp. 45-49; Butler, *Awash in a Sea of Faith,* pp. 196-99.

[19]Here and above, see Butler, *Awash in a Sea of Faith,* pp. 200-202; Nathan O. Hatch, *The Sacred Cause of Liberty: Republican Thought and the Millennium in Revolutionary New England* (New Haven, Conn.: Yale University Press, 1977), pp. 16-17.

[20]Marc Egnal, *A Mighty Empire: The Origins of the American Revolution* (Ithaca, N.Y.: Cornell University Press, 1988), pp. 6-7, 12-15, 87-101, 259-61, 333-35; Richard W. Van Alstyne, *The Rising American Empire,* paperback ed. (Chicago: Quadrangle, 1965), pp. 1-2, 8-13, 26-27.

[21]May, *Enlightenment in America,* pp. 162-63; Thomas Paine, *Common Sense,* excerpted in Marvin Meyers, John Cawelti and Alexander Kern, eds., *Sources of the American Republic: A Documentary History of Politics, Society and Thought* (Glenview, Ill.: Scott, Foresman, 1967), 1:132-35.

[22]For the Declaration as an Enlightenment document, see Garry Wills, *Inventing America: Jefferson's Declaration of Independence* (New York: Doubleday, 1978); May, *Enlighten-*

ment in America, pp. 163-64; Butler, *Awash in a Sea of Faith*, p. 196. Wills overemphasizes Jefferson's reliance on the Scottish Enlightenment but not his reliance on the Enlightenment as a whole. See Ronald Hamowy, "Jefferson and the Scottish Enlightenment: A Critique of Wills's *Inventing America: Jefferson's Declaration of Independence*," *William and Mary Quarterly* 36 (1979): 503-23. For an argument that Enlightened Americans "implicitly identified England with an unreasonable Jehovah and the old [Calvinist] Covenant of Works," see Fliegelman, *Prodigals and Pilgrims*, especially pp. 155-60. Like many secular historians, Fliegelman almost ignores the way the cross reconciles God's justice and mercy.

[23]Wood, *Creation*, pp. 127-33.

[24]Richard B. Morris, *The Forging of the Union, 1781-1789* (New York: Harper & Row, 1987), pp. 34-41, 50-51, 86-87; Bailyn et al., *Great Republic*, 1:280-85.

[25]Morris, *Forging the Union*, pp. 92-93. Attendance declined after ratification of the treaty. Jefferson complained, "We cannot make up a Congress at all. We have not sat above 3 days I believe in as many weeks. Admonition after admonition has been sent to the states, to no effect."

[26]Wood, *Creation*, pp. 135-36, 148-50, 162-67, 403-9.

[27]David Lovejoy, *Rhode Island Politics and the American Revolution, 1760-1776* (Providence, R.I.: Brown University Press, 1958), pp. 25-28, 52-53, 85-90, 93-99, 129-30.

[28]Morris, *Forging the Union*, pp. 157-58; McDonald, *Novus Ordo Seclorum*, pp. 175-76; Irwin H. Polishook, *Rhode Island and the Union, 1774-1795* (Evanston, Ill.: Northwestern University Press, 1969), pp. 108-9, 124-28.

[29]Richard Buel Jr., *Dear Liberty: Connecticut's Mobilization for the Revolutionary War* (Middletown, Conn.: Wesleyan University Press, 1980). For gentry exaggerations of the extent and consequences of "vice" in Massachusetts and Rhode Island, see McDonald, *Novus Ordo Seclorum*, pp. 176-78.

[30]Gordon S. Wood quotes Madison in "Interests and Disinterestedness in the Making of the Constitution," in *Beyond Confederation*, ed. Beeman et al., pp. 73-74; McDonald, *Novus Ordo Seclorum*, pp. 151-52; Morris, *Forging the Union*, p. 197.

[31]Wood, *Radicalism of the American Revolution*, pp. 251-52. Wood (pp. 247-52) argues that new risk-taking entrepreneurs demanded paper money, whereas the gentlemen of "old wealth"—centered in land and interest-bearing notes—opposed it.

[32]May, *Enlightenment in America*, pp. 133-35; John P. Diggins, "Slavery, Race and Equality: Jefferson and the Pathos of the Enlightenment," *American Quarterly* 28, no. 2 (Summer 1976): 206-28; Wills, *Inventing America*, pp. 66-68, 377. Wood, *Radicalism of the American Revolution*, p. 134; William W. Freehling, *Secessionists at Bay, 1776-1854*, vol. 1 of *The Road to Disunion* (New York: Oxford University Press, 1990), p. 135. Inconsistently, Jefferson attacked the king for emancipating slaves who helped British forces in the rebellious colonies.

[33]Freehling, *Secessionists at Bay*, pp. 132-34.

[34]Morris, *Forging the Union*, p. 180; Freehling, *Secessionists at Bay*, p. 130. See also Thomas Jefferson to Edward Coles, August 25, 1814, in *Thomas Jefferson: Writings*, pp. 1343-46. For St. George Tucker's Deism and proemancipation views, see May, *Enlightenment in America*, pp. 138-43.

[35]Here and above, Diggins, "Slavery, Race and Equality," pp. 213, 215, 225-26; May, *Enlightenment in America*, pp. 302, 326. For Jefferson's Deism, see May, *Enlightenment in America*, pp. 293-97.

[36]Wood, *Radicalism of the American Revolution*, pp. 145-68, 232-35, 243-51.

[37]Quoted in Wood, "Interests and Disinterestedness," p. 76.

[38]William Lee Miller, *The Business of May Next: James Madison and the Founding* (Charlottesville: University of Virginia Press, 1992), pp. 7, 14-16; May, *Enlightenment in America*, pp. 96-97, 99-100; Stephen Botein, "Religious Dimensions of the Early American State," in *Beyond Confederation*, ed. Beeman et al., pp. 317, 318-19, 320-22. For intellectual sources of the Constitution, see McDonald, *Novus Ordo Seclorum*, pp. 9-142. For classical sources (Polybius, Cicero and so on), see Richard M. Gummere, *The American Colonial Mind and the Classical Tradition* (Cambridge, Mass.: Harvard University Press, 1963), pp. 173-90. For Montesquieu as a source for the separation of powers, see Paul Merrill Spurlin, *The French Enlightenment in America: Essays on the Times of the Founding Fathers* (Athens: University of Georgia Press, 1984), pp. 86-98. See also Isaac Kramnick and R. Laurence Moore, *The Godless Constitution: The Case Against Religious Correctness* (New York: W. W. Norton, 1996), especially chap. 2. I agree with them that the Constitution "is a godless document," but not with their view that "its utter neglect of religion" was and is a good thing.

[39]Wood, *Creation*, pp. 471-564; McDonald, *Novus Ordo Seclorum*, pp. 261-91; Wood, "Interests and Disinterestedness," pp. 91-93, 107-9; Morris, *Forging the Union*, pp. 268-69, 281-83, 288-89. The classic argument for the different branches of government checking the others is given in *Federalist* 51 (written by Madison). The Constitution also prohibited state issues of paper money and state laws interfering with debtors' contractual obligations.

[40]Wood, *Creation*, pp. 513, 530-35, 544-47, 562; Morris, *Forging the Union*, pp. 305-13; McDonald, *Novus Ordo Seclorum*, pp. 277-80, 286-87. For a summary of the Anti-Federalist position (and several Anti-Federalist essays), see Herbert J. Storing, ed., *The Anti-Federalist: Writings by the Opponents of the Constitution* (Chicago: University of Chicago Press, 1985).

[41]Paul Finkelman, "Slavery and the Constitutional Convention: Making a Covenant with Death," in *Beyond Confederation*, ed. Beeman et al., pp. 194, 195-98, 201-202, 205, 207, 211, 214; McDonald, *Novus Ordo Seclorum*, pp. 236-37; Morris, *Forging the Union*, pp. 283-87.

[42]Finkelman, "Slavery and the Constitutional Convention," pp. 214-18, 220-21, 224. May (*Enlightenment in America*, p. 99) argues that the delegates who subscribed to the Moderate Enlightenment believed "that *everything* can be settled by compromise."

[43]Finkelman, "Slavery and the Constitutional Convention," p. 224; Edmund S. Morgan, *American Slavery, American Freedom: The Ordeal of Colonial Virginia* (New York: Norton, 1975), pp. 369-73, 375-76, 378-79, 380, 386.

[44]Forrest McDonald, *The Presidency of George Washington* (Lawrence: University Press of Kansas, 1974), pp. 23-26, 28-30.

[45]Wood, *Creation*, p. 513; Wood, *Radicalism of the American Revolution*, pp. 232-36, 240-43, 245-47, 248-52, 271-81, 305-17. For these basic trends, the importance (then decline) of the gentry and the outdated character of the Constitution, I am also indebted to Robert H. Wiebe, *The Opening of American Society: From the Adoption of the Constitution to the Eve of Disunion*, paperback ed. (New York: Vintage, 1985), chapters 1-7.

[46]May, *Enlightenment in America*, pp. 164-70; Jerome Blum et al., *The European World: A History* (Boston: Little, Brown, 1966), pp. 449-61.

[47]May, *Enlightenment in America*, pp. 243-45; McDonald, *George Washington*, pp. 123-29.

[48]May, *Enlightenment in America*, pp. 141-42, 181, 194-95, 192, 213-14, 236-37, 239-43, 248-49, 252-53, 261-62, 263-64; Ruth H. Bloch, *Visionary Republic: Millennial Themes*

in American Thought, 1756-1800 (Cambridge: Cambridge University Press, 1985), pp. 202-12. Bloch calls this "Francophobic reaction" and associates it with the rise of premillennialism, but it is hard to see how evangelical clergy should be blamed in political terms for necessarily criticizing an anti-Christian movement.

[49]May, *Enlightenment in America,* p. 99.

[50]For a map of the distribution of Federalist and Anti-Federalist votes and the dates of ratification by the several states, see Morris, *Forging the Union,* p. 301.

[51]Wood, *Radicalism of the American Revolution,* pp. 297-305; McDonald, *George Washington,* pp. 179-83; Ronald P. Formisano, "Federalists and Republicans: Parties, Yes—System, No," in Paul Kleppner et al., *The Evolution of American Electoral Systems* (Westport, Conn.: Greenwood, 1981), pp. 33-76. There is disagreement over whether these were true political parties, but even as factions they had similar effects.

[52]May, *Enlightenment in America,* pp. 268-74, 302-4; Jefferson to Dr. Joseph Priestley, March 21, 1801, in *Thomas Jefferson: Writings,* pp. 1085-87. For the Cane Ridge revival, see Paul K. Conkin, *Cane Ridge: America's Pentecost* (Madison: University of Wisconsin Press, 1990).

[53]May, *Enlightenment in America,* pp. 307-57.

[54]Wood, *Radicalism of the American Revolution,* pp. 365-68; Jefferson to Dr. Thomas Cooper, November 2, 1822, in *Thomas Jefferson: Writings,* pp. 1463-65.

Chapter 5: Rebel, Young Patriarch, & Go West with the Country

[1]Gary B. Nash et al., *The American People: Creating a Nation and a Society,* 3rd ed. (New York: HarperCollins, 1994), p. 428; James W. Davidson et al., *Nation of Nations: A Narrative History of the American Republic* (New York: McGraw-Hill, 1990), p. 490; James Kirby Martin et al., *America and Its People* (Glenview, Ill.: Scott, Foresman, 1989), p. 380. For an attempt to use "racism" to deconstruct American history, see Richard Drinnon, *Facing West: The Metaphysics of Indian-Hating and Empire-Building* (New York: Schocken, 1990), especially pp. xxv-xxviii, 48-57, and chapter 23. Drinnon mistakenly describes John Adams as a Puritan, despite Adams's decidedly un-Puritan views on religion (pp. 73-77).

[2]For the Appalachians as "a symbolic divide," see Robert H. Wiebe, *The Opening of American Society: From the Adoption of the Constitution to the Eve of Disunion,* paperback ed. (New York: Vintage, 1985), pp. 146-47.

[3]Quoted in Malcolm J. Rohrbough, *The Trans-Appalachian Frontier: People, Societies and Institutions, 1775-1850* (New York: Oxford University Press, 1978), p. 23.

[4]Francis Jennings, *The Founders of America: How Indians Discovered the Land, Pioneered in It and Created Great Classical Civilizations, How They Were Plunged into a Dark Age by Invasion and Conquest, and How They Are Reviving* (New York: Norton, 1993), p. 311.

[5]David J. Weber, *The Spanish Frontier in North America* (New Haven, Conn.: Yale University Press, 1992), pp. 124-27, 172-76, quote from p. 174. French political scientist quoted in William Cronon, *Nature's Metropolis: Chicago and the Great West* (New York: Norton, 1991), p. 53.

[6]Barbara Solow, "Slavery and Colonization," in *Slavery and the Rise of the Atlantic System,* ed. Barbara Solow (Cambridge: Cambridge University Press, 1991), pp. 33-35.

[7]Walter Nugent, *Structures of American Social History* (Bloomington: Indiana University Press, 1981), pp. 54-55, 134; Nathan O. Hatch, *The Democratization of American Christianity* (New Haven, Conn.: Yale University Press, 1989), p. 30. Charles Sellers points to the dynamism of semisubsistence farming in *The Market Revolution: Jacksonian America,*

1815-1846 (New York: Oxford University Press, 1991), pp. 5, 17.

[8]John Mack Faragher, *Daniel Boone: The Life and Legend of an American Pioneer* (New York: Henry Holt, 1992), pp. 9-11, 17-18; Alan Taylor, *William Cooper's Town: Power and Persuasion on the Frontier of the Early American Republic* (New York: Knopf, 1995), pp. 19-20, 22-24, 348-51.

[9]Faragher, *Daniel Boone,* pp. 23-30, 40.

[10]Ibid., pp. 15, 27, 28-29, 32, 43, 46-47, 49-50, 53-58, 311.

[11]Ibid., pp. 88, 89, 92, 109-10, 277-79.

[12]Sellers, *Market Revolution,* pp. 9, 11. Ironically, Daniel Boone was finally able to perform the patriarch's role in autocratic Spanish Missouri, where he was given large land grants and the position of local "syndic" (justice of the peace). See Faragher, *Daniel Boone,* pp. 273-85.

[13]See Winifred Barr Rothenberg, *From Market-Places to a Market Economy: The Transformation of Rural Massachusetts, 1750-1850* (Chicago: University of Chicago Press, 1992); John C. Hudson, *Making the Corn Belt: A Geographical History of Middle-Western Agriculture* (Bloomington: University of Indiana Press, 1994), pp. 10, 62, 71, 73, 92-93; Allan Kulikoff, "The Transition to Capitalism in Rural America," *William and Mary Quarterly* 46, no. 1 (1989): 121-32; James A. Henretta, "Families and Farms: *Mentalité* in Pre-industrial America," *William and Mary Quarterly* 35 (January 1978): 3-32.

[14]Sellers, *Market Revolution,* p. 29. For an extreme, off-base attack on Puritan patriarchy, see Drinnon, *Facing West,* pp. 26-29. For a text's treatment, see Martin et al., *America and Its People,* pp. 55, 58-59.

[15]Ephesians 5:21, 25-30; 6:4. Likewise, the command to wives to submit to their husbands is placed in context: "as the church submits to Christ" (see Ephesians 5:22-24).

[16]Henretta discusses the gradual shift from communal to familial to individualistic values in "Families and Farms," pp. 4-5, 21, 25-26, 28-29.

[17]Quoted in Thomas D. Clark and John D. W. Guice, *Frontiers in Conflict: The Old Southwest, 1795-1830* (Albuquerque: University of New Mexico Press, 1989), p. 190. For frontier irreligion, see also Terry G. Jordan and Matti Kaups, *The American Backwoods Frontier: An Ethnic and Ecological Interpretation* (Baltimore: Johns Hopkins University Press, 1989), pp. 73-75.

[18]Bailyn et al., *Great Republic,* 1:50, 122, 283-85; Sellers, *Market Revolution,* pp. 9-10; D. W. Meinig, *Atlantic America, 1492-1800,* vol. 1 of *The Shaping of America: A Geographical Perspective on Five Hundred Years of History* (New Haven, Conn.: Yale University Press, 1986), pp. 409-12. John Mack Faragher (*Sugar Creek: Life on the Illinois Prairie* [New Haven, Conn.: Yale University Press, 1986], pp. 50-52, 130-42, 143-45) argues that community did exist on the rectangular-grid frontier of central Illinois. However, he cites pragmatic, ad hoc cooperation, political institution-building, neighborly exchanges and kinship networks. That is "community" which has slipped a notch; it is individuals who find each other useful on occasion.

[19]Sellers, *Market Revolution,* p. 9.

[20]Alan G. Bogue, *From Prairie to Cornbelt: Farming on the Illinois and Iowa Prairies in the Nineteenth Century* (Chicago: University of Chicago Press, 1963); Hudson, *Making the Corn Belt,* pp. 7, 9, 60, 67-69, 96, 123. Hudson narrowly looks for the origins of commercial Corn Belt farming, so he mistakenly assumes that commercial corn-hog farmers were *typical* of all backcountry corn-hog farmers. He never surveys all backcountry (or "Upland South") farmers to see what was typical. In fact, the corn-hog system was suitable for both types of farming.

[21]Faragher, *Sugar Creek,* pp. 63-67, 98-103, 111; Nugent, *Structures,* pp. 57, 68-69; Sellers, *Market Revolution,* pp. 11-15. For a counterargument that claims that longer farm-to-market trips were profitable, see Rothenberg, *From Market-Places to a Market Economy,* pp. 80-95.

[22]Sellers, *Market Revolution,* p. 11; Faragher, *Sugar Creek,* pp. 101, 105-9, 111-12, 114; John Mack Faragher, *Women and Men on the Overland Trail* (New Haven, Conn.: Yale University Press, 1979), pp. 59-60, 62. For Rebecca Boone's hard life, see Faragher, *Daniel Boone,* pp. 46-50.

[23]Faragher, *Overland Trail,* pp. 115-20; Rohrbough, *Trans-Appalachian Frontier,* pp. 272-73. About two-thirds of Sugar Creek's households left the area from one decennial census to the next (Faragher, *Sugar Creek,* pp. 151-53).

[24]Faragher, *Daniel Boone,* pp. 35, 78-80, 272; Sellers, *Market Revolution,* p. 16; Faragher, *Sugar Creek,* pp. 49-52; Rohrbough, *Trans-Appalachian Frontier,* p. 273; Taylor, *William Cooper's Town,* pp. 70-75, 97-101. Cooper was a model promoter who sold land at low prices and outwitted a religious-communal promoter (p. 81).

[25]Weber, *Spanish Frontier,* pp. 11, 172-74; Jennings, *Founders of America,* pp. 177, 234; Richard White, *The Middle Ground: Indians, Empires and Republics in the Great Lakes Region, 1650-1815* (New York: Cambridge University Press, 1991); Colin G. Calloway, "Native American History and the Search for Common Ground," *Reviews in American History* 20 (December 1992): 447-52; John R. Finger, *The Eastern Band of Cherokees, 1819-1900* (Knoxville: University of Tennessee Press, 1984), pp. 4-6; Clark and Guice, *Frontiers in Conflict,* pp. 19-22, 28-29; Anthony F. C. Wallace, *The Death and Rebirth of the Seneca* (New York: Random House, 1969), pp. 111-14.

[26]Richard White, *"It's Your Misfortune and None of My Own": A New History of the American West* (Norman: University of Oklahoma Press, 1991), pp. 19-26, 29-30; Davidson et al., *Nation of Nations,* pp. 486-89. Weber's *Spanish Frontier* gives a good account of the consequences for Spain's empire.

[27]Faragher, *Daniel Boone,* pp. 19-23, 35; Faragher, *Sugar Creek,* pp. 113-16; White, *"It's Your Misfortune and None of My Own,"* pp. 44-48; Jordan and Kaups, *American Backwoods Frontier,* pp. 87-92. The mountain men were the culmination of a century of hunters' growing adoption of Indian ways. David Hackett Fischer (*Albion's Seed: Four British Folkways in America* [New York: Oxford University Press, 1989], pp. 621-30, 634, 635, 639) attributes backcountry frontiersmen's violent tendencies to the endemic violence on the English-Scottish border, whence many of them came. Undoubtedly there is some truth to this, but regional origins do not determine destiny.

[28]Richard Drinnon devotes a brief chapter to exaggerating the racism in Timothy Dwight's poetry, but Connecticut Federalists such as Dwight opposed reckless westward expansion. See Drinnon, *Facing West,* pp. 65-69.

[29]James Axtell, *Beyond 1492: Encounters in Colonial North America* (New York: Oxford University Press, 1992), pp. 110-15; Wallace, *Death and Rebirth,* pp. 125-31, 176-77; Andrew R. L. Cayton, *The Frontier Republic: Ideology and Politics in the Ohio Country, 1780-1825* (Kent, Ohio: Kent State University Press, 1986), pp. 21, 35-38; Clark and Guice, *Frontiers in Conflict,* pp. 28-39; Faragher, *Daniel Boone,* pp. 127-28, 155-56. For a critical account stressing Thomas Jefferson's enlightened inability to understand "irrational" elements in Indian cultures, see Drinnon, *Facing West,* pp. 78-98. For a fraudulent land purchase made by Pennsylvania, see Faragher, *Daniel Boone,* pp. 33-34.

[30]Faragher, *Daniel Boone,* pp. 71, 76-87, 89-94, quote from p. 80.

[31]Ibid., pp. 106-14; Rohrbough, *Trans-Appalachian Frontier,* pp. 21-24.

[32]Faragher, *Daniel Boone,* pp. 120-26.

[33]Ibid., pp. 69, 130, 145, 162-63.

[34]Daniel Goldstein, "Many Wests: A Review Essay," *The Annals of Iowa* 53, no. 2 (Spring 1994): 151. Goldstein is commenting on White's book, especially its title, *"It's Your Misfortune and None of My Own."*

[35]Faragher, *Daniel Boone,* pp. 215-24.

[36]Ibid., pp. 96-97, 222, 230.

[37]Here and above, Cayton, *Frontier Republic,* pp. 14, 21-22, 35-39; Harlan Hatcher, *Western Reserve: The Story of New Connecticut in Ohio* (Indianapolis: Bobbs-Merrill, 1949), pp. 22-26; Harry F. Lupold and Gladys Haddad, eds., *Ohio's Western Reserve: A Regional Reader* (Kent, Ohio: Kent State University Press, 1988), pp. 7-9, 32-34; Clark and Guice, *Frontiers in Conflict,* pp. 99-116; Rohrbough, *Trans-Appalachian Frontier,* pp. 194-95; D. W. Meinig, *Continental America, 1800-1867,* vol. 2 of *The Shaping of America: A Geographical Perspective on Five Hundred Years of History* (New Haven, Conn.: Yale University Press, 1993), pp. 266, 268, 269-73.

[38]Jennings, *Founders of America,* p. 334. For Southerners' settlement of southern and central Illinois, see Faragher, *Sugar Creek,* pp. 3-5, 26-27. For a map showing them pushing West the fastest, see Meinig, *Atlantic America,* p. 358. Meinig (*Continental America,* pp. 273-77) calls the land they settled "Virginia Extended" and notes its unorganized, familial, dispersed nature. For an account overstressing the English regional origins of backcountry folk, see Fischer, *Albion's Seed,* pp. 621-30, 635, 639. For an overemphasis on woodland experience and an underemphasis of the religious component, see Jordan and Kaups, *American Backwoods Frontier,* pp. 7-18. Jennings is mistaken in arguing that "homesteaders were resistless because the government intended them to be" (p. 335). Before 1812, Federalist gentry wanted to control squatters.

[39]White, *"It's Your Misfortune and None of My Own,"* pp. 85-89. See also Drinnon, *Facing West,* pp. 75-98.

[40]Here and above, White, *"It's Your Misfortune and None of My Own,"* pp. 87, 89-99; Clark and Guice, *Frontiers in Conflict,* pp. 246-53; Finger, *Eastern Band,* pp. 14-28; Jennings, *Founders of America,* pp. 331-34. For Andrew Jackson's role in Choctaw removal, see Robert V. Remini, *Andrew Jackson and the Course of American Empire, 1767-1821* (New York: Harper & Row, 1977), pp. 392-98.

[41]Here and above, see White, *"It's Your Misfortune and None of My Own,"* pp. 44-48, 139, 191-92; John D. Unruh Jr., *The Plains Across: The Overland Emigrants and the Trans-Mississippi West, 1840-60* (Urbana: University of Illinois Press, 1979), pp. 244-301; Faragher, *Sugar Creek,* pp. 49-52; Bogue, *From Prairie to Cornbelt,* pp. 33-38; Malcolm J. Rohrbough, *The Land Office Business: The Settlement and Administration of American Public Lands, 1789-1837* (New York: Oxford University Press, 1968), pp. 14-15, 43-44, 61, 197.

[42]For land speculation, town-site "booming" and leapfrogging, see Wiebe, *Opening of American Society,* pp. 138-40; Meinig, *Atlantic America,* pp. 354-57; Willard W. Cochrane, *The Development of American Agriculture: A Historical Analysis* (Minneapolis: University of Minnesota Press, 1979), pp. 54-56; Gerald W. McFarland, *A Scattered People: An American Family Moves West* (New York: Penguin, 1987), pp. 61-63; Cronon, *Nature's Metropolis,* pp. 27-41; and Wallace, *Death and Rebirth,* pp. 210-15. See also Taylor, *William Cooper's Town,* for an early promoter's career.

[43]Cronon, *Nature's Metropolis,* pp. 36-37, 41, 55-56, 63-65; Bailyn et al., *Great Republic,* 1:387-89.

[44]Cronon, *Nature's Metropolis,* p. 53; Faragher, *Daniel Boone,* pp. 294-95.

[45]Sellers, *Market Revolution,* pp. 16-18, 41-44, 154-57; Faragher, *Sugar Creek,* pp. 181-84, 199-204.

[46]Here and above, see Sean Wilentz, *Chants Democratic: New York City and the Rise of the American Working Class, 1788-1850* (New York: Oxford University Press, 1984), pp. 24-59, 87-97, 108-31, quote from p. 51.

[47]Wilentz, *Chants Democratic,* pp. 53-54, 83, 146-47, 153-57, 300-301, quotes from pp. 53, 83. See also Sellers, *Market Revolution,* pp. 23-25, 282-88 (largely based on Wilentz).

[48]Sellers, *Market Revolution,* pp. 285-88, 337-40; Gordon S. Wood, *The Radicalism of the American Revolution: How a Revolution Transformed a Monarchical Society into a Democratic One Unlike Any That Had Ever Existed* (New York: Knopf, 1992), pp. 130-34, 307-11; Wiebe, *Opening of American Society,* pp. 321-24, 337-39.

[49]Michael Feldberg, *The Turbulent Era: Riot and Disorder in Jacksonian America* (New York: Oxford University Press, 1980), pp. 3-5, 90-91, 94-99; Richard Maxwell Brown, *Strain of Violence: Historical Studies of American Violence and Vigilantism* (New York: Oxford University Press, 1975), pp. 41-57, 60-61.

[50]Roger D. McGrath, *Gunfighters, Highwaymen and Vigilantes: Violence on the Frontier* (Berkeley: University of California Press, 1984), pp. 247, 249, 251-52, 253, 255. The man is Richard Henry Lee, quoted in Wiebe, *Opening of American Society,* 133.

[51]Christopher Waldrep, "The Making of a Border State Society: James McGready, the Great Revival and the Prosecution of Profanity in Kentucky," *American Historical Review* 99, no. 3 (June 1994): 767-84, quotes from pp. 769, 778, 782.

[52]Here and above, Remini, *Andrew Jackson and the Course of American Empire,* pp. 7, 24-27, 29-30, 37, 39, 45, 54, 136-43, 161-62, 164. See also Sellers, *Market Revolution,* pp. 174-78.

[53]Remini, *Andrew Jackson and the Course of American Empire,* pp. 86-87, 132-36, 379-80; Sellers, *Market Revolution,* pp. 63-65, 170, 179, 238-39.

[54]Sellers, *Market Revolution,* pp. 35-43, 47-59, 208.

[55]Faragher, *Sugar Creek,* p. 168; Nash et al., *American People,* p. 448. The quote (from John Reynolds) that Faragher uses to prove his point does not mention God, Christianity or the church. He cites three stanzas from hymns (p. 169) as his only evidence!

[56]Faragher, *Daniel Boone,* p. 311; Henry F. May, *The Enlightenment in America* (New York: Oxford University Press, 1976), pp. 247-49; Paul K. Conkin, *Cane Ridge: America's Pentecost* (Madison: University of Wisconsin Press, 1990), pp. 57, 64. There were, however, some initial revivals in the late 1780s. See Conkin, *Cane Ridge,* p. 57. See also one observer's report on "no signs of religion among the people" of western Pennsylvania in the 1790s in Thomas P. Slaughter, *The Whiskey Rebellion: Frontier Epilogue to the American Revolution* (New York: Oxford University Press, 1986), pp. 63-64.

[57]Conkin, *Cane Ridge,* pp. 19-23, 54-61, 64. For the development of the camp meeting, see Conkin, *Cane Ridge,* pp. 85-87, and Faragher, *Sugar Creek,* pp. 162-65.

[58]Here and above, Conkin, *Cane Ridge,* pp. 76-114, 118, quote from p. 116; Waldrep, "Making of a Border State Society," pp. 769, 773-74, 777-79, quote from p. 769.

[59]Faragher, *Sugar Creek,* pp. 128-29, 161, 165, 167, 170, 195-96.

[60]Hatch, *Democratization,* pp. 30-34, 36-37, 40-43, 85-89, quote from p. 67. See also Butler, *Awash in a Sea of Faith,* pp. 236-41. Butler, however, overemphasizes bizarre, even occult, practices among Methodist itinerants and the alleged "syncretism" of early Methodism. He underemphasizes what Hatch calls "religious populism."

[61]Hatch, *Democratization,* pp. 7-8.

[62]Conkin, *Cane Ridge,* pp. 124-26, 132-34, 144-46; Hatch, *Democratization,* pp. 41-43, 170-72.

[63]Hatch, *Democratization,* pp. 113-15; Sellers, *Market Revolution,* pp. 217-21; Butler, *Awash in a Sea of Faith,* pp. 242-44; Richard L. Bushman, *Joseph Smith and the Beginnings of Mormonism* (Urbana: University of Illinois Press, 1984), pp. 20-23, 29-31, 38-39, 47-49, 58-59.

[64]Here and above, Sellers, *Market Revolution,* pp. 222-25; Butler, *Awash in a Sea of Faith,* p. 242; Hatch, *Democratization,* pp. 113-22, 167-68; Bushman, *Joseph Smith,* pp. 139, 143-48; David Brion Davis, *From Homicide to Slavery: Studies in American Culture* (New York: Oxford University Press, 1986), pp. 120-21 (reviewing Bushman's book and others on Mormonism).

[65]Sellers, *Market Revolution,* pp. 224-25; Hatch, *Democratization,* pp. 188-89; Davidson et al., *Nation of Nations,* pp. 512-13.

[66]Bailyn et al., *Great Republic,* 1:429-35; Unruh, *Plains Across,* p. 315. For interaction between overland migrants and Mormons, see Unruh (pp. 302-37).

[67]Faragher, *Sugar Creek,* p. 161.

Chapter 6: The Great Duel

[1]Thomas A. Bailey and David M. Kennedy, *The American Pageant: A History of the Republic,* 9th ed. (Lexington, Mass.: Heath, 1991), p. 474; Bernard Bailyn et al., *The Great Republic: A History of the American People* (Lexington, Mass.: Heath, 1985), 1:589. North and South "faced similar wartime problems" and used similar solutions. In that sense they were "kindred." For Union soldiers' disgust with the South, see Reid Mitchell, *Civil War Soldiers: Their Expectations and Their Experiences* (New York: Simon & Schuster, 1988), pp. 90-131.

[2]Second Inaugural Address, March 4, 1865, and Lincoln to Thurlow Weed, March 15, 1865, both in *Abraham Lincoln: Speeches and Writings, 1859-1865* (New York: Library of America, 1989), 2:686-87, 689. For Lincoln's evolving view of God's aims, see Garry Wills, *Under God: Religion and American Politics* (New York: Simon & Schuster, 1990), pp. 218-19.

[3]*Harper's Weekly,* quoted in George B. Tindall and David Shi, *America: A Narrative History,* 3rd ed. (New York: Norton, 1992), 1:646; James W. Davidson et al., *Nation of Nations: A Narrative History of the American Republic* (New York: McGraw, 1990), pp. 579, 580-81, 588; Mitchell, *Civil War Soldiers,* pp. 109, 123, 131. For the idea that the Christian suffering innocently "is done [that is, finished] with sin," see 1 Peter 4:1-2.

[4]William W. Freehling, *The Reintegration of American History: Slavery and the Civil War* (New York: Oxford University Press, 1994), pp. 178-79, 183-84; David Brion Davis, *Slavery and Human Progress* (New York: Oxford University Press, 1984), pp. 116-19; Michael F. Holt, *Political Parties and American Political Development from the Age of Jackson to the Age of Lincoln* (Baton Rouge: Louisiana State University Press, 1992), p. 319.

[5]Kenneth S. Greenberg, *Masters and Statesmen: The Political Culture of American Slavery* (Baltimore: Johns Hopkins University Press, 1985), p. 24. I am indebted to Greenberg for the insight that secession was "an act that paralleled the duel" (p. 144). I extend the metaphor to cover the war itself. Bertram Wyatt-Brown (*Yankee Saints and Southern Sinners* [Baton Rouge: Louisiana State University Press, 1985], pp. 188-213) makes much the same point as Greenberg.

[6]Wyatt-Brown, *Saints and Sinners,* pp. 185-88, 203; Gordon S. Wood, *The Radicalism of*

the American Revolution: How a Revolution Transformed a Monarchical Society into a Democratic One Unlike Any That Had Ever Existed (New York: Knopf, 1992), pp. 39-41.

[7]Here and above, Greenberg, *Masters and Statesmen,* pp. 24-28, 33-36, 40.

[8]Ibid., p. 37. Edward R. Crowther ("Holy Honor: Sacred and Secular in the Old South," *Journal of Southern History* 57, no. 4 [November 1992]: 619-36) argues that evangelicalism and the code of honor had an "interrelation and intellectual compatibility" which produced "holy honor." He is not persuasive. His definition of *evangelical* includes what should be excluded: church attenders with a "worldview," not faith; Southerners influenced but not converted; unbelievers such as James Henry Hammond; and deists discussing the "Infinite Will." For an account stressing the logical incompatibilty of "pride and piety," see Bertram Wyatt-Brown, "God and Honor in the Old South," *Southern Review* 25, no. 2 (April 1989): 283-96.

[9]John 12:43. For the two dualisms, see Richard J. Carwardine, *Evangelicals and Politics in Antebellum America* (New Haven, Conn.: Yale University Press, 1993), p. 291.

[10]The best source for these trends is Nathan O. Hatch, *The Democratization of American Christianity* (New Haven, Conn.: Yale University Press, 1989). For the Enlightenment and private values versus public facts, see Lesslie Newbigin, *Foolishness to the Greeks: The Gospel and Western Culture* (Grand Rapids, Mich.: Eerdmans, 1986), pp. 14-16, 19, 25-31, 34-38, 40.

[11]Mark A. Noll, *A History of Christianity in the United States and Canada* (Grand Rapids, Mich.: Eerdmans, 1992), pp. 219-22, 227-29, 242-43; Richard V. Pierard and Robert D. Linder, *Civil Religion and the Presidency* (Grand Rapids, Mich.: Zondervan, 1988), pp. 56-58; Robert H. Wiebe, *The Opening of American Society: From the Adoption of the Constitution to the Eve of Disunion,* paperback ed. (New York: Vintage, 1985), pp. 229-32. For church membership figures, see Carwardine, *Evangelicals and Politics,* pp. 5-6.

[12]Merrill D. Peterson, *The Great Triumvirate: Webster, Clay and Calhoun* (New York: Oxford University Press, 1987), pp. 27-29, 31, 34, 36.

[13]Ibid., pp. 105-7, 108-9, 110-11.

[14]Ibid., pp. 174-75, 178-79. For Lincoln's reverence for Founders and Union, see Charles B. Strozier, *Lincoln's Quest for Union: Public and Private Meanings* (Urbana: University of Illinois Press, 1987), pp. 55-65.

[15]Wyatt-Brown, *Saints and Sinners,* pp. 189-92; James M. McPherson, *Ordeal by Fire: The Civil War and Reconstruction* (New York: Knopf, 1982), pp. 12-19. McPherson stresses the different rates of modernization in North and South as a central cause of the Civil War, yet it is not clear why such differences must lead to conflict. Differing concepts of Union and honor provide the necessary causal link.

[16]Peterson, *Great Triumvirate,* pp. 19-23, 27; William W. Freehling, *Secessionists at Bay, 1776-1854,* vol. 1 of *The Road to Disunion* (New York: Oxford University Press, 1990), pp. 257-62, 266. Freehling's treatment of South Carolinians such as Calhoun is seriously marred by his bizarre writing style and his mocking of them. His ridicule of two disabled men, George McDuffie and Thomas Cooper (pp. 256-57), is especially cruel.

[17]Lacy K. Ford Jr., *Origins of Southern Radicalism: The South Carolina Upcountry, 1800-1860* (New York: Oxford University Press, 1988), pp. 5, 22, 37.

[18]Freehling, *Secessionists at Bay,* pp. 257-59; Charles Sellers, *The Market Revolution: Jacksonian America, 1815-1846* (New York: Oxford University Press, 1991), pp. 118-22, 305-6; Wyatt-Brown, *Saints and Sinners,* pp. 7-8; Meinig, *Continental America, 1800-1867,* vol. 2 of *The Shaping of America: A Geographical Perspective on Five Hundred Years of History* (New Haven, Conn.: Yale University Press, 1993), pp. 461-63. For

Taylor's combination of agrarianism and strict republicanism, see Robert E. Shalhope, *John Taylor of Caroline: Pastoral Republican* (Columbia: University of South Carolina Press, 1980). For John Randolph and his later conversion to Christianity, see Robert Dawidoff, *The Education of John Randolph* (New York: W. W. Norton, 1979).

[19]Peter B. Knupfer, *The Union As It Is: Constitutional Unionism and Sectional Compromise, 1787-1861* (Chapel Hill: University of North Carolina Press, 1991), pp. 2-4, 15-16, 133-38.

[20]Peterson, *Great Triumvirate,* pp. 9-11, 12-13, 15-16.

[21]Knupfer, *Constitutional Unionism,* pp. 15-16, 18, 29-31, 40-41, 45-46, 95-96, 145-46, quote from pp. 145-46. Clay tried to make the Compromise of 1850 comprehensive and final (see pp. 181-84). Clay referred to the forty-four years since Washington's 1789 inauguration, and the first session of Congress that same year.

[22]Peterson, *Great Triumvirate,* pp. 24, 98.

[23]For the spread of slave-owning cotton plantations in the "Old Southwest" of Alabama, Mississippi, Arkansas and Texas, see, for example, John Hebron Moore, *The Emergence of the Cotton Kingdom in the Old Southwest: Mississippi, 1770-1860* (Baton Rouge: Louisiana State University Press, 1988).

[24]Tocqueville is quoted by Jon Butler in *Awash in a Sea of Faith: Christianizing the American People* (Cambridge, Mass.: Harvard University Press, 1990), pp. 270, 289; Timothy Smith, *Revivalism and Social Reform: American Protestantism on the Eve of the Civil War,* 2nd ed. (Baltimore: Johns Hopkins University Press, 1980), pp. 17-21; Davidson et al., *Nation of Nations,* pp. 418-19; Noll, *History of Christianity,* pp. 171-74, 178-80.

[25]Noll, *History of Christianity,* pp. 169-70, 174-78, 227-32; Donald M. Scott, *From Office to Profession: The New England Ministry, 1750-1850* (Philadelphia: University of Pennsylvania Press, 1978), pp. 76-77; Wiebe, *Opening of American Society,* pp. 231-32, 279-80; John R. McKivigan, *The War Against Proslavery Religion: Abolitionism and the Northern Churches, 1830-1865* (Ithaca, N.Y.: Cornell University Press, 1984), pp. 19-21; Butler, *Awash in a Sea of Faith,* pp. 277-80; Davidson et al., *Nation of Nations,* pp. 412-44.

[26]Bruce Levine, *Half Slave and Half Free: The Roots of Civil War* (New York: Hill & Wang, 1992), p. 93; McKivigan, *War Against Proslavery Religion,* pp. 20-21; Davis, *Slavery and Human Progress,* pp. 136-53.

[27]Scott, *Office to Profession,* pp. 95-103; Smith, *Revivalism and Social Reform,* pp. 187-88; McKivigan, *War Against Proslavery Religion,* pp. 82-83, 85-86, 112-15; Carwardine, *Evangelicals and Politics,* pp. 139-41.

[28]Henry Adams, *The Education of Henry Adams: An Autobiography* (New York: Time, 1964), 1:51.

[29]Scott, *Office to Profession,* p. 91.

[30]Davidson et al., *Nation of Nations,* p. 444; Freehling, *Secessionists at Bay,* pp. 290-92, 308-12, 321, 322-24, 335.

[31]The subheading above is from Jeremiah 8:20.

[32]Tyler Anbinder, *Nativism and Slavery: The Northern Know Nothings and the Politics of the 1850s* (New York: Oxford University Press, 1992), pp. xiii, 3-5, 8-9; Noll, *History of Christianity,* pp. 205-6. For evangelicals' view of Catholicism and Catholic immigrants, see Carwardine, *Evangelicals and Politics,* pp. 199-204.

[33]Anbinder, *Nativism and Slavery,* pp. 43-44, 113-15; Noll, *History of Christianity,* pp. 208-10; Davidson et al., *Nation of Nations,* p. 443; William E. Gienapp, *Origins of the Republican Party, 1852-1856* (New York: Oxford University Press, 1987), p. 45; Carwardine, *Evangelicals and Politics,* p. 200.

[34]Anbinder, *Nativism and Slavery,* pp. 115-18; Gienapp, *Origins of the Republican Party,*

pp. 45-47; Carwardine, *Evangelicals and Politics,* pp. 207-12. For the Whigs and nativism, see Freehling, *Reintegration of American History,* pp. 205-6.

[35]Mark Wahlgren Summers, *The Plundering Generation: Corruption and the Crisis of the Union, 1849-1861* (New York: Oxford University Press, 1987), pp. 51-61; Anbinder, *Nativism and Slavery,* pp. 123-24. For evangelicals' disgust with partisan campaigning practices, see Carwardine, *Evangelicals and Politics,* pp. 8-14.

[36]Anson Burlingame (quoted in Anbinder, *Nativism and Slavery,* p. 45) argued that "they are in alliance by the necessity of their nature,—for one [slavery] denies the right of a man to his body, and the other [Catholicism] the right of a man to his soul. The one [Catholicism] denies his right to think for himself, the other [slavery] the right to act for himself." For the links between antislavery and nativism, see also David M. Potter, *The Impending Crisis, 1848-1861* (New York: Harper & Row, 1976), pp. 251-53; and Carwardine, *Evangelicals and Politics,* pp. 250-52.

[37]Kenneth M. Stampp, *America in 1857: A Nation on the Brink* (New York: Oxford University Press, 1990), pp. 197-208; Richard White, *"It's Your Misfortune and None of My Own": A New History of the American West* (Norman: University of Oklahoma Press, 1991), pp. 163-69.

[38]Butler, *Awash in a Sea of Faith,* pp. 284-85; Mark Y. Hanley, *Beyond a Christian Commonwealth: The Protestant Quarrel with the American Republic, 1830-1860* (Chapel Hill: University of North Carolina Press, 1994), pp. 22-23. Hanley proves that not all Protestant leaders were uncritically patriotic then.

[39]Holt, *American Political Development,* pp. 104-5; Davidson et al., *Nation of Nations,* pp. 380-81; Anbinder, *Nativism and Slavery,* pp. 10-14. Holt argues that anti-Masonry was a response to increased secularization, but that seems unlikely in the highly religious Burned-Over District in the mid-1820s. More likely, Masons were seen as a barrier to continued revival and reform.

[40]Richard H. Sewell, *Ballots for Freedom: Antislavery Politics in the United States, 1837-1860* (New York: Oxford University Press, 1976), pp. 24-79, 152-69; McKivigan, *War Against Proslavery Religion,* pp. 58-64; Carwardine, *Evangelicals and Politics,* pp. 134-39, 147-52, quotes from pp. 135, 151. Only in Massachusetts did the Liberty candidate receive 1 percent of the vote.

[41]Carwardine, *Evangelicals and Politics,* pp. 152-59. Wilmot is quoted in Sewell, *Ballots for Freedom,* p. 173. For a discussion of the mix of self-interested bias and altruism in the Free Soil party, see Sewell, *Ballots for Freedom,* pp. 170-201.

[42]Paul Kleppner et al., *The Evolution of American Electoral Systems* (Westport, Conn.: Greenwood, 1981), pp. 118-19. Carwardine (*Evangelicals and Politics,* pp. 147-52) argues that the Free Soil party had considerable evangelical support and was partly shaped by evangelicals.

[43]I am indebted to Walter Dean Burnham for the insight on capturing all power bases. See Kleppner et al., *Evolution of American Electoral Systems,* pp. 174-75. For political confidence, see Freehling, *Reintegration of American History,* pp. 178-79.

[44]Smith, *Revivalism and Social Reform,* pp. 180, 183; McKivigan, *War Against Proslavery Religion,* pp. 58-61, 66; John Demos, "The Antislavery Movement and the Problem of Violent 'Means,' " *New England Quarterly* 36 (1964): 509-14, 521-25; Mitchell Snay, *Gospel of Disunion: Religion and Separatism in the Antebellum South* (New York: Cambridge University Press, 1993), pp. 59, 64. For the willingness of Parker and others to incite slave revolts, see Jeffery Rossbach, *Ambivalent Conspirators: John Brown, the Secret Six and a Theory of Slave Violence* (Philadelphia: University of Pennsylvania Press,

1982), pp. 150-59. Carwardine (*Evangelicals and Politics,* p. 135) stresses "the more orthodox majority" and not the Garrisonian minority.

[45]Snay, *Gospel of Disunion,* pp. 24, 25-29, 31-33, 35-39, 41-42, 47-48; Carwardine, *Evangelicals and Politics,* pp. 154-55, 187-88. For Paul and Peter on Scripture, see, for example, 2 Timothy 3:16 and 2 Peter 1:20-21.

[46]Snay, *Gospel of Disunion,* pp. 24, 25-29, 31-33, 35-39, 41-42, 47-48, 44, 55-57, 59-67, 74-75, 119-20, 129-31, 133, 136; McKivigan, *War Against Proslavery Religion,* pp. 90-91; Tzvetan Todorov, *The Conquest of America: The Question of the Other,* trans. Richard Howard (New York: Harper & Row, 1984), pp. 107-8; Wyatt-Brown, "God and Honor," p. 295.

[47]Smith, *Revivalism and Social Reform,* pp. 187, 198-200, 217-18; Scott, *Office to Profession,* pp. 105-6, 108-10; McKivigan, *War Against Proslavery Religion,* pp. 22, 34, 48, 58-66, 78-79. McKivigan downplays the conventional image of Garrisonian extremism, but his figures (pp. 71-72) show that evangelical membership in Garrison's American Anti-Slavery Society dropped considerably from 1840 to 1860.

[48]I take the phrase "call and response" from Snay, *Gospel of Disunion,* pp. 12-13. Carwardine (*Evangelicals and Politics,* for example, pp. 171-72) demonstrates how Northern and Southern evangelicals alienated each other and contributed to a growing sectional hostility. See also William E. Gienapp, "The Crisis of American Democracy: The Political System and the Coming of the Civil War," in *Why the Civil War Came,* ed. Gabor S. Boritt (New York: Oxford University Press, 1996), pp. 83-84.

[49]Kleppner et al., *Evolution of American Electoral Systems,* pp. 118-19, quote from p. 118. Gienapp begins his essay by correctly noting that "only rarely has the war been considered as an understandable product of America's democratic political system" (p. 81), but he too sidesteps criticism of that system, blames true believers and faults the system on technical grounds for not preventing the rise of extremist third parties. Gienapp, "Crisis of American Democracy," pp. 81-124.

[50]Freehling, *Secessionists at Bay,* pp. 324, 344.

[51]Ibid., pp. 355, 410-11, 461-62; Greenberg, *Masters and Statesmen,* pp. 140; Potter, *Impending Crisis,* pp. 59-61; Peterson, *Great Triumvirate,* pp. 426-28; Lincoln, *Speeches and Writings,* 2:111-30. According to Freehling, "Most Southerners raged primarily because David Wilmot's holier-than-thou stance was so insulting" (p. 461).

[52]Here and above, Potter, *Impending Crisis,* pp. 27-29, 49, 61. See also Gienapp's analysis in "Crisis of American Democracy," pp. 81-124.

[53]Potter, *Impending Crisis,* pp. 64-65, 67-76; Peterson, *Great Triumvirate,* pp. 443-45, 453. Senator Thomas Hart Benton is the debater quoted.

[54]Potter, *Impending Crisis,* pp. 56-59, 69-73, 77, 81; Knupfer, *Constitutional Unionism,* pp. 174-75. Free Soil (Wilmot Proviso), slavery's right to go anywhere (Calhoun) and the Missouri Compromise's 36° 30′ line were all unambiguous, as Potter notes. They gained votes in one section but lost votes elsewhere.

[55]Potter, *Impending Crisis,* pp. 90-102; Knupfer, *Constitutional Unionism,* pp. 181-85; Peterson, *Great Triumvirate,* pp. 459-60. For the Southern convention at Nashville, see Freehling, *Secessionists at Bay,* pp. 475-86. Freehling emphasizes Southern disunity, but that was not apparent to Northerners at the time.

[56]Potter, *Impending Crisis,* pp. 106-7, 110.

[57]Here and above, for the Compromise of 1850 and the political parties, see Kleppner et al., *Evolution of American Electoral Systems,* pp. 84-94; Potter, *Impending Crisis,* pp. 108-16; Knupfer, *Constitutional Unionism,* pp. 193-95; and Freehling, *Secessionists at Bay,* pp.

487, 490-93, 509-10, 553-54. Representing the Constitutional Union position by virtue of geography, Border South representatives also provided key votes in favor of Compromise. See Freehling, *Secessionists at Bay,* pp. 508-9.

[58]Summers, *Plundering Generation,* pp. 301-2, 303; Knupfer, *Constitutional Unionism,* pp. 202-6.

[59]Gienapp, *Origins of the Republican Party,* pp. 37-67, 137; Potter, *Impending Crisis,* pp. 236-51; Anbinder, *Nativism and Slavery,* pp. 20-51, 75-102. For Northern evangelicals' growing disgust with the Whigs, see Carwardine, *Evangelicals and Politics,* pp. 197-98, 213-18, 221-22.

[60]Under the heading "The Great Question," the *North Carolina Presbyterian* (Fayetteville) asked, "What preparation have you made for eternity?" on March 23, 1861, three weeks before Fort Sumter. Quoted in Crowther, "Holy Honor," p. 636.

[61]For the Kansas-Nebraska Act, see Potter, *Impending Crisis,* pp. 145-76, 199-224; and Knupfer, *Constitutional Unionism,* pp. 202-6. For the "uprising of the clergy" against Kansas-Nebraska and missionaries in Kansas, see Carwardine, *Evangelicals and Politics,* pp. 235-37, 245-46.

[62]Here and above, see Gienapp, *Origins of the Republican Party,* pp. 273-303, quote from p. 301; Anbinder, *Nativism and Slavery,* pp. 212-19.

[63]Gienapp, *Origins of the Republican Party,* pp. 353-65, 365-67, 372-73; Davidson et al., *Nation of Nations,* pp. 541-43; Anbinder, *Nativism and Slavery,* pp. 226-32, 268-70; Carwardine, *Evangelicals and Politics,* pp. 248-54, 265. Temperance (Maine law) zeal had largely abated by 1856, according to Carwardine.

[64]For Southern threats of secession, see Potter, *Impending Crisis,* pp. 262-65. For Republicans' anti-Southernism, see Gienapp, *Origins of the Republican Party,* pp. 362-63. For Southern evangelicals' aggrieved response, see Carwardine, *Evangelicals and Politics,* pp. 255-58, 271-72.

[65]Carwardine, *Evangelicals and Politics,* pp. 292-96, 319-23, quote from p. 292.

[66]For Northern praise of Brown and Southern outrage at such praise—and fear of Northern support for slave uprisings—see Potter, *Impending Crisis,* pp. 378-84; and Carwardine, *Evangelicals and Politics,* pp. 283-85. See also Rossbach, *Ambivalent Conspirators.*

[67]Potter, *Impending Crisis,* pp. 386, 388-90.

[68]Greenberg, *Masters and Statesmen,* pp. 129, 144. Wyatt-Brown (*Saints and Sinners,* pp. 210-13) notes that "secession was a movement most attractive to the young, since honor was a martial and manly code." Reasons for "South Carolina Eccentricity," the role of that state in secession and the role of migrants from South Carolina in selling secession to other states are examined in Freehling, *Secessionists at Bay,* pp. 213-52; Meinig, *Continental America,* p. 476; and Gienapp, "Crisis of American Democracy," pp. 107-9.

[69]Potter, *Impending Crisis,* p. 523; also see p. 558.

[70]Lincoln, *Speeches and Writings,* 2:215-24.

[71]Quoted in Crowther, "Holy Honor," p. 636.

[72]Lincoln, *Speeches and Writings,* 2:686-87. To be fair, Lincoln does refer to the war's length as *the most onerous* punishment. For revivals, see Henry Steele Commager, ed., *The Blue and the Gray: The Story of the Civil War as Told by Participants* (New York: Fairfax, 1982), pp. 302-4, 414-16. For other views of the theology of the Second Inaugural, see, for example, Elton Trueblood, *Abraham Lincoln: Theologian of American Anguish* (New York: Harper & Row, 1973), pp. 135-39; and Wills, *Under God,* pp. 217-18. The phrase "marching on" comes from the Battle Hymn of the Republic: "His truth is marching on."

Chapter 7: Exodus

[1]James W. Davidson et al., *Nation of Nations: A Narrative History of the American Republic* (New York: McGraw, 1990), p. 573; Eric Foner, *Reconstruction: America's Unfinished Revolution, 1863-1877* (New York: Harper & Row, 1988), pp. 1, 73. Boston celebrated on January 1, 1863, the day the Emancipation Proclamation took effect. For the Year of Jubilee, see Leviticus 25:8-55.

[2]Foner, *Reconstruction*, pp. 77, 79-84, 87-91, 95-100, 102; William E. Montgomery, *Under Their Own Vine and Fig Tree: The African-American Church in the South, 1865-1900* (Baton Rouge: Louisiana State University Press, 1993), pp. 38-41, 42, 45, 48-55.

[3]For freedmen's desire for self-sufficiency, see Gavin Wright, *The Political Economy of the Cotton South: Households, Markets and Wealth in the Nineteenth Century* (New York: Norton, 1978), pp. 161-62; and Foner, *Reconstruction*, pp. 108-9. For the similarity in aspirations of poor Southern whites and blacks, see Jacqueline Jones, *The Dispossessed: America's Underclass from the Civil War to the Present* (New York: BasicBooks, 1992), pp. ix, 2, 3, 7, 9, 13-16.

[4]Montgomery, *Vine and Fig Tree*, pp. 53-54, 56-57, 99, 139, 148-52, 156-60, 163, 178-79, quote from p. 99; Foner, *Reconstruction*, pp. 92-93, 95.

[5]Robert G. Athearn, *In Search of Canaan: Black Migration to Kansas, 1879-1880* (Lawrence: Regents Press of Kansas, 1978), pp. 6-7, 9-11, 14-15, 16, 37-38, 43, 51-54, 61-62, 71-72, 75-79.

[6]Montgomery, *Vine and Fig Tree*, p. 188; Foner, *Reconstruction*, pp. 106, 119-21; Roger L. Ransom and Richard Sutch, *One Kind of Freedom: The Economic Consequences of Emancipation* (Cambridge: Cambridge University Press, 1977), pp. 24-31, 225-27, 229-30; Exodus 12:36; George C. Rable, *But There Was No Peace: The Role of Violence in the Politics of Reconstruction* (Athens: University of Georgia Press, 1984), pp. 4-5, 6, 9, quotes from pp. 6, 9.

[7]Robert J. Kaczorowski, "To Begin the Nation Anew: Congress, Citizenship and Civil Rights after the Civil War," *American Historical Review* 92 (February 1987): 45-68, quote from p. 49. See especially pp. 47, 49, 53-54, 66-67. For constitutionalism and laissez-faire as factors limiting Republicans (two others cited are political parties and racism), see Bernard Bailyn et al., *The Great Republic: A History of the American People* (Lexington, Mass.: Heath, 1985), 2:7-19.

[8]Foner, *Reconstruction*, pp. 178-79, 222-24, 258-60, 278-80, 556, 562-63, 581-83. Richard Bensel suggests that federal troops and civil servants in the South were effective in maintaining a Southern Republican party and discouraging white violence. See Richard F. Bensel, *Yankee Leviathan: The Origins of Central State Authority in America, 1859-1877* (New York: Cambridge University Press, 1990), pp. 387-400.

[9]Stuart E. Prall and David H. Willson, *History of England* (Orlando, Fla.: Harcourt Brace College, 1991), pp. 582-84; T. S. Ashton, *The Industrial Revolution, 1760-1830* (New York: Oxford University Press, 1964), pp. 50-54; Wright, *Political Economy of the Cotton South*, pp. 158-59.

[10]Frank McGlynn and Seymour Drescher, eds., *The Meaning of Freedom: Economics, Politics and Culture After Slavery* (Pittsburgh: University of Pittsburgh Press, 1992), pp. 5-6, 25-26, 28, 40, 42. The quote on replication of family-sized farms is from Barbara Solow, ed., *Slavery and the Rise of the Atlantic System* (Cambridge: Cambridge University Press, 1991), pp. 33-35.

[11]Bensel, *Yankee Leviathan*, pp. 301-2, 348, 361; Foner, *Reconstruction*, pp. 128-42, 153-54, 157, 162-70, 199-202.

[12]Foner, *Reconstruction,* pp. 173-75; Ransom and Sutch, *One Kind of Freedom,* pp. 65-70, 73-78, 81-105; Wright, *Political Economy of the Cotton South,* pp. 161-64. For the argument that growth in the slave population increased capital and reduced the incentive to save and that emancipation did not end the resultant capital shortage, see Roger Ransom and Richard Sutch, "Capitalists Without Capital: The Burden of Slavery and the Impact of Emancipation," *Agricultural History* 62, no. 3 (1988): 133-49, especially pp. 140-41, 148-49.

[13]Ransom and Sutch, *One Kind of Freedom,* pp. 64-65, 190-92; Wright, *Political Economy of the Cotton South,* pp. 172-73; Foner, *Reconstruction,* pp. 393, 406, 408-9. Ransom and Sutch discuss the problem at length in *One Kind of Freedom,* chaps. 7-8.

[14]Foner, *Reconstruction,* pp. 137-38, 155-56. For arguments that capitalism rests on moral foundations that it tends to undermine, see Donald A. Hay, *Economics Today: A Christian Critique* (Grand Rapids, Mich.: Eerdmans, 1990), pp. 158-60, 171-73. Wright makes the case for a need for more subsistence agriculture in the postwar South in chap. 6 of *Political Economy of the Cotton South.*

[15]Here and above, see Ransom and Sutch, *One Kind of Freedom,* pp. 106-10, 117, 120-25, 130-31, 146; Foner, *Reconstruction,* pp. 408-9; and Ransom and Sutch, "Capitalists Without Capital," pp. 148-49. For another explanation of the demise of cotton factors, see Alfred D. Chandler, *Visible Hand: The Managerial Revolution in American Business* (Cambridge, Mass.: Belknap, 1977), pp. 213-15. Chandler, however, does not address *farmers'* need for credit.

[16]This last point is suggested by Peter Kolchin's more general point that the postemancipation Southern experience was not the tragedy that historians often make of it. See McGlynn and Drescher, eds., *Meaning of Freedom,* pp. 291-308.

[17]Stuart Bruchey, *Enterprise: The Dynamic Economy of a Free People* (Cambridge, Mass.: Harvard University Press, 1990), p. 268; Charles Sellers, *The Market Revolution: Jacksonian America, 1815-1846* (New York: Oxford University Press, 1991), pp. 40-43, 44-57, 358-59. The 1840s and early 1850s (before 1857) saw great economic growth, industrialization and railroad construction. See Douglass C. North, *The Economic Growth of the United States, 1790-1860* (New York: Norton, 1966), pp. v-vii, 204-15.

[18]Sellers, *Market Revolution,* pp. 202-3, 208.

[19]For a discussion of how religion was co-opted in the push for consumerism, see William Leach, *Land of Desire: Merchants, Power and the Rise of a New American Culture* (New York: Vintage, 1993), pp. 191-224. For the influence of Darwin on Progressive reformers, see Robert M. Crunden, *Ministers of Reform: The Progressives' Achievement in American Civilization, 1889-1920* (New York: Basic Books, 1982), pp. 54, 60, 81.

[20]Bruchey, *Enterprise,* pp. 255-59; Bensel, *Yankee Leviathan,* pp. 169, 243; Roger L. Ransom, *Conflict and Compromise: The Political Economy of Slavery, Emancipation and the American Civil War* (New York: Cambridge University Press, 1989), pp. 264, 268.

[21]Bensel, *Yankee Leviathan,* pp. 61-62.

[22]Bailyn et al., *Great Republic,* 1:630; Ransom, *Conflict and Compromise,* pp. 268-71, 276-79; Bensel, *Yankee Leviathan,* pp. 69-74, 174, 178. Ransom (*Conflict and Compromise,* pp. 278-79), however, minimizes the war's role in the passage of the Homestead and Pacific Railroad Acts.

[23]Sellers, *Market Revolution,* pp. 45-46; Ransom, *Conflict and Compromise,* pp. 271-76; Bensel, *Yankee Leviathan,* pp. 239-40, 249; George Green, "Financial Intermediaries," in *Encyclopedia of American Economic History: Studies of the Principal Movements and Ideas,* ed. Glenn Porter (New York: Scribner's, 1980), pp. 711-18; William Cronon,

Nature's Metropolis: Chicago and the Great West (New York: Norton, 1991), pp. 322-24.

[24]Ransom, *Conflict and Compromise,* pp. 267-68, 272-76, 280-84; Bensel, *Yankee Leviathan,* pp. 252, 261-62, 263-65, 275-80.

[25]Ransom, *Conflict and Compromise,* pp. 274-76; Bensel, *Yankee Leviathan,* pp. 255-57, 259, 261-67. The Panic of 1873 was one such disaster.

[26]Bruchey, *Enterprise,* p. 328; Leach, *Land of Desire,* p. 32; Bailyn et al., *Great Republic,* 2:77-78.

[27]Genesis 11:1, 4.

[28]For the "democratization of desire," see Leach, *Land of Desire,* pp. 5-7. For the city as an expression of human rebellion against God, see Hay, *Economics Today,* pp. 23-25.

[29]Sellers, *Market Revolution,* p. 208. He makes this point for antebellum America, but it applies to the postwar era too.

[30]The quote and the idea of a hothouse is from Theodore Von Laue, *The World Revolution of Westernization: The Twentieth Century in Global Perspective* (New York: Oxford University Press, 1987), p. 19. The innovations are taken from Cronon, *Nature's Metropolis,* pp. 28-30, 190-91, 230-32, 259, 282-83, 374-76.

[31]Hay, *Economics Today,* p. 27.

[32]For the Lord's dispersal of the first Babel builders, see Genesis 11:5-9. For his use of idolatrous kings, see, for example, Isaiah 44:28—45:1, where the Lord calls Cyrus the Great, king of Persia, "my shepherd" who "will accomplish all that I please" (v. 28). For Paul's prophecy, see 2 Thessalonians 2:1-12 (see chapter twelve, below).

[33]Bruchey, *Enterprise,* pp. 304-5, 370-75; Herman Belz, "The Constitution and Reconstruction," in *The Facts of Reconstruction: Essays in Honor of John Hope Franklin,* ed. Eric Anderson and Alfred A. Moss Jr. (Baton Rouge: Louisiana State University Press, 1991), pp. 200-201. For the Ignatius Donnelly quote, see Martin Ridge, *Ignatius Donnelly: The Portrait of a Politician* (Chicago: University of Chicago Press, 1962), p. 315.

[34]Here and above, Chandler, *Visible Hand,* pp. 82-86, 89, 195; Cronon, *Nature's Metropolis,* pp. 72-73, 120-21. For the change from prerailroad to postrailroad mercantile worlds, see Cronon (pp. 318-32).

[35]Cronon, *Nature's Metropolis,* pp. 80-81, 92-93, 109-14; Chandler, *Visible Hand,* pp. 6-7, 240-53; Bruchey, *Enterprise,* pp. 330-34; Donald R. Hoke, *Ingenious Yankees: The Rise of the American System of Manufactures in the Private Sector* (New York: Columbia University Press, 1990), pp. 3-6, 33-41, 263-66. Hoke argues persuasively that the private sector (not government), seeking lower per-unit costs, pioneered the American system of manufacturing and interchangeable parts.

[36]Cronon, *Nature's Metropolis,* pp. 110-14, 116-19, 120-26, 143-46, 224, 230-59.

[37]Ibid., pp. 138, 163-67, 354-55; Bailyn et al., *Great Republic,* 2:86-87, 136-39, 147-49. For an account of how Gilded Age capitalists corrupted politicians, see Mark Wahlgren Summers, *The Era of Good Stealings* (New York: Oxford University Press, 1993).

[38]For the environmental effects, see Cronon, *Nature's Metropolis,* especially pp. 200-206 and 247-59.

[39]Davidson et al., *Nation of Nations,* pp. 651-52; Bruchey, *Enterprise,* pp. 313, 315-20.

[40]Bruchey, *Enterprise,* pp. 338-43; Chandler, *Visible Hand,* pp. 171-75, 181-86.

[41]Sellers, *Market Revolution,* p. 208.

[42]The command to subdue the earth is found in Genesis 1:28.

[43]Leach, *Land of Desire,* pp. 36-37, quote from p. 36; Chandler, *Visible Hand,* pp. 207-9, 238-39.

[44]Leach, *Land of Desire,* pp. 182-85; Daniel Boorstin, *The Americans: The Democratic*

Experience (New York: Random House, 1973), pp. 104-5, 130-36; Gunnar Barth, *City People: The Rise of Modern City Culture in Nineteenth-Century America* (New York: Oxford University Press, 1980), pp. 53-57, 111, 121-22.

[45]Chandler, *Visible Hand,* pp. 224-39; Cronon, *Nature's Metropolis,* pp. 336-38.

[46]Boorstin, *Democratic Experience,* pp. 108-10, 113-18.

[47]Exodus 20:17; Matthew 6:25; 1 Timothy 6:6, 9. See also, for example, 1 Peter 2:11 and Hebrews 13:5.

[48]Leach, *Land of Desire,* pp. 9, 40, 41-43, 45, 55-61; Boorstin, *Democratic Experience,* pp. 106, 137-45; 1 John 2:16.

[49]Leach, *Land of Desire,* pp. 65-67, 70, 81-83, 91, 104-7.

[50]Ibid., pp. 4-5, 91-104, 110-11.

[51]Ibid., p. 107; Hay, *Economics Today,* pp. 158-60, 171-75, 290. The "pious souls/wild pagans" quote is from the *Wall Street Journal* review of *Land of Desire,* printed on that book's inside front cover. See also Christopher Lasch, *The True and Only Heaven: Progress and Its Critics* (New York: Norton, 1991), pp. 518-22.

[52]Here and above, George M. Marsden, *Fundamentalism and American Culture: The Shaping of Twentieth-Century American Evangelicalism, 1870-1925* (New York: Oxford University Press, 1980), pp. 22-25, 48-49; Leach, *Land of Desire,* pp. 10, 195, 197, 213-16.

[53]Here and above, Marsden, *Fundamentalism,* pp. 29-31, 46-47, 54, 56-57, 60-61, 62. For the earlier rejection (and ridicule) of Calvinism, see Hatch, *Democratization.* I equate premillennialism with dispensational premillennialism, which Marsden also stresses.

[54]Leach, *Land of Desire,* p. 5.

[55]Here and above, Cronon, *Nature's Metropolis,* pp. 341-43; Reid Badger, *The Great American Fair: The World's Columbian Exposition and American Culture* (Chicago: Nelson Hall, 1979), pp. 65-69, 126.

[56]Badger, *Great American Fair,* pp. 95-102, quote from p. 98. At the Historical Congress, Frederick Jackson Turner delivered his famous essay "The Significance of the Frontier in American History."

[57]*Chicago Tribune,* September 12, 1893, pp. 1, 4, and September 13, 1893, p. 9; Badger, *Great American Fair,* pp. 97-98; Leach, *Land of Desire,* p. 227. After the Parliament ended, the Swami toured America and lectured on Hindu mind-cure techniques.

[58]Badger, *Great American Fair,* pp. 114, 119-20; Adams, *Education,* 2:117-22, quotes from pp. 118, 121; Cronon, *Nature's Metropolis,* p. 344.

[59]Badger, *Great American Fair,* pp. 105-6; Matthew 23:27.

[60]Here and above, see Phillip J. Wood, *Southern Capitalism: The Political Economy of North Carolina, 1880-1980* (Durham, N.C.: Duke University Press, 1986), pp. 12, 13, 16, 60-61, 62-64, 115, 117-20, 122-23; and Jones, *Dispossessed,* pp. 75, 89, 91, 101.

[61]Jones, *Dispossessed,* p. ix; Gilbert Osofsky, *Harlem: The Making of a Ghetto—Negro New York, 1890-1930,* 2nd ed. (New York: Harper & Row, 1971), pp. 18-24, 27-28.

[62]Osofsky, *Harlem,* pp. 13, 14-16, 22-24, 31-35.

[63]Ibid., pp. 71, 75-78, 87-88, 90-91, 93, 95, 99-102, 107-12. African-American churches were important in Harlem's growth, but Payton's (and others') speculations were crucial.

[64]Osofsky, *Harlem,* pp. 127-29, 131-35, 136-37, 143-47, 180, 183-87.

Chapter 8: Women Aim for Reform & Equality but End Up with Consumerism

[1]Gary B. Nash et al., *The American People: Creating a Nation and a Society,* 3rd ed. (New York: HarperCollins, 1994), pp. 419, 420, 616-17. The two lists do show Victorian biases. Take the treatment of 1 Corinthians 7:4: the wife's list mentions that her body also belongs

to her husband; the husband's list omits the corollary that his body also belongs to his wife. For a section on "Victorian Mores" overemphasizing their middle-class nature and neglecting their basis in Christian beliefs, see James W. Davidson et al., *Nation of Nations: A Narrative History of the American Republic* (New York: McGraw-Hill, 1990), pp. 703-4.
[2]James 4:4; Romans 8:7; 1 John 2:15. The human motive behind the crucifixion is best portrayed in Jesus' parable of the tenants (see Mark 12:7-8; Matthew 21:38-39).
[3]The passage referred to is Ephesians 5:21-33. For a brief critique of 1990s feminism, see Katherine Kersten, "How the Feminist Establishment Hurts Women: A Christian Critique of a Movement Gone Wrong," *Christianity Today,* June 20, 1994, pp. 20-25.
[4]The point about woman as "other" is made in Elizabeth Fox-Genovese, *Feminism Without Illusions: A Critique of Individualism* (Chapel Hill: University of North Carolina Press, 1991), especially pp. 117-24.
[5]Fox-Genovese, *Feminism Without Illusions,* pp. 119, 122. Christine Bolt, *The Women's Movements in the United States and Britain from the 1790s to the 1920s* (Amherst: University of Massachusetts Press, 1993), pp. 28-31; Jane Rendall, *The Origins of Modern Feminism: Women in Britain, France and the United States, 1780-1860* (New York: Schocken, 1984), pp. 59-63. For the masculine nature of republicanism, see, among others, Sara M. Evans, *Born for Liberty: A History of Women in America* (New York: Free Press, 1989), p. 47.
[6]Rendall, *Origins of Modern Feminism,* pp. 8, 12-20, 24-25, 31, quote from p. 8.
[7]Ibid., pp. 33, 45, 64, 66-68, quotes from pp. 33, 45; Bolt, *Women's Movements,* pp. 30-31.
[8]Gordon S. Wood, *The Radicalism of the American Revolution: How a Revolution Transformed a Monarchical Society into a Democratic One Unlike Any That Had Ever Existed* (New York: Knopf, 1992), p. 232; Carroll Smith-Rosenberg, *Disorderly Conduct: Visions of Gender in Victorian America* (New York: Knopf, 1985), pp. 158-59; Fox-Genovese, *Feminism Without Illusions,* pp. 119-24.
[9]Evans, *Born for Liberty,* p. 57, Rendall, *Origins of Modern Feminism,* pp. 34, 115-19, 145-46; Wood, *Radicalism of the American Revolution,* pp. 356-57, quote from p. 357; Paula Baker, "The Domestication of Politics: Women and American Political Society, 1780-1920," *American Historical Review* 89, no. 3 (June 1984): 624-25. Wood notes declining male virtue but not the diminution of the republican mother's role thereby.
[10]Timothy J. Gilfoyle, *City of Eros: New York City, Prostitution and the Commercialization of Sex, 1790-1920* (New York: Norton, 1992), pp. 26, 30-31, 46-48, 55-56, 59-61, 64, 74-75, 99, 101-5, 115, quotes from pp. 64, 99. Sean Wilentz (*Chants Democratic: New York City and the Rise of the American Working Class, 1788-1850* [New York: Oxford University Press, 1984]) sympathetically portrays this class of journeymen but barely mentions their use of prostitutes.
[11]Gilfoyle, *City of Eros,* pp. 34-36, 40, 43-45, 53, 73, 74, 109-12, 119-22, 124, 127-28, 130-34, 163, 166, 168-69, quotes from pp. 34, 74.
[12]Ibid., pp. 76-79, 86-91, 97-98, 135, 141, quote from p. 141.
[13]Phillida Bunkle, "Sentimental Womanhood and Domestic Education, 1830-1870," in *History of Women in the United States: Historical Articles on Women's Lives and Activities,* ed. Nancy Cott (Munich: Saur, 1993), 1:74-76; Wilentz, *Chants Democratic,* pp. 145-50; Smith-Rosenberg, *Disorderly Conduct,* pp. 20-21; Charles Sellers, *The Market Revolution: Jacksonian America, 1815-1846* (New York: Oxford University Press, 1991), pp. 243-45.
[14]Jon Butler, *Awash in a Sea of Faith: Christianizing the American People* (Cambridge, Mass.: Harvard University Press, 1990), pp. 281-82; Smith-Rosenberg, *Disorderly Conduct,* pp. 129-30; Bunkle, "Sentimental Womanhood," pp. 79-81; Evans, *Born for Liberty,*

p. 65; Rendall, *Origins of Modern Feminism,* pp. 78-80, 127-28; Barbara Welter, "The Cult of True Womanhood: 1820-1860," in *History of Women,* ed. Cott, 4:49-51. For masculine domination of "public space"—streets, theaters, public assemblies, parades and so on—from 1825 to 1840, see Mary P. Ryan, *Women in Public: Between Banners and Ballots, 1825-1880* (Baltimore: Johns Hopkins University Press, 1990), pp. 19, 22-27, 67-68, 132-35.

[15]For separate spheres, see Bunkle, "Sentimental Womanhood," pp. 72-73; Evans, *Born for Liberty,* pp. 68-76; Robert H. Wiebe, *The Opening of American Society: From the Adoption of the Constitution to the Eve of Disunion,* paperback ed. (New York: Vintage, 1985), pp. 270-72, 274-76, 281; Linda K. Kerber, "Separate Spheres, Female Worlds, Woman's Place: The Rhetoric of Women's History," in *History of Women,* ed. Cott, 4:173-203; Ruth Schwartz Cowan, *More Work for Mother: The Ironies of Household Technology from the Open Hearth to the Microwave* (New York: Basic Books, 1983), p. 19. The interpretation outlined here is my own. Kerber ("Separate Spheres, Female Worlds, Woman's Place,") argues that historians have allowed the nineteenth-century term "separate spheres" to shape their accounts, and she points to some problems of definition. Seeing the idea of separate spheres as one formed by men *and* women in conflict enables me to say that it was *all* of the following: "an ideology *imposed on* women, a culture *created by* women, [and] a set of boundaries *expected to be observed* by women" (pp. 181-82).

[16]Gilfoyle, *City of Eros,* pp. 99, 115; Smith-Rosenberg, *Disorderly Conduct,* pp. 159, 20-21; Bunkle, "Sentimental Womanhood," pp. 73-74, 81-82; Welter, "Cult of True Womanhood," pp. 49-66; Rendall, *Origins of Modern Feminism,* pp. 73, 74-75, 208, quote from p. 73. For the doctrine of separation of powers, see Gordon S. Wood, *The Creation of the American Republic, 1776-1787* (New York: Norton, 1969), pp. 150-61, 446-53. Ann Douglas originated the idea of the feminization of American Christianity in her book *The Feminization of American Culture* (New York: Knopf, 1977). For the debate over Douglas's concept, see David S. Reynolds, "The Feminization Controversy: Sexual Stereotypes and the Paradoxes of Piety in Nineteenth-Century America," in *History of Women,* ed. Cott, 13:113-23.

[17]Evans, *Born for Liberty,* p. 80; Rendall, *Origins of Modern Feminism,* p. 77. The fact that 5-10 percent (or more) of New York's young women prostituted might argue against natural female sexual purity or modesty. See Gilfoyle, *City of Eros,* p. 59.

[18]Nathan O. Hatch (*The Democratization of American Christianity* [New Haven, Conn.: Yale University Press, 1989]) persuasively describes evangelicals' skill in shaping their message to appeal to their culture. For changed views of conversion and mothers' role in it, see Bunkle, "Sentimental Womanhood," pp. 74-78.

[19]Bunkle ("Sentimental Womanhood," pp. 72-73) disputes the idea that capitalism was the cause of "separate spheres."

[20]Here and above, Sellers, *Market Revolution,* pp. 245-46; Evans, *Born for Liberty,* pp. 68-69.

[21]Claudia Goldin, *Understanding the Gender Gap: An Economic History of American Women* (New York: Oxford University Press, 1990), pp. 42, 45, 46-50, 50-54, quotes from pp. 42, 46.

[22]Rendall, *Origins of Modern Feminism,* pp. 155-59, 189; Sellers, *Market Revolution,* pp. 24-25; Joan M. Jensen, "Cloth, Butter and Boarders: Women's Household Production for the Market," in Cott, ed., *History of Women,* 4:264-90, especially p. 282.

[23]Rendall, *Origins of Modern Feminism,* pp. 145-46, 173; Kerber, "Separate Spheres," pp. 188-89; Jensen, "Cloth, Butter and Boarders," pp. 274-75, 280-81; John Mack Faragher, *Sugar Creek: Life on the Illinois Prairie* (New Haven, Conn.: Yale University Press, 1986),

pp. 101, 105; Virginia E. McCormick, "Butter and Egg Business: Implications From the Records of a Nineteenth-Century Farm Wife," *Ohio History* 100 (Winter/Spring 1991): 57-67.

[24]Jensen, "Cloth, Butter and Boarders," p. 282; Rendall, *Origins of Modern Feminism*, pp. 155-56.

[25]Cowan, *More Work for Mother*, pp. 22-25, 38, 42-45, 46-53, 61-63, 66-67.

[26]Quoted in Blanche Glassman Hersh, *The Slavery of Sex: Feminist-Abolitionists in America* (Urbana: University of Illinois Press, 1978), p. 189.

[27]John Demos, "The Antislavery Movement and the Problem of Violent 'Means,' " *New England Quarterly* 36 (1964): 123-25, 128; Donald M. Scott, *From Office to Profession: The New England Ministry, 1750-1850* (Philadelphia: University of Pennsylvania Press, 1978), pp. 98-99; Timothy Smith, *Revivalism and Social Reform: American Protestantism on the Eve of the Civil War,* 2nd ed. (Baltimore: Johns Hopkins University Press, 1980), pp. 180, 183, 187.

[28]Hersh, *Slavery of Sex,* pp. 85-86, 88, 97, 196-98, quotes from p. 197; Jean Matthews, "Race, Sex and the Dimensions of Liberty in Antebellum America," in *History of Women,* ed. Cott, 17:54-70; Bolt, *Women's Movements,* pp. 63-69.

[29]Hersh, *Slavery of Sex,* pp. 193-94; Matthews, "Race, Sex and the Dimensions of Liberty," pp. 58, 59. Fox-Genovese explores the consequences of feminists' reliance on Enlightened individualism in *Feminism Without Illusions.*

[30]Fox-Genovese, *Feminism Without Illusions,* pp. 29-32, 63, quote from p. 63; Matthews, "Race, Sex and the Dimensions of Liberty," p. 57; Bolt, *Women's Movements,* p. 87; Hersh, *Slavery of Sex,* pp. 121-22, 124-28; Evans, *Born for Liberty,* pp. 81, 85; Sheila M. Rothman, *Woman's Proper Place: A History of Changing Ideals and Practices, 1870 to the Present* (New York: Basic Books, 1978), p. 8. For the recollection that feminist historians of the 1960s and 1970s were "concerned with charges that our own movement was bourgeois," see Smith-Rosenberg, *Disorderly Conduct,* p. 16.

[31]Here and above, Hersh, *Slavery of Sex,* pp. 57-58, 136-38, 141-45, 148-50, 157, 193-94, quotes from pp. 136, 137, 145; Bolt, *Women's Movements,* pp. 59-60, 63-68, 86-89 (often citing Hersh); Gerda Lerner, *Creation of Feminist Consciousness: From the Middle Ages to 1870* (New York: Oxford University Press, 1994), pp. 160-65. For Shakers' use of the concept of a Father/Mother God and for the appeal to women of spiritualism's vague, nonmasculine Spirit, see Mary Farrell Benarowski, "Outside the Mainstream: Women's Religion and Women Religious Leaders in Nineteenth-Century America," in *History of Women,* ed. Cott, 13:207-31.

[32]Lerner, *Creation of Feminist Consciousness,* pp. 164-65; Bolt, *Women's Movements,* pp. 90-91; Hersh, *Slavery of Sex,* p. 104; Margaret Lamberts Bendroth, *Fundamentalism and Gender, 1875 to the Present* (New Haven, Conn.: Yale University Press, 1993), pp. 37-38.

[33]Bolt, *Women's Movements,* pp. 119-20; Hersh, *Slavery of Sex,* pp. 68-69, 189, quote from p. 189. Jean Matthews compares the drives for women's rights and African-American (male) rights in "Race, Sex and the Dimensions of Liberty," pp. 54-70.

[34]Lerner, *Creation of Feminist Consciousness,* pp. 165-66. Her comment comes in a discussion of women's biblical criticism.

[35]Some historians conflate *middle-class* and *Christian,* which is unwarranted. See Evans, *Born for Liberty,* pp. 94-96; and Davidson et al., *Nation of Nations,* pp. 703-4.

[36]Evans, *Born for Liberty,* pp. 125-30, quote from p. 126; Rothman, *Woman's Proper Place,* pp. 67-69, quote from p. 67; Bendroth, *Fundamentalism and Gender,* p. 29; Bolt, *Women's Movements,* pp. 169-71.

[37]Rothman, *Woman's Proper Place,* pp. 63-65, 70, quote from p. 70; Bolt, *Women's Movements,* pp. 166-68, 220-23; Sarah Deutsch, "Learning to Talk More Like a Man: Boston Women's Class-Bridging Organizations, 1870-1940," *American Historical Review* 97, no. 2 (April 1992): 388-95; Baker, "Domestication of Politics," p. 639; Paul Kleppner et al., *The Evolution of American Electoral Systems* (Westport, Conn.: Greenwood, 1981), pp. 165-69.

[38]Evans, *Born for Liberty,* p. 167; Baker, "Domestication of Politics," pp. 634-35; Bendroth, *Fundamentalism and Gender,* pp. 34-35; Bolt, *Women's Movements,* pp. 148-52, quote from p. 150.

[39]Bendroth, *Fundamentalism and Gender,* pp. 13-16, 17-18, 20-21, 25-29, 30, 40-41, 42-46, 48-49. Bendroth looks for secular causes of religious change, grabs for quotes, somewhat anachronistically sees American pessimism as early as the 1870s, mislabels John Nelson Darby as an "evangelist" and makes too much of the gender connotations in the idea of the church as the bride of Christ.

[40]For the introduction of the term *feminism* in 1913-1914, see Nancy Cott, *Grounding of Modern Feminism* (New Haven, Conn.: Yale University Press, 1987), pp. 13-15.

[41]Cindy Sondik Aron, *Ladies and Gentlemen of the Civil Service: Middle-Class Workers in Victorian America* (New York: Oxford University Press, 1987), pp. 3-7, 35-36, 40, 45, 56-58, 70-74, 82-83, quotes from pp. 7, 74. For another discussion of how women workers broke down separate spheres, see Evans, *Born for Liberty,* pp. 160-62.

[42]Aron, *Ladies and Gentlemen,* pp. 164-74, 177, quote from p. 166.

[43]Goldin, *Gender Gap,* pp. 17, 89-90, 91-105, 114-16, 117-18, 204-5; Rothman, *Woman's Proper Place,* pp. 47-56; Evans, *Born for Liberty,* p. 136.

[44]Elyce J. Rotella, *From Home to Office: U.S. Women at Work, 1870-1930* (Ann Arbor, Mich.: University Microfilms International Research Press, 1981), pp. 66-73; Goldin, *Gender Gap,* pp. 4, 74-75, 105-9; Evans, *Born for Liberty,* p. 135. For the telephone industry, see Kenneth Lipartito, "When Women Were Switches: Technology, Work and Gender in the Telephone Industry, 1890-1920," *American Historical Review* 99, no. 4 (October 1994): 1075-111.

[45]Goldin, *Gender Gap,* pp. 88-89, 107-14, 114-18, 214; Lipartito, "When Women Were Switches," p. 1089.

[46]Rotella, *Home to Office,* pp. 168-69; Goldin, *Gender Gap,* pp. 133-40, 179-83. Telephone operators had to be young and single in AT&T's early years. See Lipartito, "When Women Were Switches," pp. 1088-89. Goldin does not identify feminism as a cause of increased married women's labor force participation, but the change to a higher status for the working wife was partly caused by feminism.

[47]Rendall, *Origins of Modern Feminism,* pp. 211-13; Jean Gordon and Jan McArthur, "American Women and Domestic Consumption, 1800-1920: Four Interpretive Themes," in *History of Women,* ed. Cott, 4:215-43, especially pp. 224-25; William Leach, *Land of Desire: Merchants, Power and the Rise of a New American Culture* (New York: Vintage, 1993), pp. 70, 148-50, quote from p. 149; Gunnar Barth, *City People: The Rise of Modern City Culture in Nineteenth-Century America* (New York: Oxford University Press, 1980), pp. 111, 121-24, 128-30, 136-38, quote from p. 137; Ryan, *Women in Public,* pp. 76-79.

[48]Fox-Genovese, *Feminism Without Illusions,* p. 31.

[49]For the idea of a narrow "external" accounting, I am indebted to Wendell Berry's fine essay "Standing by Words," in *Standing by Words* (San Francisco: North Point, 1983), pp. 24-63, especially pp. 38-49. For married women's declining role, see Goldin, *Gender Gap,* pp. 42-43. For the masculine nature of the emerging market, see Sellers, *Market Revolution,*

pp. 205-6, 225-29, 242.

[50]Evans, *Born for Liberty,* pp. 175-76, 194-95; Cott, *Grounding of Modern Feminism,* pp. 22, 36-37.

[51]Titus 2:5. See also Ephesians 5:22-24. Many Christian writers base their ideas of sexual roles partly on physiology and psychology. See, for example, Werner Neuer, *Man and Woman in Christian Perspective* (Wheaton, Ill.: Crossway, 1991), pp. 31-58. His theological points are often well taken, but relying on scientific studies to support them seems unwise.

[52]Rosalind Rosenberg, *Beyond Separate Spheres: Intellectual Roots of Modern Feminism* (New Haven, Conn.: Yale University Press, 1982), pp. xv, 5-10, 13-16, quotes from pp. 6, 7, 9. Rosenberg sees a post-Enlightenment change from natural rights based on pure reason to rights based on the sciences of psychology and physiology (p. 15). But Enlightenment thinkers also used science to ascertain "nature"—though science at a more primitive stage of development. For Darwinians who rejected Darwin's view of female inferiority, see Carl N. Degler, "Darwinians Confront Gender: Or, There Is More to It Than History," in *Theoretical Perspectives on Sexual Difference,* ed. Deborah L. Rhode (New Haven, Conn.: Yale University Press, 1990), pp. 33-46.

[53]Rosenberg, *Beyond Separate Spheres,* pp. 18-24, quote from p. 21. For female social scientists' acceptance of evolutionary assumptions and the changing application of these to sex differences, see also pp. 103-6.

[54]Robert M. Crunden, *Ministers of Reform* (New York: Basic Books, 1982); Rosenberg, *Beyond Separate Spheres,* pp. 57-62; Ellen Fitzpatrick, *Endless Crusade: Women Social Scientists and Progressive Reform* (New York: Oxford University Press, 1990), pp. 33-34, 38, 54-55, 58-60. Ministers sympathetic to the Social Gospel played important roles in starting the discipline of sociology, though the degree to which they jettisoned doctrine for social science is debatable—depending on one's definition of true Christian doctrine.

[55]Fitzpatrick, *Endless Crusade,* pp. 101-21; Smith-Rosenberg, *Disorderly Conduct,* pp. 20-21; Gilfoyle, *City of Eros,* pp. 276-77, 311. Higher wages for women, increased emphasis on sexual satisfaction within marriage, earlier marriages and new forms of leisure such as movies also contributed to the decline.

[56]Cott, *Grounding of Modern Feminism,* pp. 38-46; Judith Schwarz, *Radical Feminists of Heterodoxy: Greenwich Village 1912-1940* (Lebanon, N.H.: New Victoria, 1982), pp. 1-3, 5-18, 21-25, 59-74, quote from p. 21; Evans, *Born for Liberty,* pp. 167-68.

[57]Cott, *Grounding of Modern Feminism,* pp. 36, 43-45, quotes from pp. 36, 45; Schwarz, *Radical Feminists,* pp. 23-25, 66, quote from p. 25.

[58]Evans, *Born for Liberty,* pp. 160, 177-78, 182-84, 195; Cott, *Grounding of Modern Feminism,* pp. 42-43. See also William H. Chafe, *The Paradox of Change: American Women in the Twentieth Century* (New York: Oxford University Press, 1991), pp. 102-6.

[59]Evans, *Born for Liberty,* pp. 175-78; Cott, *Grounding of Modern Feminism,* pp. 44-45, quote from p. 45.

[60]Evans, *Born for Liberty,* pp. 172-75, 194-96, quote from p. 194.

[61]See Patricia Grimshaw, " 'Christian Woman, Pious Wife, Faithful Mother, Devoted Missionary': Conflicts in Roles of American Missionary Women in Nineteenth-Century Hawaii," *History of Women,* ed. Cott, 13:254-85; Joan Jacobs Brumberg, "Zenanas and Girlless Villages: The Ethnology of American Evangelical Women, 1870-1910," *Journal of American History* 69, no. 2 (September 1982): 347-71; and Barbara Welter, "She Hath Done What She Could: Protestant Women's Missionary Careers in Nineteenth-Century America," *American Quarterly* 30 (Winter 1978): 624-38. For the "disintegration of the

Victorian female community," see Evans, *Born for Liberty,* p. 195.

Chapter 9: History's Accelerator
[1]Gary B. Nash et al., *The American People: Creating a Nation and a Society,* 3rd ed. (New York: HarperCollins, 1994). Other texts offer a more balanced, accurate account of America abroad. Michael Stoff's treatment in James W. Davidson et al., *Nation of Nations: A Narrative History of the American Republic* (New York: McGraw-Hill, 1990), pp. 790-820, is good. He is not obsessed with U.S. policy but compares it to that of Britain and other European powers. He does not overemphasize a few regions or events but provides a global perspective. John L. Thomas (in Bernard Bailyn et al., *The Great Republic: A History of the American People* [Lexington, Mass.: Heath, 1985], 2:255-82) balances coverage of the foreign policies of different presidents.

[2]Nash et al., *American People,* pp. 672-76. For a similar emphasis on the "City upon a Hill" speech and incidents in Samoa and Chile, see James Kirby Martin et al., *America and Its People* (Glenview, Ill.: Scott, Foresman, 1989), pp. 610, 615-16. For another lengthy treatment of Seward's failed plans, see Walter LaFeber, *The American Search for Opportunity, 1865-1913* (New York: Cambridge University Press, 1993), pp. 12-20.

[3]Nash et al., *American People,* pp. 679, 680-700, 754-55; American Social History Project Staff, *Who Built America? From the Centennial Celebration of 1876 to the Great War of 1914* (Santa Monica, Calif.: Voyager, 1993), p. 306, excursion entitled "Oceana Roll: Imperialism Goes Ragtime."

[4]Quoted in Donald Kagan, Steven Ozment and Frank M. Turner, *The Western Heritage Since 1648,* 3rd ed. (New York: Macmillan, 1987), 2:866. For other definitions and discussions of imperialism, see, for example, Marvin Perry et al., *Western Civilization: Ideas, Politics and Society,* 4th ed. (Boston: Houghton Mifflin, 1992), p. 626; LaFeber, *American Search,* p. xiii n. 2; and Heinz Gollwitzer, *Europe in the Age of Imperialism, 1880-1914* (New York: Harcourt, Brace & World, 1969), pp. 9-18. I am greatly indebted to Stuart Creighton Miller's discussion of imperialism in chap. 1 of his *"Benevolent Assimilation": The American Conquest of the Philippines, 1899-1903* (New Haven, Conn.: Yale University Press, 1982), pp. 1-12.

[5]A similar point is made by Charles S. Campbell in *The Transformation of American Foreign Relations, 1865-1900* (New York: Harper & Row, 1976), p. 86. For a forced stress on "informal imperialism" and an argument that specific crimes such as "assault, rape, theft, or business fraud" were "no more or less brutal and exploitative than westernization itself," see Eileen P. Scully, "Taking the Low Road to Sino-American Relations: 'Open Door' Expansionists and the Two China Markets," *Journal of American History* 82, no. 1 (June 1995): 62-66, quotes from pp. 65-66.

[6]Nash et al., *American People,* p. 686; Howard Zinn, *A People's History of the United States* (New York: Harper & Row, 1980), pp. 298, 302-4.

[7]For another example of a foreign-policy initiative that was soon dropped, see LaFeber's lengthy discussion of U.S. attempts to get a treaty to trade in the Congo, in *American Search,* pp. 83-87.

[8]Nash et al., *American People,* pp. 672, 678-79.

[9]D. W. Meinig, *Continental America, 1800-1867,* vol. 2 of *The Shaping of America: A Geographical Perspective on Five Hundred Years of History* (New Haven, Conn.: Yale University Press, 1993), pp. 556-57; Arrell Morgan Gibson, *Yankees in Paradise: The Pacific Basin Frontier* (Albuquerque: University of New Mexico Press, 1993), pp. 342, 365; Kinley J. Brauer, "1821-1860. Economics and the Diplomacy of American Expan-

sionism," in *Economics and World Power: An Assessment of American Diplomacy Since 1789,* ed. William H. Becker and Samuel F. Wells Jr. (New York: Columbia University Press, 1984), p. 88; Michael H. Hunt, *The Making of a Special Relationship: The United States and China to 1914* (New York: Columbia University Press, 1983), pp. 143-46.

[10]Davidson et al., *Nation of Nations,* pp. 796-97; Robert Seager II, *Alfred Thayer Mahan: The Man and His Letters* (Annapolis, Md.: Naval Institute Press, 1977), pp. 42, 95, 122; Gibson, *Yankees in Paradise,* pp. 365-66; David M. Pletcher, "1861-1898: Economic Growth and Diplomatic Adjustment," in *Economics and World Power,* ed. Becker and Wells, pp. 128-30, 154; Hunt, *Making of a Special Relationship,* pp. 15-16.

[11]Campbell, *Transformation of American Foreign Relations,* p. 107; Hunt, *Making of a Special Relationship,* pp. 12-14, 16-17, 22, generally pp. 5-61; Arnold Xiangse Jiang, *The United States and China* (Chicago: University of Chicago Press, 1988), pp. 2-13, 18; Robert Beisner, *From the Old Diplomacy to the New, 1865-1900* (Arlington Heights, Ill.: Harlan Davidson, 1986).

[12]This point is made regarding domestic reformers in Paul Kleppner et al., *The Evolution of American Electoral Systems* (Westport, Conn.: Greenwood, 1981), pp. 174, 181. For the U.S. government's inability to control its citizens' behavior in China's treaty ports and for the strange "anomaly" of the U.S. Court for China, see Scully, "Low Road to Sino-American Relations," pp. 66, 67-68, 71-76, 80-81. LaFeber (*American Search,* pp. 177, 236-37) argues that an expansionist foreign policy led to a stronger presidency. Mahan is quoted in LaFeber (p. 236).

[13]See, for example, Davidson et al., *Nation of Nations,* p. 815; Nash et al., *American People,* pp. 690, 697, quote from p. 690; and Gibson, *Yankees in Paradise,* p. 418.

[14]Campbell, *Transformation of American Foreign Relations,* pp. 146, 236. See also Foster Rhea Dulles, *America's Rise to World Power, 1898-1954* (New York: Harper, 1954), pp. 40, 42-48, 57.

[15]Clayton Roberts and David Roberts, *1688 to the Present,* vol. 2 of *A History of England,* 2nd ed. (Englewood Cliffs, N.J.: Prentice-Hall, 1985), pp. 642, 663.

[16]James C. Thomson Jr., Peter W. Stanley and John Curtis Perry, *Sentimental Imperialists: The American Experience in East Asia* (New York: Harper & Row, 1981), pp. 117-19; Dulles, *America's Rise,* p. 58; Kenton J. Clymer, *Protestant Missionaries in the Philippines, 1898-1916: An Inquiry into the American Colonial Mentality* (Urbana: University of Illinois Press, 1986), pp. 134-39, 146.

[17]Arrell Gibson (*Yankees in Paradise,* pp. 238, 246-47, 348-50) notes that the Pacific islands were not suitable for American small farmers and that U.S. citizens frequently requested government help.

[18]Stephen Neill, *A History of Christian Missions,* 2nd ed. (New York: Penguin, 1990), pp. 222, 235, 245, 248-49, 256-57, 277, 294-95; Gibson, *Yankees in Paradise,* p. 270; Kenneth Scott Latourette, *A History of Christian Missions in China* (New York: Macmillan, 1929), p. 217; Kenneth M. Wells, *New God, New Nation: Protestants and Self-Reconstruction Nationalism in Korea, 1896-1937* (Honolulu: University of Hawaii Press, 1990), pp. 27-29; John K. Fairbank, ed., *The Missionary Enterprise in China and America* (Cambridge, Mass.: Harvard University Press, 1974), pp. 36, 136. For a table on American "wives & other women" on the mission field (but no totals for other nationalities), see Fairbank (p. 37). Some 80 percent of non-Catholic missionaries since 1792 have been sent from English-speaking lands.

[19]Theodore Von Laue, *The World Revolution of Westernization: The Twentieth Century in Global Perspective* (New York: Oxford University Press, 1987), pp. 15, 16.

[20]LaFeber, *American Search,* pp. xiii, 234-35, quote from p. xiii. LaFeber's book almost totally lacks comparisons with European nations, which would show the limited nature of U.S. imperialism.

[21]Matthew 13:24-30.

[22]Gibson, *Yankees in Paradise,* pp. 103-4, 111, 113-14, 131-32, 134, 144-46, 148-49, quotes from pp. 220-21, 236-37, 258-59.

[23]Here and below, see ibid., pp. 144-46, 270, 274-75, 277-82, 379, 383, 385-86, quote from p. 386. See also Bradford Smith, *Yankees in Paradise: The New England Impact on Hawaii* (Philadelphia: J. B. Lippincott, 1956), especially pp. 130-40.

[24]Gibson, *Yankees in Paradise,* pp. 379-86, 391.

[25]See John S. Whitehead, "Writers as Pioneers," in Gibson, *Yankees in Paradise,* pp. 379-409, also p. 416; and Fairbank, ed., *Missionary Enterprise,* pp. 361-62. For one writer (Henry Adams) who did not fully appreciate paradise, see Richard Drinnon, *Facing West: The Metaphysics of Indian-Hating and Empire-Building* (New York: Schocken, 1990), pp. 243-54. Drinnon notes Adams's "racist" repression of sexual thoughts about South Seas women but does not criticize the many white males who gladly exploited them.

[26]This statement has to be qualified by limiting it to pre-1890 China, by excluding treaty ports and by allowing some exceptions. For post-1890 "American 'adventurers' and 'beachcombers' " in the treaty ports, see Scully, "Low Road to Sino-American Relations," pp. 66, 69, quote from p. 69.

[27]Hunt, *Making of a Special Relationship,* pp. 2, 6-8, 11, 42, 54; Thomson et al., *Sentimental Imperialists,* pp. 22-24.

[28]Here and above, Hunt, *Making of a Special Relationship,* pp. 42-60; Paul A. Cohen, *China and Christianity: The Missionary Movement and the Growth of Chinese Antiforeignism, 1860-1870* (Cambridge, Mass.: Harvard University Press, 1963), pp. 36-41, quotes from pp. 38, 41. Curiously, Hunt does not mention the anti-Christian bias of these books, just their pro-American bias. For an analysis of the difficulties faced by pre-1800 Catholic missionaries in communicating within Chinese culture, see Jacques Gernet, *China and the Christian Impact: A Conflict of Cultures* (Cambridge: Cambridge University Press, 1985).

[29]Cohen, *China and Christianity,* pp. 16-19, 24-27, 77, 79, 82-86; Hunt, *Making of a Special Relationship,* pp. 24-30; Neill, *History of Christian Missions,* p. 240; Ellsworth C. Carlson, *The Foochow Missionaries, 1847-1880* (Cambridge, Mass.: East Asian Research Center, 1974), pp. 45-46. Latourette (*Christian Missions in China,* pp. 6-45) has two chapters on Confucianism and Christianity seen in light of Chinese conditions.

[30]The estimate of twenty million is Tony Lambert's, as cited and endorsed by Alan Hunter and Kim-Kwong Chan in *Protestantism in Contemporary China* (Cambridge: Cambridge University Press, 1993), pp. 66-71. Hunter and Chan call Lambert's "the most consistent attempt to collate figures from all sources." *The Great Republic, Nation of Nations, American People, America and Its People* and Thomas A. Bailey and David M. Kennedy's *The American Pageant: A History of the Republic,* 9th ed. (Lexington, Mass.: Heath, 1991) do not mention missionaries after World War I. Most drop the subject well before then—judging by their indexes.

[31]Hunt, *Making of a Special Relationship,* pp. 27-30, quote from p. 29; Neill, *History of Christian Missions,* pp. 282-86, 347; Latourette, *Christian Missions in China,* pp. 382-94, 441-65; Shirley S. Garrett, *Social Reformers in Urban China: The Chinese Y.M.C.A., 1895-1926* (Cambridge, Mass.: Harvard University Press, 1970), pp. 56-67.

[32]Emily S. Rosenberg, *Spreading the American Dream: American Economic and Cultural Expansion, 1890-1945* (New York: Hill & Wang, 1982), pp. 20-21, Hunt, *Making of a*

Special Relationship, p. 396 n. 60; Davidson et al., *Nation of Nations,* p. 792. For an exaggeration of the role of American corporations in motivating overseas expansion, see LaFeber, *American Search,* pp. 28-39.

[33]Hunt, *Making of a Special Relationship,* pp. 143-46, 148-49, 151-52; John K. Fairbank, *The Great Chinese Revolution, 1800-1985* (New York: Harper & Row, 1986), p. 179; Pletcher, "Economic Growth and Diplomatic Adjustment," p. 161. For an argument disputing the idea that missions greatly aided the marketers in China, see Arthur Schlesinger Jr., "The Missionary Enterprise and Imperialism," in *Missionary Enterprise,* ed. Fairbank, pp. 342-46.

[34]Hunt, *Making of a Special Relationship,* pp. 61-64, 64-66, 69-71, 74, 96.

[35]Ibid., pp. 64-66.

[36]A similar observation, minus any Christian perspective, is made in Thomson et al., *Sentimental Imperialists,* pp. 143-44.

[37]Hunt, *Making of a Special Relationship,* pp. 73-79, 110-13.

[38]Ibid., pp. 85, 90, 92, 94, 105, 227-30, 232,

[39]Cohen, *China and Christianity,* pp. 4-6, 18-19. The extreme problems faced by Chinese converts to Christianity show the degree to which Chinese society was linked to Confucianism. See, for example, Carlson, *Foochow Missionaries,* pp. 73-75, 100-101.

[40]Gollwitzer (*Age of Imperialism,* pp. 182-89) makes the point that World War I was partly a consequence of European imperialism.

[41]Here and above, Hunt, *Making of a Special Relationship,* pp. 156-58, 160, 161-62, 165, quote from p. 161; Carlson, *Foochow Missionaries,* pp. 19, 141-45; Cohen, *China and Christianity,* pp. 44-45, 47, 48-50, 86, quotes from pp. 45, 48-49.

[42]Cohen, *China and Christianity,* pp. 266-67.

[43]Here and above, Hunt, *Making of a Special Relationship,* pp. 295-96, 286, quote from p. 296; Joseph W. Esherick, *The Origins of the Boxer Uprising* (Berkeley: University of California Press, 1987), pp. xiv, 68-79, 91-95, 226, 302-13, quote from p. 76. Hunt (*Making of a Special Relationship,* pp. 185-87, 286-88) also adroitly highlights missionary misconduct rather than Boxer atrocities, though he does mention these. For other accounts of missions, see Fairbank, *Great Chinese Revolution,* pp. 126, 137-38 (on the Boxer Rebellion); Fairbank, ed., *Missionary Enterprise,* pp. 2-10, 372-73; and Thomson et al., *Sentimental Imperialists,* pp. 44-60, which portrays missionaries as unwitting transformers of China in unintended directions. Some historians do not condemn, but virtually ignore, them. See Jack Gray, *Rebellions and Revolutions: China from the 1800s to the 1980s* (New York: Oxford University Press, 1990), pp. 126-29, 136-39; Jiang, *United States and China* (missionaries are hardly mentioned); and John K. Fairbank, *China: A New History* (Cambridge, Mass.: Harvard University Press, 1992), especially pp. 222-25, 230-32, 260-62, 320, 340 (missionaries are seen mainly as sources for Chinese reform movements).

[44]For the Chinese church in the early 1990s, see Hunter and Chan, *Protestantism in Contemporary China,* especially pp. 66-71. For the introduction, see Fairbanks, ed., *Missionary Enterprise,* pp. 1-19, quote from p. 2. For a feminist view, see Jane Hunter, *The Gospel of Gentility: American Women Missionaries in Turn-of-the-Century China* (New Haven, Conn.: Yale University Press, 1984), especially pp. xvi., 255, 263-65. For a mistaken view of missionaries as fearful (like corporations) of a glutted or resistant domestic market and hopeful of dumping their wares overseas, see LaFeber, *American Search,* pp. 95, 99-101.

[45]EP report in *Minnesota Christian Chronicle,* May 25, 1995, p. 19.

[46]Psalm 126:5-6. John Pollock, *A Foreign Devil in China: The Story of Dr. L. Nelson Bell,*

rev. ed. (Minneapolis: World Wide Publications, 1988), pp. 337-55, quote from p. 340. The estimate of two hundred thousand Christians in part of Jiangsu (p. 341) was likely overstated, given Hunter and Chan's estimate of twenty million Christians in all of China.

[47]Thomson et al., *Sentimental Imperialists,* pp. 61-63 (a rather rosy view of Tokugawa Japan); Peter Booth Wiley with Korogi Ichiro, *Yankees in the Land of the Gods: Commodore Perry and the Opening of Japan* (New York: Viking, 1990), pp. 232-55, 265-68, quotes from pp. 246, 253, 266. Wiley and Ichiro's seems the more realistic view of pre-1854 Japan.

[48]Thomson et al., *Sentimental Imperialists,* pp. 63-65, quote from p. 65; Wiley and Ichiro, *Land of the Gods,* pp. 24, 30-32, 35, 78-80, 88, 92-93, 99-104, 111-14, quote from p. 111.

[49]Quoted in Wiley and Ichiro, *Land of the Gods,* p. 282.

[50]Thomson et al., *Sentimental Imperialists,* pp. 69-70; Wiley and Ichiro, *Land of the Gods,* pp. 326-28, 344-46, 478-81.

[51]Thomson et al., *Sentimental Imperialists,* pp. 70-73, quote from p. 73; Neill, *History of Christian Missions,* pp. 276-78, quote from p. 276.

[52]Thomson et al., *Sentimental Imperialists,* pp. 73, 77-78, quote from p. 73; Neill, *History of Christian Missions,* pp. 276-80, quotes from pp. 277, 278.

[53]Thomson et al., *Sentimental Imperialists,* p. 72.

[54]Ibid., pp. 70, 74-76, quotes from pp. 75, 76; Leach, *Land of Desire,* pp. 93-94, 104-5, 185-90, quotes from p. 94. For a more complete account of how Eastern religion, occult practices and "New Thought" came together to form an "alternative religious community" in the Boston area in the 1880s and 1890s, see J. Gordon Melton, "How New Is New? The Flowering of the 'New' Religious Consciousness Since 1965," in *The Future of New Religious Movements,* ed. David G. Bromley and Phillip E. Hammond (Macon, Ga.: Mercer University Press, 1987), pp. 48-51.

[55]Thomson et al., *Sentimental Imperialists,* pp. 143-47, quote from p. 144; Campbell, *Transformation of American Foreign Relations,* pp. 230-34, 237; Nash et al., *American People,* p. 699; John Milton Cooper Jr., *Pivotal Decades: The United States, 1900-1920* (New York: Norton, 1990), pp. 106-9.

[56]Campbell, *Transformation of American Foreign Relations,* pp. 108-10. For a very critical account of American diplomatic and missionary efforts in Korea in the 1880s and 1890s, see LaFeber, *American Search,* pp. 96-98.

[57]Neill, *History of Christian Missions,* pp. 290-92; Thomson et al., *Sentimental Imperialists,* pp. 22, 31, 136-37; Wells, *New God, New Nation,* pp. 21-25, 27-29. For Catholic missions in Korea, see Neill (pp. 349-50).

[58]Here and above, Wells, *New God, New Nation,* pp. 29-32, 48-56, 57-58, 62-63, 64-65, 67.

[59]Here and above, Ibid., pp. 29, 32-33, 34-35, 37, 42-45.

[60]Ibid., pp. 89-94, 96-97, quote from p. 97. For the estimated percentage of South Koreans who were Christians in the 1980s and early 1990s, see p. 176 and Neill, *History of Christian Missions,* pp. 433-34.

[61]Stanley Karnow, *In Our Image: America's Empire in the Philippines* (New York: Random House, 1989), pp. 14-16, 59-63, quotes from p. 14; Neill, *History of Christian Missions,* pp. 142-43, 177, quote from p. 143.

[62]Richard V. Pierard and Robert D. Linder, *Civil Religion & the Presidency* (Grand Rapids, Mich.: Zondervan, 1988), pp. 114-16, 118, 122, 128-31, quotes from pp. 116, 118, 129.

[63]Karnow, *In Our Image,* pp. 12-13, 142-47, 177-80, 187-95, 196-98, 200-202, 323, quotes from pp. 12-13, 200. For a polemical attack on U.S. rule, stressing American racism and atrocities, see Drinnon, *Facing West,* pp. 279-332.

[64]Here and below, see Clymer, *Protestant Missionaries,* pp. 115, 134-39, 144-45, 146, 155, 157-58, 158-59, 162, 166, 169, 173, 174, 176, 181-82, quotes from pp. 166, 173, 174, 176.

[65]Ibid., pp. 194-95. Clymer criticizes missionaries, but his evidence shows success. Some writers criticize Americans for sending missionaries to a Catholic country. Yet they admit that Filipinos had only "after a fashion [been] Christianized." The Catholic Church had refused or failed to translate or distribute the Bible. Not until 1873 was one book (Luke) translated into a Filipino language. The first Protestant missionaries were two Spaniards, who brought Bibles in 1889, but officials ended their mission. Though Americans did not bring the first news of Jesus Christ, they did bring the Reformation, with beneficial results. The Holy Spirit has never privileged the religious status quo, as recent Pentecostal and evangelical gains in Latin America demonstrate. Neill, *History of Christian Missions,* pp. 142-43, 177, 292-93, quotes from p. 143; Clymer, *Protestant Missionaries,* pp. 93-103. Karnow *(In Our Image)* ignores Protestants. Neill implicitly attacks American ones (p. 292), except for Episcopalians, whom he commends (p. 293) for refusing to proselytize among Catholics.

[66]Lysle E. Meyer, *The Farther Frontier: Six Case Studies of Americans and Africa, 1848-1936* (Selinsgrove, Penn.: Susquehanna University Press, 1992), pp. 15-32. For an anthropologist's attack on Wycliffe Bible Translators that fits evidence into a preconceived polemic, see David Stoll, *Fishers of Men or Founders of Empire? The Wycliffe Bible Translators in Latin America* (London: Zed, 1982). Stoll ridicules Christian beliefs on pp. 22-30. For a more balanced view from an anthropologist, see Kenelm Burridge, *In the Way: A Study of Christian Missionary Endeavours* (Vancouver: University of British Columbia Press, 1991). LaFeber *(American Search,* pp. 87-88, 91) is politically correct in praising an African-American missionary and denouncing Yankee ones in Hawaii.

[67]See, for example, Clymer, *Protestant Missionaries,* pp. 14-15, 18-21, 27, 66-71, 72-73, 75-83.

[68]Quoted in Burridge, *In the Way,* pp. 26-27.

[69]2 Peter 3:4.

Chapter 10: Getting Real

[1]For an extended discussion of the idea of progress, see Christopher Lasch, *The True and Only Heaven: Progress and Its Critics* (New York: Norton, 1991), especially pp. 40-81. The quote is from 2 Peter 3:4.

[2]Ronald H. Stone, *Reinhold Niebuhr: Prophet to Politicians* (Nashville: Abingdon, 1972), pp. 10-12, 92.

[3]John Milton Cooper Jr., *Pivotal Decades: The United States, 1900-1920* (New York: Norton, 1990), pp. 222-23, 233, 235-36, 242. For the uncanny similarity, see Claude Fohlen, *Les États-Unis au XXe siècle* (Paris: Aubier, 1988); Thomas Jefferson to John Langdon, March 5, 1810, in *Thomas Jefferson: Writings,* ed. Merrill D. Peterson (New York: Library of America, 1984), pp. 1218-19. For the 1805-1812 debate, see Henry Adams, *History of the United States During the Administration of Thomas Jefferson [and] of James Madison* (New York: Library of America, 1986).

[4]Cooper, *Pivotal Decades,* pp. 233-35, 238-39, 255-56, 264-67; Kathleen Burk, *Britain, America and the Sinews of War, 1914-1918* (London: G. Allen & Unwin, 1985). The description of Wilson is Reinhold Niebuhr's, as quoted in Donald Meyer, *The Protestant Search for Political Realism, 1919-1941,* 2nd ed. (Middletown, Conn.: Wesleyan University Press, 1988), pp. 219.

[5]Fohlen, *Les États-Unis;* Cooper, *Pivotal Decades,* pp. 228, 230-31, 270-73.

[6]For mobilization and its effects, see Cooper, *Pivotal Decades,* pp. 268-70, 287-305; and Ellis W. Hawley, *The Great War and the Search for a Modern Order: A History of the American People and Their Institutions, 1917-1933* (New York: St. Martin's, 1979), pp. 20-30. Hawley calls it "war collectivism" (p. 45), Theodore Von Laue (*The World Revolution of Westernization: The Twentieth Century in Global Perspective* [New York: Oxford University Press, 1987], p. 56) labels it "war socialism."

[7]Hawley, *Great War,* pp. 21-27, 45-46; Cooper, *Pivotal Decades,* pp. 287-96; Robert D. Cuff and Melvin I. Urofsky, "The Steel Industry and Price Fixing During World War I," *Business History Review,* Autumn 1970, pp. 291-306; Paul A. C. Koistinen, "The 'Industrial-Military Complex' in Historical Perspective: World War I," *Business History Review,* Winter 1967, pp. 378-403; Robert F. Himmelberg, "The War Industries Board and the Antitrust Question in November 1918," *Journal of American History* 52 (June 1965): 59-74; Charles Gilbert, *American Financing of World War I* (Westport, Conn.: Greenwood, 1970), p. 216.

[8]Cooper, *Pivotal Decades,* pp. 297-302, 304-5, 307-12; Hawley, *Great War,* pp. 27-30; Norman H. Clark, *Deliver Us from Evil: An Interpretation of American Prohibition* (New York: Norton, 1976), pp. 124-25, 127. For one state's mobilization effort and repression of dissent, see Carl H. Chrislock, *Watchdog of Loyalty: The Minnesota Commission of Public Safety During World War I* (St. Paul: Minnesota Historical Society Press, 1991).

[9]David M. Chalmers, *Hooded Americanism: The First Century of the Ku Klux Klan, 1865-1965* (Garden City, N.Y.: Doubleday, 1965), pp. 24-27, 29-31; Michael E. Parrish, *America in Prosperity and Depression, 1920-1941* (New York: Norton, 1992), pp. 114-15; Paul Avrich, *Sacco and Vanzetti: The Anarchist Background* (Princeton, N.J.: Princeton University Press, 1991), pp. 94-96, 104-6, 109-11, 137, 139, 141-42, 149-56, 165-67, 174-75. Some anarchist bombings occurred during the war.

[10]Here and above, James W. Davidson et al., *Nation of Nations: A Narrative History of the American Republic* (New York: McGraw-Hill, 1990), pp. 889, 892-93; Bernard Bailyn et al., *The Great Republic: A History of the American People* (Lexington, Mass.: Heath, 1985), 2:315-20; Jonathan M. Nielson, "The Scholar as Diplomat: American Historians at the Paris Peace Conference of 1919," *International History Review* 14, no. 2 (May 1992): 236 (quoting White); Cooper, *Pivotal Decades,* pp. 333-42; Fohlen, *Les États-Unis;* Meyer, *Protestant Search,* p. 219.

[11]Cooper, *Pivotal Decades,* pp. 343-50; *Congressional Record* 66:1:8135 (November 8, 1919). The senator was Knute Nelson, Republican from Minnesota. See Millard L. Gieske and Steven J. Keillor, *Norwegian Yankee: Knute Nelson and the Failure of American Politics, 1860-1923* (Northfield, Minn.: Norwegian-American Historical Association, 1995), pp. 323-30.

[12]Robert S. McElvaine, *The Great Depression: America, 1929-1941* (New York: Time Books, 1984), p. 10; Meyer, *Protestant Search,* p. 219.

[13]Von Laue, *World Revolution,* pp. 5-6, 43, 61-63, 68-72, 75; Hannah Arendt, *The Origins of Totalitarianism,* 2nd ed. (Cleveland, Ohio: World, 1958), pp. 158-60, 208, 267, 270-76. I do not agree with Von Laue that Germany should be seen as non-Western. Germany's defeat and Versailles, not its alleged non-Western status, motivated its frantic mobilization to catch up.

[14]Here and above, see Arendt, *Origins,* pp. 159-60, 234-35, 308-10, 315, 328, 333-35.

[15]Here and above, Von Laue, *World Revolution,* p. 66; Harvey Klehr, *The Heyday of American Communism: The Depression Decade* (New York: Basic Books, 1984), p. 4; H. W. Brands, *The Devil We Knew: Americans and the Cold War* (New York: Oxford

University Press, 1993), pp. 3-4.

[16]Cooper, *Pivotal Decades,* pp. 324-30; Klehr, *Heyday,* pp. 7-13; Avrich, *Sacco and Vanzetti,* pp. 149-56, 165-67, 174-77.

[17]Parrish, *Anxious Decades,* pp. 41-46, 72, 74-78, 147-52, 153-57; Clark, *Deliver Us from Evil,* p. 152; Evans, *Born for Liberty,* pp. 176-79; Stanley Coben, *Rebellion Against Victorianism: The Impetus for Cultural Change in 1920s America* (New York: Oxford University Press, 1991), pp. 36-49 (Coben defines Victorianism on p. 4).

[18]Lary May, *Screening Out the Past: The Birth of Mass Culture and the Motion Picture Industry* (New York: Oxford University Press, 1980), pp. 36-38, 64, 66, 67, 71, 73, 95.

[19]Here and above, ibid., pp. 96, 99-100, 103, 109-14, 119, 121-25, 142-43, 146.

[20]Ibid., pp. 38-39, 165, 167, 183, 186-89, 196, 234; Parrish, *Anxious Decades,* pp. 71-74; Davidson et al., *Nation of Nations,* p. 919. Thomas Doherty (*Projections of War: Hollywood, American Culture and World War II* [New York: Columbia University Press, 1993]) writes that "classical Hollywood cinema might be flippantly defined as a Jewish-owned business selling Roman Catholic theology to Protestant America" (p. 5).

[21]Jean Gordon and Jan McArthur, "American Women and Domestic Consumption, 1800-1920: Four Interpretive Themes," in *History of Women in the United States: Historical Articles on Women's Lives and Activities,* ed. Nancy Cott (Munich: Saur, 1993), 4:233-36; Ruth Schwartz Cowan, *More Work for Mother: The Ironies of Household Technology from the Open Hearth to the Microwave* (New York: Basic Books, 1983), pp. 174-75, 182-88; George Soule, *Prosperity Decade, from War to Depression: 1917-1929* (New York: Rinehart, 1947), pp. 116, 276-77, 324.

[22]Soule, *Prosperity Decade,* pp. 295, 326-27; William E. Leuchtenberg, "The Second Industrial Revolution," in *American Economic History, Essays in Interpretation,* ed. Stanley Coben and Forrest G. Hill (Philadelphia: J. B. Lippincott, 1966), pp. 462-63, 464-65, 473, quote from p. 464; Parrish, *Anxious Decades,* pp. 74-78; McElvaine, *Great Depression,* pp. 39-41.

[23]Gary Gerstle, "The Protean Character of American Liberalism," *American Historical Review* 99, no. 4 (October 1994): 1045-47, 1049-59; Klehr, *Heyday,* pp. 4-5, 8, 28-31; Phillip J. Wood, *Southern Capitalism: The Political Economy of North Carolina, 1880-1980* (Durham, N.C.: Duke University Press, 1986), pp. 85-89; Parrish, *Anxious Decades,* pp. 423-25.

[24]Parrish, *Anxious Decades,* pp. 200-203, poem quoted on p. 203; Cooper, *Pivotal Decades,* p. 325; Avrich, *Sacco and Vanzetti,* pp. 56-57, 159-61, 165-67, 204-5, and p. 245 n. 32, quotes from pp. 56, 159.

[25]Parrish, *Anxious Decades,* p. 200.

[26]Robert L. Dorman, *Revolt of the Provinces: The Regionalist Movement in America, 1920-1945* (Chapel Hill: University of North Carolina Press, 1993), pp. xiii, 1, 6-25. Mumford quoted on p. 7.

[27]For places, see William Cronon, *Nature's Metropolis: Chicago and the Great West* (New York: Norton, 1991), p. 259; for the hothouse, see Von Laue, *World Revolution,* p. 19.

[28]It is clear in the case of one set of regionalists, the Southern Agrarians, that in seeking a moral, personal, human-scale alternative to mass industrial society they were really seeking Christian faith but could not recognize or admit that. See John L. Stewart, *The Burden of Time: The Fugitives and Agrarians, the Nashville Groups of the 1920s and 1930s, and the Writing of John Crowe Ransom, Allen Tate and Robert Penn Warren* (Princeton, N.J.: Princeton University Press, 1965).

[29]Meyer, *Protestant Search,* pp. 5-7, 11, 12-13, 19-25, 27, 55-57, 78-79, 109, quotes from

pp. 27, 109. A look at Henry Ford's treatment of his workers briefly led Reinhold Niebuhr to advocate the mild socialism of the Social Gospel. See Stone, *Niebuhr,* pp. 27-31. For a contemporary Catholic critique of capitalism, see Amintore Fanfani, *Catholicism, Protestantism and Capitalism* (reprint Notre Dame, Ind.: Notre Dame University Press, 1984).

[30]Meyer, *Protestant Search,* pp. 10-12, 61-69, 80, 81, 116-17, quotes from pp. 57, 80, 117.

[31]Here and above, Stone, *Niebuhr,* pp. 39, 44-48, quote from p. 39; Meyer, *Protestant Search,* pp. 134-35, 141-43, quote from p. 135. His first book, *Does Civilization Need Religion?* "rested finally on the very sentimentality about man that the book ostensibly condemned." See Richard Wightman Fox, *Reinhold Niebuhr: A Biography* (New York: Pantheon, 1985), p. 103. See Stone, Meyer and Fox for Niebuhr's shifting stands.

[32]Fox, *Reinhold Niebuhr,* pp. 88-89, quote from p. 89; Leo P. Ribuffo, *Right Center Left: Essays in American History* (New Brunswick, N.J.: Rutgers University Press, 1992), pp. 106-8, 114-19; Leo P. Ribuffo, *The Old Christian Right: The Protestant Far Right from the Great Depression to the Cold War* (Philadelphia: Temple University Press, 1983), pp. 25-26, 28-31, 34-35, 43-46, 48-50, 57-58, 61-62; Meyer, *Protestant Search,* pp. 145-48, 160-61; David F. Wells, *The Person of Christ: A Biblical and Historical Analysis of the Incarnation* (Westchester, Ill.: Crossway, 1984), pp. 9-10, quote from p. 10. "New Age" is anachronistic for the 1920s, but it seems to fit Ward's "theology of immanence cast as radical humanism" (Meyer, *Protestant Search,* p. 148). Ribuffo's "Old Christian Right" is misnamed; Pelley was no Christian, either before or after he became a right-wing zealot.

[33]Ribuffo, *Old Christian Right,* pp. 81-87; Ribuffo, *Right Center Left,* p. 120; Paul Boyer, *When Time Shall Be No More: Prophecy Belief in Modern American Culture* (Cambridge, Mass.: Harvard University Press, 1992), pp. 94-95, 100-102.

[34]Here and above, Chalmers, *Hooded Americanism,* pp. 33, 34-35, 43, 51-52, 85, 113-14, 165-66, 236-37, 246-48, quotes from pp. 33, 248; William D. Jenkins, *Steel Valley Klan: The Ku Klux Klan in Ohio's Mahoning Valley* (Kent, Ohio: Kent State University Press, 1990), pp. 46-50; Parrish, *Anxious Decades,* pp. 116, 119. For fundamentalist ministers' attempts to assert masculinity, see Margaret Lamberts Bendroth, *Fundamentalism and Gender, 1875 to the Present* (New Haven, Conn.: Yale University Press, 1993), pp. 64-66, 76.

[35]Here and above, Parrish, *Anxious Decades,* pp. 116-19, quote from p. 116; Chalmers, *Hooded Americanism,* pp. 32, 43, 51-52, 71, 81-83, 109, 114-15, 166-69, 180-81, 215, 281-82, 299, quotes from pp. 51, 166, 169, 299. Niebuhr attacked the Klan when it ran a candidate in the 1925 Detroit mayoral race. See Fox, *Reinhold Niebuhr,* pp. 91-92. For the KKK as a fraternal order and the nature of fraternalism, see Mary Ann Clawson, *Constructing Brotherhood: Class, Gender and Fraternalism* (Princeton, N.J.: Princeton University Press, 1989), pp. 4, 11, 218-19.

[36]In a similar way, the Italian upper and middle classes were using Fascist thugs to oppose communists. See F. Lee Benns and Mary Elisabeth Seldon, *Europe 1914-1939* (New York: Appleton-Century-Crofts, 1965), pp. 215, 219-20.

[37]Quotes from Parrish, *Anxious Decades,* pp. 41, 48-49.

[38]Here and above, Soule, *Prosperity Decade,* pp. 278-80, 284-85, 294-95, quotes from pp. 280, 294; McElvaine, *Great Depression,* pp. 42-46.

[39]Here and below, see Peter Temin, *Lessons from the Great Depression: The Lionel Robbins Lectures for 1989* (Cambridge, Mass.: MIT Press, 1989), pp. 7-9, 10-15, 86. As Temin points out, this was technically the gold exchange standard. For an article linking ideas of sound money and racial "purity," see Michael O' Malley, "Specie and Species: Race and

the Money Question in Nineteenth-Century America," *American Historical Review,* April 1994, pp. 369-95.

[40]Parrish, *Anxious Decades,* pp. 233-35, 243-45, 248-53, 257-58; Temin, *Lessons,* pp. 43-46, quotes from pp. 43, 45; Akira Iriye, *The Globalizing of America, 1913-1945* (Cambridge: Cambridge University Press, 1993), pp. 64-68, 96-100, 118-19. Temin is not persuasive in arguing that the lack of an economic downturn after the 1987 stock market crash proves that the 1929 crash was "not a strong or independent force" in causing the Great Depression.

[41]Quoted in McElvaine, *Great Depression,* p. 139. For the lack of shock among liberal intellectuals, see also Gerstle, "American Liberalism," pp. 1067-68.

[42]McElvaine, *Great Depression,* pp. 130, 138-69, quote from p. 130.

[43]Ibid., pp. 117-18. For the different components in the 1933-1936 New Deal, see Alan Brinkley, *The End of Reform: New Deal Liberalism in Recession and War* (New York: Knopf, 1995), pp. 4-6. Brinkley notes that "liberals in the 1930s were reshaping their convictions in response to the realities" (p. 4).

[44]John Patrick Diggins, *The Promise of Pragmatism: Modernism and the Crisis of Knowledge and Authority* (Chicago: University of Chicago Press, 1994), pp. 2-4, 8, 24-25, 256, 269, quotes from pp. 2, 3, 256, 269.

[45]Klehr, *Heyday,* pp. 93-95, 167-72, 179, 186-87, 206, 207-8; Gerstle, "American Liberalism," pp. 1043-45, 1059, 1067-69.

[46]Meyer, *Protestant Search,* pp. 12-13, 19-25, 166-67, 170-71, 188-94, 203-6, 209-12, 214, 318-19; Stone, *Niebuhr,* pp. 55-56, 59-66, 68-69, 71. McElvaine, *Great Depression,* pp. 98-99, 105, 112-17, 124-28, quotes from pp. 127, 128. Some liberals and Christian Marxists traveled to the Soviet Union to see the future firsthand.

[47]Dorman, *Revolt of the Provinces,* pp. 148-49, 151, 154-205, 232, 251-53, 280, 284, 292-302, 304, quotes from pp. 167, 284, 301, 304.

[48]Ribuffo, *Old Christian Right,* pp. 13-16, 17-18, 80-81, 86-87, 99-124. This book is unfairly titled, for only one of its four main figures, Gerald B. Winrod, was clearly motivated by Christian doctrine and belief.

[49]Here and above, Eduard Mark, "October or Thermidor? Interpretations of Stalinism and the Perception of Soviet Foreign Policy in the United States, 1927-1947," *American Historical Review,* October 1989, pp. 937-45, quote from p. 939; Ribuffo, *Old Christian Right,* pp. 19-24, 180-83.

[50]Parrish, *Anxious Decades,* pp. 439-40, 443-46.

[51]Diggins, *Promise of Pragmatism,* pp. 273-75. For the idea of a "Second Thirty Years' War" (apparently first used by Winston Churchill), see Temin, *Lessons,* p. 1, and Von Laue, *World Revolution,* p. 51.

[52]I am indebted to Iriye, *Globalizing of America,* pp. 134-35, for the point about Fascism as preparation for war. See also his point that "American action made little immediate difference" (p. 125) in affecting Japan's growing expansionism in the 1930s (pp. 122-27).

[53]Parrish, *Anxious Decades,* pp. 451-57, 458-72, quotes from pp. 459, 461.

[54]Steve Fraser and Gary Gerstle, eds., *The Rise and Fall of the New Deal Order, 1930-1980* (Princeton, N.J.: Princeton University Press, 1989), pp. 16-19, 88-91, 94-97, 102-9, 111, 130, 141-42; Brinkley, *End of Reform,* pp. 143-46, 147, 164, 173-74, 177, 198-99, 235, 257-58. For a brief intellectual biography of Thurman Arnold that shows the role of religious skepticism in causing one New Dealer to move away from fundamental (antitrust) principles to pragmatism, see pp. 109-12.

[55]Randall B. Woods and Howard Jones, *Dawning of the Cold War: The United States' Quest*

for Order (Athens: University of Georgia Press, 1991), pp. 4, 16-21; William Graebner, *The Age of Doubt: American Thought and Culture in the 1940s* (Boston: Twayne, 1991), pp. 70-74.

[56]John Patrick Diggins, *The Proud Decades: America in War and Peace, 1941-1960* (New York: Norton, 1988), pp. 44-47, 48-49; Doherty, *Projections of War,* pp. 247-49, quote from p. 249; Ronald Schaffer, *Wings of Judgment: American Bombing in World War II* (New York: Oxford University Press, 1985), pp. 26, 37, 64-69, 73-79, 95-100, 105.

[57]Brands, *Devil We Knew,* pp. 3-4; Woods and Jones, *Dawning of the Cold War,* pp. 83-84, 98, 104-6, 110-12, 112-17.

[58]Woods and Jones, *Dawning of the Cold War,* pp. 56-58, 69, 72, 74, 98, 101, 103; Brands, *Devil We Knew,* p. 30. Brands sees the American use of the U.N. as destroying its usefulness.

[59]For a revisionist critique of U.S. policy, see, for example, Edward Pessen, *Losing Our Souls: The American Experience in the Cold War* (Chicago: Ivan R. Dee, 1993), especially pp. 12, 20-22, 24-25, 46-47, 51-52, 68-70, 76, 78, 88-91.

[60]William L. O'Neill, *American High: The Years of Confidence, 1945-1960* (New York: Free Press, 1986), pp. 56-57.

[61]Woods and Jones, *Dawning of the Cold War,* pp. 61, 66, 78-81, 249-51, quotes from pp. 61, 78; O'Neill, *American High,* pp. 225-28, 232-33.

[62]Quoted in Stone, *Niebuhr,* p. 174.

[63]Fox, *Reinhold Niebuhr,* pp. 238, 244, 246; Stone, *Niebuhr,* pp. 46-48 (discussing an early Niebuhr book).

[64]Ursula M. Niebuhr, *Remembering Reinhold Niebuhr: Letters of Reinhold and Ursula M. Niebuhr* (San Francisco: HarperSanFrancisco, 1991), p. 403. This July 18, 1960, letter was a response to one from British MP John Strachey (p. 400). For the quote on (in)security, see Fox, *Reinhold Niebuhr,* pp. 240-41. For policymakers and this paradox, see H. W. Brands, "The Age of Vulnerability: Eisenhower and the National Insecurity State," *American Historical Review* 94, no. 4 (October 1989): 963-89.

[65]For a similar interpretation, see Warren Susman's essay in *Recasting America: Culture and Politics in the Age of Cold War,* ed. Lary May (Chicago: University of Chicago Press, 1989), especially pp. 20-22. George Lipsitz's effort to turn a few limited "general strikes," some songs and films made by folks with day jobs, some car customizing and roller derby matches, and some red-baiting in the late 1940s into a hypothetical opportunity for working-class militancy is not convincing. He ignores the long history of corporate control of the economy. That chance may have existed in the 1870s-1890s, but not in 1945-1957. See Lipsitz, *Rainbow at Midnight: Labor and Culture in the 1940s* (Urbana: University of Illinois Press, 1994).

[66]O'Neill, *American High,* pp. 12-18, 24-27, quote from p. 27; Elaine Tyler May, "Cold War—Warm Hearth: Politics and the Family in Postwar America," in *New Deal Order,* ed. Fraser and Gerstle, pp. 156-59; Diggins, *Proud Decades,* pp. 181-85.

[67]O'Neill, *American High,* pp. 29-30, 32, 40-41, quotes from pp. 32, 41; Diggins, *Proud Decades,* pp. 212-14, 216-18; May, "Cold War—Warm Hearth," pp. 166-68, 170-71.

[68]Diggins, *Proud Decades,* pp. 209-10, Eisenhower quoted on p. 209; O'Neill, *American High,* pp. 212-13, quote from p. 213. For private values and public facts in general, see Lesslie Newbigin, *Foolishness to the Greeks: The Gospel and Western Culture* (Grand Rapids, Mich.: Eerdmans, 1986).

[69]My interpretation is influenced by Warren Susman's view of Disneyland in *Recasting America,* ed. May, pp. 31-33; by Elaine Tyler May's essay in *New Deal Order,* ed. Fraser and Gerstle, especially pp. 165-69; and by O'Neill, *American High,* pp. 40-41. For the

1950s "conformist" youth culture, see Simon Frith, *Sound Effects: Youth, Leisure and the Politics of Rock 'n' Roll* (New York: Pantheon, 1981), pp. 187-89, 192.

[70]O'Neill makes this point in *American High,* p. 289.

[71]Ribuffo, *Old Christian Right,* pp. 13-16, 181, quote from p. 181; O'Neill, *American High,* pp. 197-98; Diggins, *Proud Decades,* pp. 105-7.

[72]Allen J. Matusow, *The Unraveling of America: A History of Liberalism in the 1960s* (New York: Harper & Row, 1984), pp. 3-9, 18; David Steigerwald, *The Sixties and the End of Modern America* (New York: St. Martin's, 1995), pp. 5-8. At the start of his book, Matusow recognizes 1960s liberals' agreement with the realist consensus, but his book examines the failure of liberalism, not realism. Steigerwald is closer to my view.

[73]Matusow, *Unraveling of America,* pp. 13-14, 30; Steigerwald, *The Sixties and the End,* pp. 11-12.

[74]Robert A. Divine, ed., *The Cuban Missile Crisis,* 2nd ed. (New York: Markus Wiener, 1988), pp. 9-11, 16-17, 151-54, 206-7, 230; Robert F. Kennedy, *Thirteen Days: A Memoir of the Cuban Missile Crisis* (New York: Norton, 1969), p. 25; John Morton Blum, *Years of Discord: American Politics and Society, 1961-1974* (New York: Norton, 1991), pp. 37-42, 45-46, 76-78. For a balanced analysis of JFK's feeling that he needed to show resolve in October 1962, see Richard Ned Lebow's essay in *The Cuban Missile Crisis Revisited,* ed. James A. Nathan (New York: St. Martin's, 1992), especially pp. 169-73.

[75]Kennedy, *Thirteen Days,* p. 62; Divine, ed., *Cuban Missile Crisis,* p. 36; Diggins, *Proud Decades,* p. 339; Nathan, ed., *Cuban Missile Crisis Revisited,* pp. 169-70, quote from p. 170.

[76]Nathan, ed., *Cuban Missile Crisis Revisited,* pp. 4, 12-14, quote from p. 4.

[77]Divine, ed., *Cuban Missile Crisis,* pp. 20-25, 30-31, 54, 189-92, 197-202, 204; Kennedy, *Thirteen Days,* pp. 33-39, 43-45, 48-49.

[78]Divine, ed., *Cuban Missile Crisis,* pp. 61-64, 203; Kennedy, *Thirteen Days,* pp. 67-71, 83; Blum, *Years of Discord,* pp. 85-91.

[79]Kennedy, *Thirteen Days,* pp. 99, 105-6. See also Divine, ed., *Cuban Missile Crisis,* p. 223.

[80]Nathan, ed., *Cuban Missile Crisis Revisited,* pp. 16, 19-23, 138-40, 143, 144-52, 166, quotes from pp. 21, 143. Laurence Chang's essay (pp. 131-53) is especially helpful on misinformation during the crisis on both Russian and American sides.

[81]Nathan, ed., *Cuban Missile Crisis Revisited,* p. 153. For God's promises of a coming messianic rule, see Craig A. Blaising and Darrell L. Bock, *Progressive Dispensationalism* (Wheaton, Ill.: Victor, 1993), chaps. 5-6.

Chapter 11: "At Sixes & Sevens"

[1]I am thinking of James Davison Hunter's two excellent books *Culture Wars: The Struggle to Define America* (New York: BasicBooks, 1991) and *Before the Shooting Begins: Searching for Democracy in America's Culture War* (New York: Free Press, 1994) and of Haynes Johnson's *Divided We Fall: Gambling with History in the Nineties,* paperback ed. (New York: Norton, 1995).

[2]Stanley Rothman and S. Robert Lichter, *Roots of Radicalism: Jews, Christians and the New Left* (New York: Oxford University Press, 1982), pp. 392-93. For two activists in academia, see James Miller, *"Democracy Is in the Streets": From Port Huron to the Siege of Chicago* (New York: Simon & Schuster, 1987), pp. 319, 321, 323. For a critical account with a youthful, idealistic aura, see Todd Gitlin, *The Sixties: Years of Hope, Days of Rage* (New York: Bantam, 1987). The aura makes for good memoir but poor history.

[3]Allen J. Matusow, *The Unraveling of America: A History of Liberalism in the 1960s* (New

York: Harper & Row, 1984), pp. xiv, 3-9, 18; David Steigerwald, *The Sixties and the End of Modern America* (New York: St. Martin's, 1995), pp. 5-8.

[4]Gitlin, *Sixties,* pp. 31, 32-33, 37-42, 47-48, 74-75, 83, quotes from pp. 31, 83; Steigerwald, *The Sixties and the End,* p. 122; Miller, *"Democracy Is in the Streets,"* pp. 79-89, 168-69; John Patrick Diggins, *The Proud Decades: America in War and Peace, 1941-1960* (New York: Norton, 1988), pp. 194-207, 249-50, 267-71; Simon Frith, *Sound Effects: Youth, Leisure and the Politics of Rock 'n' Roll* (New York: Pantheon, 1981), pp. 181-87, 191-92.

[5]John Morton Blum, *Years of Discord: American Politics and Society, 1961-1974* (New York: Norton, 1991), pp. 96-97; Steigerwald, *The Sixties and the End,* p. 134.

[6]Frith, *Sound Effects,* p. 192; Blum, *Years of Discord,* p. 97; Miller, *"Democracy Is in the Streets,"* p. 180.

[7]Miller, *"Democracy Is in the Streets,"* pp. 23, 31-32, 35, 43, 50, 73; Gitlin, *Sixties,* pp. 26-27, 60, 66-67, 69, 73, 84.

[8]Paul Booth is the reminiscing activist. He is quoted in Miller, *"Democracy Is in the Streets,"* pp. 71-72.

[9]Miller, *"Democracy Is in the Streets,"* pp. 139, 162, 330-31, quotes from pp. 139, 331. The entire Port Huron Statement is reprinted on pp. 329-74. Mills is quoted in John Patrick Diggins, *The Promise of Pragmatism: Modernism and the Crisis of Knowledge and Authority* (Chicago: University of Chicago Press, 1994), p. 402.

[10]Miller, *"Democracy Is in the Streets,"* pp. 16, 23, 77-78, 94-95, 146-47, 148-49, quotes from p. 146. According to Miller (p. 103), participatory democracy was not a concept derived from the civil rights movement, so I discuss it before dealing with that movement, even though Port Huron came after the movement began to influence the New Left.

[11]Miller, *"Democracy Is in the Streets,"* pp. 51, 96-98, 98-99, 147; Diggins, *Proud Decades,* pp. 259-61; Gitlin, *Sixties,* p. 84; Diggins, *Promise of Pragmatism,* pp. 404-5.

[12]Miller, *"Democracy Is in the Streets,"* pp. 89, 142-43, 145, 151, 152, quote from p. 89.

[13]Quoted in ibid., p. 148.

[14]Michael J. Klarman, "How *Brown* Changed Race Relations: The Backlash Thesis," *Journal of American History* 81, no. 1 (June 1994): 90. For liberals' reemphasis on racial and ethnic issues in the 1940s and their move away from class issues, see Gary Gerstle, "The Protean Character of American Liberalism," *American Historical Review* 99, no. 4 (October 1994): 1070-72.

[15]Matusow, *Unraveling of America,* pp. 60-61; Steigerwald, *The Sixties and the End,* pp. 38-39; David R. Goldfield, *Black, White and Southern: Race Relations and Southern Culture 1940 to the Present* (Baton Rouge: Louisiana State University Press, 1990), pp. 43-44; Aldon D. Morris, *The Origins of the Civil Rights Movement: Black Communities Organizing for Change* (New York: Free Press, 1984), pp. 81, 105, quote from p. 105.

[16]Bernard Bailyn et al., *The Great Republic: A History of the American People* (Lexington, Mass.: Heath, 1985), 2:496-500, 522-25; James Kirby Martin et al., *America and Its People* (Glenview, Ill.: Scott, Foresman, 1989), pp. 895-97, 900-904; James W. Davidson et al., *Nation of Nations: A Narrative History of the American Republic* (New York: McGraw-Hill, 1990), pp. 1142-47, 1166-72; Gary B. Nash et al., *The American People: Creating a Nation and a Society,* 3rd ed. (New York: HarperCollins, 1994), pp. 954-59, 1006-18; Diggins, *Proud Decades,* pp. 275-96. For a stress on the black church that partly subsumes it under middle-class and Southern values, see Christopher Lasch, *The True and Only Heaven: Progress and Its Critics* (New York: Norton, 1991), pp. 393-98.

[17]Goldfield, *Black, White and Southern,* pp. 48-49, 63, 67-69, 70, 72-73, 114, 116; Klarman, "Backlash Thesis," pp. 81-82; Adam Fairclough, *To Redeem the Soul of America: The*

Southern Christian Leadership Conference and Martin Luther King Jr. (Athens: University of Georgia Press, 1987), pp. 20-21.

[18]Goldfield, *Black, White and Southern,* pp. 79-80, 84-85, quote from p. 80; Klarman, "Backlash Thesis," pp. 102-3. The columnist quoted was James J. Kilpatrick.

[19]Goldfield, *Black, White and Southern,* pp. 87-89, 100, 107-9; Klarman, "Backlash Thesis," pp. 82, 98-104, 106, quote from p. 82.

[20]Morris, *Origins of the Civil Rights Movement,* pp. xii-xiii, 5-6, 74, 79-80; Goldfield, *Black, White and Southern,* p. 101; Fairclough, *To Redeem the Soul of America,* pp. 1, 7, 17-18.

[21]Steigerwald, *The Sixties and the End,* pp. 41-47, 53-54, 69-71; Blum, *Years of Discord,* pp. 192-93, 145-48; Diggins, *Proud Decades,* pp. 286-88, 306. The classic exposition of the movement's use of nonviolent direct action and its need to bypass politics is Martin Luther King Jr., "Letter from Birmingham Jail" (1963).

[22]Goldfield, *Black, White and Southern,* pp. 2-3, 21, 89-90, quote from p. 21 and quoting Benjamin Mays on pp. 89-90; Taylor Branch, *Parting the Waters: America in the King Years, 1954-63* (New York: Simon & Schuster, 1988), p. 119 (this quote regarding the furniture describes what King did not preach and, by implication, what other black ministers did preach); Morris, *Origins of the Civil Rights Movement,* pp. 79-80, 97.

[23]For liberal, Social Gospel campus ministries' role in recruiting white young women to the civil rights cause in the 1950s, see Sara Evans, *Personal Politics: The Roots of Women's Liberation in the Civil Rights Movement and the New Left* (New York: Knopf, 1979), pp. 29-36. For the Social Gospel and mainline Northern churches in the early 1960s, see James F. Findlay, "Religion and Politics in the Sixties: The Churches and the Civil Rights Act of 1964," *Journal of American History,* June 1990, pp. 66-92, especially 66-70, 87-89.

[24]Branch, *Parting the Waters,* pp. 3-5, 9, 57-58, 61-63, 65, 68-69, 71-74, 81-87, 110, 119, quotes from pp. 62, 119; Goldfield, *Black, White and Southern,* pp. 89-90, 97-98, 103; Lasch, *True and Only Heaven,* pp. 387-93; Steven F. Lawson, "Freedom Then, Freedom Now: The Historiography of the Civil Rights Movement," *American Historical Review* 96, no. 2 (April 1991): pp. 460-62; Eugene D. Genovese, "Martin Luther King Jr.: Theology, Politics, Scholarship," *Reviews in American History* 23 (March 1995): 1-11. Genovese gives an excellent brief analysis of King's theology and philosophy as well as a critique of his scholarship.

[25]Branch, *Parting the Waters,* pp. 178, 203; Goldfield, *Black, White and Southern,* pp. 163-64. The MIA was the Montgomery Improvement Association, the umbrella organization leading the Montgomery bus boycott. For the "spiritual discipline against resentment" and for an insightful analysis of King, see Lasch, *True and Only Heaven,* pp. 386-98.

[26]Morris, *Origins of the Civil Rights Movement,* pp. 97-99; Branch, *Parting the Waters,* p. 195.

[27]Morris, *Origins of the Civil Rights Movement,* pp. 189, 198, 207, 215-18, 220, quote from p. 189; Steigerwald, *The Sixties and the End,* pp. 48, 50-51, 56, 58-59, 61, quote from p. 61; Doug McAdam, *Freedom Summer* (New York: Oxford University Press, 1988), pp. 26-34; Branch, *Parting the Waters,* pp. 275, 279, 291, 301.

[28]Miller, *"Democracy Is in the Streets,"* pp. 34-36, 38, 56, 57-61 (quoting Hayden); Gitlin, *Sixties,* pp. 127-28, 139, 147, 163, quotes from pp. 127-28, 163; McAdam, *Freedom Summer,* p. 4.

[29]McAdam, *Freedom Summer,* pp. 4-5, 41-49, 65, 131, 137, quote from p. 65; Gitlin, *Sixties,* p. 165 (quoting Hayden). I, not McAdam, am inferring from liberal views an inadequate explanation of evil and an inadequate eschatology.

[30]Gitlin, *Sixties,* p. 165 (quoting Hayden); McAdam, *Freedom Summer,* pp. 131, 138-44,

quotes from pp. 131, 140.

[31]McAdam, *Freedom Summer,* pp. 161, 163-69, 172-73, 178-85, quote from p. 161; Steigerwald, *The Sixties and the End,* pp. 132-33. For the search for community, sexual liberation and nonconformity in the early years of SDS, see Gitlin, *Sixties,* pp. 105-9.

[32]Steigerwald, *The Sixties and the End,* p. 133.

[33]Miller, *"Democracy Is in the Streets,"* pp. 39, 51 (quoting Haber and Hayden); Gitlin, *Sixties,* pp. 21-24, quotes from p. 23.

[34]Brands, *Devil We Knew,* pp. 73-74.

[35]H. W. Brands, "The Age of Vulnerability: Eisenhower and the National Insecurity State," *American Historical Review* 94, no. 4 (October 1989): 963-89, quotes from pp. 964, 973; Allan M. Winkler, *Life Under a Cloud: American Anxiety About the Atom Bomb* (New York: Oxford University Press, 1993), pp. 81-83.

[36]Winkler, *Life Under a Cloud,* pp. 105-7; Gitlin, *Sixties,* pp. 86-96, quote from p. 94; Miller, *"Democracy Is in the Streets,"* pp. 329, 336, 340, 345, 346-48, 355.

[37]Winkler, *Life Under a Cloud,* pp. 173-76, 178; Miller, *"Democracy Is in the Streets,"* pp. 163-64, quote from p. 163; Gitlin, *Sixties,* pp. 97-101, Moore quote from p. 100.

[38]Gitlin, *Sixties,* pp. 99-100.

[39]Miller, *"Democracy Is in the Streets,"* pp. 163-64, quotes from p. 164; Gitlin, *Sixties,* pp. 100-101. Ussher's overly specific date for creation was Sunday, October 23, 4004 B.C. See Ernst Breisach, *Historiography: Ancient, Medieval and Modern* (Chicago: University of Chicago Press, 1983), p. 177.

[40]Miller, *"Democracy Is in the Streets,"* pp. 164-65. For pacifists' feelings of powerlessness and their candidates' poor showings, see Charles DeBenedetti, *An American Ordeal: The Antiwar Movement of the Vietnam Era* (Syracuse, N.Y.: Syracuse University Press, 1990), pp. 60-61.

[41]Miller, *"Democracy Is in the Streets,"* pp. 148-49 (quoting Lippmann) and 224 (quoting Shero). I take "democratic dogma" from Henry Adams, *The Degradation of the Democratic Dogma.* For Boomers, New Leftists and the Bomb, see Gitlin, *Sixties,* pp. 22-24.

[42]James William Gibson, *The Perfect War: Technowar in Vietnam* (Boston: Atlantic Monthly, 1986), p. 8.

[43]George C. Herring, *America's Longest War: The United States and Vietnam, 1950-1975* (New York: Knopf, 1986), pp. 15, 44, 55, 61, 66-69, 108, 110, 118-19, 158-59, 191.

[44]Herring, *America's Longest War,* pp. 48-49, 55, 61, 66-69, 87, 108, 110, 153-54, 186-87, 190-91, quotes from pp. 61, 153; William J. Duiker, *The Communist Road to Power in Vietnam* (Boulder, Colo.: Westview, 1981), p. 170, quote from p. 170; Steigerwald, *The Sixties and the End,* pp. 87-88.

[45]Kennedy quoted in Steigerwald, *The Sixties and the End,* p. 75.

[46]Herring, *America's Longest War,* pp. 145-46, 177 (quoting McNamara); Steigerwald, *The Sixties and the End,* pp. 80-85.

[47]Duiker, *Communist Road to Power,* pp. 7-9, 324. For the "powerful moral charge" of Marxism, see Theodore Von Laue, *The World Revolution of Westernization: The Twentieth Century in Global Perspective* (New York: Oxford University Press, 1987), p. 43.

[48]Gibson, *Perfect War,* pp. 15-16.

[49]Diggins, *Promise of Pragmatism,* pp. 24-25, 253, 269-70, quotes from pp. 269, 270; Herring, *America's Longest War,* p. 125; Gibson, *Perfect War,* pp. 14, 103, 124, 156.

[50]Here and above, Diggins, *Promise of Pragmatism,* pp. 214-16, 253, 256, 403, quotes from pp. 256, 403; Herring, *America's Longest War,* pp. 22, 31-32, 37-42, 79, 82-84, 93, 104, 127, 131-33, 140-42; Steigerwald, *The Sixties and the End,* pp. 91-93; James

A. Nathan, ed., *The Cuban Missile Crisis Revisited* (New York: St. Martin's, 1992), pp. 1-2, 23-24, 26-27, 180.

[51]See, for example, Herring's account of Johnson's pragmatic use of the Gulf of Tonkin incident in *America's Longest War,* pp. 119-22.

[52]Santayana quoted in Diggins, *Promise of Pragmatism,* p. 403.

[53]Steigerwald, *The Sixties and the End,* pp. 85-87, 92, 116-18; Herring, *America's Longest War,* pp. 147, 149-50, 151, 161-63; Gibson, *Perfect War,* pp. 109-18, 121, 158-62, 166, 262-65, 265-69, 299-303. That is not to downplay NLF atrocities.

[54]For mainstreaming, see Steigerwald, *The Sixties and the End,* pp. 134-34.

[55]Gitlin, *Sixties,* pp. 184-85, quote from Potter on p. 184; Miller, *"Democracy Is in the Streets,"* pp. 231, 260-61, 264-69, 278-80, 283; Steigerwald, *The Sixties and the End,* pp. 133-35.

[56]Herring, *America's Longest War,* p. 171; Steigerwald, *The Sixties and the End,* pp. 246-47; Gitlin, *Sixties,* p. 344. The phrase "oversimplified logic" is also a quote from Gitlin (p. 186).

[57]This comparison is suggested by Samuel Huntington's remarks, quoted in Miller, *"Democracy Is in the Streets,"* p. 320; and by Gordon S. Wood, *The Radicalism of the American Revolution: How a Revolution Transformed a Monarchical Society into a Democratic One Unlike Any That Had Ever Existed* (New York: Knopf, 1992), p. 232. For the attempt in the seventies to reconstruct authority and tradition, see Peter N. Carroll, *It Seemed Like Nothing Happened: America in the 1970s* (New Brunswick, N.J.: Rutgers University Press, 1990), pp. 297-99.

[58]Miller, *"Democracy Is in the Streets,"* pp. 296-99, 305-6, 312; Gunter Lewy, *Peace and Revolution: The Moral Crisis of American Pacifism* (Grand Rapids, Mich.: Eerdmans, 1988), pp. vii, 20-22, 37-40, 44-47, 50, 59, 109, quote from p. 59; DeBenedetti, *American Ordeal,* p. 200. New Left radicals were only one part of a broader antiwar movement. See Steigerwald, *The Sixties and the End,* pp. 105-6, and Herring, *America's Longest War,* p. 171.

[59]DeBenedetti, *American Ordeal,* pp. 153-54; Gitlin, *Sixties,* pp. 290, 335-36.

[60]Quoted in DeBenedetti, *American Ordeal,* p. 194. See also p. 257.

[61]Gitlin, *Sixties,* pp. 197-201, 204, 206-7, 213; Matusow, *Unraveling of America,* pp. 290-92, 295-97; Frith, *Sound Effects,* pp. 52-55, 73-74, 100; Miller, *"Democracy Is in the Streets,"* pp. 277-78. For apocalyptic themes in rock music and popular culture, see Paul Boyer, *When Time Shall Be No More: Prophecy Belief in Modern American Culture* (Cambridge, Mass.: Harvard University Press, 1992), pp. 8-9.

[62]Gitlin, *Sixties,* pp. 105-9, 262, quotes from pp. 107, 262; Todd Gitlin, "1968: The Two Cultures," in *An American Half-Century: Postwar Culture and Politics in the USA,* ed. Michael Klein (London: Pluto, 1994), pp. 64, 67-68; Steigerwald, *The Sixties and the End,* pp. 137-39, quotes from pp. 137-38; Matusow, *Unraveling of America,* pp. 321-22. For the asceticism and mutual love of a quasi-church, see Miller's description of the SDS's ERAP project in *"Democracy Is in the Streets,"* pp. 198-99, 207, 208. For the search for salvation and social justice in the sixties, see Peter Clecak, *America's Quest for the Ideal Self: Dissent and Fulfillment in the Sixties and Seventies* (New York: Oxford University Press, 1983), pp. 115-25.

[63]Quoted in Miller, *"Democracy Is in the Streets,"* p. 307.

[64]Gitlin, *Sixties,* pp. 347, 382, 401, quotes from pp. 347, 382; Steigerwald, *The Sixties and the End,* pp. 137, 139-40; DeBenedetti, *American Ordeal,* pp. 189, 224; Miller, *"Democracy Is in the Streets,"* pp. 273-77, quote from p. 276.

[65]Glenn W. Jones, "Gentle Thursday: An SDS Circus in Austin, Texas, 1966-1969," in *Sights on the Sixties,* ed. Barbara L. Tischler (New Brunswick, N.J.: Rutgers University Press, 1992), pp. 75-80, quotes from pp. 77-78. Jones seems to ascribe more practical efficacy to this event than I do.

[66]Gitlin, *Sixties,* pp. 387-88.

[67]Clecak, *Quest for the Ideal Self,* p. 116 (quoting Goodman), pp. 125-27, 136-38; Wade Clark Roof, *A Generation of Seekers: The Spiritual Journeys of the Baby Boom Generation* (San Francisco: HarperSanFrancisco, 1993), pp. 59, 102-4, quote from p. 102; Richard Quebedeaux, *The Young Evangelicals: Revolution in Orthodoxy* (New York: Harper & Row, 1974), pp. 49-51, 90-96.

[68]Quebedeaux, *Young Evangelicals,* p. 27; Boyer, *When Time Shall Be No More,* p. 5.

[69]Gitlin writes of two cultures existing in 1968, but Steigerwald shows the splintering of society into many subcultures (partly after 1968). See Gitlin, "Two Cultures," pp. 59-61; and Steigerwald, *The Sixties and the End,* pp. 222-40. The phrase "cultural civil war" is from Steigerwald (p. 154).

[70]Here and above, Steigerwald, *The Sixties and the End,* pp. 164-67, 168-70, 171-73, 175-78, quotes from pp. 164-65, 167; Robert M. Crunden, *A Brief History of American Culture* (New York: Paragon House, 1994), pp. 300-301, 319-22, quote from p. 320.

[71]For the term "new culture" and for Hell's Angels as antiheroes, see Steigerwald, *The Sixties and the End,* pp. 154, 182.

[72]Steigerwald, *The Sixties and the End,* pp. 148-50, 152-53, 183, quote from p. 183; Miller, *"Democracy Is in the Streets,"* p. 257; Gitlin, *Sixties,* pp. 109, 363-75, quotes from p. 375; Carroll, *It Seemed Like Nothing Happened,* pp. 267-68, 289-94. Carroll notes a "visual treatment of women as sex objects" in the 1970s, but fails to link that to the 1960s loosening of traditional morality. The classic account of the origins of sixties feminism in the civil rights movement and the New Left is Evans, *Personal Politics* (see pp. 78-82, 85-88, 98-101, 116-19, and chaps. 7-8).

[73]Steigerwald, *The Sixties and the End,* pp. 248-50; Carroll, *It Seemed Like Nothing Happened,* pp. 264-66; Frith, *Sound Effects,* pp. 190-92, quote from p. 192.

[74]Steigerwald, *The Sixties and the End,* pp. 222-37; Carroll, *It Seemed Like Nothing Happened,* pp. 246, 255-57, 287-89, 307, 315, quotes from pp. 246, 315.

Chapter 12: Splinter-New

[1]For example, James Davison Hunter's otherwise excellent book *Culture Wars: The Struggle to Define America* ([New York: BasicBooks, 1991], especially pp. 132, 177-78) points to the Enlightenment as the crucial divide and analyzes progressive versus orthodox views, but he does not note that progressives broke decisively with the orthodox on morality in the sixties. The term *splinter-new* is from Danish (*splinterny,* "brand-new").

[2]Quoted in Peter N. Carroll, *It Seemed Like Nothing Happened: America in the 1970s* (New Brunswick, N.J.: Rutgers University Press, 1990), p. 339.

[3]For an excellent discussion of the splintering of the Left into many identity enclaves, each with its own perspective, see Todd Gitlin, *The Twilight of Common Dreams: Why America Is Wracked by Culture Wars* (New York: Henry Holt, 1995), pp. 128-50, 200-202.

[4]Mansel G. Blackford, *A History of Small Business in America* (New York: Twayne, 1991), pp. 106-9. Alvin Toffler and Heidi Toffler (*Creating a New Civilization: The Politics of the Third Wave,* rev. ed. [Atlanta: Turner, 1995], pp. 31-32, 37-40, 43-46) call this process "de-massification" and attribute it largely to changing technology. See also Michael Barone, *Our Country: The Shaping of America from Roosevelt to Reagan* (New York: Free

Press, 1990), pp. 599-602, 615-16. Barone refers to a big-unit and small-unit economy.

[5]Quoted in Barone, *Our Country,* p. 607.

[6]James L. Baughman, *The Republic of Mass Culture: Journalism, Filmmaking and Broadcasting in America Since 1941* (Baltimore: Johns Hopkins University Press, 1992), pp. 109-10, 113, 126-29; Simon Frith, *Sound Effects: Youth, Leisure and the Politics of Rock 'n' Roll* (New York: Pantheon, 1981), pp. 118-19.

[7]Frith, *Sound Effects,* pp. 121-22, quote from p. 121; Baughman, *Republic of Mass Culture,* pp. 132-37, 196-99.

[8]Baughman, *Republic of Mass Culture,* pp. 140, 143-45, 203-4, quotes from pp. 140, 145.

[9]Gitlin, *Twilight of Common Dreams,* pp. 160-63.

[10]Carroll, *It Seemed Like Nothing Happened,* pp. 295-96; Rob Shields, ed., *Lifestyle Shopping: The Subject of Consumption* (London: Routledge, 1992), pp. 1, 7, 16, and chap. 8.

[11]Michael Dunne, *Metapop: Self-Referentiality in Contemporary American Popular Culture* (Jackson: University Press of Mississippi, 1992), pp. 4-5, 6, 13-16, 18, 52, 62, 100, 111-22. Neil Postman suggests something similar by writing of the "decontextualized fact" and the "pseudo-context" in *Amusing Ourselves to Death: Public Disclosure in the Age of Show Business* (New York: Viking, 1985), pp. 76, 99-113, quote from p. 76.

[12]E. Ann Kaplan, *Rocking Around the Clock: Music Television, Postmodernism and Consumer Culture* (New York: Methuen, 1987), pp. 1, 11, 12-13, 21, 30, 33-48, 54, 82-83, 90, quotes from pp. 12, 21. For a different view that stresses music, lyrics and "star identities" as well as visual images, see Andrew Goodwin, *Dancing in the Distraction Factory: Music Television and Popular Culture* (Minneapolis: University of Minnesota Press, 1992).

[13]Dunne, *Metapop,* pp. 12-15, 62, 95, quote from p. 95. I am indebted to David F. Wells (*No Place for Truth: Or, Whatever Happened to Evangelical Theology?* [Grand Rapids, Mich.: Eerdmans, 1993]) for the idea that entertainment versus boredom has replaced truth versus falsehood. For the blurring of lines between fantasy and reality, see, for example, Haynes Johnson, *Sleepwalking Through History: America in the Reagan Years* (New York: Norton, 1991), pp. 139-41, 145-46, 159-62.

[14]Dunne, *Metapop,* pp. 183-89; Donald Lazere, "Introduction: Entertainment as Social Control" and "Conservative Media Criticism: Heads I Win, Tails You Lose," in *American Media and Mass Culture: Left Perspectives,* ed. Donald Lazere (Berkeley: University of California Press, 1987), pp. 1-26, 81-94, especially pp. 1-3, 8-11, 17-18, 81-87, 92-93. For this debate as it relates to Internet popular culture, see Howard Rheingold, *The Virtual Community: Homesteading on the Electronic Frontier,* rev. ed. (New York: HarperCollins, 1994), pp. 279-81, 285-86, 297-99.

[15]David F. Wells, *God in the Wasteland: The Reality of Truth in a World of Fading Dreams* (Grand Rapids, Mich.: Eerdmans, 1994), pp. 216, 218-19.

[16]John Morton Blum summarizes the Watergate affair and Nixon's long struggle to retain the presidency in *Years of Discord: American Politics and Society, 1961-1974* (New York: Norton, 1991), pp. 436-44, 447-53, 461-75.

[17]Herbert D. Rosenbaum and Alexej Ugrinsky, eds., *The Presidency and Domestic Policies of Jimmy Carter* (Westport, Conn.: Greenwood, 1994), pp. 7-8, 18-19, 45-46, 65-67, quote from p. 8; Erwin C. Hargrove, *Jimmy Carter as President: Leadership and the Politics of the Public Good* (Baton Rouge: Louisiana State University Press, 1988), pp. 15-16, 31-32, 34, 47-48. Todd Gitlin (*Twilight of Common Dreams,* pp. 73-79, 185) all but ignores Jimmy Carter as a one-time unifying figure.

[18]Gaddis Smith, *Morality, Reason and Power: American Diplomacy in the Carter Years*

(New York: Hill & Wang, 1986), p. 32. In the NIV the text from 2 Chronicles reads, "If my people, who are called by my name, will humble themselves and pray and seek my face and turn from their wicked ways, then will I hear from heaven and will forgive their sin and will heal their land." The Lord is addressing Solomon and referring to Israel, and the occasion is the consecration of the temple. The context rules out any application to the United States.

[19]Hargrove, *Jimmy Carter as President,* pp. 47-49, 51-52, 101-2, quotes from pp. 47-48, 52; Carroll, *It Seemed Like Nothing Happened,* pp. 187-89, 216-21, quote from p. 216; Barone, *Our Country,* pp. 556-58, 562-63.

[20]Hargrove, *Jimmy Carter as President,* pp. 94-96, 101-3; James W. Davidson et al., *Nation of Nations: A Narrative History of the American Republic* (New York: McGraw-Hill, 1990), p. 1254. For the energy issue and the 1978-1980 OPEC price increases, see Marilu Hunt McCarty, "Economic Aspects of the Carter Energy Program," in *Domestic Policies of Jimmy Carter,* ed. Rosenbaum and Ugrinsky, pp. 555-70 (especially p. 565).

[21]Hargrove, *Jimmy Carter as President,* pp. 111-13; Smith, *Morality, Reason and Power,* pp. 4, 16-17, 19-20; Gary Sick, *All Fall Down: America's Tragic Encounter with Iran* (New York: Random House, 1985), pp. 38-39, 81-85, 112-13, 164-65, quotes from pp. 38-39, 165.

[22]Sick, *All Fall Down,* pp. 38-39, 84-85, 89, 150-51, 164-65; Michael M. Gunter, "The Iranian Hostage Case: Its Implication for the Future of the International Law of Diplomacy," in *Jimmy Carter: Foreign Policy and Post-Presidential Years,* ed. Herbert D. Rosenbaum and Alexei Ugrinsky (Westport, Conn.: Greenwood, 1994), pp. 191-210. Gunter makes the point about Khomeini's messianic role on pp. 194-95.

[23]Carter's national security adviser, Zbiegniew Brzezinski, favored the use of troops against demonstrators; Secretary of State Cyrus Vance opposed it. See Sick, *All Fall Down,* pp. 71-72; and Hargrove, *Jimmy Carter as President,* pp. 138-41. For the lack of any good, effective policy options in Iran, see also Smith, *Morality, Reason and Power,* pp. 180, 187-88. Sick describes the hostage crisis in detail.

[24]For the abortion issue and feminism, see, for example, William H. Chafe, *The Paradox of Change: American Women in the Twentieth Century* (New York: Oxford University Press, 1991), pp. 204, 216; and Winifred D. Wandersee, *On the Move: American Women in the 1970s* (Boston: Twayne, 1988), pp. 18-19, 28-32, 182-85. Neither book, however, shows how central abortion rights was to feminism. For an unbiased look at the issue, see James Davison Hunter, *Before the Shooting Begins: Searching for Democracy in America's Culture War* (New York: Free Press, 1994). He gives devastating evidence on pp. 174-80 as to why liberal historians cannot be trusted to write dispassionately and fairly on this issue.

[25]Blum, *Years of Discord,* pp. 459-60.

[26]Hunter, *Before the Shooting Begins,* pp. 86-94, 96-97, 106-7, 147. By arguing that such a consensus was politically possible in the early 1970s, I am not saying that I personally feel it is morally acceptable. I do not feel such a compromise is morally acceptable.

[27]I am indebted here and above to Hunter's excellent analysis in *Before the Shooting Begins,* pp. 29-30, 160, 246-49 nn. 1-3, quotes from pp. 29-30, 248, 249. Having just testified against Robert Bork's confirmation, historian William E. Leuchtenberg called *Roe* "laughably reasoned" in a speech at the Mid-America Conference on History on September 24, 1987. Notes in author's possession.

[28]Steve Fraser and Gary Gerstle, eds., *The Rise and Fall of the New Deal Order, 1930-1980* (Princeton, N.J.: Princeton University Press, 1989), pp. 259, 261-62, 278, 284; Hunter, *Culture Wars,* pp. 280-81; Barone, *Our Country,* pp. 508-9, 565, 577, quote from p. 577.

Richard Jensen describes the cultural conflict as one between moderns and postmoderns, in Paul Kleppner et al., *The Evolution of American Electoral Systems* (Westport, Conn.: Greenwood, 1981), pp. 227-30, with the "climax" in 1972 "as Nixon rallied modernists to destroy the McGovern crusade" (p. 228).

[29]Barone, *Our Country,* pp. 594, 613-17; Carroll, *It Seemed Like Nothing Happened,* pp. 343-44; Fraser and Gerstle, eds., *New Deal Order,* p. 279. For the supply-side thinking and promoting behind the tax cut, see Johnson, *Sleepwalking,* pp. 97-115.

[30]Johnson, *Sleepwalking,* p. 131; Barone, *Our Country,* pp. 616, 621, 630.

[31]Postman, *Amusing Ourselves to Death,* pp. 108-10. For direct-mail techniques and distortions, see Hunter, *Culture Wars,* pp. 163-67. For Reagan as FDR, see Barone, *Our Country,* pp. 594-95. Johnson's *Sleepwalking* is an extended argument that reality was ignored in the 1980s.

[32]Barone, *Our Country,* pp. 614, 622.

[33]Haynes Johnson, *Divided We Fall: Gambling with History in the Nineties,* paperback ed. (New York: Norton, 1995), pp. 80-86; John Mueller, *Retreat from Doomsday: The Obsolescence of Major War* (New York: BasicBooks, 1989), pp. 202-5, quote from p. 205; Davidson et al., *Nation of Nations,* p. 1282; Bernard Bailyn et al., *The Great Republic: A History of the American People* (Lexington, Mass.: Heath, 1985), 2:621; Barone, *Our Country,* pp. 610-11, 651-53.

[34]Richard Butsch, ed., *For Fun and Profit: The Transformation of Leisure into Consumption* (Philadelphia: Temple University Press, 1990), pp. 220-21; Davidson et al., *Nation of Nations,* p. 1297; Barone, *Our Country,* pp. 660-61; Johnson, *Sleepwalking,* pp. 377-86; Rheingold, *Virtual Community,* pp. 6-7, 67-70, 76-80, 264-66.

[35]For the inability to control the border with Mexico, see Johnson, *Divided We Fall,* pp. 261-75. For abortion as an industry, see Hunter, *Before the Shooting Begins,* pp. 75-78.

[36]Warren I. Cohen, *America in the Age of Soviet Power, 1945-1991* (New York: Cambridge University Press, 1993), pp. 217-18, 225-26, 231-33, 237, 239-45. For a brief analysis of communism's fall, see, for example, Francis Fukuyama, *The End of History and the Last Man,* paperback ed. (New York: Avon Books, 1993), pp. 23-38, 40-41.

[37]Here and above, Baughman, *Republic of Mass Culture,* pp. 195-99, 203-4, 216-17, 219; Philip Elmer-Dewitt, "The Amazing Video Game Boom," *Time,* September 27, 1993, pp. 67-72; Hunter, *Culture Wars,* p. 229; Davidson et al., *Nation of Nations,* pp. 1297, 1298-302, quote from p. 1297; Johnson, *Divided We Fall,* p. 37. For Branson, see Arthur Frommer, *Arthur Frommer's BRANSON!* (Old Tappan, N.J.: Macmillan Travel, 1995). I rely on a review in the Minneapolis *Star-Tribune,* June 4, 1995, pp. G1, G9. See also "The Christian Capitalists," *U.S. News & World Report,* March 13, 1995, pp. 52-63.

[38]Michael B. Katz, ed., *The "Underclass" Debate: Views From History* (Princeton, N.J.: Princeton University Press, 1993), pp. 57, 74-76, 87-88, 98, 101-17, 162-63, 169, 175-79, 181-93, 249, 393-401.

[39]Ibid., p. 85.

[40]Ibid., pp. 104, 185-86; Johnson, *Divided We Fall,* pp. 39, 78, 103, 278-80, 288-93; Jonathan Tilove, "Teens Americanized into an Underclass," *St. Paul Pioneer Press,* December 18, 1994, p. 20A, quote from Professor Rafaela Santa Cruz. Tilove also cites sociologists Alejandro Portes, Min Zhou and Ruben Rumbaut.

[41]For a look inside inner-city street-gang culture, see Johnson, *Divided We Fall,* pp. 183-92, 193-204, 206-21.

[42]For the bus tour, see Peter Goldman et al., *Quest for the Presidency: 1992* (College Station: Texas A&M University Press, 1994), pp. 483-85.

[43]Christopher Lasch, *The True and Only Heaven: Progress and Its Critics* (New York: Norton, 1991), pp. 117-19, quote from p. 118. For the debate over revisionist history in the classroom, see, for example, "Whose America?" *Time,* July 8, 1991, pp. 12-21. For leftists' assault on revisionists' textbooks in Oakland, California, see Gitlin, *Twilight of Common Dreams,* pp. 7-36.

[44]Daniel T. Rodgers, "Republicanism: The Career of a Concept," *Journal of American History* 79, no. 1 (June 1992): 23-24, 32-34; Robert N. Bellah et al., *Habits of the Heart: Individualism and Commitment in American Life* (New York: Harper & Row, 1985), pp. 221, 281-83, 286-90, 296, quotes from pp. 221, 281, 296; Goldman et al., *Quest,* pp. 74, 254, 292; Gitlin, *Twilight of Common Dreams,* pp. 210-19, 234-37.

[45]Hunter, *Before the Shooting Begins,* pp. 10-11, 34-36, 234-44; Bellah et al., *Habits of the Heart,* pp. 27-28, 290, quote from p. 27.

[46]Gitlin's account of the textbook debate in Oakland is a graphic example of this splintering on the Left. See Gitlin, *Twilight of Common Dreams,* pp. 7-36.

[47]Goldman et al., *Quest,* pp. 489-90; Fukuyama, *End of History,* pp. xi, xiii-xvi, 39-51, 314-16. Fukuyama admits the deficiencies of a purely economic view of history, but he supplements it with a drive for recognition that is also an inadequate explanatory factor.

[48]Fukuyama, *End of History,* pp. 59-61, 143-52, 196-98. Hegel's (and Fukuyama's) "struggle for recognition" is derived from a hypothetical portrayal of the "First Man" (p. 146).

[49]*Time,* May 15, 1995, pp. 30-35, quotes from pp. 30, 35.

[50]For a rather negative look at Christian lawyers, see *Time,* March 13, 1995, pp. 57-58, 65.

[51]Hunter, *Culture Wars,* pp. 300-302, quotes from pp. 301, 302. He analyzes the prochoice sympathies of the press in *Before the Shooting Begins,* pp. 154-63. His devastating account of how 281 historians distorted the evidence of nineteenth-century American views on abortion in order to support abortion rights is proof that a Christian interpretation of U.S. history is needed. See pp. 174-80 and the endnotes on pp. 279-80.

[52]John C. Burnham, *Bad Habits: Drinking, Smoking, Taking Drugs, Gambling, Sexual Misbehavior and Swearing in American History* (New York: New York University Press, 1993), pp. 230-42.

[53]*U.S. News & World Report,* March 13, 1995, pp. 54-59, quote from p. 54; 2 Corinthians 2:17; Wells, *No Place for Truth,* p. 79; Wells, *God in the Wasteland,* pp. 218-19, 220, 221, quotes from pp. 220, 221.

[54]Lasch, *True and Only Heaven,* p. 516; *U.S. News & World Report,* March 13, 1995, p. 63. I am indebted to Wells's *No Place for Truth,* which portrays consumerism as a threat to evangelical theology. Other evangelical critiques see more enemies than merely a "new class": for example, Os Guinness and John Seel, eds., *No God but God: Breaking with the Idols of Our Age* (Chicago: Moody Press, 1992), and Michael Scott Horton, ed., *Power Religion: The Selling Out of the Evangelical Church?* (Chicago: Moody Press, 1992). But see Richard J. Mouw's whistling-through-the-cemetery review of them in *Christianity Today,* March 8, 1993, pp. 37-38.

[55]Hunter, *Culture Wars,* pp. 304-5, quotes from p. 305; Matthew 7:13-14. See also Wells, *No Place for Truth,* pp. 72-75, 79. Alister McGrath (*Evangelicalism and the Future of Christianity* [Downers Grove, Ill.: InterVarsity Press, 1995], p. 43) sees some problems in today's evangelicalism, but not this danger, which was partly created by young evangelicals' wish to be seen as an "*intellectually respectable* Christian option" (McGrath's italics).

[56]McGrath, *Evangelicalism and the Future,* p. 103; Wells, *God in the Wasteland,* pp. 222-23. To be fair, McGrath's viewpoint is a biblical one, and he does not sidestep the "truth question" himself. Yet Wells's pessimistic analysis of evangelicalism's future is more

persuasive than McGrath's rather optimistic one. McGrath's is a largely sociological analysis which argues that evangelicalism will triumph over its competitors *within* the church; Wells's is a primarily theological one that argues for (post)modernity's seductive appeal—greater than that of any Christian viewpoint. McGrath talks of an intramural contest, Wells of a more challenging varsity match with real foes.

[57]Vishal Mangalwadi, *When the New Age Gets Old: Looking for a Greater Spirituality* (Downers Grove, Ill.: InterVarsity Press, 1992), pp. 14-16; Rheingold, *Virtual Community,* pp. 12-14; Peter Leyden, "On the Edge of the Digital Age" (pt. 1), Minneapolis *Star-Tribune,* June 4, 1995, p. 6T (quoting Schwartz). For an early prediction of a "Computopia" or Computer Utopia, see Yoneji Masuda, *The Information Society as Post-industrial Society* (Washington, D.C.: World Future Society, 1981), especially pp. 146-56.

[58]Wells, *No Place for Truth,* pp. 71-72.

[59]Rheingold, *Virtual Community,* pp. 85, 109; Fukuyama, *End of History,* pp. 72-81; Neil Postman, *Technopoly: The Surrender of Culture to Technology* (New York: Vintage, 1993), p. 7; *Time,* June 5, 1995, pp. 50, 52. Gates seems to be Netheads' Nixon, the hated and feared infocapitalist (see Rheingold, *Virtual Community,* p. 304).

[60]Postman, *Technopoly,* p. 10; Rheingold, *Virtual Community,* pp. 68, 121-27, 131-39, 145-50, 176-77, 221-25, 251-58; Philip Elmer-Dewitt, "On a Screen Near You: Cyberporn," *Time,* July 3, 1995, pp. 38-45 (the study on which this article is based has been severely criticized, however); "Battle for the Internet," *Time,* July 25, 1994, pp. 50-55; "Censoring Cyberspace," *Time,* November 21, 1994, pp. 102-4; "Technomania," *Newsweek,* February 27, 1995, pp. 25-33 (summarizing five basic issues on pp. 27-29); *Chronicle of Higher Education,* March 1, 1996, pp. A25, A27; Joshua Quittner, "Betting on Virtual Vegas," *Time,* June 12, 1995, pp. 63-64; and "Back to the Real World," *Time,* April 17, 1995, pp. 56-57. Computer buff Rheingold downplays negatives on the Internet, such as sex chat, MUD addiction and pornography. "MUD" stands for Multi-User *Dungeon,* but more games are played than that one. For a list of human-centered concerns about computerization, see Charles Dunlop and Rob Kling, eds., *Computerization and Controversy: Value Conflicts and Social Choices* (San Diego: Academic Press, 1991), pp. 2-3; for a censorship debate at Stanford, see pp. 325-26, 376-78.

[61]*Time,* April 11, 1994, pp. 28-35; *Time,* March 13, 1995, pp. 40-47; *U.S. News & World Report,* March 13, 1995, pp. 68-71.

[62]*Time,* September 27, 1993, pp. 67-72, quotes from pp. 69, 71; *Time,* May 22, 1995, p. 66.

[63]Peter Leyden, "The Electronic Elite Take Over the World," Minneapolis *Star-Tribune,* April 15, 1994, p. 16A, and "Technology Redefining Haves and Have-Nots," *Star-Tribune,* June 4, 1995, p. 6T; *Newsweek,* February 27, 1995, pp. 50-53, quote from p. 51; Richard M. Krieg, "Signed Off: Information Apartheid Blocking Black Communities," *Chicago Tribune,* October 23, 1995, sec. 1, p. 13.

[64]*Time,* July 3, 1995, p. 45; *Time,* July 25, 1994, pp. 52, 54-55; Rheingold, *Virtual Community,* pp. 171-72; Steve Lohr, "Protecting Youngsters from Internet Dangers," *The New York Times,* September 21, 1995, pp. B1, B2; *Newsweek,* February 27, 1995, p. 52; Krieg, "Signed Off," p. 13.

[65]A strong anticapitalist spirit is evident in Rheingold's *Virtual Community.* He notes that "the hacker ethic was that computer tools ought to be free" (p. 102), and he is very critical of large corporations seeking profit from the Net. For a discussion of "technological utopianism" regarding computerization and "technological anti-utopianism," see Dunlop and Kling, eds., *Computerization,* pp. 14-29. This is a debate, however, between machine-centered and human-centered views. There is no God-centered view expressed.

[66]Matthew 15:19-20.

[67]Rheingold, *Virtual Community,* p. 3; Dunlop and Kling, eds., *Computerization,* pp. 322-24, 335-37, 342. See Dominic Papatola, "Cyberworld Shrinks Your Individuality," *Duluth News-Tribune,* April 8, 1995, p. 1B. For "Internet's testosterone-heavy demographics," see *Time,* July 25, 1994, p. 56.

[68]Leyden, "On the Edge of the Digital Age," Minneapolis *Star-Tribune,* June 25, 1995, pp. 1T, 4T, and June 4, 1995, p. 6T; Rheingold, *Virtual Community,* pp. 106-7. For WELLites' amazingly arranging a medical evacuation for a sick friend in New Delhi, see Rheingold, *Virtual Community,* pp. 28-32.

[69]Stephen L. Talbott, *The Future Does Not Compute: Transcending the Machines in Our Midst* (Sebastopol, Calif.: O'Reilly & Associates, 1995), p. 359. He also discusses how the computer changes our sense of reality.

[70]Postman, *Amusing Ourselves to Death,* pp. 9-15, 16-29; Postman, *Technopoly,* pp. 7, 22-29, 107-22, quote from p. 7.

[71]Rheingold, *Virtual Community,* pp. 28-32, quotes from pp. 31, 32.

[72]Genesis 11:1-9, quote from v. 4; Leyden, "On the Edge," Minneapolis *Star-Tribune,* June 4, 1995, p. 6T, and June 25, 1995, p. 4T. For the Gaia thesis and its attendant spirituality, see also Rosemary Radford Ruether, *Gaia and God: An Ecofeminist Theology of Earth Healing* (San Francisco: HarperSanFrancisco, 1992), pp. 4, 254-58.

[73]Christopher John Farley, "HIStory and Hubris," *Time,* June 19, 1995, p. 58.

[74]Toffler and Toffler, *Creating a New Civilization,* p. 12. Ironically, the computer software that produced the index for the 1995 paperback edition picked up the running footers (authors and title)—giving the impression that the Tofflers and civilization are the two main topics covered. That's computer-generated hubris! Kling and Iacono (*Computerization,* pp. 63-74) discuss how those who report on computerization are often strong, biased advocates of it.

[75]Mangalwadi, *When the New Age Gets Old,* pp. 12-14, 18, 25, quote from p. 14.

[76]Ibid., pp. 12-16, 18, 21-26, 32, 54-55, 108-9, quotes from p. 13. For the sixties as the key decade, see Wade Clark Roof, *A Generation of Seekers: The Spiritual Journeys of the Baby Boom Generation* (San Francisco: HarperSanFrancisco, 1993), pp. 21-22, 63-67. He cites the many Renaissance fairs as sixties reunions (pp. 117-18). Some experts sidestep and play down the sixties-New Age link. See, for example, J. Gordon Melton, "How New Is New?" in *The Future of New Religious Movements,* ed. David G. Bromley and Phillip E. Hammond (Macon, Ga.: Mercer University Press, 1987), pp. 46-56.

[77]This syncretism is made clear in Mangalwadi's *When the New Age Gets Old,* which opposes the New Age movement as well as New Age books. See, for example, Matthew Fox, *The Coming of the Cosmic Christ: The Healing of Mother Earth and the Birth of a Global Renaissance* (San Francisco: HarperSanFrancisco, 1988); and Ruether, *Gaia and God.* Fox and Ruether would likely deny that they are New Age thinkers, of course.

[78]Bromley and Hammond, eds., *New Religious Movements,* pp. 11-45, quote from p. 13, referring to Mormonism's appeal to Christians, but applying as well, I argue, to the New Age movement broadly defined. Wells, *God in the Wasteland,* p. 222.

[79]Fox, *Coming of the Cosmic Christ,* pp. 5, 8, 24-27, 45-46, 135, 145, 154-55, 164, 178-85, 206-7, 225-27, 235, 240, quotes from pp. 135, 154, 207. Fox's one quibble with New Agers seems to be their belief in reincarnation.

[80]Second Thessalonians 2:3-12, quote from v. 12. Implied is the idea that the global proclamation of the gospel is a necessary precondition for the Rebellion and the Lie, for how could people refuse to believe a truth that they had never heard? See also Daniel

9:26-27 and Mark 13:14-22, 26-27 for the Rebellion and Lie.

[81]Revelation 22:13.

[82]Paul Boyer, *When Time Shall Be No More: Prophecy Belief in Modern American Culture* (Cambridge, Mass.: Harvard University Press, 1992), pp. 325-39; Fox, *Coming of the Cosmic Christ,* pp. 245-46.

[83]Wells, *God in the Wasteland,* p. 170.

[84]First Peter 2:7, quoting Psalm 118:22. Of course Peter is referring specifically to Israel's leaders, but the words can be broadly applied to all human rejection of the Christ.

[85]For changing meanings of "democracy" throughout U.S. history, see Russell L. Hanson, *The Democratic Imagination in America: Conversations with Our Past* (Princeton, N.J.: Princeton University Press, 1985).